BLOOD & ROSES

Helen Castor is a Fellow in History at Sidney Sussex College, Cambridge.

Further Praise for *Blood & Roses*:

'Helen Castor's affectionate, detailed history offers a compelling portrait of the life and times of an upwardly mobile family which, however grand it became, was forever trying to escape the ignominy of its humble origins.' *Sunday Times*

'There are two schools of thought regarding the past: that it's just a foreign country, but its inhabitants are different from us in outlook, psyche and behaviour; and that there is only a hairline track of difference between our ancestors' ways and our own. If ever the second school needs a confidence boost, they should reach for Helen Castor's book . . . The history of these times is complex, and this is not a book to read with one eye on the sports results. But it rewards concentration.' *The Herald*

'Castor sustains the narrative, admirably simplifying where necessary, to carry the reader along. She cleverly weaves explanation of contemporary social structure, legal procedure, marital customs and other aspects of fifteenth-century life into the story and makes just the right level of reference to and exposition of the unfolding political context.' *History Today*

'Castor's artful writing means that the Pastons' opinions, the squabbles, trials and tribulations emerge from this delightful text to bring the family to life. It's a human, compelling story of a family surviving internal and external pressures and it makes 500 years seem not so very long ago.' *Good Book Guide*

'This absorbing account of a family living through the Wars of the Roses is based on a remarkable collection of private letters . . . a fascinating book and an invaluable resource for anyone wanting to know more about England during this period.' *Historical Novels Review*

BLOOD & ROSES

The Paston Family in the Fifteenth Century

HELEN CASTOR

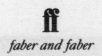

faber and faber

First published in Great Britain in 2004
by Faber and Faber Limited
3 Queen Square London WC1N 3AU
This paperback edition published in 2005

Typeset by Faber and Faber Limited
Printed in England by Mackays of Chatham plc,
Chatham Kent

The right of Helen Castor to be identified as author
of this work has been asserted in accordance with Section 77
of the Copyright, Designs and Patents Act 1988

A CIP record for this book
is available from the British Library

ISBN 0–571–21671–4

2 4 6 8 10 9 7 5 3 1

for Julian and Luca

Contents

List of Illustrations

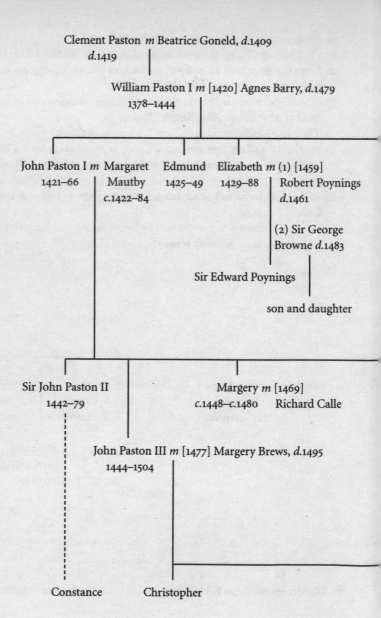

Clement Paston *m* Beatrice Goneld, *d*.1409
d.1419

William Paston I *m* [1420] Agnes Barry, *d*.1479
1378–1444

John Paston I *m* Margaret   Edmund   Elizabeth *m* (1) [1459]
1421–66   Mautby   1425–49   1429–88   Robert Poynings
   c.1422–84   *d*.1461

(2) Sir George
Browne *d*.1483

Sir Edward Poynings

son and daughter

Sir John Paston II   Margery *m* [1469]
1442–79   *c*.1448–*c*.1480   Richard Calle

John Paston III *m* [1477] Margery Brews, *d*.1495
1444–1504

Constance   Christopher

The Paston Family

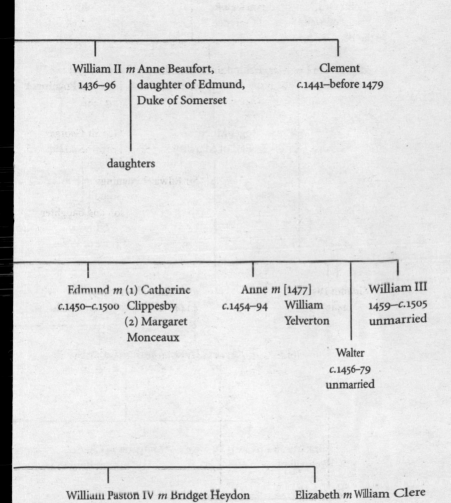

William II *m* Anne Beaufort,
1436–96   daughter of Edmund,
Duke of Somerset

Clement
*c.*1441–before 1479

daughters

Edmund *m* (1) Catherine
*c.*1450–*c.*1500   Clippesby
(2) Margaret
Monceaux

Anne *m* [1477]
*c.*1454–94   William
Yelverton

William III
1459–*c.*1505
unmarried

Walter
*c.*1456–79
unmarried

William Paston IV *m* Bridget Heydon

Elizabeth *m* William Clere

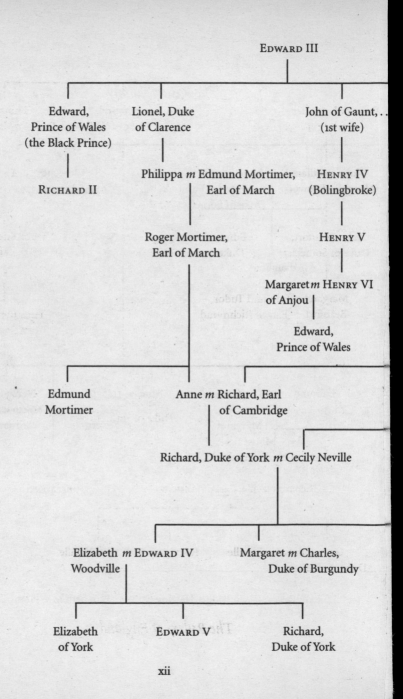

EDWARD III

Edward,
Prince of Wales
(the Black Prince)

Lionel, Duke
of Clarence

John of Gaunt, . .
(1st wife)

RICHARD II

Philippa *m* Edmund Mortimer,
Earl of March

HENRY IV
(Bolingbroke)

Roger Mortimer,
Earl of March

HENRY V

Margaret *m* HENRY VI
of Anjou

Edward,
Prince of Wales

Edmund
Mortimer

Anne *m* Richard, Earl
of Cambridge

Richard, Duke of York *m* Cecily Neville

Elizabeth *m* EDWARD IV
Woodville

Margaret *m* Charles,
Duke of Burgundy

Elizabeth
of York

EDWARD V

Richard,
Duke of York

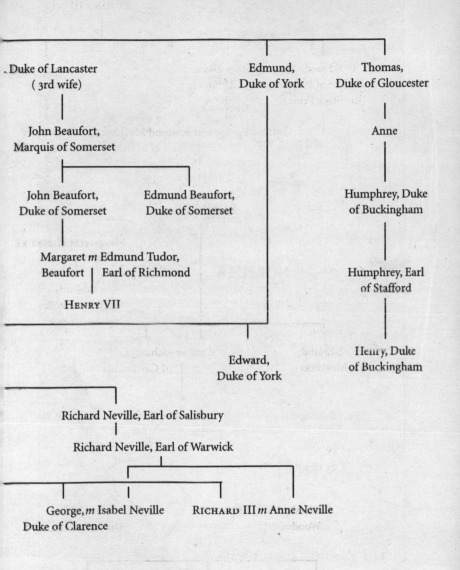

. Duke of Lancaster
(3rd wife)

Edmund,
Duke of York

Thomas,
Duke of Gloucester

John Beaufort,
Marquis of Somerset

Anne

John Beaufort,
Duke of Somerset

Edmund Beaufort,
Duke of Somerset

Humphrey, Duke
of Buckingham

Margaret *m* Edmund Tudor,
Beaufort | Earl of Richmond

HENRY VII

Humphrey, Earl
of Stafford

Edward,
Duke of York

Henry, Duke
of Buckingham

Richard Neville, Earl of Salisbury

Richard Neville, Earl of Warwick

George, *m* Isabel Neville
Duke of Clarence

RICHARD III *m* Anne Neville

The Rulers of England

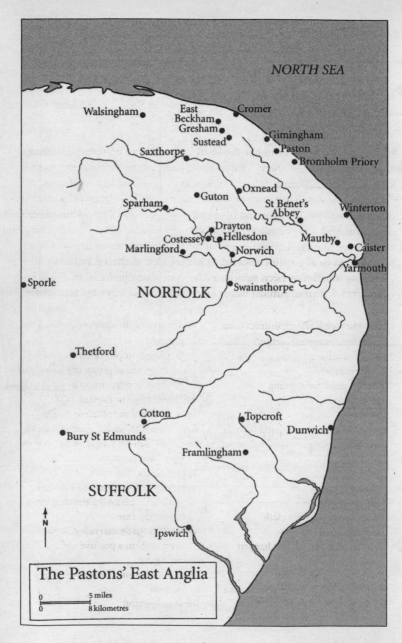

NORTH SEA

Walsingham

East
Beckham
Cromer
Gresham
Gimingham
Sustead
Paston
Saxthorpe
Bromholm Priory

Oxnead

Guton
St Benet's
Abbey
Winterton
Sparham

Drayton
Costessey
Hellesdon
Mautby
Caister
Marlingford
Norwich
Yarmouth

Sporle

NORFOLK
Swainsthorpe

Thetford

Cotton
Topcroft
Dunwich
Bury St Edmunds
Framlingham

SUFFOLK

N

Ipswich

The Pastons' East Anglia

0   5 miles
0   8 kilometres

Author's Note & Glossary

The units of currency in late medieval England were pounds (£), shillings (s) and pence (d); there were twelve pence to the shilling and twenty shillings to the pound. Money could also be accounted in marks, each of which was equivalent to two-thirds of a pound (13s 4d). Among the coins in circulation were the groat, worth a third of a shilling (4d), and the noble, worth a third of a pound (6s 8d).

The spelling of all quotations from contemporary sources has been modernised. As far as possible, vocabulary has been left unaltered, but a few now-obsolete words have been substituted for ease of comprehension. Some less familiar words, and familiar words used in unfamiliar ways, are listed below.

advertise warn, notify, instruct (also *advertisement*, instruction)

assoil absolve, pardon

avoid remove

brothel good-for-nothing

but if unless

con know how to

conceive think, understand (also *conceit*, opinion or understanding)

crazed ill

devoir duty

divers several

fain glad, gladly

frieze coarse woollen cloth

fumous angry

hap (n.) happening; (v.) happen

harness armour

heavy sad or oppressive

journey either in modern sense, or a day's work

labour (v.) try to achieve or seek to persuade

large liberal, ample: can have positive connotations of generosity or negative ones of offensiveness

let either allow or prevent

lewd ignorant or foolish or vulgar

liefer rather (from *lief*, glad or willing)

livelihood landed estates or the income from such property

lumish malicious

maintenance support of a litigant by someone with no legitimate connection to the case

marvellous to be marvelled at, not necessarily in a positive sense

move urge

noise (n.) rumour; (v.) to spread a rumour

noyous harmful

obloquy bad repute

paid pleased (as in 'well paid' and 'evil paid')

pipe roll

proper one's own

sad wise, sensible, serious

sans without

shrew malevolent person

shrewd malicious or dangerous or poor in quality

simple plain or humble or foolish

strange alien, other; or unfriendly

therefor for that object or purpose

treat (v.) negotiate

trow (v.) believe, think

unsitting unsuitable, unbecoming

very true

vouchsafe (v.) graciously agree

weal well-being

wicket small opening in a door or wall

worship qualities characteristic of gentility, or the respect in which someone displaying those qualities is held

wroth furious

Acknowledgements

I could not have been more fortunate in my agent, Patrick Walsh, and my editors, Jon Riley and Walter Donohue: they have made the impossible happen, several times over. To them, and to Charles Boyle, Ron Costley, Josine Meijer, and the remarkable team at Faber, I am extremely grateful.

Christine Carpenter introduced me to the Pastons sixteen years ago; for that, as for so much else, I am profoundly in her debt. As always, she has been unfailingly generous with her expertise and her friendship, as have Richard Partington, Caroline Burt, John Watts, Benjamin Thompson and Rosemary Horrox. Richard Beadle first made me think about telling the Pastons' story, and Colin Richmond offered kind encouragement along the way. Sidney Sussex College, Cambridge, has been a happy academic home for me for ten years, and I must thank everyone there – master, fellows, staff and students, and particularly the historians – for making it so.

I owe more than I can say to the people who have seen me through the writing of this book from its very beginnings: Rachel Aris, Lucyann Ashdown, Tony Badger, Gary Beggerow, Sarah Beglin, Nigel Blackwood, Katie Brown, Melissa Calaresu, Virginia Crompton, Russell Davies, John Foot, Robert Gordon, Harriet Hawkes, Grace Hodge, David Jarvis, Emily Lawson, Jo Marsh, Rosemary Parkinson, Barbara Placido, Anne Shewring, Keith Straughan, Catherine Taylor, Thalia Walters and Simon Whiteman. Without Allison Weild, the book could not have been written: thank you.

My family, and especially my sisters Harriet and Portia, have been a constant source of encouragement and inspiration. Very special thanks to my parents, Grahame and Gwyneth, for a truly extraordinary combination of emotional, practical and intellectual support.

Julian Ferraro has helped in more ways than I can begin to describe. The book is dedicated to him and to Luca, with all my love.

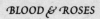

BLOOD & ROSES

– the most curious papers of the sort I ever saw –

In the late spring of 1735 the Reverend Francis Blomefield, a noted antiquarian and local historian, was summoned to give an expert opinion on the family papers of William Paston, the second Earl of Yarmouth, who had died a little over two years earlier. The Earl had been staving off bankruptcy by the narrowest of margins for the last thirty years of his life, and the task of liquidating his estate to pay off his vast debts now fell to his son-in-law Thomas Weldon, the husband of his daughter Charlotte. By the time Blomefield arrived in the muniment room at Oxnead Hall – the Paston family seat in Norfolk, now in a state of ruinous disrepair – the Earl's books, paintings and furniture had already been sold. Before the remaining lands were disposed of and the house abandoned, Blomefield spent two weeks 'among the old writings' in the Paston archive, gathering material for the *Topographical History of the County of Norfolk* which he planned to publish, and bringing order to the jumbled piles of documents for the benefit of the Earl's executors. At the end of the fortnight, he wrote to Major Weldon to report his findings.

> There are innumerable letters, of good consequence in history, still lying among the loose papers, all which I laid up in a corner of the room on a heap, which contains several sacks full; but as they seemed to have some family affairs of one nature or other intermixed in them, I did not offer to touch any of them, but have left them to your consideration, whether, when I go to that part of the country, I shall separate and preserve them, or whether you will have them burned, though I must own 'tis pity they should; except it be those (of which there are many) that relate to nothing but family affairs only. I have placed everything so that now the good and bad are distinguished and preserved from the weather, by which a great number have perished entirely.[1]

Whether any of the letters which had miraculously survived the elements and the late Earl's indifference were in fact burned is not clear. What is known is that Blomefield himself acquired a good number, while others passed into the hands of rival collectors; and that, in 1771, many of the manuscripts were bought by John Worth, a chemist from Diss in Norfolk, as a speculative investment. When Worth himself died three years later, the papers were acquired by a local gentleman and amateur historian named John Fenn.

In May 1782, Fenn showed the collection – which consisted largely of letters written three hundred years earlier, during the Wars of the Roses, by the Earl of Yarmouth's ancestors – to a friend, the literary connoisseur Horace Walpole, who responded with some excitement:

> *I have brought you back your manuscripts myself, for I was afraid of keeping them they are so valuable, especially the Paston Letters, which are the most curious papers of the sort I ever saw, and the oldest original letters I believe extant in this country. The historic picture they give of the reign of Henry VI makes them invaluable, and more satisfactory than any cold narrative. It were a thousand pities they should not be published, which I should be glad I could persuade you to do.*[2]

Fenn took him at his word, and embarked on the challenging process of preparing the manuscripts for publication. He was initially overwhelmed by the scale and complexity of the task which faced him: the sheer number of letters, and the difficulty of deciphering archaic English in centuries-old handwriting. '*I must read much and I must write much, for I would not willingly publish them either in a slovenly or a careless manner*', he told another friend. '*I have been in some measure arranging them lately, but the heap and the crincum crancum hands fright me. However, if my friends encourage me, I think I shall venture.*'[3] He was engagingly modest about his own abilities, but – in an era when a number of early manuscript collections were destroyed by antiquarians who cut up the documents, filed away the topographical references and used what was left as scrap paper – Fenn proved to be a historian of unusual sensitivity and rigour. He transcribed a selection of the letters in their original spelling, and produced a modernised version of the text of each one, to be printed on the facing page. It took three years from the date of his first discussions with Walpole to complete his work, nine months to agree terms with a publishing house, and another year for the two volumes to go through the press. Finally, in January 1787, the first edition of the Paston letters appeared in print (cumbersomely entitled *Original Letters, written during the reigns of Henry VI, Edward IV, and Richard III, by various persons of rank or consequence; containing many curious anecdotes relative to that turbulent and bloody, but hitherto dark period of our history; and eluci-*

4

dating, *not only public matters of state, but likewise the private manners of the age: digested in chronological order; with notes, historical and explanatory; and authenticated by engravings of autographs, paper marks and seals*).[4] It sold out within a week.

The Paston letters rapidly became the literary sensation of the year. Walpole rhapsodised over them: '*The Letters of Henry VI's reign etc are come out, and to me make all other letters not worth reading*', he said; '*I have gone through above one volume, and cannot bear to be writing when I am so eager to be reading.*'[5] He was not alone in his enthusiasm. '*It is with more pleasure than I can describe that I have seen your Original Letters*', another antiquarian told Fenn; '*I think them one of the richest treasures in the English language; my attention is captivated; they cause me to forget to eat and to sleep*'.[6] Nor was it only those who already shared Fenn's historical interests who were entranced by the correspondence. The Paston letters became the talking-point of the season in polite society: '. . . *so fast went the first edition that we could not procure a copy so soon as we wished, though a friend had been written to in town upon the very first advertisement*', a Suffolk gentleman wrote in May, adding that, '*for several visits, the chat of the day was given up for the anecdotes of our ancestors*'.[7]

The letters were an instant success, both critically and commercially, because they offered a unique and compelling perspective on the dramatic events of the Wars of the Roses: the experiences of a family who lived through the conflict, recounted in their own words. '*It is very curious indeed, I did not know that there was so much as a private letter extant of that very turbulent period*', Walpole wrote.[8] He was right to be surprised. A vast wealth of documentation survives from late medieval England: voluminous legal and governmental records; accounts and deeds recording the property transactions of individual families; works of literature and scholarship; and narratives written by contemporary chroniclers. In none of these texts, however, can individual voices be heard speaking for themselves *in private*, without the constraints of technical form or the consciousness of a public readership. The gap in the sources between the dry impersonality of formal administrative records and the self-consciously dramatic accounts of writers and chroniclers means that it is impossible to know for certain what even the most eminent members of medieval society – monarchs, nobles and prelates – thought and felt about their lives. In the case of men and women below this exalted level in the social hierarchy, evidence even of their actions can be difficult to find and harder to interpret. The one great exception is provided by the Paston letters, in which, as Fenn told his readers, '*the private life of individuals is laid open; we become acquainted with family occurrences; we see the transitions from joy to sorrow, from pain to pleasure'.*[9]

Given the ephemeral nature of such personal papers, the continued existence of the Paston correspondence is little short of miraculous. It was the chance result of an unforeseeable combination of circumstances: the carefulness with which the fifteenth-century Pastons kept their letters, and the carelessness of later generations who failed to clear their archive of documents which had no further practical use. Even when the papers came to light in the 1730s, it was not a foregone conclusion that they would be preserved. The antiquarian Blomefield thought it entirely possible – if regrettable – that the Earl of Yarmouth's executors would choose to burn them, and even he saw no particular value in *'those (of which there are many) that relate to nothing but family affairs only'.*[10] Forty years later, it was happy accident which brought the collection into the careful hands of John Fenn. Since the first publication of the letters in the 1780s, four other fifteenth-century correspondences have been discovered – those of the Stonors, an Oxfordshire gentry family; the Plumptons of Yorkshire (whose letters survive only in seventeenth-century transcript); the Celys, a family of wool merchants; and the Armburghs of Warwickshire. Invaluable though they are, none can match the Paston correspondence in scale or depth. Around three hundred Stonor letters survive from the fifteenth century, and a similar number of Plumpton papers from the fifteenth and early sixteenth centuries; the smaller Cely collection covers only two decades, and the Armburgh papers – found and published as recently as the 1990s – relate to a single highly complex legal dispute.[11] The Paston archive, meanwhile, consists of more than a thousand documents, written by three generations of the family over a period of seventy years. The fact that the Pastons themselves were caught up in the civil wars which convulsed England in the second half of the fifteenth century has reinforced both the enduring appeal of the letters and their exceptional value as a historical source.

Once transcribed from the *'crincum crancum hands'* which so intimidated Fenn, the language of the correspondence is direct and vivid. The vagaries of late medieval spelling lend a disconcertingly alien appearance to the Pastons' writing in unedited form, but the grammar and vocabulary of the period present few difficulties: if, for example, *'I haue do yowre herrendys to myn moder & myn hunckyl'* requires a second glance from modern readers, *'I have done your errands to my mother and my uncle'* does not.[12] However, the content of the letters is not always so easy to interpret. In some instances, references which were abundantly clear to both writer and recipient are now irretrievable ('*I have delivered the other thing that you sent me ensealed in the box as you commanded me . . .*').[13] Nor is it a straightforward matter to fit the correspondence together in sequence: not all of the letters are dated, and, even where they are, the contemporary practice of calculating time in relation to the Church's extensive calendar of holy days leaves plenty of room for confusion. A letter written on '*the Thursday before St Peter's Day*' might refer to the feast of St Peter and St Paul on 29 June, or that of St Peter's Chair on 22 February, or St Peter in Chains on 1 August, even without taking into account other saints who shared the apostle's name.[14] Despite the richness of the letters, it also has to be accepted that much remains unknown – and unknowable – about the Pastons. There are no surviving portraits or images of any member of the family in the fifteenth century, for example, and the letters provide no descriptions of personal appearance beyond a single mention of '*the gallant with the great chin*' – disappointingly, an acquaintance rather than a relative.[15]

Nevertheless, even if we cannot picture the Pastons' faces, the extraordinary fact is that, at a distance of more than five hundred years, we can hear their individual voices with the immediacy of an overheard conversation. The writers and recipients of the letters are real people – husbands and wives, parents and children, friends and enemies – who act, think and express themselves in instantly recognisable ways. Since the late sixteenth century, Shakespeare's epic cycle of history plays has exercised such a tenacious grip on the imagination that it is scarcely possible to think of the Wars of the Roses without conjuring up hectic images of poetry and melodrama, but the letters operate in a very different register of thought and speech. '*England hath long been mad, and scarred herself*', Shakespeare's King Henry VII declares after his victory on Bosworth field; for the Pastons, on the other hand, living in the midst of the conflict, '*the world, I assure you, is right queasy*'.[16] That world was a complex and competitive place, and they encountered its challenges with matter-of-fact pragmatism, sceptical intelligence and wry humour. But the Pastons were far more than passive observers of their times. In their letters, the tumultuous upheavals of civil war form the setting for the drama of the Pastons themselves – an ambitious *nouveau riche* family striving to leave their humble origins behind as the Wars of the Roses unfold around them.

This is their story.

– *a worshipful man grown by fortune of the world* –

In 1378, in a small village near the north-east Norfolk coast, there lived '*a good plain husbandman*' named Clement, who took his surname, Paston, from the place where he lived. Clement was a peasant farmer who held some arable land and '*a little poor watermill running by a little river*'. That was the sum total of his estate; '*other livelihood nor manors had he none, there nor in none other place*'. He was a careful man who worked hard to make his living from the land. The single surviving document describing his life tells how he '*went at one plough both winter and summer, and he rode to mill on the bare horseback with his corn under him, and brought home meal again under him*'. After the harvest each year he drove his cart the fifteen miles or so down the coast to Winterton to sell his grain, '*as a good husbandman ought to do*'.[1] Perhaps it was at Winterton market that he met a woman named Beatrice Goneld, whose family came from the neighbouring village of Somerton. Clement and Beatrice married, and in 1378 Beatrice gave birth to their only surviving child, a son named William. More than six hundred years later, there is little more that can be said about the lives of Clement and Beatrice Paston. Even the fact that these few details survive makes the couple unusual; most people of their time and class have left no trace in the written records which would allow even the sketchiest outline of their life stories to be drawn. One thing, however, can be concluded with some certainty: Clement and Beatrice were determined to do everything they could to give their son greater opportunities than they had ever had.

The figure of the self-made man from a poor background whose success founds a dynasty has become one of the iconic archetypes of modern fact and fiction, but the phenomenon is centuries old. Medieval English culture was deeply infused with the belief that the order of God's creation manifested itself in a social and political hierarchy within which every man should know and keep his place, but behind this image of rigid social stratification lay a wealth of opportunities for those with ability and ambition, even if their origins were humble. This was true more than ever at the end of the fourteenth century. The Black Death, which struck England in 1348, killed

nearly half the country's population – perhaps three million people – in little more than eighteen months. Contemporary chroniclers, in shock,
described how those left alive struggled to bury the corpses of the scores
who died each day. The plague itself was no respecter of persons; it *seizes
young and old alike, sparing no one, and reducing rich and poor to the same
level*, King Edward III wrote after his fourteen-year-old daughter succumbed to the disease in the autumn of 1348.[2] Even if their bodies remained
unscathed, the aristocracy soon made the uncomfortable discovery that
their purses might not escape the effects of mortality on such a horrifying
scale. The sudden and overwhelming shortage of peasant labour gave those
who survived an economic bargaining-power unimaginable in previous
centuries. Only a year after the epidemic's first outbreak, the government
reacted by trying to fix the cost of labour at pre-plague levels – the imposi-
tion of a maximum rather than a minimum wage – but population loss was
so immense that the economic tide could not be held back for long. Once
the immediate crisis was over, those who were left in the towns and the
countryside began to take advantage of the new opportunities for advancement which had opened up all around them. The futility of the government's attempt to block social mobility altogether was already becoming
apparent by 1363, when a statute was passed specifying detailed restrictions
to the *'outrageous and excessive apparel'* which many people were now affect-
ing, *'contrary to their estate and degree'*.[3]

For those who were determined to improve their lot, there were few better places to be than Norfolk at the turn of the fifteenth century. It was one
of the most prosperous counties in England, with rich soils to grow grain,
and pastureland for the thousands of sheep on which the flourishing local
wool and cloth industries depended. The flat East Anglian landscape offered
easy transport by river and road, and ships laden with cloth and grain sailed
from the ports of Yarmouth and Lynn to markets elsewhere in England, and
to the continent via Calais, the Low Countries and the Baltic. The sea coast
provided opportunities to make money in fishing as well as shipping, and
sea water was used for the production of salt, a valuable commodity essen-
tial for preserving meat, fish, butter and cheese. The commercial centre of
the shire was the city of Norwich, which suffered badly during the plague,
but recovered so rapidly that during the fifteenth century it overtook York
and Bristol to become the second-largest city in England after the capital,
with more than 10,000 inhabitants. If there was plenty of money to be made,
there was also enough flexibility in local society to accommodate those who
made it. The Norfolk gentry were numerous, wealthy and independent-

minded. While several great magnates had estates in the county, none had an interest large enough to guarantee a controlling stake in the social and political life of the region. As a result, successful merchants, tradesmen and professionals – clerics, lawyers or administrators – who aspired to convert their earnings into the status and influence conferred by landownership had a better chance of establishing themselves among the landed classes in Norfolk than in most other parts of the country.

If the young William Paston was to be one of them, he would first of all need an education. Clement scrimped, saved and borrowed to send his son to school, perhaps at Bromholm Priory, only a mile from Paston, or perhaps to a grammar school in Norwich. Such schools, often established on a very small scale, were springing up in increasing numbers in towns around the country; the boys who attended were taught to read and write and given instruction in Latin, the formal language of the Church and the law – two of the potential careers to which the acquisition of such skills gave an entrée. William chose the latter. In doing so, he was following in the footsteps of his maternal uncle Geoffrey Goneld, or Somerton as he now called himself, after his family's home village. Geoffrey Somerton was a modestly successful attorney with no children of his own, and he helped his brother-in-law Clement with the cost of sending William to London to train as a lawyer.

The four great central law courts sat a mile and a half outside the City of London in the Great Hall of the royal palace of Westminster: the court of Common Pleas on the west side of the Hall, the Chancery and the court of King's Bench on the dais at the south end, and the Exchequer in antechambers to the north. When all four were in session the vast space was filled with a hum of voices rising from the press of people to the magnificent hammerbeam roof forty feet above their heads. This was where William Paston came with his fellow students to sit in the 'crib', the place reserved for lawyers-in-training to observe the courts in action. Legal proceedings were conducted in English but recorded in Latin; until as recently as 1362 they had been conducted in French, the language of aristocratic society since the Conquest three hundred years earlier, although it was now being superseded by English in everyday use even among the highest social classes. William and the other students were expected to take notes on the cases they observed, and on the explanatory comments which the judges from time to time aimed in their direction. In the evenings, the students returned to their lodgings in one of the four Inns of Court – Gray's Inn, Lincoln's Inn, and the Inner and Middle Temple – which lay between Westminster and the City. The Inns had first developed as a convenient form of accommodation in the capital for lawyers working away from home, but by the early fifteenth century they were also offering courses of instruction in the intervals between the legal terms, when the courts were not in session. Students attended 'readings' given by senior members of the Inn – seminars where statutes were discussed in detail, clause by clause – and took part in 'moots', mock-trials in which they themselves had the chance to argue cases before their peers and their teachers.

William was a clever young man who made the most of the opportunities which his parents and his uncle had worked so hard to give him. His choice of career was a shrewd one. The English legal system in the late Middle Ages was the most centralised and sophisticated in Europe, with a network of royal officials which reached into every corner of local society. However, while the power of the law was theoretically all-encompassing, the reality was somewhat different. The state had no police force or standing army at its disposal through which decisions taken in royal courts could be directly enforced. Even had such a force existed, its deployment would have presented insuperable problems: the difficulties of communication – at a time when it took three days by road for a message to reach Norwich from London, for example – meant that government could be effective only if some means of enforcement were available rapidly, on the spot, wherever and whenever required. For that, the King had to rely on the private power of the nobility and gentry, whose estates gave them not only wealth and status, but authority over the peasant tenants who lived and worked on their lands. This authority – which contemporaries described as 'lordship' – was partly economic, since tenants owed rents and services to their lord in return for the land they cultivated; partly social, since deference to one's superiors was a religious as well as a cultural obligation; and partly jurisdictional, since the lord of each manor had the right to hold a court through which he regulated various aspects of his tenants' lives. At the most fundamental level, this direct control over people meant that, in any given region, the leading landowners could raise men quickly and effectively to enforce the King's commands. Of course, they could raise men quickly and effectively under other circumstances too; the capacity of landowners to use force for their own ends was an inescapable fact of medieval life.

The King's ability to rule therefore depended on his ability to harness the power of the landed hierarchy to serve his government – something which, under normal circumstances, was not difficult to achieve. If power depended on the possession of land, then the King's law – as the authority which guaranteed the security of landownership – had an overriding power of its own. All landowners needed the law to justify their possession of their estates; all landowners had a great deal to lose if order were allowed to disintegrate into anarchy. Their power was therefore the King's to command, a relationship in which political pragmatism merged seamlessly with their accepted duty of obedience to the anointed monarch. So long as the nobility and gentry were confident that the King would protect their interests by defending the realm from external attack and upholding the framework of law within it, they could get on with the important business of competing with one another for position and influence. Landownership brought with it endless possibilities for conflict – over title to estates, rights of inheritance, contested boundaries, competing jurisdictions, and so on *ad infinitum* – and landowners of all ranks did not hesitate to turn to the courts if they felt their rights were under threat. Even if disputes were eventually settled, as they often were, by private means – negotiation, mediation or arbitration – the law invariably played some part in the process. The courts could be used to pressurise an opponent to come to terms, or to validate a settlement once agreement had been reached. In this profoundly law-minded and litigious society, lawyers would never be short of opportunities to make money.

It was always likely, therefore, that William Paston would succeed in making a good living once he completed his training, but, as it turned out, he achieved a great deal more than that. He returned to Norfolk to start his legal practice, and the extent of his abilities rapidly became clear as he began to outstrip his uncle's achievements. By 1412 he had been retained as legal counsel to the powerful city corporation of Norwich. The Bishop of Norwich appointed William steward of his courts in 1413, and two years later he added the stewardship of the Duke of Norfolk's East Anglian estates to his portfolio. He was a justice of the peace in Norfolk from 1418, and the number of landowners for whom he acted as lawyer and trustee (or feoffee, to use the contemporary term) steadily increased. The widow of one such gentleman told William in 1426 of '*the great trust that my lord had in you, making you one of his feoffees and also one of his attorneys, as for one of his best trusted friends*'.[4] By that time, William's local influence was developing into an impressive career at national level. In 1418, at the age of forty, he was raised to the ranks of the serjeants-at-law, an elite group of senior lawyers from among whom judges were selected when there was a vacancy on the bench. The Year Book for 1422–3, in which notes were compiled on the year's most significant cases, makes clear that William was by then one of the five most prominent and influential lawyers practising in the court of Common Pleas.

William's workload was diverse and challenging. Lawsuits which reached a hearing at Westminster were often complex in both legal and political terms, requiring a great deal of expertise in the interpretation of statute and case law, as well as rhetorical agility and an adroit sense of diplomacy. Many were highly technical cases concerning the intricacies of land law, but others were more colourful. In 1422–3, for example, William became embroiled in a domestic dispute between Joan Holland, the dowager Duchess of York, and her fourth husband Henry Broomfleet, Lord Vescy. Broomfleet had spent four years serving overseas on Henry V's campaign in northern France, and told his servants to take orders from his wife while he was away, presuming, it seems, that she would stay at her manor of Cottingham in East Yorkshire during his absence. However, the dowager Duchess decided to leave Cottingham, and took with her more than a thousand pounds' worth of the couple's silver plate. Her husband was furious, allegedly because she had put such valuable possessions at risk by moving them – although it seems safe to assume that this particular disagreement formed part of a more general rift between the couple, since, rather than dealing with the matter in private, Broomfleet responded by bringing charges of theft against several members of his wife's household on the grounds that they had removed the silver without his permission. The dowager Duchess engaged William Paston to defend her men, but despite doing everything he could – arguing, for example, that the wrong writ had been served on his clients – he eventually lost the case. It is possible that, by this stage, the couple had made up their differences, and that the lawsuit was resolved by collusion between the litigants themselves.[5]

If the idea of lawyers making capital out of failing marriages is instantly recognisable from a modern perspective, another case in which William was involved in the summer of 1423 seems altogether alien – a reminder that the legal system within which he worked was rooted in a society where force might play a variety of roles, both public and private, in the pursuit of justice. William represented a knight named Sir Peter Tilliol in a dispute with Henry Percy, Earl of Northumberland, over the title to the manor of Torpenhow in Cumberland. For some reason which, frustratingly, the surviving records do not explain, it was decided that the case should be resolved not in the usual way, by summoning a jury of local men who would draw on their local knowledge in deciding between the two sides' claims, but instead by combat between two 'champions', one representing each of the litigants. Trial by battle was an ancient practice, which entrusted the complex task of deciding guilt to divine rather than human judgement. By the fifteenth century, however, it had almost entirely fallen out of use, certainly for cases of disputed landownership such as this one. As a result, the imposing ceremonial which attended a judicial battle was already so antique and unfamiliar that the court found itself uncertain of some of the finer points of detail.[6]

The main outline of the ritual, however, was clear enough for the case to proceed. On the first day of the hearing, at the judges' command, each of the two champions placed five pennies into the fingers of a glove. Then, using their right hands with their arms uncovered to the elbow, they threw the gloves into the court. The following day, they returned to the hall, '*bareheaded and ungirdled, well-hosed and without shoes*'.[7] The two men climbed over the bar at which the serjeants-at-law stood to plead cases; one was directed to stand at the western side of the court, the other to the east. William Paston and his opposite number, the Earl of Northumberland's lawyer, were called upon to confirm that the champions were ready to fight, and that there was no legal reason to delay the duel. Once they had done so, battle was awarded to take place three days later. The champions were not to meet or communicate in the meantime; one was sent westwards to Westminster Abbey, the other east to St Paul's Cathedral, to pray that God would give victory to the rightful claimant. On the appointed day, Saturday 3 July, William appeared in court with Tilliol's champion, who stood at the bar dressed, as was traditional, in red leather over his armour (in order, according to a contemporary treatise, that, if he were to be injured, '*his adversary shall not lightly espy his blood*', and thereby gain an advantage by playing on the injury, '*for in all other colours blood will lightly be seen*').[8] Once they were ready, Northumberland's champion was summoned into the hall. The order was given three times, but neither the Earl nor his man appeared. The court therefore judged that Northumberland had defaulted, and the disputed manor was awarded to Tilliol. The Earl's non-appearance was almost certainly the result of a settlement negotiated behind the scenes; in public, however, William had won the case without a blow being struck.

The fact that William acted for the plaintiff in probably the last case of English land law ever tried by combat – even if the duel itself did not ultimately take place – is a curiosity among the many distinctions of what was fast becoming a remarkable legal career. In 1426, he was appointed a King's serjeant – one of a select group from among the serjeants-at-law who were retained by the crown to act for the King in his courts. Those whose expertise and experience were recognised in this way could confidently expect in due course to be raised to the bench, and William was no exception. Three years later, at the age of fifty-one, he exchanged the white coif and striped gown of a serjeant-at-law for the red robes of a justice in the court of Common Pleas.

William had reached the top of his profession. The peasant's son from Paston village was now one of the King's most senior judicial representatives. He was also a rich man, earning money on a scale which gave him a standard of living far removed from his father's life at Paston, riding to mill *'on the bare horseback with his corn under him'*. A labourer or peasant farmer working on the land in the favourable economic conditions of the fifteenth century might earn something of the order of £3 a year. When Clement Paston himself died in June 1419, he left charitable bequests, mainly to St Margaret's church at Paston where he was buried, which came to a total of not much more than £1.[9] A minor member of the gentry, meanwhile, might find himself with a disposable income of perhaps £20 a year. William, on the other hand, received an annual sum of more than £70 for his work as a justice of Common Pleas, to replace the substantial fees from the landowners, religious institutions and town corporations by whom he had previously been retained as legal counsel. However, wealth alone was not enough to establish himself securely in the aristocratic circles in which he now moved: for that, he needed to use his money to buy himself an estate.

Landownership was the defining mark of a gentleman, but it was landownership of a particular kind that counted; simply accumulating farmland of the type which Clement Paston had held would not do. Aristocratic landholders owned whole manors, which brought with them the privileges of manorial lordship, and the acquisition of lands of this kind would not necessarily be a straightforward business. Despite the massive population loss, competition for such properties remained fierce. The increase in social mobility meant that, for every gentry family which died out or mismanaged its affairs, there was a wealthy newcomer – or, more likely, several wealthy newcomers – waiting to snap up its estates. Even once a purchase had been secured, the new owner might still face further challenges. The political, social and financial value of manorial land was such that no one would willingly relinquish any sort of a claim to its possession, and the heirs of whoever sold the property, or of those who had owned it in the past – even the distant past – might allege that they had been unlawfully deprived of their rights. Claims of this kind could embroil a purchaser for years in troublesome and costly litigation, and a particularly unwise or unlucky buyer, who failed to check the seller's title to the estate with sufficient care or faced a particularly powerful challenger, might even lose the land altogether. The irony of the situation – that his professional success had now brought him to a point where he would have to confront the very difficulties which had been such a fruitful source of employment in his legal practice – cannot have been lost on a man as astute as William.

The residual power of lineage and inheritance, even in the face of lawful purchase, presented rising professionals like William with a further problem. Social mobility in late medieval England took place within a culture which publicly proclaimed that power, wealth and status were inextricably linked with birth, however great the evidence to the contrary. In theory, gentlemen were born, not made, and land handed down from generation to generation of irreproachably blue blood. In practice, of course, gentlemen were ever more frequently made rather than born. The trick was to cover the traces of such transactions as quickly and deftly as possible, in order that social appearances could be preserved by allowing new blood to be accepted as old. The Pastons themselves later took great pains to suppress the story of Clement Paston's labour on the land, not because it was inaccurate, but precisely because it was true. The single surviving account of his life, which makes his hard work sound so impressive to modern ears, was compiled in the middle of the fifteenth century by an anonymous enemy of the family to demonstrate that Clement's descendants had no right to the exalted social status they were attempting to claim. The document had both a sarcastic title – '*A Remembrance of the Worshipful Kin and Ancestry of Paston*' – and a far from subtle theme: much of Clement's land, the author says, was '*bond land*'; his wife Beatrice was '*a bond woman*'; '*and as for Geoffrey Somerton, he was bond also*'.[10] The word 'bond' came from Old Norse, and had equivalents deriving from each of the other languages which had contributed to the formation of late medieval English – 'serf' from Latin, 'churl' from Old English, and 'villein' from Old French. All four were equally unwelcome to Paston ears: a bondman, serf, churl or villein was an unfree man, who could be regarded in some senses at least as the property of the lord of the manor on which he lived. Unfreedom was an inherited, personal status which imposed unwelcome obligations: unfree peasants were in theory required to work on their lord's land as well as their own holdings; they also had to pay for his permission to marry, to move away from the manor, or even to send their sons to school. In practice, the changed economic climate after the Black Death meant that it was becoming much harder for lords to enforce their rights over their unfree tenants, or even to identify who was free and who was not. If Geoffrey Somerton was indeed a bondman, for example, it did not stop him pursuing a career as a local attorney. Nevertheless, the allegation was a serious threat to the family's standing or 'worship' (a term laden with significance for contemporaries, meaning both the qualities characteristic of gentility and the respect in which someone who displayed those qualities was held). It might also be a dangerous weapon in the hands of a resourceful opponent, since unfreedom brought with it specific legal disabilities – bondmen technically had no right of access to the King's courts, for example, and no right to exercise jurisdiction in a manor court – which might be used to challenge the family's right to hold manorial land.

Despite these many complications, William Paston proved more than equal to the task he faced. He set about building up a landed estate with the same shrewd and at times ruthless efficiency with which he pursued his legal career. Most of the properties he bought over a twenty-year period from the late 1410s onwards were concentrated in his home region of northern Norfolk, not far from the land he inherited from his father Clement and his uncle Geoffrey Somerton. Paston itself was not a manor in its own right, but William began to buy up as much land as he could in and around the village, with the intention of creating a new manor there to serve as the ancestral home of his dynasty. This was an ambitious project in political as well as practical terms, but by no means unrealistically so. William's timing was good: during the 1420s there were relatively few great magnates in the region on whose toes he might risk treading. The Duke of Norfolk and the Earl of Suffolk spent much of the decade fighting in France, and their estates were in any case concentrated mainly in Suffolk. The only nobleman with a major estate in northern Norfolk was the Duke of Lancaster, who from 1399 – when Henry Bolingbroke, the heir to the duchy, seized the throne from his cousin Richard II to become Henry IV – was also the King. William had powerful connections within the royal administration, and was himself retained as legal counsel to the Duchy of Lancaster by 1420. This association was not the only way in which his career helped to facilitate his transition from wealthy professional to landed gentleman. He had the contacts to help him find manors to buy, the expertise to see purchases safely through, and the influence to defend his new possessions. By the early 1440s, he had succeeded in accumulating estates which brought him a landed income of about £250 a year.

Nevertheless, his success was not achieved without effort and persistence. There may have been no noblemen blocking his path, but competition among the Norfolk gentry and would-be gentry – men like William himself – was intense. With demand for manorial estates so consistently high, every step forward for William inevitably represented a reverse for someone else, whether a reluctant seller or a rival buyer. Land purchases could be hard-fought affairs, and it was easy to make enemies. William's acquisition of the north Norfolk manor of East Beckham, for example, took a decade to complete, and the hostilities provoked by the saga lingered for many years after that. The estate was offered for sale in 1434 by a widow named Joan Mariot. Her husband had made money in the fishing industry at Cromer, but his aspirations to gentility had not yet removed him from the dangers of his trade; he drowned '*by tempest of the sea*',[11] and Joan was forced to sell off land in the attempt to clear his debts. East Beckham was well placed for Paston interests – it lay a little more than ten miles up the coast from Paston, but only a mile from Gresham, a valuable manor which William had bought seven years earlier – and he immediately made Joan Mariot an offer for the property. However, a rival bid came just as quickly from a gentleman named Edmund Winter, from whose family the Mariots had originally bought the manor twenty years before.

Edmund's father William Winter, like William Paston a generation later, was a lawyer from a poor family, who made himself a fortune and used his money to buy estates, including East Beckham, in northern Norfolk. After his death, East Beckham was sold to pay for religious bequests in his will, but the loss of the manor rankled with his son, whose fortunes were on the slide by the early 1430s. As Edmund struggled to defend his family's interests, he did not give up his attachment to what had once been Winter property, but at least he had the consolation that East Beckham in the hands of a Cromer fisherman posed little threat to what remained of the Winters' local influence. The prospect that the estate might now be taken over by Judge William Paston – whose star was rising as rapidly as Winter's was falling – was an entirely different matter. Edmund was so desperate that, when it became clear at the end of 1434 that his bid to buy back the manor had failed, he took it by force.

Winter seized East Beckham before its sale to William Paston had been completed. William therefore offered to act for Joan Mariot in her legal battle to recover the manor, on the basis that his costs would be offset against the purchase price he had already agreed to pay her. The lawsuit was tortuous, and, despite Judge William's eminence and expertise, Edmund Winter scored some early successes. The Mariots' frustration with Winter – and perhaps William's too – spilled over in the course of proceedings in Chancery in 1436: '*another so great a forswearer*,' they declared, '*nor so damnable a slanderer, nor so shameless usual languager, visager and contriver of untrue, feigned and slanderous tales and matters as he is, was never in his days of his degree in that shire*'.[12] The case was still not resolved when Joan Mariot died in 1441. Her son John rapidly realised that, even if the final verdict were to go his way, virtually all of the money his family desperately needed to raise by selling East Beckham would now be eaten up by William's costs for seven years of litigation. Mariot saw no alternative but to back out of the sale – and immediately found an unlikely ally in his opponent Edmund Winter. Despite his success in spinning out the lawsuit thus far, Winter knew his claim to the manor was technically weak; his overriding priority all along had been to protect his wider interests by stopping William from taking possession of the estate, and he stood a much better chance of doing so if he now backed John Mariot's decision to keep it for himself. However, after seven years in court, William was not about to walk away without a fight. His own claim to East Beckham was shaky, to say the least, given that the purchase agreement had never taken legal effect. On the other hand, he did hold all the title deeds – which the Mariots had given to him when he agreed to represent them against Winter – and had no intention of returning them. He dug in his heels, and brought to bear all the political and judicial influence he could muster. He managed to secure custody of the manor in 1442, and finally, in July 1444, nearly ten years after his first attempt to buy it, William's title to East Beckham was confirmed by the courts.

As Edmund Winter and John Mariot had discovered to their cost, William was pursuing his campaign of upward social mobility with absolute focus and single-minded ambition. As an experienced lawyer and now a royal judge, he knew that litigation was as much a political process as a legal one, and he was prepared to use all the means at his disposal – both inside and outside the courtroom – to further his interests. None of his other legal battles is as well documented as the fight for East Beckham, but what scraps of information survive confirm that he was a tough and totally uncompromising opponent. Juliana Herberd, a Norwich widow, claimed that, in order to get his hands on her property, William had her imprisoned for three years '*in the pit within the castle of Norwich in great mischief, in so much that she had not but a pint of milk in ten days and ten nights and a farthing loaf*'.[13] Herberd clearly believed that he was pitiless; another opponent during the 1420s, a former soldier named Walter Aslak, also found William to be a relentless adversary. William alleged that, in the course of their dispute, Aslak posted up anonymous notices around Norwich threatening him and his servants with '*menaces of death and dismembering*', threats which were made doubly terrifying, he said, by allusions to a recent unsolved and particularly vicious murder in the county. As if that were not enough, William pointed out that the notices contained '*also these two words in Latin, "et cetera", by which words commonly it was understood that the forgers and makers of the said bills imagined to the said William, his clerks and servants, more malice and harm than in the said bills was expressed*'.[14] Aslak protested his innocence and, under some political pressure, William was persuaded that the case should go to arbitration. At that point it would have been usual to halt legal proceedings until the appointed arbiters had given their judgement, but William refused to withdraw the suit on which he had already embarked. At his insistence, it was agreed that the lawsuit should proceed – and, further, that Aslak would not resort to procedural defences or invoke political protection when the case was heard, but simply answer the charge brought against him. Aslak complied with this highly unusual stipulation on the understanding that, whatever happened in court, William would stand by the outcome of the arbitration, and that Aslak would therefore '*not be damaged in his body nor his goods, whatsoever the inquest said*'.[15]

The two sides gave very different accounts of what happened next. Aslak said that William '*broke his faith and his troth*' and secured a court order for his imprisonment. William, on the other hand, protested that he was '*at all times ready to obey and perform*' the arbiters' award, but that Aslak '*plainly refused*'.[16] Whatever the rights and wrongs of the case – which are now impossible to recover – the ruthlessness of William's tactics is apparent. He knew his strengths and he played to them. The law courts were his home territory, from which he would not budge even in circumstances where it would have been both normal and expected for him to do so. Like any other landowner, he was prepared to go to arbitration in the hope of an advantageous settlement and to use all of his political weight in the attempt to influence the outcome, but, for William, negotiations of this kind were an adjunct to litigation, not an alternative to it. In this instance, he even managed to engineer a situation in which his opponent had already promised not to avail himself of several possible lines of legal defence by the time the case came to court. '*And under this colour*', Aslak later complained, '*the said Walter was deceived*'.[17]

William's uncompromising approach was a necessary condition of his success, both as a lawyer and as a newcomer to the competitive world of the gentry. However, by his own lights at least, an uncompromising approach was not the same as an unscrupulous one. Most of the information which has survived about the Herberd and Aslak cases comes from petitions submitted in the course of the hearings, complete with legal jargon and overheated rhetoric, but William also mentioned the disputes in a private letter written in the spring of 1426, when both cases were in full flood. His brief comments give pause for thought about the machiavellian figure described by his opponents. In his letter, William talked of his *'three adversaries'* – Herberd, Aslak, and a priest named John Wortes, who was harassing the Prior of Bromholm by claiming to have been appointed prior there himself. *'I have not trespassed against none of these three, God knows'*, William said, *'and yet I am foully and noisingly vexed with them to my great unease, and all for my lords' and friends' matters and not for my own'.*[18] In other words, he had become involved in all three cases not on his own account, but in his professional capacity as a lawyer. This was certainly true in the Wortes case: William was the priory's legal representative, and became personally embroiled as a result when Wortes – who was clearly something of a loose cannon – not only began proceedings to have William excommunicated, but claimed that his own real name was Paston and that he was William's cousin (*'God defend that any of my poor kin should be of such governance as he is of'*, William said feelingly).[19] But the same was also true in the cases of Aslak and Herberd. Aslak's hostility was rooted in the fact that William represented Norwich Priory against him in a dispute over the right of appointment to a local benefice; and Juliana Herberd's lands were caught up in a lawsuit in which, again, William was acting on behalf of someone else. Not only that, but William clearly believed that he had done nothing wrong in the course of these disputes, either legally or morally. Of course, his healthy confidence in the rectitude of his own position did not necessarily mean that his conduct was beyond reproach, but the gulf between his perspective and those of his opponents is an indication of the complexities of a world where the personal, the professional and the political could not easily be distinguished, let alone separated.

The fact that the William of the 1426 letter – weary at the harassment he felt he was enduring, and eloquent in his irritation – is so much more human than the villain of his enemies' petitions emphasises the difficulties of drawing conclusions from evidence that is fragmentary at best. The voices of later generations of Pastons speak clearly in their letters, but very little of William's correspondence has survived: only seven letters in all, six of them concerning his legal affairs, and one specifying the masonry he required for a mill he was building at Mundesley near Paston village. His domestic life has left so few traces in the existing documents that it is almost touching to find, among his legal papers, a note in his own handwriting of a recipe for a *'wholesome drink of ale'* given to him by a Norfolk gentlewoman named Sybilla, Lady Boys. Various herbs, including sage, rosemary, thyme, cloves, mace and spikenard, should be placed in a bag inside each barrel of ale, Sybilla told him, together with '*a new-laid hen's egg*' which would '*keep the ale from souring*'.[20] Sybilla Boys was a friend, but by the 1420s there was another, much more important woman in William's life: his wife, Agnes.

As a young man, William seems to have made no attempt to marry, preferring instead to dedicate himself to his career. Like everything else he did, that was a matter of calculation; after all, a wealthy lawyer and landowner in his forties could secure a much better marriage than a legal student from a poor background in his twenties. Finally, in 1420, at the age of forty-two – newly promoted to the rank of serjeant-at-law after two decades of single-minded devotion to his work – William was ready to commit himself to family life. The match he made was an excellent one. His bride was the elder daughter of a Hertfordshire knight named Sir Edmund Barry. As co-heiress of her father's estates, Agnes brought William three manors, and, at more than twenty years his junior, she could reliably be expected to produce the heirs who would secure the future of the Paston name. William was not disappointed: their first child, a son named John, was born on 10 October 1421.

Frustratingly, almost nothing of the couple's personal relationship beyond those bare facts can now be recaptured. None of William's letters to his wife has survived, and only one written by Agnes to William. That one, at least – so far as it is possible to tell from a single short note, scribbled in haste, years into their marriage – seems to confirm the impression Agnes gave in later life of being matter-of-fact, unromantic and thoroughly practical. William was away in London, which gave Agnes the opportunity to ask him to do some shopping for her. In this case, it was gold thread she wanted: '*I pray you do buy for me two pipes of gold*', she wrote, before adding news of her husband's fishponds ('*Your stews do well*').[21] Pragmatism rather than imagination in his young wife probably suited William well, and certainly their partnership proved both lasting and fruitful. Over the next twenty years, Agnes gave birth to three more sons, Edmund, William and Clement, and one daughter, Elizabeth. At least one more boy, Henry, died in childhood.

By the early 1440s, Judge William Paston – now in his sixties – had good reason to survey his achievements with satisfaction. While his father had '*lived upon his land that he had in Paston, and kept thereon a plough all times in the year*',[22] William was building a manor house there, complete with its own chapel. The one gamble this intelligent and ambitious man had taken was the decision to postpone starting a family until middle age. His late marriage had brought him many advantages, but it also meant that his son and heir would probably be no more than a young man when he took his place as head of the family. It remained to be seen whether the gamble would pay off.

CHAPTER TWO

– no will of them in writing –

William Paston's decision to invest two decades in his spectacularly successful career before marrying and starting a family meant that his son's
upbringing was dramatically different from his own. John Paston was not
born into village life, but into the luxurious and cosmopolitan world of the
gentry. William had succeeded in giving his son all the advantages of birth
which he had lacked, but he could not let go of his driving ambition: his own
father's life at the plough was too fresh in the memory for the family's position yet to be secure. He was determined that John should have an education
which would mark him out as a gentleman, and give him the skills he would
need to defend Paston interests against rivals for whom such a recently constructed estate represented rich potential pickings.

Like his father – but without the financial struggles which dogged
William's education – John was first taught at home in Norfolk, either within the Paston household itself or at a grammar school in Norwich. In his
mid-teens, however, he was sent to study at Cambridge. The university
there, like its counterpart in Oxford, was already more than two hundred
years old. All the scholars who taught at the universities were members of
the clergy, whether priests or monks, and almost all of those who undertook
the four years of study required to graduate to the degree of Bachelor of
Arts, or seven to become a Master of Arts, were also destined for a career in
the Church. However, by the early fifteenth century it was increasingly common for the sons of noblemen and gentlemen to further their education by
spending a year or two sampling the courses on offer – which included
grammar, logic, rhetoric, arithmetic, music, geometry, astronomy and philosophy, as well as more advanced tuition in theology, canon law, civil law
and medicine – without proceeding to a degree. Most such students lived in
private lodgings and worked under the individual direction of one of the
university's Masters of Arts, but by the later 1430s, when John Paston arrived
in Cambridge, there were also six colleges in the town: Peterhouse, Clare,
Pembroke, Gonville Hall, Trinity Hall and Corpus Christi.[1] The colleges
were religious foundations which provided a privileged academic environ-

ment for the scholars who made up their fellowships, but they also accommodated a limited number of undergraduates. Supporting a student at a college was a particularly costly business, but Judge William's wealth meant that expense was no bar to his ambitions for his family. John was sent to Trinity Hall, a college which had Norfolk connections – its founder was William Bateman, Bishop of Norwich in the mid-fourteenth century – and which specialised in the study of civil and canon law.

At seventeen, newly equipped with this academic grounding, John spent a year serving as a Yeoman of the Stable in the royal household. The Stable was – exactly as it sounds – the division of the household establishment responsible for the care of the King's horses, a major enterprise given the number of animals needed to transport the court when it moved, as it regularly did, between the royal palaces. Under the overall command of the Master of the Horse, the Yeomen of the Stable worked under the immediate supervision of the Avener, whose title derived from the Latin word for the oats with which the horses were fed. Looking after horses was too menial a job for John to have undertaken in his own family home, but menial jobs became gentlemanly ones if they were performed in a noble household, or especially in the service of the King.[2] Placements of this kind offered gentlemen's sons the chance to cultivate the polished manners of the court, and to observe at close hand the workings of political life at the very highest level. William Paston had in abundance the influential contacts needed to secure such an appointment for his son. He had served the Lancastrian dynasty for years, and his professional career had flourished under the government of Henry V, an outstandingly able man whose commanding rule in England was matched by his military successes in France. By the later 1430s, the hopes of the political establishment rested on King Henry's son, Henry VI, a teenager a couple of months younger than John Paston, but, until the boy King was old enough to rule for himself, the responsibilities of government lay in the hands of his leading nobles – for the most part men of William's generation, many of whom William knew well. Thanks to his father's success, John therefore had the opportunity to pursue his political education with the same degree of privilege as his academic schooling.

By the time he turned eighteen in the autumn of 1439, John Paston had had a taste of the best education money could buy, and of the sophisticated culture and complex politics of the court. However, William – whose legal expertise had been so crucial to his dealings in land as well as his professional success – also wanted his son to acquire a working knowledge of the law. As the heir to a valuable estate, John would have no need to follow in his father's footsteps as a practising lawyer, but William nevertheless believed that a legal training was an indispensable part of his son's preparation for his future responsibilities; *'he said many times'*, Agnes later recalled, *'that whosoever should dwell at Paston should have need to con defend himself'*.[3] John therefore went to Westminster, as his father had done forty years earlier, to study the common law. His time at the Inns of Court was socially as well as educationally productive: *'And when your leisure is, resort again unto your college the Inner Temple'*, a friend wrote warmly in November 1440, *'for there be many which sore desire your presence'*.[4] By then, back in Norfolk at just turned nineteen, John had other responsibilities: he was now a married man.

Judge William, the son of a peasant, had waited twenty years to marry, until his professional success allowed him to make an advantageous match. In doing so, he helped to ensure that his son would not have to wait nearly so long for a wife. As the eldest son of a wealthy gentleman, John had a great deal to offer as a prospective husband. Not only that, but he had a responsibility to marry sooner rather than later, to secure his family's future by providing a new generation of Paston heirs. His parents lost no time in searching for a suitable bride, and the young woman on whom their choice fell was an heiress named Margaret Mautby. She was an only child, whose father had died when she was ten or eleven; she was now living with her mother and stepfather at his manor of Geldeston in south-eastern Norfolk. In prospect, it was a fine match. The Mautby estates which Margaret would inherit were worth around £150 a year – a major addition to the annual landed income of £300 or so which William and Agnes between them now commanded – and their location in the north and east of the county complemented that of the Paston lands. By the time the young couple met for the first time in April 1440, plans for the wedding were already well advanced; they had probably been under discussion for years, since William had known Margaret's father and grandfather well and was a trustee in the Mautby estates. However, an arranged marriage of this kind would serve the two families' interests only if it became a lasting partnership; husband and wife would need to work as a team to manage their household and estates, and it was vital that the relationship should produce children. The hope was always that affection or even love would grow once the couple had spent some time together. In this case, the omens looked good. *'And as for the first acquaintance between John Paston and the said gentlewoman'*, Agnes reported to her husband, *'she made him gentle cheer in gentle wise, and said he was verily your son. And so I hope there shall need no great treaty between them'*.[5]

Agnes's instincts could not be faulted. Neither John nor Margaret was prone to romantic fantasy; even as eighteen-year-olds, they were sensible, pragmatic people who understood and appreciated their parents' reasons for bringing them together. Perhaps as a result, their compatibility was obvious and immediate. Within six months of meeting they were married. After the wedding, John returned to Cambridge to continue his studies – this time at Peterhouse, the oldest college in the university – and also spent time in London with his father on family business. Margaret, meanwhile, remained at home in Norfolk. She was an intelligent young woman, who had been educated as befitted an heiress who would one day be mistress of a wealthy household. However, in a culture where oral traditions of learning still had deep roots, education did not necessarily imply literacy. Margaret almost certainly knew how to read, but, like most gentlewomen, she was not taught the technical business of writing with a quill pen on parchment or paper; even the handwriting of her expensively educated husband was much cruder than that of a trained clerk, for whom writing was a professional skill. While John usually dictated his letters and then corrected and signed them himself before they were sent, Margaret was wholly reliant on the few members of their household who could write if she wished to send messages to her husband while he was away. However, the impossibility of completely private communication – something of which, of course, she had no expectation – did not stop Margaret composing letters which were both personal and engagingly characterful.

In December 1441, a little more than a year after their marriage, Margaret was staying with her mother-in-law Agnes at Oxnead, a manor nine miles north of Norwich which William had bought more than twenty years earlier, and which was now one of the family's principal residences. John was away in London and Margaret was looking forward to his return, but his absence did at least raise the enticing prospect of the fine shopping which the capital had to offer. Judge William had promised her a new girdle, and was blaming his failure to produce it on John's forgetfulness, an explanation which Margaret was reluctant to believe: '*I suppose that is not so,*' she wrote; '*he said it but for a scusation*'. There was a connection, it transpired, between her eagerness to have John home and her impatience to have the new girdle: she was almost six months pregnant with their first child. '*I am waxed so elegant,*' she said wryly, '*that I may not be girt in no bar of no girdle that I have but of one*'. A close family friend, John Damme, had visited the house, and when he heard the news '*he said by his troth that he was not gladder of nothing that he heard this twelvemonth than he was thereof*', Margaret told her husband, sounding both excited and self-conscious about her changing shape: '*I may no longer live by my craft; I am discovered of all men that see me*'.[6]

Childbirth was a process managed exclusively by women – usually an experienced midwife with the help of the expectant mother's female relatives. Unnervingly, the local midwife had been incapacitated by a bad back for the best part of four months, but Margaret was reassured to receive a message that she would nevertheless come when needed, '*though she should be pushed in a barrow*'. Despite the fact that John himself would have no part to play at the birth, it was clear how glad Margaret would be to have him home for the later stages of her pregnancy. '*I pray you*', she asked, '*that you will wear the ring with the image of St Margaret that I sent you for a remembrance till you come home*' – St Margaret being the patron saint of pregnant women as well as her own namesake. She added a rueful afterthought: '*You have left me such a remembrance that makes me to think upon you both day and night when I would sleep*'.[7]

The baby, who was born safely by the middle of April 1442, was a boy, named John like his father. Fatherhood did not mean that John could spend all of his time at home, however, any more than William had been able to do so when John himself was growing up. During his frequent absences, Margaret had to take responsibility for the running of their household in Norfolk. Officially, their main home was now Gresham, a valuable estate near the north Norfolk coast, which William had bought in 1427. Gresham was Margaret's jointure – property settled jointly on the couple when they married, to provide them with a home and an income until John came into his inheritance, and to ensure that Margaret would still have a home and an income for her lifetime if she were left a widow. In practice, however, she and the baby spent a good deal of time staying with her mother Margery at Geldeston, and probably more still with her mother-in-law Agnes at Oxnead and Norwich. Margaret and Agnes got on well, despite the twenty-year age gap. They were similar in temperament – direct, straightforward and down to earth – and also had babies very close in age, since Agnes gave birth to her fifth surviving child, Clement, not long before the arrival of John and Margaret's little boy. Margaret's letters give the distinct impression that the two women could be a formidable combination when they chose. '*My mother greets you well and sends you God's blessing and hers, and she prays you, and I pray you also, that you be well dieted of meat and drink, for that is the greatest help that you may have now to your health ward*', Margaret told John firmly in the autumn of 1443. He had been seriously ill, and she and Agnes had done everything they could think of to intercede for his recovery; Agnes promised a wax statue weighing as much as John himself to the shrine of the Virgin Mary at Walsingham, and Margaret vowed to travel there on pilgrimage. '. . . *by my troth*', she told him, '*my mother and I were not in heart's ease from the time that we knew of your sickness till we knew verily of your amending*'. At twenty-one, Margaret was still very young, and her affection for her husband was expressed in endearingly blunt fashion. '*If I might have had my will I should have seen you before this time. I would you were at home*', she said, '. . . *liefer than a new gown, though it were of scarlet*'.[8]

At least she had news to cheer John during his convalescence. She was pregnant again, and in the spring of 1444 gave birth to another boy. Confusingly – and for reasons which are not at all clear – this second son was also named John like his father and brother. Christian names often ran in families, but they normally did so in succeeding generations, and to find three Johns in only two generations is extremely rare. The most likely explanation is that John and Margaret observed a widespread custom in naming each of their two sons after his chief godparent, and happened to choose two godfathers who shared the same name as John himself. No information survives about the boys' baptisms or the identity of their godparents, but there were a number of plausible candidates named John in the Pastons' circle: Sir John Fastolf, for example, a wealthy relative of Margaret's, for whom William Paston acted as a legal adviser; her maternal uncle John Berney of Reedham; or perhaps Judge William's friend John Damme of Sustead, who had been so delighted to hear the news of Margaret's first pregnancy. Whatever the reason for the repetition, the family themselves never seem to have had problems distinguishing between father and sons. Years later, Margaret saw no difficulty in writing a letter to John Paston to let him know that '*I received a letter . . . from John Paston, in the which letter he wrote that you desired that I should have John Paston . . . look in the great standing chest in one of the great canvas bags which stand against the lock*'.[9] It was clear to her when she wrote the letter, and to her husband when he read it, that she had passed on instructions sent by her elder son, staying with his father in London, to her younger son, at home with her in Norwich. Even in the family's most informal correspondence, there is no sign of diminutives or nicknames; the boys usually signed themselves '*John Paston the elder*' and '*John Paston the younger*' or '*the youngest*', to distinguish themselves from their father, who was simply '*John Paston, esquire*'. The younger son once signed a letter to his mother as '*John of Geldeston*' – Margaret's mother's home after her remarriage, and the place where he was born – but it was an isolated attempt to write in private code at a time of political danger, rather than a reflection of any need to differentiate himself from his brother.[10]

By the summer of 1444, Margaret, at twenty-two, was growing up fast. She had two young sons and increasing domestic responsibilities, including the often pressing need to manage the family budget. Their income from the manor of Gresham, like all estate revenues, was sporadic. Like most of the gentry and nobility, the Pastons leased out nearly all of their lands rather than farming them directly themselves, but rents were paid seasonally, and – wealthy though they were – cash might run short as rent-day approached, or even after that, if the harvest was bad or prices low and the tenants could not pay what they owed. '*I suppose I must borrow money in short time but if you come soon home*', Margaret told her husband that July. '*So God help me, I have but four shillings, and I owe near as much money.*' She was confident enough of their finances to ask John to do some shopping for her in London, but she was clearly under strain; she could not suppress her irritation, for example, at his inability to remember that the boys might grow while he was away: '*As for caps that you sent me for the children, they be too little for them. I pray you buy them finer caps and larger than those were.*'[11]

Such domestic worries were about to be swept aside, however, by the dramatic changes which engulfed her life, and that of her husband, only weeks later. Her father-in-law, Judge William, was now in his mid-sixties, and beginning to suffer from serious ill-health – so much so that six months earlier he had been forced to take sick-leave from his judicial duties, which included not only sitting to hear cases in the court of Common Pleas, but serving on commissions of assize. Assize judges, appointed from among the justices and serjeants-at-law of the Westminster courts, travelled on circuits around the country twice a year to bring the King's justice directly to the localities. William was due to ride the south-eastern circuit in the early spring of 1444, but had to withdraw from the commission because of his illness. Quite apart from the demands of hearing the cases themselves, the physical strain of moving between the towns where the sessions were to be held was too much to contemplate. John stayed with him in Norfolk, helping to write his letters, while in London his legal clerk James Gresham conveyed his apologies to John Fortescue, the chief justice of King's Bench. Fortescue was particularly sympathetic since he too was unwell. '*He has had a sciatica that has letted him a great while to ride,*' Gresham reported, '*and dares not yet come on no horse's back. And therefore he has spoken to the lords of the council and informed them of your sickness, and his also.*' Gresham's own concern for his master's health was evident: '*Almighty Jesu make you hale and strong'*, he wrote.[12] William did recover – he was back in court later in the spring – but the episode was serious enough to convince him that he should update his will. That summer, he was in London, staying with Agnes at his lodgings near St Bride's church in Fleet Street, when he again fell ill. On Thursday 13 August, not long before midnight, William died.

William's career had brought him a long way from his roots in Paston village. His parents were buried in the church there, and his father had left bequests in his will of a few shillings apiece. William's body was brought back from London to Norfolk and buried, as he had wanted, in the Lady Chapel of Norwich's great cathedral; he left a landed estate which had made him a powerful man in northern Norfolk, and personal possessions, including a great deal of cash, which were worth a few thousand pounds. Nevertheless, the legacy he left his heir was not a straightforward one. William's success had ensured that his son was a gentleman born, not a professional lawyer trying to clothe himself in the trappings of gentility, and William had done everything he could to give him a privileged training for the role he was about to take up. However, John was just twenty-two years old, and what he lacked was time: time to gain experience of the political world, and to develop his own standing within it. He had none of the personal influence which his father had built up as a result of his long and distinguished career. Over the course of four decades William had demonstrated that he was a shrewd operator who knew exactly how best to pursue and defend his own interests. John, on the other hand, was an unknown quantity. Fresh from his studies, in August 1444 he was left alone and exposed at the head of a family which had powerful enemies as well as powerful friends. Inexperienced though John was, he was not a fool, and he must have anticipated that the Pastons' local rivals would try to take advantage of his loss. Even if he was prepared for trouble, however, he cannot have expected the first challenge he faced as head of the family to come from within the family itself, in the form of his father's will.

The problem which had confronted Judge William as he lay on his sickbed that summer was how to reconcile all the different demands on the estate he would leave when he died. He had five children to provide for, ranging in age from John, now married to Margaret with two boys of his own, to Clement, a toddler not much older than John and Margaret's first son. William's ambitions for the future of the Paston name dictated that he should leave the bulk of his estates in the hands of his eldest son, to preserve the wealth and security of the senior line of the family. As a father, however, he also wanted to provide generously for all of his children. Here the concerns of a caring parent merged with the preoccupations of the ambitious dynast: if the junior Pastons were not given the means to sustain themselves among the ranks of the gentry, not only would their own lives be a struggle, but they might drag the Paston name down with them – a risk to which a family whose status was so recently acquired would be particularly vulnerable. William also had to provide for his wife Agnes in her widowhood, which might well be lengthy, given that she was only in her early forties. Once all of these claims had been accounted for, he also had to consider the needs of his own soul. Only a very few people – the saintly, in the literal sense of the word – could expect to be admitted directly to heaven when they died; the majority of repentant sinners would first be cleansed of their sins in purgatory, a place of unspeakable torment. The anticipation of purgatory was a powerful encouragement to live a good Christian life, but deathbed bequests provided testators with one final chance to shorten their stay there: they could help themselves by leaving money for penitential works of piety and charity; and they could enlist the help of those who would survive them, by paying for prayers to be said and masses to be sung for their souls after they had died.

William had drafted his will a couple of years earlier, in late 1441 or 1442. The division of the Paston estates on which he settled was characteristically careful. Agnes's share was a large one, reflecting the benefit her name and her inheritance had brought to the family. She of course retained possession of her own three manors, as well as the Pastons' home at Oxnead which she had received as her jointure when she married; but William also gave her his estates in and around Paston on the north-east Norfolk coast, including the land which his father Clement had left him, and other properties bought in the 1420s as his career gathered pace. All in all, Agnes would have an annual income of around £100. To his eighteen-year-old son Edmund, William left the manor of Snailwell in Cambridgeshire, worth a little more than £26 a year, a sum which would allow him to sustain a comfortable, if modest, living. William intended that Edmund should have the means to supplement this income, if he chose, by practising as a lawyer; he would receive his inheritance when he was twenty-one, and until then, William directed, he was to study law – dialectics for six months, civil law for a year, and the common law after that. His third son, seven-year-old William, was to have lands in mid-Norfolk, west of Norwich, worth about £16 a year. The baby of the family, Clement, would receive lands in eastern Norfolk, just north of Yarmouth, also valued at around £16 a year. Both were to be educated well enough to allow them to embark on professional careers. To his only daughter, twelve-year-old Elizabeth, William left a dowry of £200 in cash, so long as she married with Agnes's consent, and so long as the marriage agreement provided her with a landed income of at least £40 a year.

John, his eldest son, was to have what was left. The only property specifically allocated to him in the will was Gresham in north Norfolk, of which he and Margaret had already taken possession as Margaret's jointure. By law, however, anything not specifically bequeathed elsewhere in William's will would automatically pass to his heir. By that token, John would receive three more manors: East Beckham, a couple of miles from Gresham, which William finally succeeded in wresting from Edmund Winter and John Mariot just before his death; Sporle, in western Norfolk; and Swainsthorpe, just south of Norwich. The last remaining issue was that of William's own spiritual needs: he left a bequest – modest, by contemporary standards – to pay for masses to be celebrated for his soul for seven years after his death. William had pulled off a complex balancing act. The settlement could not be said to be overgenerous to his eldest son, who would need all the resources he could muster for the difficult task of protecting William's legacy, particularly given that there was every chance that Agnes might hold her share of the estates for another twenty years at least; but then again, as William was well aware, John did also have the benefit of Margaret's Mautby inheritance. Prompted by his bout of illness, William confirmed and dated the will in January 1444.

Seven months later, with death this time close at hand, he seems to have had second thoughts. It was Agnes who claimed to have been privy to her husband's thinking as he lay dying. He was afraid, she said, for the future of the youngest Paston boys, telling her repeatedly that '*the livelihood which he had assigned to his two youngest, William and Clement, by his will in writing was so little that they might not live thereupon without they should hold the plough by the tail*'.[13] That his sons might go straight back to the life his own father had lived on the land was a possibility which Judge William could not easily accept, having worked so hard to ensure that they were born to something very different. He was also, understandably, more deeply preoccupied than he had previously been with the imminent sufferings of his soul. At the eleventh hour, Agnes said, he decided to use the three manors he had not mentioned in his written will to buy himself some peace of mind, castigating himself as he did so for his sloth '*that his will was not made up*'. '"... whatsoever come of me, dame,*"' he told her, '"*I will you know my will*"'.[14] It is, on the face of it, surprising that a lawyer of William's talents had not made sure that every last item among his affairs was in perfect order well before his last illness – but perhaps the reality of death had been at once too uncomfortable and too remote a prospect to contemplate for such an energetic man.[15] Now, Agnes claimed, he instructed that East Beckham, Sporle and Swainsthorpe should be divided between their two youngest sons, and that the revenues of Swainsthorpe should also pay for masses for his soul, not for the modest term of seven years specified in his will, but instead in perpetuity. These arrangements – if they were allowed to stand – would leave John with Gresham, and little else.

Agnes's version of the events leading up to her husband's death was written two decades later. It was by no means an impartial account; Agnes, the proud heiress, took care to report William's concern that '*if he had done too little to any, it was to me*' – although he could spare her nothing more, since '*he had more to care for which were mine as well as his*'.[16] Her story was also confusing, if not confused: she described her husband on his sickbed telling John of his intentions – '*asking him the question whether he held him not content, so saying to him in these terms, "Sir, if thou do not, I do, for I will not give so much to one that the remnant shall have too little to live on"*'[17] – but later said that she herself had '*opened and declared*' the new will to their eldest son after William's death. Elizabeth Paston, asked to testify to the facts many years later, confirmed that she had been at the St Bride's house in London during her father's last illness, but that her older brother had not.

What is not in doubt is John's reaction. On Friday 21 August, a week after William's death, his four executors – his wife Agnes; his son John; his cousin William Bacton, the son of Clement Paston's sister Martha; and his friend John Damme – gathered to read his will. '*I let them see it*', Agnes wrote, '*and John Damme read it. And when he had read it, John Paston walked up and down in the chamber; John Damme and I kneeled at the bed's feet.*'[18] The difficulty was that the properties about which Judge William had allegedly changed his mind were not mentioned in the written will in the first place. When Agnes explained what she claimed were William's last wishes, John reacted with fury, utterly refusing to countenance the suggestion that his inheritance should be so drastically reduced. '*And the said John Paston would in no wise agree thereto*', she reported, '*saying that by the law the said manors should be his, in as much as my husband made no will of them in writing*'.[19]

John's response was uncompromising, but understandable. If Agnes was right about her husband's final intentions, William had placed his eldest son in an extraordinarily difficult position. It had always been clear that John would face many challenges on his father's death, but William now proposed that he should meet them with both hands tied behind his back. If he had to defend Paston interests not only without the benefit of his father's experience, reputation and connections, but also without most of his lands, his chances of maintaining the family's standing were slender. This was the first test John had to face as head of the family, and he responded with more than a hint of his father's toughness. He took immediate steps to make sure that it was the written will which was put into effect, securing the deeds to the estates, and initiating the process by which he would receive possession of the lands from William's trustees. He also retrieved the valuables which his father had deposited for safekeeping in Norwich Priory – said to be nearly £1,000 in cash, as well as jewellery and silver plate – without reference to Agnes or the other executors. His prompt action saved him: despite his mother's protests, probate was awarded on William's written will, without modification, on 24 November 1444.

However, the cost in personal terms was high. His unequivocal rejection of Agnes's version of his father's last wishes caused a major breach within the family. '*After that my son John Paston had never right kind words to me*', Agnes wrote years later.[20] That was not quite true: she and John found a way to paper over their differences, and her relationship with Margaret remained close. Equally, the issue did not disappear. Agnes would not forget about it – something which might come back to haunt John, given that she held such a substantial part of his inheritance – and his brothers, with encouragement from their mother, might well feel hard done by in years to come. But his behaviour was not purely, or even mainly, rooted in selfishness. Generosity to his siblings, his mother, even his father's soul, would benefit no one if the position of the whole family were so compromised that they all sank back to the ranks of the peasantry as a result. John had confronted the reality of what he believed to be necessary to safeguard Paston interests, and had shown that he was willing to face the consequences, however personally unpleasant. It was not the last time in his life that he would be required to do so.

Hardheaded as he was prepared to be within the family, however, to the wider world he was young, and inexperienced in the political and legal manoeuvring at which his father had excelled. How serious the consequences of the loss of Judge William might be on this broader political stage was all too soon apparent. William's long fight for East Beckham against Edmund Winter and John Mariot had finally ended with a judgement in his favour only a month before he died. His opponents had been resourceful and determined, but the combination of William's legal expertise and his powerful connections in the end proved too much for them to overcome. However, in the autumn of 1444, only weeks after William's death, Mariot initiated new proceedings in the court of Common Pleas to retrieve the manor. It took a year, but he won his case. East Beckham was one of the estates for the sake of which John had endured such bitter confrontation with his mother, and he had managed to hold on to it for only a matter of months. And – as John must have realised as he surveyed the lands for which his father had fought so hard – this was only the beginning.

CHAPTER THREE

– *a perilous dwelling* –

On the morning of Friday, 17 May 1448, Margaret and her mother-in-law Agnes went to hear mass in their parish church in Norwich. The Pastons' new chaplain, a young man named James Gloys, did not accompany the two women to the service, but spent the morning in town and then walked alone back towards Agnes's house. He was not far from home when his route took him past the door of a townhouse belonging to a gentleman named John Wyndham.[1]

Wyndham was a self-made man from a background so obscure that he had only recently settled on Wyndham as his surname. He had made a great deal of money in trade and, like William Paston before him, he was rapidly converting his wealth into land and the status that came with it. Relations between Wyndham and the Pastons were not warm. Their ambitions to tread the path of social advancement at the same time in the same place were always likely to cause friction, and their rivalry had found a flashpoint the previous summer in a quarrel over the services of a shepherd at Margaret's manor of Sparham. As a result of the incident, Wyndham had brought a prosecution in King's Bench against two of the Pastons' tenants which was still pending in the courts.[2]

It became clear on this particular Friday morning that Wyndham's campaign of self-assertion could be pursued in town just as well as in the country or a court of law. He stood at his gate, a servant at his side, as James Gloys approached. Another of his men, Thomas Hawes, stood beyond the open drain which ran down the middle of the narrow street, so that Gloys had no option but to run the gauntlet between them. If this was provocation, the young chaplain – a forceful character with competitive instincts of his own – was quick to accept the challenge. Gentlemen acknowledged one another with a doffed cap, but Gloys made no move to tip his hat as he walked towards them. The slight could not be ignored. As Gloys drew level with the gate, Wyndham drew attention to his rudeness with a witheringly sarcastic instruction – '*Cover thy head!*' – using the insultingly familiar '*thy*' instead of the respectful '*your*'. Gloys's response – '*So I shall for thee!*' –

threw the insult back, and he had taken only three or four more steps when Wyndham said, '*Shall thou so, knave?*' and drew his dagger. Gloys turned, his own blade in his hand, but a barrage of stones flung by Wyndham and Hawes forced him to run for shelter up the street to Agnes's house. Hawes dashed after him, '*and cast a stone as much as a farthing loaf into the hall after Gloys, and then ran out of the place again*'. Gloys gave chase as far as the gate, '*and then Wyndham called Gloys thief and said he should die, and Gloys said he lied and called him churl, and bade him come himself or else the best man he had, and Gloys would answer him one for one*'.[3] Wyndham was only too willing to take Gloys up on this suggestion, and sent Hawes to fetch his sword and spear.

Margaret and Agnes heard the shouting from inside the church, and slipped out of the service to investigate the disturbance. When she realised what was happening, Margaret intervened immediately, sending Gloys back into the house and away from the confrontation. She succeeded in stopping the fight, but also in drawing Wyndham's abuse onto herself and her mother-in-law: '*then Wyndham called my mother and me strong whores, and said the Pastons and all their kin were churls of Gimingham, and we said he lied, knave and churl that he was*'. There was more, which Margaret did not have time or inclination to commit to paper: '*And he had much large language, as you shall know hereafter by mouth*'.[4]

Wyndham might trade insults with women, but he would not threaten them with physical harm. Margaret could hold her own when it came to defending the family's honour, but she remained concerned about her hot-headed chaplain's safety, and, as events turned out, she was right to be apprehensive. That afternoon she and Agnes went to tell the Prior of Norwich what had happened, and to seek his help. Wyndham was summoned to explain himself, but while he was with the Prior trouble erupted again between Gloys and Thomas Hawes. Gloys, who clearly had no intention of backing down from the fight, was standing in the street at Agnes's gate, where Hawes could see him from inside Wyndham's house. Hawes '*came down with a two-hand sword and assaulted again the said Gloys and Thomas my mother's man,*' Margaret reported, '*and let fly a stroke at Thomas with the sword and rippled his hand with his sword*'. Although Gloys himself escaped unharmed, Margaret decided to take no more chances. '*And for the perils of that might hap by these premises, and the circumstances thereof to be eschewed*', she wrote to her husband in London, '*by the advice of my mother and others I send you Gloys to attend upon you for a season, for ease of my own heart, for in good faith I would not for £40 have such another trouble.*' Not that this was necessarily the end of her worries. She had heard that Wyndham would soon be travelling to London, and feared that he would take the opportunity to attack John himself. '*I pray you beware how you walk if he be there, for he is full cursed-hearted and lumish*,' she warned her husband. '*I know well he will not set upon you manly, but I believe he will start upon you or on some of your men like a thief.*'[5]

It was an unnerving incident. Private though the substance of the quarrel was, it was played out in public, on a city street, and Margaret's account of what happened gives a clear sense of the extent to which reputations were at stake:

> *When Wyndham said that James should die, I said to him that I supposed that he should repent him if he slew him or did to him any bodily harm; and he said nay, he should never repent him, nor have a farthing worth of harm, though he killed you and him both. And I said yes, if he slew the least child that belongs to your kitchen, and if he did he were like, I suppose, to die for him.*[6]

Gentlemen were men to be reckoned with, who could command respect and defend themselves, their families and their honour – and, for John Paston and John Wyndham, the need to demonstrate that they were indeed gentlemen was at the heart of the argument. Both Wyndham and the Pastons lived in glass houses when it came to their families' origins, and on this occasion both started throwing stones. One word, '*churl*', was repeated over and over as gibes were traded: '*Gloys said he lied and called him churl*', '*the Pastons and all their kin were churls of Gimingham*', '*we said he lied, knave and churl that he was*'. This accusation – that the would-be gentleman was in fact a peasant, and an unfree peasant at that – was extremely dangerous territory. An unfree man had no right to exercise manorial lordship, precisely the kind of authority which allowed rising men to claim gentility. The Pastons were so sensitive to the charge that, at some point after Margaret's account of the confrontation was written, the words with which Wyndham had struck so close to the bone were excised from the letter, leaving a hole in the paper where '*churls of Gimingham*' had been.[7] The irony was that both Margaret and Agnes, the targets of this tirade, were better born than either their husbands or Wyndham himself, even if they had little choice but to accept that their status was now defined by the family into which they had married.

What was disquieting above all was that few people would have dared to insult the Pastons so openly when Judge William was alive. The loss of his influence was everywhere apparent in the family's new vulnerability to attack, of which the street fight with Wyndham was only the most spectacularly public manifestation. Agnes was finding that being William Paston's widow was not at all the same as being his wife. The vicar of Paston had agreed in the spring of 1444 that a road in the village should be diverted to allow the Pastons' new manor house there more privacy, but after William's death a few months later he reneged on the deal, plunging Agnes into a vitriolic dispute which poisoned her relations with the villagers for years ('*All the devils of hell draw her soul to hell for the way that she has made!*', a woman cried in the churchyard after mass one Sunday).[8] A couple of miles away at the village of Trunch, a man named Palmer who had leased some land from the family for seven or eight years suddenly refused to pay eight shillings of what he owed, claiming it was rent due to the overlord of the land. '*Geoffrey asked Palmer why the rent was not asked in my husband's time*,' Agnes reported, '*and Palmer said, for he was a great man and a wise man of the law, and that was the cause men would not ask him the rent*'. Six months after William's death, it was with feeling that Agnes told their son Edmund, studying at Clifford's Inn in London, '*to think once of the day of your father's counsel to learn the law*', and recalled her husband's maxim that '*whosoever should dwell at Paston should have need to con defend himself*'.[9]

It was an inescapable problem for the family that so many of their estates had been bought so recently. Purchase, however legally sound, did not mean that the new owner was safe against challenge from the family to which the land had previously belonged. The commercial market in land, booming though it was, sat uneasily within a culture steeped in the concept of inheritance, and the heirs of those who had offered estates for sale often acted as though such transactions were an illegitimate interruption of their rightful possession. The trick, for such 'cheated' heirs, was to watch and wait for the opportunity to make a claim good. Edmund Winter thought that he had found just such an opening in 1434 when he seized the manor of East Beckham before Judge William's purchase of the property had been completed – but, after ten acrimonious years in the courts, he discovered he was wrong. What Winter needed was a political opportunity, not a technical one. It was a political opportunity which William's death represented – and within months East Beckham was back in the hands of Winter's ally John Mariot.

The resuscitation of existing disputes was not the only difficulty with which John Paston had to contend. His father's death also gave opportunists the chance to come forward with fresh claims which, however spurious, might cause the family problems in their newly exposed state. The manor of

Oxnead, which Agnes held as her jointure, was claimed by a friar named John Hauteyn on the grounds that his ancestors had owned it in the time of Edward III, a century earlier. Hauteyn made little headway – he lacked sufficiently powerful backing to make a specious case stick – but he was persistent in his efforts. It was an irritant which the family could well have done without, particularly given that her sons were concerned that Agnes was not reliably discreet about her legal affairs. '*I pray write to my mother of your own head as for to counsel her how that she keep her privy and tell nobody right naught of her counsel,*' Edmund asked his elder brother John, '*for she will tell persons many of her counsel this day, and tomorrow she will say by God's fast that the same men be false*'.[10]

Hauteyn was a nuisance, but John Paston's greatest enemy, a friend of John Wyndham's named John Heydon, was much more than that. Had Judge William still been alive, he would have recognised Heydon as a rival cast in his own image: a clever and hugely ambitious young lawyer from a poor background, working hard to establish his family among the Norfolk gentry with the help of powerful patrons for whom he acted as legal counsel. Heydon, like Wyndham, had changed his name during his professional rise, swapping the tradesman's surname of Baxter (meaning 'baker') for the more genteel place-name of Heydon, the manor where his father had lived and worked on the land. It was as John Heydon, lawyer and gentleman, that he bought the manor of Baconsthorpe in northern Norfolk, only three miles from the Pastons' estate at Gresham. Heydon's professional career was spectacularly successful, but his personal life was a mess. His marriage broke down in 1444 when his wife Eleanor gave birth to a child by another man. '*Heydon's wife had child on St Peter's Day. I heard say that her husband will none of her, nor of her child that she had last neither,*' Margaret reported to John that summer. '*I heard say that he said, if she comes in his presence to make her excuse, that he should cut off her nose to make her to be known what she is, and if her child comes in his presence he said he would kill it. He will not be entreated to have her again in no wise, as I heard say.*'[11] However, the circumstances of his wife's disgrace meant that Heydon, as the wronged party, remained on good terms with her family. When his father-in-law wrote his will four years later he failed to mention his daughter Eleanor, but left Heydon a book of chronicles and made him supervisor of the will itself. It was the identity of Heydon's friendly father-in-law which was unfortunate from the Pastons' point of view: he was Edmund Winter, their opponent in the bitter fight for East Beckham.

If Heydon's relationship with Winter was one reason for him to be hostile to the Pastons, the location of his own estates was another. He was buying up properties around his new home at Baconsthorpe to create an estate which would make him a landowner of substance in northern Norfolk – exactly the same area where William Paston had concentrated his own acquisitions. The Paston manor of Gresham and the disputed manor of East Beckham, as well as Margaret's Mautby estates at Matlask and Bessingham, all lay within a radius of three miles from Baconsthorpe.[12] Trying to expand their holdings in the same small area was always likely to set Heydon and the Pastons on a collision course, but Heydon – as a mere attorney, however up-and-coming – stood little chance of denting the regional standing of a man of Judge William's influence. William's son John, however, was a different matter. William's death could not have coincided more neatly with the blossoming of John Heydon's political career, and John Paston, fresh out of university at the age of twenty-two, could not hope to compete. It was almost certainly Heydon, working for his father-in-law Winter, who engineered the Pastons' loss of East Beckham to John Mariot in the year after Judge William died, and three years later he instigated a yet more devastating attack.

Gresham was a valuable property, with a fine manor house, which William Paston had bought two decades earlier in 1427. The circumstances which brought the estate on to the market were convoluted in the extreme, but, unlike the case of East Beckham, there was no question that William's purchase was both legal and completed. In theory, the Pastons should have encountered no difficulties there. In fact, it was crucial for John Paston that no problem should arise; Gresham had been settled on himself and Margaret when they married, and it was one of the few manors to which his mother and brothers could have no claim, whatever the debates about his father's will. He needed the house as a home for his family, and the estate as a substantial source of income. A watertight legal title, however, proved no defence when Heydon decided to seize the opportunity to make trouble which Judge William's death presented.

Until the end of the fourteenth century, Gresham had belonged to a Buckinghamshire family named Moleyns. By the 1440s, the Moleyns heiress Eleanor was married to Robert Hungerford, heir to a Wiltshire barony, who took the title of Lord Moleyns in right of his wife and with it her residual claim (such as it was) to the manor of Gresham. There was good reason why the young Lord Moleyns might want to make the most of his wife's inheritance: his father and grandfather were still alive, and it might be years before he succeeded to his own title and estates. On the other hand, northern Norfolk was a long way from either Wiltshire or Buckinghamshire, and it would be difficult for any lord to make a dubious claim stick at such a distance from his own 'country'. Difficult, that is, unless he had local help. Moleyns was making a career for himself at Henry VI's court, where he met the well-connected Norfolk lawyer John Heydon. The combination of Heydon and Moleyns proved lethal for the Pastons. On 17 February 1448 Moleyns – *'by the excitation and procuring of John Heydon',* as John Paston later claimed[13] – sent a posse of men from Wiltshire to seize Gresham for himself. John and Margaret were not there and, with no warning of Moleyns's plans, had no chance to organise any attempt at defence. Gresham was gone before they knew what had happened.

It was disastrous news. John knew, at least, that his title was good, but as soon as he started proceedings to retrieve the estate he discovered quite how heavily the cards were stacked against him. Heydon and Moleyns had friends in very high places – most importantly William de la Pole, Earl (and, from 1448, Duke) of Suffolk, in whose service Heydon had already been active for more than a decade. Suffolk was one of the most powerful landowners in East Anglia, and since his return to England from the French wars in 1430 had established himself as the leading political figure in the region. Not only that, but by the mid-1440s he had also emerged as the King's chief minister – and, when the King in question was Henry VI, that meant a very great deal. Henry had inherited the throne more than twenty years earlier at the age of only nine months, but he was proving to be no more capable of leadership as an adult than he had been as an infant. The great nobles had hoped for a worthy successor to his father, the charismatic warrior Henry V, but found that he bore a much closer and much more unfortunate resemblance to his maternal grandfather, the mentally unstable King Charles VI of France. It gradually became apparent that they would have to continue to manage his rule for him, since Henry – a naïve, unworldly and childlike figure – did little more than smile and agree to every suggestion his advisers made. So it was that Suffolk took charge of Henry's government, as steward of the King's household and the leading voice on the royal council. It was a role which gave him enormous power and responsibility, but little time to pay detailed attention to local disputes. Suffolk scarcely had a chance even to set foot in East Anglia, making his home instead at his wife's estate of Ewelme in Oxfordshire, from where the royal palaces at Westminster and Windsor were more easily accessible. John Paston, without access to the absent but apparently all-powerful Duke, stood little chance of defending himself against John Heydon, who was one of Suffolk's chief local servants.

If there was no prospect of securing help from the Duke of Suffolk, John needed to look for alternative sources of lordship – and there were precious few on the horizon. In theory, the Duke of Norfolk, John Mowbray, should have been able to offer some support, given that he too held a massive East Anglian estate. In practice, though, Norfolk was struggling to make any political impact at all in a region so overwhelmingly dominated by his rival Suffolk – besides which, his ambitious but ill-judged efforts to assert himself in local politics had so far proved almost laughably incompetent. In any case, what John Paston desperately needed was access to the very top of the political hierarchy, if he were to have any hope at all of standing up to enemies who could call on the towering figure of Suffolk as their patron. Given the peculiarities of Henry VI's government, that meant finding a patron of his own at court, someone who had direct access to the malleable King but owed nothing to Suffolk, and might therefore be able to circumvent the Duke's apparent stranglehold on royal authority. Luckily for John, he already knew the man he believed he needed: an esquire of the royal household named Thomas Daniel.

Daniel, who was originally from Cheshire, arrived in East Anglia in the autumn of 1446 through one of the most outrageous acts of fraud perpetrated even in this increasingly flexible political world. The victims of his chicanery were the Woodhouse family of Roydon near King's Lynn. Henry Woodhouse, the head of the family, was the son of one of Henry V's closest aides – so close that the King himself stood godfather to his young Woodhouse namesake. Henry Woodhouse was not the politician his father had been, however, and he had made little impact in the wider world by the time he began negotiating a marriage for himself in 1446. The bride on whom he set his sights was Thomas Daniel's sister Elizabeth. Woodhouse was so keen to secure the match that he handed over his estates in trust to Daniel before the wedding had taken place, in preparation, presumably, for a resettlement on the happy couple once they were married. As soon as Daniel's name was on the deeds, however, he broke the news to Woodhouse that Elizabeth was already married to someone else. Daniel himself, meanwhile, had no intention of giving back the lands. Henry Woodhouse was distraught, but there was little he could do. Technically, he had handed over the estates to Daniel of his own free will, and Daniel lost no time in exploiting his access to the King to reinforce his new East Anglian power base. In November 1446 he secured his own appointment as sheriff for Norfolk and Suffolk – an office for which, as a landholder in the region, he was now of course well qualified – and five months later obtained royal permission to fortify 'his' manor house at Roydon.

Daniel had not only defrauded a gentleman out of his entire inheritance, but then decided, with breathtaking chutzpah, to use the estates as a base from which to challenge the Duke of Suffolk in his own backyard. His methods were unappealing – particularly for a family who were themselves victims of a courtier helping himself to a Norfolk estate – but the prospect of a court insider who might allow them to mobilise royal support against their opponents proved too much for the Pastons to resist, and in the spring of 1448 John Paston showed no qualms about attaching himself to Daniel. '*I pray you that you will vouchsafe to send me word how you speed in your matter touching Gresham, and how Daniel is in grace,*' Margaret wrote in April to her husband, who had just left Norwich for London, adding, '*I pray you that I may be recommended to my lord Daniel.*' It was not yet clear how successful their new patron would prove to be in chipping away at Suffolk's regional dominance, and Margaret at least was anxious. '*It is said in this country that Daniel is out of the King's good grace,*' she reported, '*and he shall down, and all his men and all that be his well-willers. There shall no man be so hardy to do neither say against my lord of Suffolk, nor none that belong to him; and all that have done and said against him, they shall sore repent them.*'[14] But it was not that easy for the Duke, at the head of a regime beset by problems at home and abroad, to see off Daniel's persistent and focused ambition in one small corner of his empire. By the summer of 1448, Daniel's success in thumbing his nose at Suffolk was causing much local comment, and the Pastons were doing what they could to encourage others to follow their lead in joining him. Edmund Paston, back in Norwich after completing his legal studies in London, reported to his brother that a local official had '*inquired me of the rule of my master Daniel and my lord of Suffolk, and asked which I thought should rule in this shire, and I said both, as I trow, and he that survives to hold by the virtue of the survivor, and he to thank his friends and to acquit his enemies. So I feel by him he would forsake his master and get him a new if he thought he should rule.*' That was certainly what John wanted to hear – as was Edmund's optimistic afterthought: '*And so I think much of all the country is so disposed*'.[15]

Despite all their hopes, however, it gradually became clear during the summer that the Pastons' alliance with Daniel was producing very little in the way of practical benefit. It was perhaps always likely that an opportunist as ruthlessly self-serving as Daniel would have little energy to spare for other people's troubles. The further problem was that, however unrewarding Daniel's lordship was turning out to be, it also came at a price. By identifying themselves with Daniel and supporting his unsavoury behaviour, the Pastons involved themselves in a much wider web of rivalries and hostilities than simply their own fight with John Heydon. They already knew that Heydon had friends who could help to make their lives unpleasant – the recent incident with John Wyndham in the street in Norwich had made that all too clear – but through their association with Daniel they invited even more hostile attention.

Daniel had probably seen the inept Henry Woodhouse as an easy target, but Woodhouse was not without allies of his own. His brother-in-law Sir Thomas Tuddenham was a powerful man who held major offices both at court and in Norfolk, a trusted adviser of the Duke of Suffolk, and a close friend of John Heydon. Remarkably, Tuddenham's marriage had broken down in a very similar way to Heydon's own, when his wife, Henry Woodhouse's sister Alice, gave birth to a son as a result of an affair with her father's chamberlain. Unlike Heydon, Tuddenham put himself through the public humiliation of a divorce, but like his friend he remained on good terms with his estranged wife's family.[16] Despite his closeness to Heydon, Tuddenham had not previously concerned himself with the Pastons, but, once they had associated themselves with Daniel's appalling treatment of his brother-in-law, Tuddenham joined the campaign of harassment which the family and their servants and tenants now faced. '*It is told me that he that keeps your sheep was outlawed on Monday at the suit of Sir Thomas Tuddenham*', Margaret reported to her husband in April 1448, '*and if it be so you are not like to keep him long*.'[17]

John was becoming deeply frustrated. Moleyns's men were living in his manor house at Gresham and collecting rents from the tenants there, and Daniel had so far failed to do anything at all to help. In June, John sought arbitration in the case through the good offices of William Wainfleet, the Bishop of Winchester, a proposal to which Moleyns declared himself amenable, although with no result.[18] It was increasingly clear that procrastination was entirely in Moleyns's interests. He was in charge at Gresham, and the status quo therefore suited him. Given the weakness of his claim, he was not at all interested in bringing the case to speedy judgement in the courts. The longer he could take the profits of the manor and postpone formal hearings into its ownership, the better it would be. John Paston was a stubborn man who believed in the process of law, but even he was beginning to realise that he could not depend on the authority of a court in

which he simply could not persuade his adversary to appear. Direct negotiation was working no better: sixteen separate meetings took place between
lawyers representing the two sides, and John believed he had answered
every claim Moleyns's advisers raised. When opposing counsel admitted
'*they could no further in the matter*', John himself rode to Salisbury to petition Moleyns in person, but '*none answer had but delays*'.[19] By the autumn,
he decided more assertive action was needed to bring pressure to bear on
Moleyns's occupation of Gresham. He, of course, could not leave their legal
business at London for long, so that it was Margaret and their two sons,
now aged six and four, who went on 6 October 1448 to take up residence at
a house in Gresham almost on the doorstep of the men who were occupy-
ing their home.

Margaret's presence at Gresham served as a physical embodiment of the
Pastons' claim to the manor – she had re-entered the property, even if not
their own manor house, and was demanding rent payments from the tenants in recognition of her husband's rights. From her position on the front
line, she was also able to send John detailed information about what
Moleyns's men were doing there. Their house was held by a small company of Moleyns's servants from Wiltshire led by a man named John
Partridge, with help from a few local men, including John Mariot.
Margaret's arrival, she told her husband, had spurred Moleyns's men into
a frenzy of activity:

> *Partridge and his fellowship are sore afeared that you would enter again*
> *upon them, and they have made great ordinance within the house, as it is*
> *told me. They have made bars to bar the doors crosswise, and they have*
> *made wickets on every quarter of the house to shoot out at, both with bows*
> *and with handguns; and the holes that be made for handguns they be*
> *scarce knee high from the floor, and of such holes be made five. There can*
> *no man shoot out at them with no hand bows.*

Confronted with these alarming preparations, Margaret felt that she too
needed to make ready her defences. She asked her husband to send crossbows, '*for your houses here be so low that there may no man shoot out with no*
long bow, though we had never so much need'. Two or three short poll-axes she
also thought would be useful, '*to keep with doors*', and '*as many jacks*' –
armoured jackets, made of quilted fabric or leather into which metal plates
were sewn – '*as you may*'. However disconcerting her situation, Margaret was
practical and resourceful, and she was not panicking. Together with the
weapons and body-armour, she asked John to send her a pound of almonds

and a pound of sugar, and material to make gowns for the children, as well as '*a yard of broad cloth of black for a hood for me of 44d or 4s a yard, for there is neither good cloth nor good frieze in this town*'.[20]

Others were not so sanguine. On 5 November Margaret's uncle Philip Berney came to visit her at Gresham, and was visibly shocked when he saw her servants wearing their helmets and leather '*jacks*'. He left as soon as he decently could after lunch, promising Margaret that he would come again soon, but a week later sent his servant Davy instead with a tale of woe. Her uncle '*had hurt his own horse that he rode upon, and he had Davy saddle another horse, and he stood by and made water while he saddled him*', but while Berney was relieving himself, disaster struck. Without warning, the horse '*slinked round and took his master on the hip such a stroke that never man may trust him after, and broke his hip*'. Margaret was full of sympathy over this unfortunate accident, but her chaplain James Gloys – now back in Norfolk after his Wyndham-inspired exile – was incensed at Berney's cowardice. '*I know well that it was not so*', he told John; he had heard in Norwich the very next day that Berney was '*hale and merry*'. He wanted to warn his master of such feeble friendship, but could not bear to tell Margaret of her uncle's duplicity: '*if my mistress knew that I sent you such a letter I were never able to look upon her, nor to abide in her eyesight*'.[21]

However, Margaret was not completely without support. John Damme, their good friend only a mile away from Gresham at Sustead, kept in close touch with her and spoke to Partridge and Mariot on her behalf, even if the conversation all too easily turned into a pantomime of threats: '*I bade him remember him that he might not abide there if you would have him out*', Damme reported later to John in London; '*and he said he knew well that – but he said, if you put them out, you should be put out soon after again. And I said, if it hap it so, they should not long rest there.*' Damme still hoped that their arrogance would be misplaced – '*Partridge and his fellow bear great visage and keep great junkets and dinners, and say that my Lord Moleyns has written plainly to them that he is lord there and will be and shall be, and you not to have it; but I trust to God's righteousness of better purveyance*' – but he was fearful, particularly of what John Heydon might do. '*Like it you to remember what Heydon does and may do by colour of justice of the peace*,' he warned John, '*being of my lord's counsel and not your good friend nor wellwiller*'. He left it to a postscript to suggest that now might be a good time for John to order an elegant '*jack defensible*' for himself.[22]

It was not John, however, but Margaret who would need that kind of protection. In the early morning of Tuesday, 28 January 1449, a small army arrived to drive the Pastons completely from Gresham. Margaret, at home with a household of twelve, was in no position to resist. John later described her attackers as a thousand strong and fully equipped for a military assault, and, even allowing for the margin of exaggeration which every petitioner to parliament permitted himself, it was clearly a terrifying onslaught. The Paston servants were under-equipped and vastly outnumbered. Moleyns's men *mined down the wall of the chamber wherein the wife of your said beseecher was,'* John wrote, *'and bore her out at the gates, and cut asunder the posts of the houses and let them fall, and broke up all the chambers and coffers within the said mansion, and rifled and in manner of robbery bore away all the stuff, array and money that your said beseecher and his servants had there'.*[23] Margaret and the children were unhurt, but it was abundantly clear that Moleyns was no longer prepared to tolerate their presence at Gresham. The small and beleaguered Paston household fled to Sustead to seek shelter with John and Elizabeth Damme.

The Paston strategy of using direct action to force Moleyns to show his hand had worked a little too well, but John could at least now claim with substantial justification that Moleyns was guilty of an overt and violent breach of the peace, and he lost no time in pursuing the charge. He rode immediately to Winch, the Norfolk home of John de Vere, Earl of Oxford, and asked the Earl to come in his capacity as a justice of the peace to challenge Moleyns's occupation. Oxford had promised John Damme a couple of months earlier that he would visit Gresham if he were needed (*'if it were fair weather he would not tarry, and if it rained he would not spare'*), and now he was as good as his word.[24] The Earl arrived at the manor the day after the assault, but Moleyns's men barred the gates of the manor house against him, declaring that neither he nor anyone else should come in except by permission of their lord. Oxford did nothing more, claiming that he had no time because of his imminent departure to attend parliament, but he did at least send a report into King's Bench detailing John's allegations and certifying that the doors of the house at Gresham had been closed against him by Moleyns's servants.[25]

It was better than nothing, but not much. John returned to London, accompanied by John Damme, to pursue his complaints against Moleyns at the parliament which opened on 12 February, while Margaret and the boys remained at Sustead with Damme's wife Elizabeth. Those tenants at Gresham who continued to support the Pastons were harassed with physical threats and lawsuits; for many, it was easier simply to pay Moleyns's agents the rent they demanded. At Sustead, Margaret was still close enough at least to try to protect the villagers who had supported her, and to exert pressure on Moleyns's men. An esquire from Wiltshire named Walter Barrow had taken over from John Partridge in command at Gresham since the events of the previous month, and on John's instructions Margaret sent him a message to complain about the threatening behaviour of his men.

Margaret dispatched her own servant Katherine to speak to Barrow, '*for I could get no man to do it*'. There were at least some benefits of being a woman in this situation. Where the conversation between John Damme and John Partridge two months earlier had degenerated rapidly into macho posturing, communication from Margaret via a female servant allowed Barrow to be gracious. He received Katherine with '*great cheer*', and told her politely that he would like to speak to her mistress, suggesting that he should pass by the house at Sustead on a hunting trip that afternoon. When Barrow and his servants arrived, they waited outside and sent, again politely, to ask if Margaret would see them. Unsurprisingly, Margaret was extremely wary. She refused to invite them into the Dammes' home – '*in as much as they were not well-willing to the good man of the place, I would not take it upon me to bring them in to the gentlewoman*' – but she went out herself to speak to Barrow at the gate. He was all charm, responding to Margaret's message with '*such an answer as they hoped should please me*', and giving his word that none of her servants or tenants would be harmed. Rumours she had heard that she was vulnerable even at Sustead – '*that I should not long dwell so near them as I do*' – were also vehemently denied. Barrow and his man '*spoke to me in the most pleasant wise*,' Margaret reported, and '*said they would do me service and pleasure, if it lay in their powers to do anything for me*'.[26]

Margaret was not convinced, however, and remained resolutely unimpressed by Barrow's blandishments. '*I trust not to their promise*', she told John, '*in as much as I find them untrue in other things*'. The Pastons' belongings which had been in the house at Gresham had by now been sold or given away, but Barrow told her she could have had whatever she liked, had she only asked. '*I said nay, if I might have had my desire I should neither have departed out of the place nor from the stuff that was therein*'. This sharp retort, at least, drew a stinging reply: '*They said as for the stuff, it was but easy. I said you would not have given the stuff that was in the place when they came in, not for £100. They said the stuff that they saw there was scarce worth £20.*' Before they parted, she took care to let Barrow know that she was well aware of the role John Heydon was playing behind the scenes of Lord Moleyns's manoeuvres. '*I told him I knew well he set never thereupon by no title of right that he had to the manor of Gresham,*' she said stoutly, '*but only by the information of a false shrew. I rehearsed no name, but methought by them that they knew who I meant*'.[27]

Margaret was holding her own with extraordinary courage and dignity, but she was now genuinely frightened, especially – and amazingly, given that it was she who had faced an armed attack – for her husband's safety:

> *I hear say that you and John Damme are sore threatened always, and say though you are at London you shall be met with there as well as though you were here; and therefore I pray you heartily beware how you walk there and have a good fellowship with you when you shall walk out. The Lord Moleyns has a company of brothel with him that reck not what they do, and such are most for to dread. They that are at Gresham say that they have not done so much hurt to you as they were commanded to do.*

Under the circumstances, she was finding it increasingly difficult to cope with their enforced separation. '*I pray you heartily that you will send me word how you do and how you speed in your matters,*' she wrote, '*for by my troth I cannot be well at ease in my heart, nor not shall be, till I hear tidings how you do.*'[28]

Two weeks later, at the end of February, her fears finally became too much to bear. Word reached her that Moleyns's men were planning to kidnap her from Sustead and hold her captive at Gresham, whether as a tactical move to force John into confrontation or simply for their own entertainment ('*they said it should be but a little heart-burning to you*', she told her husband). Either way, their motives hardly mattered: Margaret was profoundly unnerved. She gathered her possessions and left Sustead for Norwich, telling no one of her departure except Elizabeth Damme, and pretending even to her that she would be away only two or three weeks while she had some clothes made for herself and the children. She was worried that John would be angry that she had left – '*beseeching you that you be not displeased, though I am come from that place that you left me in*' – but too anxious to stay so near Gresham any longer. She sounded, for once, shaken and very scared. '*After that I heard these tidings I could no rest have in my heart till I was here*', she wrote from Norwich, '*nor I dared not out of the place that I was in till that I was ready to ride*'. On her journey from Sustead she stopped at Oxnead to see Agnes, who offered her house in Norwich to Margaret and the children for as long as they needed, a suggestion which was accepted with gratitude. At least now they were physically safe, although she continued to worry about

John's vulnerability in London. '*At the reverence of God,*' she told him, '*beware of the Lord Moleyns and his men, though they speak never so fair to you, trust them not, nor eat nor drink with them, for they are so false it is not for to trust in them.*'[29]

It is a measure of the strain they were under that their letters make no mention of happier news. At some point in 1448 or 1449 Margaret gave birth again, to a girl named Margery, after her own mother. The new baby may have arrived even before Margaret took up residence at Gresham in October 1448, or Margaret may have been pregnant during some or all of the upheavals there. Either way, it is clear that Margaret, now twenty-six, was a remarkably brave and resourceful woman – and also that she and her husband had almost no time to enjoy their growing family. From March 1449, while Margaret and the children stayed in Norwich, John did what he could to press their case in London, but, in the absence of any help from influential men, it was not much. He submitted a petition to the King in parliament describing the assault on Gresham and detailing their losses there – which for these purposes he put at £200, rather than the £100 Margaret had claimed to Walter Barrow or Barrow's own disparaging estimate of £20 – but to little effect. One infuriating problem he faced in trying to press charges in the courts was that, by law, indictments required the name, status and place of residence of each man accused – and, because Moleyns's men came from Wiltshire, no one locally knew who they were. As he pointed out in his petition, '*your said beseecher can have none action by your law against the said riotous people for the goods and chattels by them so riotously and wrongfully taken and borne away, because the said people be unknown, as well their names as their persons, unto him*'.[30]

While John struggled with legal technicalities, Lord Moleyns himself, who had not once set foot in Norfolk since the conflict began, sent an expansively authoritative letter designed to reassure his supporters and intimidate those who were still daring to defy him, which John Heydon was showing around polite society in Norwich. '*The lord Moleyns wrote in his foresaid letter that he would mightily with his body and with his goods stand by all those that had been his friends and his well-willers in the matter touching Gresham,*' Margaret had heard, '*and prayed Heydon that he would say to them that they should not be afeard in no wise, for that was done it should be abided by.*'[31] Walter Barrow too had been irritatingly complacent when Margaret talked to him last before leaving Sustead, telling her that no one in England held better evidence than his master had to justify his claim to Gresham. Margaret did what she could to puncture his self-assurance – she knew exactly what kind of documents Moleyns had, she told him, and '*the seals of them were not yet cold*' – but without much success. Barrow was still all public smiles: '*if he came to London while you were there he would drink with you for any anger that was between you*,' Margaret told John. '*He said he did but as a servant, and as he was commanded to do.*' Nevertheless, rumours were circulating in Norfolk that '*you have had one shot, and unless you beware you shall have more before Easter*': now Gresham had gone, word had it that the manors of Sporle and Swainsthorpe would be next, on what grounds Margaret had no idea, although on past experience grounds of any kind were hardly needed.[32] And of course, now that the Pastons had been forced on to the back foot, the blows might come from more directions than one. The friar John Hauteyn thought he saw an opportunity to revive his campaign to wrest Oxnead from Agnes, and began to issue renewed threats. '*There was a person warned my mother within these two days that she should beware*,' Margaret told her husband on 2 April, '*for they said plainly she was like to be served as you were served at Gresham within right short time*'.[33]

One deeply distressing blow had already fallen by the time Margaret wrote with this news. John's brother Edmund was taken ill suddenly at London and died on 21 March, at the age of only twenty-five. The will he dictated hours before his death was short – he had no wish to occupy his mind with the things of this world, he said, now that he had so little time to prepare himself for the next – and simply left everything he had to his elder brother. John took pains to make sure that Edmund's gravestone should be finely made – '*it is told me that the man at St Bride's is no cleanly portrayer, wherefore I would fain it might be portrayed by some other man*' – but had almost no time to mourn.[34] He was having to concentrate on the Hauteyn claim to Oxnead when he could ill afford to divert any of his attention from Moleyns and Gresham, and he had no effective lordly support on which to call in either case. He tried to impress a lawyer at the papal court in Rome, whose advice he wanted, by sending word that '*my lord of Winchester and Daniel owe goodwill to the part that he shall labour for*',[35] but the truth was that the Bishop of Winchester had not been able even to persuade Lord Moleyns to the negotiating table, and Thomas Daniel was a chancer who looked after no one but himself. Even one of their tenants at Swainsthorpe had heard as much, Margaret told John after a visit to the manor in May: '*he said he supposed that D. would do for you, but he said he was no hasty labour-er in no matter. He said by his faith he knew where a man was that laboured to him for a matter right a long time, and always he promised that he would labour it effectually, but while he sued to him he could never have remedy of his matter*.[36]

Margaret felt the time had come for a change of strategy, even if her uncharacteristically convoluted way of saying so indicated how hesitant she was about suggesting it: *'folks that be your right well-willers have counselled me that I should counsel you to make other means than you have made, to other folks that would speed your matters better than they have done that you have spoken to thereof before this time'*. Her husband was both stubborn and proud, and the implication that his efforts over the last year had had no appreciable effect could hardly be welcome, particularly given that Margaret wanted to propose that it was the patron of their enemy Heydon to whom they should be suing for help: *'Sundry folks have said to me that they think verily, but if you have my lord of Suffolk's good lordship while the world is as it is, you can never live in peace without you have his good lordship.'* Once she had summoned up the courage to broach the subject, her usual fluency returned as she tried to persuade John of the urgent need to follow this course. *'Therefore I pray you with all my heart that you will do your part to have his good lordship and his love in ease of all the matters that you have to do, and in easing of my heart also,'* she wrote. *'For by my troth, I am afeared else both of these matters the which you have in hand now, and of others that be not done to yet, but if he will do for you and be your good lord.'*[37] As a reading of their experiences over the last year, Margaret's analysis had a lot to recommend it – even if, given Heydon's closeness to Suffolk, it seemed unlikely that the Duke might be persuaded to intervene.

Margaret's conclusions could not be faulted, but the timing of her suggestion could scarcely have been worse. One of the reasons why her husband had struggled so much to interest anyone of influence in their problems at Gresham was that much greater troubles were threatening to engulf the very highest levels of Henry VI's government. For almost thirty years, the most pressing issue which the great nobles had faced was how to defend Henry V's conquests in France in the name of a King who could not lead his own army, at first because he was a child, and then because his engagement with the world was so vague that his presence on a battlefield would be nothing but a liability. Henry VI set foot on French soil only once, at the age of nine, when he travelled to Paris for his coronation as King of France in 1431. Six months earlier, Joan of Arc had been burned as a witch and a heretic by the English at Rouen, but her death came too late to stop the French military resurgence which she had inspired by driving the English from the gates of Orléans in 1429. The English commanders in France held the line for a few more years against the armies of the French Dauphin, now crowned as Charles VII, but by the 1440s it was apparent that the question could only now be how best to protect English interests in retreat.

Peace was the only realistic option. In 1444 the Duke of Suffolk led an embassy to France which agreed a temporary ceasefire and a marriage alliance between King Henry, now twenty-two, and the French King's fifteen-year-old niece Margaret, daughter of the Duke of Anjou. Given the strength of the French position, English chances of securing a lasting settlement now depended on combining resolute defence of those French territories which were still in English hands with a willingness to put something concrete on the table which might persuade the French to come to terms. The attempt failed on both counts. A secret deal was made during 1445 whereby England agreed to cede the county of Maine to the French in return for an extended truce, an agreement which in theory should have allowed the English forces in Normandy time to establish themselves on a soundly defensive footing, and provided France with a reason to settle for peace. In practice, the difficulty of enforcing a single, clear policy in the name of a vacuous King ensured that neither happened. No advantage was taken of the breathing-space afforded by the truce to regroup in Normandy, while at the same time the surrender of Maine did not take place as the treaty had promised, giving Charles VII legitimate reason to consider the agreement broken and himself absolved of the need to abide by its terms. In August 1449 he sent his armies into Normandy, and the result was a rout. Rouen fell to the French at the end of October, and by the beginning of 1450 almost all of Normandy had been overrun. In only four months, Henry V's spectacular conquests had been lost for ever.

Recriminations in England began even while the disaster in France was still unfolding. When parliament convened in November 1449, the Commons could not contain its outrage that a war which had cost thousands upon thousands of pounds in taxation was ending in such devastation and ignominy. It was clear that, for once, the Lower House was speaking not only for the lesser landowners and rich merchants who made up its members but for the mass of the King's subjects in blaming those closest to the King for the catastrophe. Inside parliament, leading courtiers were subjected to lacerating criticism; outside, the hostility they met could take much more brutal form. The Keeper of the Privy Seal, the Bishop of Chichester, was fatally unlucky to find himself in the wrong place at the wrong time in Portsmouth on 9 January 1450, when he was hacked to death by a mob of mutinous soldiers. A month later, however, the consensus in both country and parliament was that principal responsibility for the calamitous failure of English policy in France lay squarely with William de la Pole, Duke of Suffolk. Treason was the only possible explanation for what had happened, and the only person whose treason could have led to such terrible consequences was the man at the King's right hand.

On 7 February articles of impeachment were presented against Suffolk by the Commons in parliament which claimed, with righteous anger and total indifference to the lack of either evidence or plausibility, not only that the Duke had plotted the destruction of English interests in France, but that he had sought to depose King Henry in favour of his own son. Fundamentally, the charges amounted to the fact that a scapegoat was needed for the loss of France, and Suffolk's pre-eminence in government made him the only possible candidate. His fall was now both inevitable and necessary in order to defuse the political crisis – and yet his fellow magnates were deeply uneasy at the prospect of handing him to a lynch mob for a policy in which they had all been involved, a shared responsibility which Suffolk would expose as publicly as he could if the treason charges were pursued against him. The accusations could not be ignored completely, but Suffolk's trial was postponed for several weeks, a delay which gave rise to rumours in Norfolk that '*the Duke of Suffolk is pardoned, and has his men again waiting upon him, and is right well at ease and merry, and is in the King's good grace and in the good conceit of all the lords as well as ever he was*'.[38] The Commons used this interval to come up with a further slew of allegations against the Duke, this time concerning domestic misgovernment and financial impropriety. Rather than compounding the pressure on Suffolk as the Commons must have hoped, however, these additional charges offered the lords a way out of the public process of impeachment. On 17 March, a declaration was made in King Henry's name dismissing the charges of treason, but accepting the second set of articles against the Duke which the Commons had produced, those '*touching misprisions which be not criminal*'.[39] There would be no formal judicial hearing; instead, Suffolk was sentenced to banishment for a term of five years.

It seemed as though the worst of the political storm was over. On Thursday 30 April the Duke of Suffolk left England. His two ships took up position in the Channel near the Kent coast while he sent ahead to Calais to see what reception awaited him there. At some point during the day he wrote a touching letter to his only child, his seven-year-old son John, charging him to be true and faithful to God, the King, and his mother; '*and last of all, as heartily and as lovingly as ever father blessed his child on earth, I give you the blessing of our Lord and of me, which of his infinite mercy increase you in all virtue and good living . . . Written of my hand, the day of my departing from this land. Your true and loving father, Suffolk.*'[40] The Duke was still waiting for an answer from Calais when his ship was approached by another, the *Nicholas of the Tower*. At the insistence of the master of the *Nicholas*, the Duke came aboard the ship to speak with him. He was greeted with a cry of '*Welcome, traitor*.'[41]

Suddenly, shockingly, it was clear that neither the charges of treason which had been levelled at the Duke in parliament nor the violent anger which had precipitated them could be side-stepped quite so easily. The sailors on Suffolk's own ship disowned him, and when the Duke asked the name of the craft on which he was now held prisoner he fell into despair. A prophecy had been made before he left England that, '*if he might escape the danger of the Tower, he should be safe*'. On board his own ship en route to Calais, the Tower of London had seemed comfortingly distant, but the *Nicholas of the Tower* had been close at hand to intercept him, '*and then his heart failed him, for he thought he was deceived*'.[42] Two days later, the crew of the *Nicholas* used their ship as a makeshift court to try Suffolk for treason, declaring that, '*as the King did not wish to punish these traitors of his own will, nor to govern the aforesaid realm better, they themselves would do it*'.[43] The verdict was never in doubt. In full view of Suffolk's men, the Duke was taken from the *Nicholas* into its small launch, where a stock and an axe had been laid out. One of the sailors, '*one of the lewdest of the ship*', ordered the Duke to '*lay down his head, and he should be fair fared with and die on a sword*'. The sword was rusty, and it took half a dozen strokes to cut Suffolk's head from his body. The shipmen '*took away his gown of russet and his doublet of velvet mailed, and laid his body on the sands of Dover*'. As news spread that Suffolk's mutilated corpse lay on Dover beach, the political world was temporarily paralysed with shock. '*The sheriff of Kent does watch the body*', it was reported three days later, '*and sent his undersheriff to the judges to wit what to do*'.[44]

At Norwich, the Pastons received word of what had happened from their friend William Lomnor. '*I recommend me to you and am right sorry of that I shall say*', he wrote, '*and have so washed this little bill with sorrowful tears that scarcely you shall read it*'.[45] John and Margaret themselves had little cause to weep for Suffolk. The regime over which he had presided, battered from without by the French advance and eroded from within by the strain of Henry VI's incompetence, had utterly failed to bring Lord Moleyns to heel or to offer them justice at Gresham. And yet the Duke's power had seemed so unassailable that their only hope, Margaret had believed, lay in securing his favour – at least *'while the world is as it is'*.[46] In May 1450, the world, it seemed, had changed.

CHAPTER FOUR

– *the world is changed greatly* –

The Duke of Suffolk's murder unleashed chaos across the country. Little more than two weeks after his headless body was thrown on to the Kent shore, revolt erupted in the shire under the leadership of a man named Jack Cade. As disturbances spread across the south, eventually reaching as far west as Somerset, the Kentish rebels, thousands strong, marched on London. Margaret Paston's seventy-year-old kinsman Sir John Fastolf, an old soldier who had made a fortune in the French wars, found himself caught in the eye of the storm. He was living in retirement less than a mile downriver from London Bridge while his Norfolk home was being rebuilt, and was forced to take refuge in the Tower when the rebels surged into Southwark on their way towards the city. Many of the specific grievances of the Kentish contingent were local ones – particularly their hatred of the courtier Lord Saye, whom they accused of oppression and extortion in their county – but what made them so dangerous was that they also espoused the more general demand for reform which had been made by the Commons in parliament only a few months earlier. As the rebels were approaching Southwark, Fastolf sent out a servant to see if he could secure a copy of their manifesto. The poor man barely escaped with his life, but the document he brought back encapsulated the popular perception of the past few months' events in stark terms. King Henry, the rebels declared, '*has had false counsel, for his lands are lost, his merchandise is lost, his commons destroyed, the sea is lost, France is lost, himself so poor that he may not for his meat nor drink*'. And they were in no doubt where the blame should fall: '*he owes more than ever did King in England, and yet daily his traitors that be about him wait wherever thing should come to him by his law, and they ask it from him*'.[1]

With the government in disarray, the King was dispatched to the midlands for safety, leaving the rebels to storm across London Bridge and into the city itself. Cade was determined to demonstrate that his programme of reform was legitimate, and presided over quasi-judicial hearings at the Guildhall at which twenty leading courtiers were formally indicted for treason. Violence could not be restrained for long, however. Lord Saye and his equally reviled son-in-law, the sheriff of Kent, were executed and their heads paraded on pikes through the streets, from time to time being made to kiss each other in gruesome pantomime as the crowds jeered.

But the bloodshed and looting proved the rebels' undoing. Many Londoners were sympathetic to their complaints, but the mayor and leading citizens would not simply stand by and watch their city being destroyed. On the night of 5 July, they decided to seize control of London Bridge, intending to leave Cade and his men shut out of the city, marooned in the lodgings they had commandeered for themselves among the inns of Southwark on the south bank of the Thames. Hundreds were killed in a battle which raged all night, but, when light came and the smoke cleared, the city gates had finally been closed against the insurgents. Negotiations followed, during which the rebels were allowed a formal opportunity to present their complaints, and many took up the offer of a pardon for those who would return to their homes. Cade himself, knowing by now that a pardon would not save him, retreated first to Kent and then to Sussex. He was wounded and captured on 12 July, and died shortly afterwards of his injuries. His naked body was brought back to London for formal identification, and on 16 July his corpse was publicly beheaded at Newgate; his head was then placed on a spike on London Bridge, and his body dragged through the streets before being cut into pieces to be displayed in towns around the country as a dreadful reminder of the fate of traitors.

Cade's part in the revolt was over, but unrest continued across the southeast, fuelled by the anger of the soldiers and settlers who were straggling home as the last outposts of English rule in northern France fell to the French. News reached London on 19 August that '*Cherbourg is gone, and we have not now a foot of land in Normandy*'.[2] Calais, and the beleaguered remains of the Duchy of Aquitaine around Bordeaux, were all that was now left of the English empire in France. The loss of naval control in the Channel made southern England, already staggering under the impact of revolt, a yet more dangerous place. That much had been frighteningly clear in Norfolk even as early as the spring, when French ships were raiding the coast from Yarmouth to Cromer, stealing English boats and kidnapping anybody, man or woman, who was foolish enough to walk on the beaches. '*The said enemies be so bold that they come up to the land and play them on Caister sands and in other places as homelily as they were Englishmen*,' Margaret told her husband.[3]

And yet, despite the terror of these upheavals, the disintegration of the Duke of Suffolk's regime also represented a huge opportunity for anyone who had suffered under his rule. Political structures which had seemed immovable and invulnerable were suddenly in flux. The situation was dangerous and chaotic, but the sweeping away of old certainties meant that those who had been excluded from power might now have a real chance to assert themselves. John Paston, a small fish in a small pond, certainly thought so, but it was equally true for much greater men. For the Duke of Norfolk, the way was now open to step out of his rival's shadow and claim the place he believed was rightfully his at the centre of East Anglian politics. Sir John Fastolf, too, harboured an acute sense of grievance against Suffolk's regime, believing both that his vast military experience had been overlooked in government policy-making, and that he had been victimised in Norfolk by the Duke's servants, especially John Heydon and Sir Thomas Tuddenham.

For others, such as Thomas Daniel, the situation was more complicated. As a prominent member of the court, Daniel had been a target of fierce hostility in the wake of Suffolk's fall, but he was no friend of the Duke's, and in the summer of 1450 saw the possibility of manoeuvring for his own advantage as well as the need for self-defence. He had been friendly with the Duke of Norfolk for a couple of years already, and now began to cultivate an acquaintance with John de Vere, Earl of Oxford, whose Norfolk home at Winch was only a couple of miles from Daniel's fraudulently acquired house at Roydon. All in all, these developments could scarcely have seemed more positive for John Paston. His connections with Thomas Daniel had been little use before this point, but the alliance of Daniel with Oxford, who had at least been sympathetic when he visited Gresham in the previous year, and the association of both men with the Duke of Norfolk and Margaret's cousin Fastolf, seemed a great deal more promising, especially given that Suffolk's death had left the Pastons' enemies Heydon and Lord Moleyns suddenly vulnerable. After two years of struggle, whatever the chaos that surrounded him, it finally seemed possible that John might find a way to expel Moleyns's men from his property.

It was a summer of frantic activity on all fronts. Sir John Fastolf set to work within days of Suffolk's death to compile an exhaustive list of all the wrongs he felt he had suffered over the previous twelve years. His temporary displacement from his Southwark home at the hands of the rebels did nothing to deflect him from his purpose, although it did encourage him to stock up on weaponry, so long as it could be done economically and discreetly: 'purvey me at the least five dozen longbows, with shot belonging thereto', he told his chaplain in Norfolk, 'and purvey also quarrel heads' – bolts for crossbows – '*to be made there, for the price is dearer here than there; and let no language be had of ordinances making*'.[4] John Paston, meanwhile, presented a petition to the Chancellor, John Kemp, Archbishop of York, asking that a special judicial commission should be appointed specifically to investigate Moleyns's seizure of Gresham. He proposed that Lord Moleyns should be compelled to remove his men from Gresham immediately, and that the profits of the estate should go to a neutral party until the commission could sit and the matter be decided.

Chancellor Kemp was not unsympathetic to the suggestion, and wrote to Moleyns accordingly, but the very circumstances which were finally giving John this access to the heart of government also told heavily against him. With the country engulfed in chaos, powerful men had more important things to think about than injustices perpetrated in a small corner of northern Norfolk. Rumours were sweeping the south of more risings to follow Cade's revolt, and word came to London that as many as ten thousand rebels were massing in Wiltshire. The rumour subsided as rapidly as it had developed, but by then it had already served Lord Moleyns's purpose. The Pastons' lawyer James Gresham wrote in the middle of August to report Moleyns's response to the Chancellor's letter. Of course, Moleyns said, '*if he might attend to be in Norfolk and leave the necessary service that he did to the King now in Wiltshire, he would be but well pleased that you had your assize*'; but, he explained in tones of the utmost sincerity, he simply could not leave Wiltshire, since he '*had sore been laboured in his country to peace and still the people there to restrain them from rising, and so he was daily laboured there about in the King's service*'.[5] James Gresham's advice was that – given the ongoing unrest, and Moleyns's obvious determination to continue stonewalling for as long as he could – John should abandon his campaign for a special investigation into his own case, and rely instead on the fact that general judicial commissions were being appointed to deal with disorder across the south of England. When the justices sat in Norfolk, John could present his complaints against Moleyns to them.

In the circumstances, it was a hardy man who would argue with that; but John was, if nothing else, hardy. He had heard all Moleyns's fine words before, and he was angry. In John's mind, the situation was clear: he had a right to Gresham which he could establish in law, and he wanted his day in court to prove it. Not for the last time, his conviction that right as he saw it should prevail made him incapable of negotiating the complex politics of the situation. He could not accept that he might have to take the pragmatic route and cede some ground to a man who had less right but more power than he. Moleyns had indicated that he would consider the possibility of arbitration, but the two sides could not even agree on what that should mean. In John's eyes, arbitration was a chance to put his case to an impartial referee for judgement – *'before this time I have agreed to put it in two judges so they would determine by our evidences the right,'* he explained, *'moving neither party to give other by any means, but only the right determined, he to be fully recompensed that has right'* – while for Moleyns it represented an opportunity to bargain from a position of strength with all the leverage he could muster. *'He would not agree',* John wrote angrily, *'but all times would that those judges should entreat the parties as they might be drawn to by offer and proffer, to my conceit as men buy horses'.* John was so infuriated, and so impatient with the sprawling mess of his affairs, that he urged James Gresham to press the Chancellor for a decision one way or the other on the question of the special commission, even if to do so was to risk a negative response: *'I pray you heartily labour you so to my lord Chancellor',* he wrote, *'that either he will grant me my desire or else that he will deny it'.*[6]

In the end, as James Gresham had foreseen, the answer was no. All John's hopes now rested on the general commission of *oyer* and *terminer* – a judicial inquiry appointed to sit outside Westminster with the power not only to hear indictments but to determine verdicts on them – which would convene at Norwich in September 1450. Norwich itself had been a focus of deep hostility to John Heydon for more than ten years, ever since Heydon, serving as a judge in the city in 1437, had become embroiled in two interminably bitter disputes, one between rival factions within the city government, and the other between the city corporation and the cathedral priory. Now, when the commissioners held preliminary hearings there on Thursday 17 September, that hostility came flooding out in a deluge of allegations against Heydon which smacked more of pent-up antagonism than any kind of factual accuracy. Heydon had conspired with his friend Thomas Tuddenham and other associates, it was said, to pervert justice and extort money in Norfolk and Suffolk, a malevolent compact which dated back to 1439 (or 1441, or 1434, or 1435, or perhaps 1436, depending on which of the mass of indictments one consulted). He had committed treason in the spring of 1450 by expressing the view that the King had no right to Normandy, and that it might be a good idea to get rid of Calais too, given that its defence was costing £10,000 a year (although privately there was anxiety that the witness who had heard Heydon utter these treasonable words was proving difficult to produce in court). On 6 September, less than a fortnight before the start of the hearings, Heydon had ridden into Norwich with sixty armed men and tried to encourage the townspeople to rebel. It was further alleged that, ten days later, on the very night before the sessions began, he had secretly removed the piece of Jack Cade's body which had been strung up on the town gate, both to scandalise the inhabitants and to bring them into the King's displeasure. This macabre accusation was made by the Pastons' friend John Damme; other cases were brought against Heydon and Tuddenham by Sir John Fastolf's chaplain Thomas Howes, complaining of wrongs done to Fastolf and his servants over a period of more than ten years. While this array of charges was being presented, another hearing took place at Swaffham, where John Paston's complaints were finally put before the court. Men from Wiltshire including Walter Barrow and John Partridge, together with local associates including John Mariot of East Beckham, were indicted for seizing the Pastons' manor of Gresham by force on 28 January 1449, on the instructions, the indictment alleged, of both Heydon himself and Robert, Lord Moleyns.[7]

Once the charges had been presented, the first substantive hearings were held at Norwich on Tuesday 22 September. This was the beginning of a lengthy legal process. Local juries had to be summoned to give a verdict on the charges, and it could take months after the summonses had been issued to get both the jurors and the defendants into court. Nevertheless, there were encouraging signs for the Pastons and their friends. The commissioners sitting to hear the charges were the Duke of Norfolk, the Earl of Oxford, and Justice William Yelverton, a Norfolk-born judge in the court of King's Bench who was a friend and counsellor to Sir John Fastolf. None of the three had any reason to be sympathetic to Heydon and his former colleagues in the Duke of Suffolk's service. On the other hand, Suffolk's fall had not at a stroke cut off their opponents' access to the King. Lord Moleyns, for example, had procured a royal letter four days earlier commanding that legal process against himself and his servants should be halted until Moleyns could be present in person at the Norfolk hearings – and that would not be for some time, since '*our right trusty and wellbeloved Lord Moleyns is by our special desire and commandment waiting upon us*'.[8] There seemed little that John Paston could do but wait to see how the indictments would proceed.

Meanwhile, Thomas Daniel's view of the situation was almost entirely different. John and his patron could hardly have been more temperamentally mismatched. All John's instincts reinforced his belief that due process of law would eventually vindicate the rightfulness of his position, whereas the law seemed at best an irrelevance to Daniel's policy of anarchic self-interest. Having succeeded with so little apparent difficulty in taking over the Woodhouse estates at Roydon, Daniel set his sights next on the manor of

Bradeston in eastern Norfolk, halfway between Norwich and Yarmouth. Bradeston belonged to the Berneys of Reedham, the family of Margaret Paston's mother Margery. The head of the family, Margaret's oldest Berney uncle Thomas, had died nine years earlier, leaving his young son as his heir. Thomas's widow Elizabeth remarried, and Bradeston and the other Berney estates were therefore temporarily in the custody of her new husband Osbert Mundford. Daniel had no more claim to Bradeston than he had to Henry Woodhouse's property at Roydon, and this time he did not even bother to resort to quasi-legal subterfuge. Unabashed by the venomous criticism of grasping courtiers at the parliament which met at Leicester in May 1450, Daniel sent his men to occupy Bradeston while parliament was still sitting. It took three months before Mundford succeeded in recovering the manor, on 6 September, with the help of John Heydon. In fact, it was this expedition to expel Daniel's men from Bradeston which resulted in Heydon's indictment for attempted insurrection at Norwich that day. As Heydon himself explained later in court, he had gathered twenty-six armed men – *defensibly* armed, he pointed out – to assist him in his capacity as a justice of the peace in helping Mundford recover Bradeston, and had simply ridden through the city on his way to the manor.[9]

Mundford's success in thwarting Daniel's aggression encouraged Henry Woodhouse to feel that he too might at last stand a chance of recapturing his own home at Roydon. Daniel himself was occupied in London, but persuaded a servant of the Earl of Oxford named Thomas Denys to take command at Roydon on his behalf. Denys, whom John Paston knew slightly, was an impulsive man of great energy and very little judgement. A year earlier, trying to be helpful, Denys had come up with a strategy to expel Lord Moleyns's men from Gresham, but in view of his tendency to act first and think later it was perhaps not surprising that John was unenthusiastic. ('*Thomas Denys asked me why you observed not the purpose that he moved you of for the removing of the strength at Gresham, etc,*' James Gresham told John in October 1449; '*he would it should yet be done.*')[10] By 4 October 1450, Denys himself was bitterly regretting that he had ever agreed to help Daniel at Roydon. Henry Woodhouse was gathering forces on all sides of the manor with the help of his brother-in-law, Heydon's friend Thomas Tuddenham, but Denys's own lord, the Earl of Oxford, had refused to send help against them. Denys appealed frantically to John Paston for support – '*I think if they get the place upon me there helps my life no pardon*' – and invoked their shared enmity to Heydon and Tuddenham as a cause for common defence. '*If you help not now*', he wrote in a desperate postscript, '*Tuddenham and Heydon shall* achieve in their dis-ease the conquest that they could never achieve in their prosperity'.[11] For all the history of hostility between Heydon and John Paston, and for all John's hopes of help from Thomas Daniel, the recent trouble at Bradeston was more than enough to warn him off trying to help Denys defend Daniel's occupation of Roydon. Osbert Mundford and the Berneys were old friends and relations – close enough that Margaret was godmother to Mundford's daughter Mary – and, if Heydon had helped to expel Daniel from their property, then that, at least, had to be a mark in his favour to set against the long list of Paston complaints.

There was another reason, apart from events at Bradeston, why John Paston's adherence to Thomas Daniel was under strain. In the autumn of 1450, a new hope appeared amid the political chaos in the person of Richard, Duke of York, one of the greatest magnates in the realm and a close relative of the King. Where King Henry was descended from the third son of his ancestor Edward III, York was descended in the male line from Edward III's fourth son – and, until such time as the young and so far childless Queen gave her husband a son, that made York the heir to the throne. The Duke was also descended, through his mother, from the second son of Edward III. Although there could be no serious suggestion that a claim through the female line might supersede the authority of the anointed King, this concentration of royal blood in his veins gave York confidence that he could speak for the realm more authoritatively than any other nobleman. In 1450, there was much to speak about. York had spent years fighting to defend the English conquests in France, until in 1447 he was appointed the King's lieutenant in Ireland, an office which he took up in person in the summer of 1449. Despite the fact that he had been involved in policy-making throughout the 1440s, his absence from both England and France at this specific point in 1449–50 – during both the catastrophic losses in France and the subsequent terrors of Cade's rebellion – allowed him to claim that his hands were clean in the aftermath of the disasters, as few other noblemen could. When he returned to England in early September, he aligned himself immediately with the House of Commons in denouncing leading members of the court for their destructive greed and evil counsel, and presented himself as the champion of reform in the interests of the 'common weal' of the realm. '. . . *my lord was with the King, and he visaged so the matter there that all the King's household was and is afeared right sore*', Justice Yelverton's clerk William Wayte told John on 6 October; '*and my said lord has put a bill to the King and desired much thing, which is much after the Commons' desire, and all is upon justice*'. With parliament in session, the extent to which York could call on widespread support from the gentry and leading townsmen was plain, and under his influence a number of the most hated members of the royal household, including Thomas Daniel, were formally charged with treason. The implications were not lost on John Paston and his friends. '*Sir, speak to Denys that he avoids his garrison at Roydon*,' Wayte advised John urgently, '*for there is none other remedy but death for Daniel and for all those that are indicted*.'[12]

The scramble for position around York was frantic. It was reported that John Heydon and Thomas Tuddenham were ready to pay £2,000 to win the favour of the Duke's right-hand man Sir William Oldhall, and gossip had it that they had earmarked another £1,000 to secure a sympathetic sheriff. Neither rumour was financially plausible, but it was certainly true that Heydon and his friends, like John Paston and his allies, were doing everything they could to procure the appointment of a sheriff they thought likely to be favourable to their own cause. For the first time in years, Heydon was having to work extremely hard in his own defence, and he met some unaccustomed challenges along the way. At London he visited Justice John Markham, one of the judges of the King's Bench, hoping presumably to solicit some legal support, and instead received an unexpected moral lecture: '*he told H. his part how that he lived ungoodly in putting away of his wife and kept another, etc*'. Heydon was taken aback, but defended himself stoutly ('*he turned pale colour, and said he lived not but as God was pleased with, nor did no wrong to no person*'), and was equally robust in his repudiation of the Pastons' version of events at Gresham. He had had nothing to do with what happened there, he said, but would not give an inch, all the same, on the justice of Moleyns's claim: '*he enforced greatly and said his title was better than yours*', John was told.[13]

Despite Heydon's bravado, the news of Lord Moleyns seemed more heartening now that the Duke of York was dictating the political agenda. William Wayte reported that Moleyns was '*sore out of grace, and that my lord of York loves him not*' – or, as Judge Yelverton himself more laconically put it, '*some men suppose that my lord of York cherishes not much the said Lord Moleyns*'.[14] Not, of course, that York's antipathy to Moleyns could in itself guarantee victory for the Pastons. Moleyns had still not appeared in Norfolk in person at any stage in the two and a half years of the contest over Gresham, but continued to issue threats from a distance. Some of his men had been taken into custody at Norwich, and Moleyns was said to be furious, swearing that he would have his revenge on those who had dared attack him. He was reported to be on his way to Norfolk with more than a hundred men, and '*if he comes to Norwich, look there be ready to wait upon the mayor a good fellowship*', William Wayte told John, '*for it is said here that they are but beasts*'.[15] The Pastons' friends were taking the threats seriously. Wayte and his master Judge Yelverton both warned John to be careful, particularly of Heydon's influence behind the scenes: '*Sir, beware of Heydon*,' Wayte wrote on 6 October, '*for he would destroy you, by my faith*'.[16] On the other hand, Moleyns had so far gone to great lengths to avoid setting foot in Norfolk and therefore having to face any judicial process against him, and the hearings were after all continuing, with the next sessions scheduled for November.

Sure enough, Moleyns and his '*great people*' failed to appear in the county to back up his bluster. The manoeuvring around the Duke of York intensified, however, as news came that the Duke was on his way to visit Norfolk. Even the great and the good were feeling the pressure in the frenetic activity which preceded his arrival: '*Sir, it were wisdom that my lord of Oxford wait on my lord of York*', Wayte told John.[17] '*Spend somewhat of your goods now, and get you lordship and friendship there*,' Judge Yelverton advised, '*for thereupon depends all law and profit*'.[18] Such feverish anticipation, however, could only meet with disappointment. The roots of the political crisis were too deep to be susceptible of a quick fix, even had the Duke been the saviour some wished to paint him. In practice, York's self-promotion as the champion of popular grievance meant that he was regarded with increasing suspicion by many of his fellow magnates – and, without broad support among the nobility, the Duke would find it difficult either to create a workable regime or to establish the legitimacy of his own leadership in government. It was perhaps unsurprising, therefore, that nothing conclusive happened as a result of his visit to East Anglia, other than that he decided, in conclave with the Duke of Norfolk, on the candidates he wished to see elected as the local MPs at the next parliament.

So much was now happening at once that it was hard to know where to be. The next sessions of the judicial hearings in Norwich were scheduled for Monday 16 November, but one could not be there and at parliament, which opened at Westminster on 6 November, at the same time. John Damme and James Gresham wished that John were there to defend himself when '*the Lord Moleyns had language of you in the King's presence*' – '*your absence does no ease here*', they wrote on 11 November – and as a result John hurried to join them in London.[19] On the other hand, absenting himself from the legal sessions in Norwich was equally problematic: '*also that my cousin Paston be so hastily helped in his matters that he may soon come hither again*', Justice

Yelverton requested in a letter to Sir John Fastolf on the eve of the hearings.[20] The judges themselves faced the same dilemma. The Duke of Norfolk travelled to London to attend parliament, but the Earl of Oxford was given permission to miss the parliamentary session in order to sit at Norwich with Yelverton when the court reconvened. Meanwhile, the Pastons' opponents tried to argue that Yelverton himself should be removed from the hearings, and it was not hard to see why. He was an unarguably partisan presence, sending a constant stream of information and advice to John Paston and Sir John Fastolf, to whom he was so close that Fastolf called him '*my brother*'.[21] Both Fastolf and John Paston worked frantically behind the scenes to make sure that Yelverton would in the end be allowed to sit, and, once the decision had been confirmed, Fastolf sent a manservant and horses to convey the judge safely to Norwich.

Yelverton was as worried as anyone else about the opportunities his departure from London would give his enemies in this agitated political atmosphere, asking Fastolf to '*be my shield and my defence against all false noises and slanders moved against me by their means in my absence*'. On the other hand, he was also convinced that, now the commissions had begun their work, there was a real opportunity to strike a blow against their enemies. '*Here is a marvellous disposed country*,' he told Fastolf, '*and many evil-willed people to Sir Thomas Tuddenham and Heydon*.' His only concern was that people would lack the confidence to come forward with their complaints unless they were sure of a well-disposed sheriff who could be relied on to empanel a sympathetic jury – or, in Yelverton's eyes, of course, simply an honest sheriff, '*that neither for good favour nor fear will return for the King nor between party and party none other men but such as are good and true*'.[22] The annual appointment of sheriffs in each county would normally have been made at the beginning of November, but in these wildly abnormal circumstances the decision was delayed until after the Duke of York's return to London at the end of that month. York himself, who had staked his claim to power on a call for justice and good government, could not afford to be seen to support the nomination of partisan office-holders, and the gentleman who was appointed as sheriff of Norfolk and Suffolk on 3 December, John Jermyn, does seem to have been a genuinely neutral figure, in the sense that neither the Pastons' friends nor their opponents could claim him as one of their own. As soon as his name had been confirmed, therefore, Fastolf suggested that they should shift their efforts to campaigning for '*a good undersheriff which were not inclining to the party of T.H.*'.[23]

The hearings went ahead as planned in November in the presence of Justice Yelverton and the Earl of Oxford, and more sessions were held in Norwich in December.[24] As always, however, getting all parties and a jury into court for each case was a laborious business. Very little was resolved, and legal process was postponed again to further hearings to be held at King's Lynn after Christmas. There Oxford and Yelverton would be joined as judges by Thomas, Lord Scales, whose home at Middleton lay only a couple of miles away from the town. There was good news – John Heydon and Thomas Tuddenham would at last appear before the court, it was said – but also bad: '*it is like that great labour and special pursuit shall be made to the Lord Scales that he will maintain the said Tuddenham and Heydon in all he can or may*', Fastolf heard.[25] It was hard to know what to make of this. Lord Scales, now about fifty, had returned to England in 1449 after spending the best part of thirty years fighting in France. During that time he had become so close to John Fastolf, with whom he commanded the campaign in Maine after the English victory at Verneuil in 1424, that he addressed him respectfully as '*father*'.[26] He had also developed a strong relationship with the Duke of York, and stood godfather to York's eldest son Edward when he was born at Rouen in 1442. Scales's commitment to the war, including a decade spent as lieutenant-general of western Normandy, meant that he cannot have been sanguine about the collapse of English policy there at the end of the 1440s. However, that in itself did not mean that he would blame the Duke of Suffolk for the disaster. Suffolk himself had fought in France for fifteen years – he lost three brothers in the war and was captured briefly in 1429 – and Scales might well view him as his brother-in-arms just as much as Fastolf or York. Moreover, Scales's closest political connections in East Anglia – so far as it was possible to tell, given his limited involvement in domestic affairs up to this point – were with Suffolk's men. Most ominously for the Pastons, he was related by marriage to their enemy Lord Moleyns, Scales's wife Emma being the aunt of Moleyns's wife Eleanor. Both sides therefore had much to hope for from Scales, and neither could be sure – on this, his first real foray into the snake-pit which Norfolk politics had become – which way he would jump.

It was nerve-racking to have a new element introduced into the already complex political equation at this late stage in proceedings, but John Fastolf at least was hoping that the presence of Oxford and Yelverton would be enough to secure a favourable outcome, whatever Scales chose to do or say. Yelverton was certainly a dependable ally, and Oxford was sufficiently on side to write to the sheriff, who was responsible for the crucial task of recruiting juries, explaining his concern in case '*true favour in your office to the people that have complained by many and great horrible bills against certain persons should not be showed at this next sessions at Lynn*'.[27] Indeed, new charges against Heydon and Tuddenham were still coming in – enthusiastically encouraged, of course, by John Fastolf and John Paston – including a bill of complaints from the town of Swaffham, where Tuddenham had been the King's steward for the past sixteen years. A petition detailing the Swaffham allegations was even submitted to parliament, asking that, because '*the said Sir Thomas is a common extortioner*', and because he '*would never appear in his person, nor by his attorney*' at the commission's hearings in Norfolk, he should be arrested and held in prison until the Lynn sessions.[28] The prospect of a man as well connected as Thomas Tuddenham awaiting the verdict of a Norfolk court under lock and key was never a realistic one, but it is striking that those in the town who had grievances against him now felt bold enough to demand it.

Meanwhile, Heydon and Tuddenham were trying everything they could think of to extricate themselves from the charges. It had been widely reported in London that their opponents in Norfolk were (potentially literally) up in arms, and it therefore seemed less likely that they would choose to appear in person at the Lynn sessions. Fastolf's servant John Bocking reported that Tuddenham had lost his prayer-book on Tower Hill and sent a servant back to look for it, '*and a good fellow wished it in Norfolk, so he would fetch it there*'; '*men think that Norfolk men were hardier than they be*', he added ruefully.[29] As Bocking implied, a key factor in the campaign on both sides was the attempt to control the flow of information between Norfolk and London. For the Pastons and their allies, it was crucially important that the lords around the King at Westminster should be convinced that the county was convulsed with popular resentment of their opponents. Their hope was that, in the aftermath of the revolts of the previous summer, the fall of Tuddenham and Heydon would seem a small price to pay to avoid further unrest. Tuddenham and Heydon themselves, on the other hand, knew that every report which reached Norfolk of the powerful support on which they could call at court made it less likely that any jury would dare to convict them. In the meantime, most of the region's gentry – who had no personal stake in the grievances between the two sides, and whose overriding concern in these chaotic months was political survival – were simply waiting to see what the political landscape looked like once the dust finally settled.

At the beginning of January 1451, it was impossible to tell who had the upper hand. The Pastons' hopes received a sudden boost from Simon Blake, a King's serjeant and member of the royal household who had held office for the past six months as bailiff of Swaffham, where feeling against Thomas Tuddenham was running so high. Blake arrived in London on Saturday 27 December and launched into a public-relations offensive, telling the Chancellor that, if Tuddenham and Heydon were pardoned or the hearings in Norfolk overridden, '*London should have as much for to do as they had for to keep London Bridge when the Captain*' – Jack Cade – '*came thither, for he told him that there was up in Norfolk ready to rise 5,000 and more*'. It seemed as though Blake had arrived just in time, Tuddenham and Heydon having almost convinced the lords that the charges against them were a political vendetta and that they should be pardoned. Lord Scales, meanwhile, had not yet shown his hand in public, but Yelverton's clerk William Wayte believed that he would back Heydon and Tuddenham, and was seeking to settle the grievances between Tuddenham and the towns-people of Swaffham – the risk being that, if he succeeded, other complaints might fall by the wayside. To counter this threat, Yelverton and John Paston therefore did what they could to mobilise support from the strongly anti-Heydon faction at Norwich. '*My master prays you*', Wayte told John, '*that you will speak with the mayor and his brethren that they purvey that there be at Lynn a sufficient fellowship together, and that there be made a great noise upon the Lord Scales both of Tuddenham and Heydon and for all those that are of that sect*'.[30] However, this was a dangerous game which could be exploited by their enemies. Just as John Heydon's role in helping Osbert Mundford reclaim the manor of Bradeston was parlayed into an armed riot in the indictments which John Paston helped frame, John's own attempts to ensure that Norwich's grievances were well represented at the Lynn hearings were seized on by his old rival John Wyndham. '*And sir, at the reverence of God, labour your matters wisely and secretly*', Wayte – who was now sending him weekly bulletins from Yelverton's side – urged him, '*for Wyndham noised you sore before my lord of Oxford and my lord Scales that you should raise much people with great array out of Norwich; and therefore, sir, let the people be wisely and manly guided in their speaking and demeaning*'.[31]

In public, John Heydon was all confidence. '*It seems by their countenance that they trust of a good year*', Wayte reported gloomily. By 9 January he had also heard that two of Heydon's servants, Thomas Bridge and William Prentice, were '*at home with the Lord Scales*', which was truly bad news. On the other hand, Scales's attempt to mediate between Tuddenham and the town of Swaffham had broken down acrimoniously, so that the town's representatives would be at the hearings '*in their best array*' to put forward their complaints. After months of raised hopes and interminable delays, the wait for judgement was becoming acutely frustrating. '*Sir, I would there were a thousand of good manly men to cry out on Tuddenham, Heydon, Prentice, and Bridge for their false extortions*', Wayte wrote in a rare moment of departure from measured analysis of the latest developments. In the meantime, there was still much to fear. '*I beseech you beware to whom you show your letters. Let them be burned*', he added – not that John, an inveterate filer of correspondence, complied.[32]

The sessions at Lynn finally opened on Tuesday 13 January, but yet again Paston hopes that the charges might come to judgement were dashed almost immediately. Once more, Heydon and Tuddenham failed to appear at the hearings, and process was respited, this time for three months, to Norwich in Easter week. If there was a silver lining to be found, it was that this postponement did at least allow a slightly longer time to regroup and plan for the next round. For John Paston, that meant focusing on Gresham. He had considered the possibility of trying to re-enter the estate four months earlier, but decided against it, put off both by the intimidating noises Moleyns was making, and by his own determination to settle for nothing less than full judicial restitution for all the wrongs he had suffered: '*the manor is so decayed by the Lord Moleyns's occupation*', he complained, '*that, where it was worth to me 50 marks by year, I could not now make it worth £20*'.[33] By the end of January 1451, however, the situation looked a little different. Despite all Moleyns's sound and fury, it was now clear that his repeated threats to arrive in Norfolk armed to the teeth were not about to materialise, something which left his servants still holding out at Gresham in an increasingly precarious position. At the same time, judicial restitution had not proved as easy to secure as John had hoped, and direct action seemed correspondingly more appealing. In February, after three long years, John Paston finally sent his servants into Gresham and took back his manor.

Moleyns's response was prompt and predictable. He sent word via his man John Partridge that he would '*come down himself and enter in the said manor within a short time*'. Magnanimously – a well-worn stratagem in the battle for hearts and minds among the villagers – he added that, when he reclaimed his property, he would not demand any rents which the tenants had paid to John Paston in the meantime. Even though John was back in possession, Moleyns's continuing threats affected his dealings there in a major way. After Margaret's experiences at Gresham two years earlier, there was no suggestion that she and the children should move back to the manor house, but no tenant could be found who was prepared to live there either. The villagers remained nervous, and one at least was refusing to pay his rent unless he was forced to do so – something which would indicate his resistance to John Paston if he later had to deal again with Moleyns. The Paston chaplain James Gloys, who was managing the estate for John, tried to seize some of the man's goods but was routed by his formidable mother ('*I have been there divers times for to distrain him, and I could never do it but if I would have distrained him in his mother's house; and there I dared not for her cursing*').[34]

Meanwhile, there were worrying signs that the campaign against their enemies was beginning to fray around the edges. News arrived in Norwich at the beginning of March of their opponents' latest tactic: a time-honoured device, of bringing indictments in a completely different county – charges which were difficult even to find out about, let alone defend oneself against. Word had it that John Paston, his friend John Damme, Judge William Yelverton and even the Earl of Oxford himself had been indicted in Kent for maintenance – that is, unlawful support of one party to litigation by people unconnected with the case – at the Norfolk hearings. Damme was in particular trouble, indicted for treason on the grounds that he had falsely charged John Heydon with treason by accusing him of taking down the dismembered part of Jack Cade's body from the gates of Norwich. Margaret was worried about what this all meant. '. . . *the people that be against Sir Thomas Tuddenham and Heydon be sore afeared*,' she told John, '*because of this noise and of other language that is had both in this town and in the country that these said Tuddenham and Heydon should be as well at ease and have as great rule as ever they had*'.[35] There was even a rumour that Heydon was about to be knighted, '*and much other language there is which causes men to be afeared, thinking that he should have a rule again*'. Heydon himself was doing all he could to stoke the fears of the people of Norwich and create uncertainty about his movements. He had his men bring his horse and saddle into Norwich Abbey in full view of the city, '*thinking to men of the town that Heydon had gone over the ferry and so into the Abbey*'; it was two whole days before they admitted he was not there, but still in London.[36]

The debilitating uncertainty continued throughout March. Margaret at least had some domestic issues to occupy her time – whether John wanted red for the livery gowns he would distribute to his servants that year, for example – and brought her own shrewd perspective to John's attempts to recover property that had gone missing from Gresham as a result of Moleyns's occupation. *'As for that you desired that I should enquire where any stuff is of yours, I know not how to do therewith,'* she told her husband, *'for if one were espied that has of your stuff, and we had it from him, others that have more thereof would beware by him and avoid such stuff as they have of yours'.* Rumours were getting stronger, however, that both Heydon and Tuddenham, as well as Lord Moleyns, had secured their positions and would shortly be back in Norfolk in full force. John was in London, staying at the Inner Temple, where Margaret sent him the latest news from Norwich. *'It is said here',* she wrote on Monday 15 March, *'that the King should come into this country, and Sir Thomas Tuddenham and Heydon are well cherished with him; and also it is said they shall have as great rule in this country as ever they had, and many more folks are sorry therefor than merry. Sir Thomas Tuddenham's men and Heydon's sow this seed all about the country, that their masters shall come home in haste in their prosperity and be as well at ease as ever they were'.* The propaganda battle would play a vital part in determining what happened when the court finally came to judgement. So many people were waiting to gauge the political climate before committing themselves to one side or the other that being perceived to be confident of success might go more than halfway towards achieving it. Unfortunately, it was a battle the Pastons' enemies seemed to be winning. The tenants at Gresham, Margaret reported, were terrified, *'the language is so great on the other party'.*[37] By the end of the month, the manor was awash with rumours that Moleyns himself would be there very soon. *'Other tidings have we none',* Margaret said wearily, *'but that Tuddenham and Heydon should have again the rule in this country as much as ever they had, or more'.*[38]

Easter week – the new date set for the hearings – fell in the last week of April. By the middle of the month, John Fastolf received information at London that Heydon and Tuddenham would definitely be at Norwich to appear in court – good news in itself, in that it offered a chance of proceeding with the indictments at long last, but only so long as those who had brought the allegations forward could be kept steadfast when the time finally came for the charges to be heard. There was bad news too, however. Neither the Duke of Norfolk nor the Earl of Oxford would be present at the sessions, and their place on the bench would be taken by John Prisot, chief justice in the court of Common Pleas, who had long-standing connections with both Heydon and Tuddenham. It was a blow, but not necessarily a decisive one. Prisot would, after all, be sitting with the Pastons' staunch ally

William Yelverton. Whatever happened, it was clear that this, at last, would be the final showdown.

The court convened in the Guildhall of Norwich on Thursday 29 April. Counsel for the city of Norwich spoke, followed by the lawyers for the town of Swaffham. Sir John Fastolf's cases were put forward, then John Paston's, and many others. But it rapidly became apparent that Justice Yelverton's determination to see these cases through was more than matched by Justice Prisot's determination to head them off. Yelverton did what he could – objecting, for example, when Prisot declared that he would hear all cases except those presented by the city of Norwich, which he would put in continuance, '*which words Yelverton thought right partial*' – but Prisot nevertheless '*would suffer no man that was learned to speak for the plaintiffs, but took it as a venom, and took them by the nose at every third word, which might well be known for open partiality*'. The worst news of all was Prisot's decision that the hearings should not, after all, go ahead at Norwich as planned, but should be adjourned for a few days and then reconvene at Walsingham. Fastolf's chaplain Thomas Howes, who was in court to report back to his master, saw this as a blatantly partisan move. Walsingham, in north-western Norfolk, was deep in Duchy of Lancaster territory, where Thomas Tuddenham and John Heydon had been powerful for years, or, as Howes put it, '*where they have greatest rule*'.[39] The trouble was that Tuddenham and Heydon could easily make the converse claim about Norwich, a town where they faced more hostility than anywhere else in the county. Either way, the endgame had begun with a shattering setback for the Pastons and their friends. Justice Prisot's decision stood: the hearings would reopen the following week, on Tuesday 4 May, at Walsingham.

Some of the Duke of Norfolk's men arrived in Walsingham over the weekend, and sent news back to John Paston in Norwich. '*The sheriff is not so whole as he was,*' they told him, '*for now he will show but a part of his friendship.*' Now that it was clear that the court would give its judgement on territory dominated by Heydon and Tuddenham, the drift of support away from the Pastons and their allies was reaching a critical mass: '*there is great press of people*', Norfolk's men reported, '*and few friends as far as we can feel yet*'. They would do their best, they said, but John ought to think carefully about whether or not he should be there himself. The information they had already gathered about his own case was devastating. '*The sheriff informed us that he has writing from the King that he shall make such a panel to acquit the Lord Moleyns. And also he told us, and as far as we can conceive and feel, the sheriff will empanel gentlemen to acquit the lord, and jurors to acquit his men;*

and we suppose that it is by the motion and means of the other party.'[40] Victory through this court now seemed an impossibility.

When the sessions finally reopened on Tuesday morning, any last remaining embers of hope were extinguished. The Pastons had been so full of excited optimism when the hearings began at Norwich more than seven months earlier, with their allies the Duke of Norfolk, the Earl of Oxford and Justice Yelverton on the bench. Now, at Walsingham, the judges were Justice Prisot and Lord Scales, both of whom had already made plain their support for the Pastons' opponents. Sir John Fastolf's chaplain Thomas Howes wrote to the elderly knight in despair at the wrecking of all their hopes:

> . . . *it was the most partial place of all the shire, and thither were called all the friends, knights and esquires and gentlemen that would in no wise do otherwise than they would. And the said Tuddenham, Heydon and other oppressors of their sect came down thither, as I understand, with four hundred horse and more; and considering how their well-willers were there assembled at their instance, it had been right jeopardous and fearful for any of the plaintiffs to have been present, for there was not one of the plaintiffs nor complainants there, but your right faithful and trusty well-willer John Paston.*[41]

The scene he met when he arrived at Walsingham can only have been a bitter blow for John. But even he, hardy soul that he was, had not been there at the start of the sessions. By the time he arrived, Moleyns had already been acquitted on the charge of commanding his servants to enter Gresham illegally. On this, Moleyns's first, belated visit to Norfolk, he had had to push hard before the verdict had gone his way. No local jury, however bold, could easily reject the word of one of the King's courtiers, and this in the end was what the case came down to: *'the Lord Moleyns should not have been acquitted of his commandment had he not sworn on a book, such evidence was against him'*, John was told.[42] Even after his arrival, John's lone, if sturdy, presence was no help to his cause or those of his friends. Thomas Howes was disgusted at what he saw as the perfidy of men from whom they had hoped for support in the heady days after the Duke of Suffolk's death. *'Also to know some of your faint friends,'* he told Fastolf, *'at that time that my lord Norfolk sat upon the oyer determiner, Sir John Heveningham might not find it in his heart to go four furlongs from his dwelling place to the shirehouse, but now he could ride from Norwich to Walsingham'* – a distance of about thirty miles – *'to sit as one of the commissioners'.* Fastolf's cases, like John Paston's, had ended in disappointment. *'. . . this I know well'*, Howes wrote, '*that they found none obstacle nor impediment in their conscience in all your matter*'.[43]

The problem was that the situation had never really been as simple as the moral outrage of Fastolf and his servants made it sound. Fastolf himself had not lived in Norfolk for years. After decades serving in France, he spent years more staying at his Southwark house while he waited for his grand new castle at Caister to be finished. During all that time, he had been engaged from a distance in an ambitious programme of land purchase, converting the fortune he had made in the French wars into an extremely valuable Norfolk estate. As the Pastons had discovered, it was impossible to buy significant amounts of land without encountering legal challenges of one kind or another – and, if the rights and wrongs of the disputes in which he became embroiled looked black-and-white to Fastolf at a distance of more than a hundred miles, not all of them appeared so clear-cut from other perspectives. Lord Scales, whose friendship with Fastolf did not long survive his own return to England in 1449, clearly felt that right was not entirely on one side. '*Father, if you had been to me as faithful and kind since I came into England as you were in France,*' Scales told him in January 1452, '*by my troth there had been no man of your estate that so much I would do for*'.[44] Fastolf, like John Paston, had undoubtedly suffered in the later 1440s at the hands of unscrupulously acquisitive courtiers, and both men blamed John Heydon and Thomas Tuddenham for their losses. But some of their friends and neighbours had good reason to value Tuddenham and Heydon's support in the face of exactly the same sort of attack. Osbert Mundford, for example, would not have been able to defend himself against the outrageous belligerence of Thomas Daniel – a subject on which Fastolf and John Paston remained strangely silent – had it not been for John Heydon's help. It was hardly surprising, then, that Mundford was prepared to serve at the Walsingham sessions on the jury which acquitted Heydon of the charges brought against him by Fastolf.

The reality was that disputes – even bitter and violent disputes – were facts of life in such a competitive and highly mobile society. What was increasingly apparent, however, was that conflict could not be resolved, nor even kept within acceptable limits, under the rule of a King who had the unchallenged authority to maintain order and dispense justice but was incapable of exercising it. Under those circumstances, judicial process became as susceptible to political control as the King himself. And by the spring of 1451 it was clear that, after a year of chaos, political control was back with the court. The person of the King – totally ineffective though he was – remained the only source of legitimate authority. The Duke of York had ridden a wave of popular support in the autumn of 1450, but in the long run his attempt to seize control of government from the lords closest to the King could not succeed, given that they, not he, were the ones who could plausibly claim to speak for King Henry himself. It was Henry's cousin Edmund Beaufort, Duke of Somerset, who emerged to take the Duke of Suffolk's place at the King's right hand, and with it his ability to demand the co-operation of the nobility in government. The re-emergence of the power of the royal household meant a return to the structure of power which had sustained Suffolk's rule in the 1440s. In Norfolk, the acquittal of Suffolk's men at Walsingham in May 1451 was the inexorable result.

However inescapable the wider political realities, the outcome of the Walsingham sessions was devastating for the Pastons. Stubborn and dogged as ever, John did not stop trying to impose the sanctions of the law on his opponents. By the end of the month his servant John Osbern was making renewed overtures to the sheriff to try to hold him to his promise that he would help prosecute the Paston case against Moleyns's men, even if their lord had escaped punishment. It was no longer possible, however, to cling to the belief that the world was now a different place. Sheriff Jermyn 'said he would do for you that he may', Osbern wrote on 27 May, 'except for the acquittal of the Lord Moleyns's men, in so much as the King has written to him for to show favour to the Lord Moleyns and his men. And, as he says, the indictment belongs to the King and not to you, and the Lord Moleyns a great lord.' A clearer summing-up of the situation could hardly be imagined. John Paston professed to be unimpressed by the constraints of royal commands – the sheriff had sent him a copy of the King's letter, and John replied dismissively that 'a man should get such one for a noble', a coin worth six shillings and eightpence – although Osbern pertinently suggested that, if it was that easy, John should himself 'get a commandment of the King to the sheriff for to show you favour'. Whatever John said, all the signs were that the tide had turned conclusively. The sheriff claimed, for example, to have received a letter from the Duke of Norfolk, originally apparently such a strong supporter of the complaints of 1450, requiring him to show favour to Lord Moleyns and his men in the indictments. Osbern found this hard to believe ('I suppose he had no writing from my lord of Norfolk as he said'), but it was not beyond the bounds of possibility that Norfolk, who was never the most dependable of lords, might simply have changed sides.[45] If he had switched his sympathies at the eleventh hour, it might help to explain why he stayed secretly at the home of one of his squires near Ipswich when he returned from London, summoning his wife to meet him there, rather than riding on with his retinue to his castle at Framlingham where Osbern and others were waiting to speak to him.

John had to face the fact that his campaign was over. In the summer months which followed, he attempted to negotiate terms with Moleyns over the Paston belongings which had been looted from Gresham, but it was clear now that Moleyns and Heydon were successfully blocking further legal process against them. However bruised Heydon and Thomas Tuddenham had been by the events of the previous eighteen months, they and their former colleagues in the Duke of Suffolk's service were now finding their feet again as a political force in the region under the new leadership of Lord Scales, whose support had been so vital to their victory at Walsingham. Suffolk's men could also call upon the backing of the Duke's widow, Alice Chaucer. The Duchess's grandfather was the author of the *Canterbury Tales*, and her father had risen to a position of great wealth and influence in the service of the Lancastrian crown. Alice herself inherited a keen intelligence and a shrewd political brain along with the Chaucer family fortune, and, finding herself a widow at the age of forty-six, she applied her formidable talents to the defence of her husband's legacy on behalf of their young son.[40] She was more than a match for the Duke of Norfolk, whose ambition vastly outstripped his abilities, and who was discovering that he could not, as he had hoped, simply step into Suffolk's shoes as the dominant force in East Anglian society. With Norfolk still shadow-boxing the ghost of a dead rival, and Sir John Fastolf at Southwark doggedly pursuing the lawsuits he still had in train, John Paston was left to find his place as best he could in a world which turned out to have changed very little.

CHAPTER FIVE

– *a squire of worship* –

1451, which had started with such promise, had turned into a year of bitter disappointment for John and Margaret Paston. John remained in London, staying at the Inner Temple, for much of June and July, and Margaret tried to cheer him with news of good wishes from Norwich. At a lunch party she attended at the end of June the other ladies present '*desired to have had you there,*' she told her husband; '*they said they should all have been the merrier if you had been there*'. The idea that John would be a cheerful presence at the dining table seemed unlikely given the circumstances, but the inhabitants of Norwich had worries of their own from which any distraction might be welcome. There was sickness in the town; Margaret and their daughter Margery, now a toddler, had both been ill, and Margaret asked John to send them a pot of treacle, a costly medicinal paste credited with curing everything from insomnia to the effects of poison.[1] One of Sir John Fastolf's closest friends from the French wars, Sir Henry Inglose, had died the night before Margaret wrote, and, practical as ever, she told her husband that, '*if you desire to buy any of his stuff, I pray you send me word thereof in haste*'.[2]

The resolution of their legal struggle, however unfavourable it seemed, did at least offer the opportunity to concentrate for a while on more domestic concerns. They had a new baby – Edmund, named after John's dead brother – and one pressing question was where their growing family was going to live. After the events of the past three years, Gresham was too dilapidated and too insecure to be a realistic option. Margaret's manor of Mautby, near Yarmouth, would be a possibility in the future, but not until building work had been completed on the house. Margaret supervised operations there during John's absences, and as a result was a more realistic judge of progress – which was inevitably slow, given the difficulties of bad weather and unreliable workmen – than her husband. '*As for your work at Mautby,*' she wrote in November, '*it is not like that there shall no more be made thereof this year but the gables of the chamber and the chapel windows, and the reeder has done well his part to the hall. As for the little house that you wrote to me for,*' *my uncle and Sir Thomas say it is not for your avail for to have workmen on it till winter be passed. The masons failed till more than a fortnight after I came thence.'* What they really needed was a home in Norwich. They were actively looking for a place to buy, and in the meantime Margaret and the children could find lodgings with friends in the town, but it was not a long-term solution. '*I shall abide in Talvas's place till you come home,*' she told John, '*but as for your being there when you come home, the houses be too small for your men and your horses, and therefore you had need come home the sooner to pur-vey you of another place.*'[3]

As the year dragged on, the old heavyweights of the Norfolk political scene were not only finding their feet again, but re-emerging in new alliances. Thomas Daniel was engaged in a bravura display of political escapology, for which he turned out to have a remarkable talent. In the spring of 1451 he was acquitted of the charges of treason laid against him the previous autumn. Not only had he survived the tidal wave of public hostility which engulfed the court in 1450, but he came up clutching the hand of a powerful new patron, the Duke of Somerset, Suffolk's successor as the leading figure in King Henry's government. When Daniel's formerly close relationship with the Duke of Norfolk became strained in the autumn of 1451, Somerset persuad-ed Norfolk's mother, the dowager Duchess, to ask her son to take Daniel back into his favour. This intervention was so successful that Daniel married Norfolk's cousin, Margaret Howard, at Framlingham Castle shortly after-wards. More startling were reports that Lord Scales had taken Daniel under his wing at the end of 1451. Given the enmity between Daniel and the Duke of Suffolk's servants, whose lord Scales now was, this development was both unexpected and perplexing. It may have been an indication that the political dislocation caused by the upheavals of 1450 was taking time to play itself out; or it may just have been the latest surprise in a career which was full of them. Thomas Daniel consistently did – and got away with – things which other people would not even have thought of, let alone attempted. Perhaps he was extremely able, as well as unpredictable and unreliable; perhaps he had enor-mous personal charm; or perhaps he simply dared to do what other people did not, and had the nerve to brazen out the consequences. Whatever the explanation, there seemed to be a real prospect that Daniel's hostility to Suffolk's men, and his defrauding of Henry Woodhouse at Roydon, might now be swept under the carpet, and an accommodation brokered between Daniel, Tuddenham and Heydon. If that did happen, the Duke of Norfolk's servant Richard Southwell had heard that Daniel '*shall be suffered to enter into Bradeston*' – the manor from which he had temporarily expelled the Pastons' friend Osbert Mundford in 1450 – '*and keep it, to the intent that the country shall think, and my lord also, that he has great favour among the lords of the Council and cause men to fear him the more*'. This seemed extraordinary, and Southwell was not convinced that it was true – '*whether it be thus or not I cannot say*', he told John – but, as he pointed out, there would be an acid test for all the speculation: '*methinks you shall soon know if Mundford will agree that he shall enter into Bradeston, and if that be true all the remnant shall seem the more likely*'.[4]

Mundford did not agree, but it happened nonetheless. On 8 February 1452 Daniel sent some of his servants, led by Charles Nowell, an esquire from Shelland in Suffolk, to seize Bradeston for the second time. Osbert Mundford, a distinguished soldier who was currently serving in the English garrison at Calais, was furious, but unable to leave his post. '*I may not come, nor I will not come, though I should lose all Bradeston*', he wrote, ' . . . *considering that the enemies draw daily hitherward*'. It was doubly outrageous, he felt, that Daniel should choose to take advantage of the fact that he could not defend himself in Norfolk because he was busy defending his country. He petitioned the King for help – although, given Daniel's relationship with the Duke of Somerset, that seemed unlikely to produce immediate results. He also therefore wrote to his friend John Paston to ask advice on how best to bring legal action against Daniel, promising, touchingly, to buy him a drink for his pains if ever he came to Calais ('*you shall have a stoop of beer to comfort you after your travail of the sea*').[5] With characteristic effrontery, Daniel meanwhile sought to forestall any local resistance by claiming that the Duke of York was his trustee in the manor and would help him hold on to it. It was a bare-faced lie, and York, incensed that his name had been used in this way, wrote immediately to a group of Norfolk gentlemen, including John Paston, to distance himself from the whole situation ('*we certify unto you and to every of you for truth that we knew never such feoffment made, nor we consented never to such forcible entry, and we disavow it by these our letters signed with our own hand*').[6] It soon became clear, however, that Daniel's hold on the manor itself could not be shaken off so easily.

He did not come to Norfolk in person, but installed Charles Nowell at Bradeston as his bailiff. Nowell and his supporters – principally his brothers Otwell and Arthur, and a lawyer named Robert Ledham from the neighbouring village of Witton – rapidly began to throw their weight about in the surrounding area. This was the usual attempt at intimidation, designed to deter local people from daring to support Mundford's right to the estate, just as Moleyns's servants had done at Gresham. Being Daniel's men, however, Ledham and the Nowells engaged in the campaign of threats with unusual enthusiasm. Their main objective was to follow Daniel's orders in protecting Bradeston, but that mission also offered them a chance to pursue their own quarrels. Ledham, for example, had fallen out several years earlier with a neighbour at Witton named John Wilton. Ledham accused Wilton of assaulting him in the summer of 1447; Wilton's account of events was that a fight had broken out after he had *'peacefully and modestly'* asked Ledham's men to stop trampling his crops.[7] When the opportunity to reopen hostilities presented itself five years later, Ledham took it with gusto, fighting with Wilton in a local churchyard, knocking his heavily pregnant wife to the ground, and seizing his cattle and sheep in lieu of what Ledham claimed were rent arrears. To add insult to injury, not only did Ledham take the animals but he *'killed them and laid them in salt, and afterwards ate them'*.[8]

The surviving accounts of the alleged crimes of Ledham and the Nowells and their men are not, of course, impartial documents. Accusations were presented with no explanation of context but plenty of circumstantial detail designed to provoke horror and outrage. During a late-night assault on the house of John Coke, another tenant at Witton, for example, they allegedly *'gave him seven great wounds'*, and then hit his eighty-year-old mother on the crown of her head with a sword, *'which wound was never whole to the day of her death'*. One poor soul, Thomas Baret of the nearby village of Burlingham, was said to have been beaten so badly *'that he kept his bed a month'*, and when he had the temerity to complain about the beating, Ledham's men lay in wait for him and *'beat him again'*. Some of the charges were patently weak, little more than attempts to pin anything bad that happened in the area on the people who had become the local bogeymen. An unsolved murder near Framlingham in Suffolk, for instance, was included among the complaints with the comment that, *'whether any of the said fellowship were there or not, men cannot say, there be of them so many, of which many be unknown people'*.[9] Nevertheless, it is clear that the attempt to strike fear into the inhabitants of neighbouring villages was both concerted and successful. Some of the men who were targeted by Nowell and Ledham were too afraid of ambush to move about with confidence on public roads, and in some cases they were vulnerable even in their own homes. *'And so, for salvation of their lives and in eschewing of such inordinate costs as never was seen in that country before,'* a petition to parliament later alleged, *'many of them forsook and left their own habitation, wife and child, and withdrew to fortresses and good towns as for that time'*, John Wilton and Thomas Baret among them, the former to Norwich and the latter to Yarmouth.[10]

John Paston, who had once hoped for so much from Thomas Daniel, had supported his friend Osbert Mundford from the beginning in the fight with Daniel over Bradeston. On Monday, 3 April 1452, however, the issue suddenly became much more personal when John was assaulted outside the door of Norwich Cathedral by Charles Nowell and five other men. John's account did not record the circumstances of the attack, whether words were exchanged or provocation given on either side, but it was a frightening confrontation, with Nowell *'smiting at me while one of his fellows held my arms at my back'.*[11] He suffered no serious injury, but later the same day Osbert Mundford's brother-in-law Philip Berney – Margaret's timorous uncle, who had told her his hip was broken in order to avoid having to brave a return visit to Gresham – was ambushed near his home by Nowell and his men. They shot and injured Berney's horse, allowing them to ride him down, and then *'broke a bow on the said Philip's head'*, before taking him and his two servants prisoner with the words, *'traitors, you shall die!'*. Their excuse for the attack – or justification, from their point of view – was that they were arresting Berney, and took him to the Bishop of Norwich, before whom they required him to provide security that he would keep the peace. At that point, they let him go. Berney too did not dare to go home to Reedham, but took refuge instead in the greater safety of Sir John Fastolf's castle at Caister.[12]

The campaign of intimidation was as frightening as it was unsubtle. The message that no one should dare challenge, or even question, Daniel's possession of Bradeston was underscored with violence at every possible opportunity. Even the activities of Lord Moleyns's men at Gresham had been more recognisably within the bounds of 'normal' behaviour than this, in that Moleyns had some sort of claim to Gresham – however far-fetched and atavistic – which he chose, as many people did, to pursue by direct action, even if the ejection of Margaret and her household from the estate was direct action of a particularly forceful kind. What Daniel's men were engaged in was much more like a reign of terror, in both its nature and its intensity: what Moleyns had only threatened, Daniel was putting into practice. And the peculiarly frightening thing from John Paston's point of view was that there was nowhere to turn for help. Daniel himself had been John's major hope for support when it came to his battle with Heydon and Moleyns, even if it was hope which was ultimately disappointed. Even worse, the Duke of Norfolk was also implicated in what was now happening. The willingness of Daniel's men to involve themselves in violently disruptive tactics had come in handy for the Duke in 1450, when they joined some of

Norfolk's own retainers in launching an aggressive campaign of harassment against the Duke of Suffolk's estates and servants in the aftermath of Suffolk's death. The association between Daniel and Norfolk was already a couple of years old by this point, and both men stood to gain from the attempt to overthrow the local power of Suffolk's men. Although they subsequently fell out briefly in 1451, by the beginning of 1452 Daniel's marriage to Norfolk's cousin had cemented their alliance. Only weeks later, Daniel sent his men – who were now also part of Norfolk's entourage – into Bradeston, and the violent reprisals against anyone who opposed them began.

John Paston had had reason enough before this to be sceptical about Daniel's reliability as a patron, but he was baffled by the Duke of Norfolk's apparent willingness to condone the victimisation of gentlemen such as himself who had been willing to offer the Duke their service in his struggle against Suffolk's dominance. Quite apart from the breach of the bond of mutual loyalty which was supposed to underpin the relationship between lord and servant, it seemed ludicrous that Norfolk would be prepared simply to throw away gentry support when it had been so hard for him to attract any in the first place. The only possible explanation, John thought, was that the Duke was unaware of what was happening – and the perfect opportunity to seek redress seemed to be about to present itself, since Norfolk would shortly be arriving at Framlingham Castle, his ancestral home in Suffolk.

At least, that was what John had been told. By 23 April, having waited for ten days for the Duke's coming, and being assured each day that his arrival was imminent, John was becoming frantic. He wrote to the sheriff, this year a Suffolk man named John Clopton, to explain his predicament, in the process sketching out several different versions of the letter with different levels of detail and desperation. In one draft John described the attack he had suffered at Charles Nowell's hands outside Norwich Cathedral, and tried, respectfully, to point out why it might be a matter of concern to the Duke. It *'was to me strange case'*, he wrote, *'thinking in my conceit that I was my lord's man and his homager before Charles knew his lordship, and that my lord was my good lord'*. He was all the more confused, he explained, since he had seen Norfolk in London only two months earlier, in the middle of February, when Nowell was already in occupation at Bradeston, and even then the Duke had *'granted me his good lordship so largely that it must cause me ever to be his true servant to my power'*. The rest of the letter maintained this tone of genteel bewilderment rather than anger. Either the constraints of courtesy and policy were keeping John's pen under iron discipline, or he genuinely believed that Norfolk would clear up the whole sorry mess as soon as he realised what had happened:

> *I thought also that I had never given cause to none of my lord's house to owe me evil will, nor that there was none of the house but I would have done for as I could desire any man to do for me, and yet will, except my adversary. And thus I and my friends have mused of this, and thought he was hired to do thus, and, this notwithstanding, as soon as knowledge was had of my lord's coming to Framlingham, never attempted to proceed against him as justice and law would, but to trust to my said lord that his Highness would see this punished.*[13]

If his faith in Norfolk was genuine, he was about to be sadly disappointed.

At the end of the month, the Duke finally arrived at Framlingham. Before John and the other gentlemen who had suffered at the hands of Ledham and the Nowells had a chance to present any of their complaints, however, it became clear that Daniel's men had laid plans for just this eventuality, and now they set their scheme in motion. Three months earlier – before Nowell had even entered Bradeston on Daniel's behalf – an associate of his named Roger Church had gathered fifteen local men in a wood at Postwick, a couple of miles from Ledham's home at Witton. It is not at all clear what happened there. The villagers later claimed '*they were innocent, and knew not why they assembled but only by the excitation of the said Church and his men*'.[14] On the other hand, Church was subsequently charged with inciting rebellion as a result of this meeting; he allegedly planned to set fire to two monasteries just outside Norwich to draw the townspeople out, so that he and his men could enter the city to loot it.[15] The truth is probably somewhere in between. It seems likely that the men were promised some kind of campaign to right wrongs in the county under the captaincy of Church, who allegedly named himself '*John Amend-All*', one of the pseudonyms used by the rebel leader Jack Cade in 1450.[16] Nothing further happened in January – unsurprisingly, given that Church was faking this reformist zeal as part of the plan which Nowell and Ledham had concocted in case they were challenged in their occupation of Bradeston. At the end of April, with the Duke of Norfolk newly arrived at Framlingham and John Paston and his friends waiting to tell him of Nowell and Ledham's thuggery, Roger Church allowed himself to be arrested by his own friends – on a promise that he would be protected and pardoned '*by the means of Daniel*' – and brought to the Duke. In Norfolk's presence, Church confessed his part in the 'rising' at Postwick, and named 'many notable and thrifty men that were well willed to the said Mundford for the said manor of Bradeston', including John Paston, as his co-conspirators in an attempted rebellion, he said, of 300 men. A number of the villagers who had gathered with Church in Postwick wood were brought in to corroborate his story under the intimidating gaze of Daniel's men. By this means Nowell and Ledham hoped 'that the substantial men of the country should be by that means so troubled and endangered that they should not be of power to let and resist the misrule of the said Ledham and his misgoverned fellowship'.¹⁷

It was in many ways a well-conceived plan. An accusation of treason could do a lot of damage in these uncertain times. At the very least, John and his friends would be deflected from pursuing their complaints against Daniel's men by the need to defend themselves against the charges. All Nowell and Ledham now needed was for the Duke of Norfolk to take the story seriously – and, right on cue, he ordered that a bill of Church's allegations should be drawn up and delivered to the sheriff. It was Sheriff Clopton who smelled a rat. He summoned the witnesses who were said to have corroborated Church's account and, in their relief at finally being able to speak freely, the truth came tumbling out. 'The substance of the tale told by the said Roger Church was untrue and feigned and imagined by the same Church,' one said. Church himself had instigated the meeting at Postwick wood, and John Paston and the other gentlemen named in Church's bill had neither been present nor even spoken of on that occasion, 'but that they and other thrifty men were noised by the said Church and by his counsellors since the time of the gathering of the said fellowship'.¹⁸ Sheriff Clopton immediately sent an account of his whole investigation to the King and Council, and John travelled to London to be on the spot to rebut the story of the rebellion in case of any sign that it might be taken seriously.

The Duke of Norfolk, around whom Daniel's men would have run rings had it not been for Clopton's intervention, had been less than no help. John sent his servant John Osbern instead to see Walter Lyhert, the Bishop of Norwich, a consummate politician who had been prominent in the Duke of Suffolk's regime, and who was temporarily therefore keeping his head down, away from Westminster in the safety of his own diocese. The Bishop's closeness to Suffolk would have made him an unlikely source of assistance under normal circumstances, but these circumstances were far from normal. In supporting his friend Mundford at Bradeston, John Paston found himself in an improbable alliance with Suffolk's men, including John Heydon and Thomas Tuddenham, against opponents who had the protection of Daniel and the Duke of Norfolk. In this context, Bishop Lyhert – who must have been alerted to the fact that trouble was brewing a month earlier when Nowell dragged the unfortunate Philip Berney before him – provided a sympathetic ear. '*I had great cheer*', Osbern reported, clearly impressed by the quality of the Bishop's hospitality, with '*wine and ale both*'. Publicly, John was holding firm to the line that the Duke of Norfolk would not in the end let Nowell and Ledham go unpunished – '*I trusted to my lord of Norfolk's lordship and righteousness that he would see that Charles should be sharply corrected for his trespass and misrule*', Osbern told the Bishop on John's behalf – but also sought to make clear that he would not let the matter rest if Norfolk failed to act ('*or else the gentlemen of the shire must together purvey another means*'). Bishop Lyhert was shrewd enough to see exactly what was happening. '*He said it would none otherwise be*', Osbern reported, '*but, if he had spoken with you before you rode to London, he hoped by your advice he should have purveyed a means to have set that in correction, and also the trouble for the manor of Bradeston, for that was cause of all*'. The Bishop also told Osbern that John could count on support from Lord Scales, whose brief rapprochement with Daniel the previous December, if it had ever existed, had not survived the renewal of trouble at Bradeston. Scales '*is well disposed to you and in the best wise*', Osbern wrote, '*and will do for you that he can, so that you would forsake Daniel*' – a stipulation with which John was presumably now only too happy to comply.[19]

Four days later, the rot seemed to have spread even further. Margaret told John on 18 May that Daniel's methods had rubbed off on another of the Duke of Norfolk's men, their old acquaintance Richard Southwell, who had seized the manor of Holme Hale near Swaffham from Sybilla Boys, the friend who had sent Judge William her recipe for ale many years earlier. Southwell '*keeps it with strength with such another fellowship as has been at Bradeston*,' Margaret reported, '*and wastes and despoils all that there is*'. '*It seems it was not for naught that he held with Charles and his fellowship*', she added tartly.[20] Southwell had been due to marry Lady Boys's widowed daughter-in-law Jane until she was kidnapped and forcibly married in the summer of 1451 by a gentleman named Robert Langstrother, a neighbour of Jane's parents. Langstrother was charged with abduction, but legal process against him was blocked when Jane Boys testified that she had consented to the marriage. Southwell had lost both his bride and her share of the Boys estates, and it was presumably in frustration at this injustice that he decided to help himself to Holme Hale.[21] Margaret was concerned about what the spreading disorder might mean – '*as for tidings*,' she wrote, '*we have none good in this country; I pray God send us good*' – but was not worried enough to let the practicalities of family life slip her mind. She reminded John of the shopping she needed from London, including a new girdle for their small daughter Margery, and added the nearest she ever came these days to a sentimental word (*'I hope you shall be at home so soon that I will do write no more tidings to you'*).[22]

In London, John was busy preparing a petition detailing all of Nowell and Ledham's offences, and appealing to the Chancellor for a special inquiry into Roger Church's faked rebellion, *'so that they that be guiltless in this may be so declared, and that they that be guilty may be punished according to their demerits'*.[23] Despite John's efforts, rumours that he was *'one of the captains of the risers in Norfolk'* reached Cambridge, where his brother William was a student, by the middle of June.[24] On 3 July Bishop Lyhert of Norwich arrested Roger Church and imprisoned him in Norwich Castle, but Church was still defiant, declaring not only that he stood by his story, but that he had another, yet more eminent name, still to produce. *'Men think that have spoken with him that he hopes to have good help'*, Margaret told her husband; *'I pray God that the truth may be known'*. It seemed hardly surprising that John had still not remembered Margery's girdle.[25]

There was no immediate relief from the pressure. That autumn Daniel's hold over the Duke of Norfolk was demonstrated still further. His men were present in threateningly large numbers at court hearings in Norwich and Walsingham, which John believed had been *'set of purpose to have by indictments defouled such persons as were of the old counsel with the said lord, and such as keep Woodhouse land, or such as help or comfort Osbert Mundford, marshal of Calais, in his right of the manor of Bradeston, of which he is now late wrongfully disseised; and generally to have hurt all others that would not follow the opinions of the said new counsel'*.[26] Only two years earlier, immersed in the labyrinthine process of trying to secure convictions against Heydon and Moleyns in the autumn of 1450, it must have seemed to John scarcely imaginable that the political world in which he lived could become any more tortuous and complex. But that was exactly what had happened. The grievances held by John and his friends against Heydon and his associates had been suppressed, not resolved, by the outcome of the inquiries of 1450–1. Those tensions had now been compounded by the combination of Daniel's anarchic opportunism and the Duke of Norfolk's misjudgements and mismanagement. Norfolk's retainers had been stampeding across the late Duke of Suffolk's estates in Suffolk, vandalising his parks and threatening his servants, in an attempt to intimidate the widowed Duchess and demonstrate what Norfolk hoped was his new supremacy in local affairs. Meanwhile, Daniel and his men, with the Duke's support, or at least his acquiescence, were causing chaos in Norfolk.

What was needed was a king who would stamp his authority on this mess by making clear to the chief protagonists that their behaviour would no longer be tolerated, while at the same time creating conditions in which an accommodation between all the warring parties could be reached and enforced to prevent the violence recurring. A king of that kind, however, was exactly what the country did not have. The Duke of Somerset had been able to establish his leadership in government, but his regime was more fragile than his predecessor Suffolk's had been. The crisis of 1450 had begun to expose King Henry's deficiencies to public view, something which made the task of ruling in his name all the more difficult, especially now that the Duke of York had made himself a figurehead for criticisms of the court. As a result, East Anglia was not the only region disintegrating into serious disorder, and it was apparent that something had to be done. On 8 January 1453, a huge judicial commission was issued to deal with crime and disorder across south-eastern England. This should have been a powerful statement of royal intent to bring offenders to heel, but Somerset's hands were tied by the need to sustain noble support for his regime across the political spectrum, even if members of the nobility were themselves implicated in the trouble which the commission was supposed to be investigating. The noblemen named among the commissioners therefore included the Duke of Norfolk, the Earl of Oxford, Lord Scales and even Lord Moleyns. It hardly seemed likely that a tribunal in which Norfolk could claim an official role would be able to take a strong lead in dealing with violence for which his men were responsible, but Somerset did at least ensure that, when the sessions began in East Anglia in February, it was three professional royal justices who would sit to hear the indictments, rather than any of the noble commissioners. If nothing else, this opened the way for formal charges to be presented, whatever might or might not happen thereafter.

If any doubt remained about the need for some kind of royal intervention to deal with the increasingly unruly state of local politics, it was dispelled on 12 February when Thomas Daniel, at the head of a menacingly large group of the Duke of Norfolk's retainers and servants, attended the county court at Ipswich where the Suffolk MPs for the forthcoming parliament were to be elected. Their plan – that Daniel himself should be nominated as one of the knights of the shire – did not get very far. The sheriff reported back to

Westminster that he had been unable to hold a valid election '*because of menaces and threats*', and pointed out that Daniel was in any case not qualified to represent the county in parliament because he held no lands there; it was in Norfolk, not Suffolk, that he had managed, however fraudulently, to acquire some estates.[27] Nevertheless, it was precisely this kind of casual assumption on Daniel's part that he could get what he wanted by bullying and intimidation which had caused such problems for more than a year, and when the King's judges arrived in the region three days later they were inundated with complaints against the servants of both Daniel himself and the Duke of Norfolk, who was now looking more like Daniel's stooge than his patron.

It took Justices Prisot, Bingham and Danvers two weeks to hear all the indictments which the gentlemen of Norfolk and Suffolk were waiting to present to them. Charles Nowell and Roger Ledham were charged with a string of offences committed in and around Bradeston, including the assault on Philip Berney at Thorpe wood. The whole story of Roger Church's treacherous behaviour was also told in court. In Suffolk, meanwhile, the Duke of Norfolk's men, with Nowell and his brothers among their number, were accused of violent attacks on the Duchess of Suffolk's parks and servants going back as far as February 1450. For good measure – presumably on the principle that a treason charge was always a useful weapon – several of Norfolk's leading retainers, including Charles Nowell, were accused of planning to kill the King and make the Duke of York '*king and governor*' of the realm. There could be no better demonstration of the political convulsions which Daniel and Norfolk had precipitated in only twelve months than the fact that, during the course of these hearings, John Paston found himself serving on a presenting jury shoulder-to-shoulder with his old enemies Sir Thomas Tuddenham and John Wyndham.[28]

Despite the fact that Daniel and Norfolk between them had inspired a chorus of complaint among the region's gentry more general than any of the grievances expressed in 1450–1, the Duke of Somerset could not afford to alienate Norfolk and risk driving him into the arms of the Duke of York, who had been forced for the time being to retreat to the safety of his own estates but would surely seize any opportunity to reassert himself in government. Norfolk was therefore able to secure letters from King Henry ordering that legal process against his leading retainers should be halted – a decision justified, with magnificent vagueness, by '*certain causes and considerations moving us*'.[29] However, even if there was no prospect that any of the accused would ever be convicted, the very fact that so many of the Duke's servants had been hauled into court represented a slap on his wrist. Not only that, but the extent to which he was under pressure from his peers was apparent in the manoeuvring which surrounded the court hearings. All the main protagonists demanded that their opponents bind themselves to keep the peace, on pain of financial penalties ranging from a couple of hundred to a couple of thousand pounds. Not only did this process confirm that former allies, such as the Earl of Oxford, were now ranged against him, but Norfolk himself was the only one of all those involved who was required to bind himself in the humiliatingly large sum of £10,000.[30] As a result, the February inquiries did mean that the freedom of action which Daniel and Norfolk had enjoyed up to this point was at last curtailed. Daniel's men were still in occupation at Bradeston, but their reign of terror was over. Finally, after years of subordinating family life to the pressing demands of self-defence, the Pastons had a chance to catch their breath.

Two months later, when the Queen, Margaret of Anjou, visited Norwich, Margaret Paston had new worries to face, but for once they were sartorial rather than political. She was concerned not to look like the poor relation among the great and the good who assembled for the royal reception, and in the end had to borrow a necklace from her close friend Elizabeth Clere, '*for I dared not for shame go with my beads among so many fresh gentlewomen as here were at that time*'. It was a difficulty she was determined would not be repeated: '*I pray you that you will do your cost on me against Whitsuntide that I may have something for my neck*', she asked her husband firmly.[31] In the summer she finally found the family a home in Norwich, even if the house was to rent rather than buy and a little more expensive than they had hoped, despite Margaret's best efforts at negotiation over the price. '*He would not let it in no wise less than 5 marks*', she told John. '*I told him that surely you should not know but that I hired it of him for £3. I said, as for the noble, I should pay it of my own purse, that you should have no knowledge thereof.*' However, her pleasure in their new home was tempered by sad family news. '*As for the chamber that you assigned to my uncle*', she wrote on 6 July, '*God has purveyed for him as his will is*'.[32] Philip Berney had died four days earlier, '*with the greatest pain that ever I saw man*', Agnes told John – a loss which was immediately counted among Charles Nowell's crimes, on the grounds that Philip had never been the same since the attack on the road at Thorpe fifteen months earlier. Margaret herself had been ill again, and she was not the only one. The day after Philip Berney's death, Sir John Heveningham – their '*faint friend*' from the judicial proceedings of 1450–1 – '*went to his church and heard three masses, and came home again never merrier, and said to his wife that he would go say a little devotion in his garden and then he would dine; and forthwith he felt a fainting in his leg and sank down. This was at nine of the clock, and he was dead before noon.'*[33]

The rest of that autumn passed peacefully enough. Margaret and John had a small falling-out, about what is not clear from their letters, but it was enough for an unusual and contrite apology from Margaret: *'beseeching you that you be not displeased with me, though my simpleness caused you for to be displeased with me. By my troth it is not my will neither to do nor say that should cause you for to be displeased, and if I have done I am sorry thereof and will amend it; wherefore I beseech you to forgive me, and that you bear no heaviness in your heart against me, for your displeasure should be too heavy to me to endure with'.*[34] Otherwise she was busy stocking up provisions for their new household. By November, frustrated at the lack of choice she found in Norwich, she was delegating purchases to John in London:

> *As for cloth for my gown, I can none get in this town better than that is that I send you an example of, which methinks too simple both of colour and of cloth; wherefore I pray you that you will vouchsafe to do buy for me three yards and a quarter of such as it pleases you that I should have, and what colour that pleases you, for in good faith I have done sought all the drapers' shops in this town and here is right feeble choice. Also I pray you that you will do buy a loaf of good sugar and half a pound of whole cinnamon, for there is none good in this town.*[35]

Meanwhile, building work continued at Mautby, although Margaret was still having trouble with supplies: *'I can neither be purveyed of joists nor of board not yet'*, she wrote in January.[36] By then, she knew she was pregnant for the fifth time. She was already thinking ahead about names for the new baby. *'I pray you if you have another son'*, she asked her husband a few days later, *'that you will let it be named Henry in remembrance of your brother Henry'*, William and Agnes's son who had died in childhood. Margaret, at thirty-one, was not having the easiest time in this pregnancy – she signed the letter *'by your groaning wife, M.P.'*[37] – and wished that John did not have to be away from home so much. *'I pray you that you be not strange of writing of letters to me between this and that you come home'*, she wrote. *'If I might, I would have every day one from you.'*[38]

One particular reason for wishing John in Norwich was that Margaret was increasingly concerned about the predicament of his sister Elizabeth, still not married at the advanced age of twenty-four and trapped at home with her increasingly irascible mother Agnes. *'It seems by my mother's lan-*

guage that she would never so fain to have been delivered of her as she will now', Margaret told her husband in January 1454.[39] The relationship between Agnes and Elizabeth had not been good for a long time. Five years earlier Margaret's friend Elizabeth Clere had implored John to pay some attention to his sister's plight, 'for she was never in so great sorrow as she is nowadays'. Agnes shared the prevailing contemporary view that disobedient children should be physically chastised by their parents, but the occasions on which Elizabeth incurred her displeasure were becoming worryingly frequent. 'She has since Easter the most part been beaten once in the week or twice,' Elizabeth Clere reported, 'and sometimes twice on one day, and her head broken in two or three places'. She was anxious about the effect her own intervention might have on a valued friendship – 'I pray you burn this letter', she asked John, 'for if my cousin your mother knew that I had sent you this letter she should never love me' – but she was increasingly concerned that his sister would accept an unsuitable match simply to escape from Agnes. '. . . sorrow often times causes women to beset them otherwise than they should do,' she wrote, 'and if she were in that case I know well you would be sorry'.[40]

As Elizabeth Clere had suspected, Elizabeth Paston proved willing to countenance any of the suitors suggested for her, however apparently unappealing. She had even been prepared, at not quite twenty, to contemplate marriage to Sir John Fastolf's stepson Stephen Scrope, a pox-scarred widower more than twice her age, whose estates were still in the hands of his elderly but tenacious stepfather. Not that these potential objections made the match unacceptable, in Elizabeth Clere's judgement: 'methinks he were good for my cousin your sister', she told John, 'without that you might get her a better'.[41] The difficulty was that, absorbed first by his struggle with Moleyns over Gresham and then by the outrages of Daniel and his men, John had neither the time to give any thought to his sister's misery, nor the inclination to set aside the money she would need as a dowry. Several more matches were proposed over the next few years, but nothing concrete had come of any of the discussions by the autumn of 1454, when Scrope's name was put forward for a second time. John's younger brother William was not convinced that the suggestion was a good one, but he too urged John to rescue their sister one way or another. 'You know who is most worshipful better than I,' he wrote. 'At the reverence of God draw to some conclusion, it is time.'[42]

By then, however, political events were once again engrossing John's attention. At the beginning of August 1453, King Henry suddenly suffered a total mental collapse, so severe that it could not be kept hidden. Although he could still walk and eat, he did not speak, and showed no flicker of recognition or understanding. Five months later, news reached East Anglia that even the birth of his son and heir, Prince Edward, had not been able to penetrate the King's catatonic state:

> . . . *at the Prince's coming to Windsor, the Duke of Buckingham took him in his arms and presented him to the King in goodly wise, beseeching the King to bless him; and the King gave no manner answer. Nevertheless the Duke abode still with the Prince by the King; and when he could no manner answer have, the Queen came in, and took the Prince in her arms and presented him in like form as the Duke had done, desiring that he should bless it; but all their labour was in vain, for they departed thence without any answer or countenance, saving only that once he looked on the Prince and cast down his eyes again, without any more.*[43]

With the King so completely incapacitated, it could no longer be claimed with any plausibility that he was a functional part of government. At a stroke, the basis of the Duke of Somerset's power was cut from under him. If the King was ill, then – just as had been the case when he was an infant – his rule would have to be delegated formally to a noble council. Under those circumstances, the claims of the Duke of York to a leading role in government could no longer be dismissed. By November, York was back in London, and this time he found a new ally in his campaign to bring Somerset down. The latter's attempt to make the Duke of Norfolk toe the line in East Anglia without alienating him completely had failed. Norfolk denounced Somerset for assuming '*over-great authority in this realm*', and declared that the Duke was responsible for the English losses in France. With all the melodrama he could muster, he petitioned his fellow magnates to take action: '*I have required to have overture of justice by you, which you have not yet done to me, whereof I am so heavy that I may no longer bear it, specially since the matter by me pursued is so worshipful for all the realm, and for you, and so agreeable to God, and to all the subjects of this realm, that it may be no greater*'.[44] On 23 November, Somerset was arrested and committed to the Tower on suspicion of treason.

The mid-winter months were tense and uncertain. The atmosphere was so jumpy that many of the lords were arming themselves; the Duke of Buckingham, for example, was reported to have had 2,000 livery badges made, '*to what intent men may construe as their wits will give them*'. York had succeeded in removing his rival from power, but it was much less clear that the rest of the nobility would allow him to take formal control of government during the King's illness; and, although Somerset was in custody, he had not completely lost the means to make his influence felt. He was reported to have '*spies going in every lord's house of this land*', and the Duke of Norfolk was warned to be careful of his own security: '*the Duke of Somerset makes him ready to be as strong as he can make him, wherefore it is necessary that my lord look well to himself, and keep him among his household, and depart not from them, for it is to dread lest ambushments be made for him*'. Daniel and some of his colleagues in the royal household sought to safeguard their positions by requesting funds for a garrison to guard the King and his baby son, a garrison which would, of course, be under their own command. Meanwhile, Queen Margaret realised that her new role as the mother of the heir to the throne might allow her to claim the right to govern in her son's name, and she did so in January 1454 in what would turn out to be characteristically resolute and unsubtle fashion. '. . . *she desires to have the whole rule of this land*', it was reported, along with the authority to name all the officers of state, all sheriffs and all bishops.[45] The alarming prospect of the French-born Queen taking unfettered rule for herself went a long way to persuading the nobility that the Duke of York's claim to lead the council of the lords was in fact the best available option, and on 27 March 1454 York was named Protector of the realm.

York's influence in government was good news for John Paston, just as it had been in the autumn of 1450. The Duke's ascendancy meant the retreat of the power of the royal household, something which was apparent as early as the beginning of November 1453, when Osbert Mundford at last succeeded in reclaiming his manor of Bradeston from Thomas Daniel's men. Once York became Protector, John lost no time in drafting a petition which detailed yet again all of Nowell and Ledham's activities, including harassment which Mundford's men had suffered in the few months since they had returned to Bradeston.[46] Robert Ledham's establishment at Witton was a disorderly house full of criminals, John said – '*six or seven of the said Ledham's men daily, both workday and holiday, used to go about in the country with bows and arrows, shooting and playing in men's closes among men's cattle, going from alehouse to alehouse and menacing such as they hated, and sought occasion and quarrels and debates*' – and the indictments against them should therefore be allowed to proceed.[47] Daniel himself was outlawed in the spring of 1454 because he failed to appear in court to answer the Earl of Oxford for a debt of £100. Although sentence of outlawry was little more than an inconvenience for a man of Daniel's standing, the fact that process had been awarded against him was a clear sign that his influence was fading.[48] Not only that, but his alliance with the Duke of Norfolk, which had caused so much havoc in East Anglia, was stretched to breaking point by their different reactions to the Protectorate. Unimpressed by Somerset's attempt to discipline him, Norfolk was one of York's strongest supporters in the autumn of 1453. Daniel, on the other hand, derived his influence from his position in the royal household, and therefore had a fundamental interest in supporting Somerset. However much damage they were each capable of causing on their own, they would never again join forces as they had done to such disruptive effect in 1452.

The enforced retreat of Daniel's men from Bradeston was not the only benefit of York's rule from the Paston point of view. The end of Somerset's household-based regime also meant that John Paston's old enemy John Heydon was now more vulnerable than at any point since 1450, and some of the charges which Heydon and Thomas Tuddenham had faced in that year – and thought they had seen off for good at the Walsingham sessions in 1451 – were revived in King's Bench early in 1454.[49] By that stage, John Paston had also received welcome news of Lord Moleyns. Moleyns had neither given up his claim to Gresham, nor paid any compensation for the damage his men had done there, but at least he was no longer in a position to cause the Pastons further trouble. He went to France early in 1453 to take part in the last-ditch defence of Gascony, and was captured by the French shortly after his arrival. He remained a prisoner there for six years until his family had gathered the vast ransom demanded for his release.

By the summer of 1454 John had good reason to feel that he was in a better position than he had been for years. Since 1448, when Moleyns had first seized Gresham, John had been almost constantly on the defensive, desperately trying to protect both his family, and the estates which his father had so painstakingly assembled, from predatory rivals and the effects of political chaos. Now, at thirty-two, he had a chance at last to emerge from his father's shadow as a man of influence in his own right. His new standing was the subject of a gratifying conversation which his brother William reported from London in July. Thomas Billing, a serjeant-at-law, had spoken sharply to Daniel's man Robert Ledham on the subject of his feud with John. '*It is the guise of your countrymen*', Billing told Ledham,

> to spend all the good they have on men and livery gowns and horse and harness, and so bear it out for a while, and at the last they are but beggars; and so will you do ... As for Paston, he is a squire of worship, and of great livelihood, and I know he will not spend all his good at once, but he spares

yearly 100 marks or £100. He may do his enemy a shrewd turn and never fare the worse in his household, nor the less men about him. You may not do so, but if it be for a season. I counsel you not to continue long as you do.[50]

It made a pleasing change for John to be spoken of with such respect. Just as pleasing was the imminent arrival in Norfolk of Margaret's kinsman Sir John Fastolf. His magnificent new home at Caister, less than two miles from John and Margaret's manor of Mautby near the east Norfolk coast, was finally finished and ready for his occupation, and Fastolf was preparing to move his household there permanently from his London house at Southwark. The events of the past few years, and particularly their joint enterprise in trying to bring down the Duke of Suffolk's men in 1450–1, had made Fastolf appreciative of John's loyalty and tenacity. *'He says you are the heartiest kinsman and friend that he knows'*, John's brother William told him in the summer of 1454. *'He would have you at Mautby dwelling.'*[51] John's experiences at the hands of the Duke of Norfolk and Thomas Daniel had given him little cause before this to feel that the friendship of great men was worth having. In Fastolf, however, he had at last found a mentor whose influence on his career, and his life, would be profound.

CHAPTER SIX

– *the heartiest kinsman and friend* –

If his inheritance from his father was the first defining relationship of John Paston's career, then his service to Sir John Fastolf was the second. By the 1450s Fastolf was one of the richest men in England outside the ranks of the nobility, and his connections with the Paston family already went back decades. It was not until Fastolf came to live in Norfolk in 1454, however, that his relationship with John Paston began to take on much greater significance for both men.

Fastolf was later immortalised by Shakespeare as Prince Hal's disreputable friend Sir John Falstaff, but Shakespeare took major liberties with the life-story of his model. The debauched and cowardly old knight dying in Mistress Quickly's care on the eve of the Battle of Agincourt bears little relation to a man who, in fact, fought at Agincourt as a soldier in his prime at the age of thirty-five. Fastolf's grandfather Alexander was a shipowner at Yarmouth, who made enough money in trade for his son John, Fastolf's father, to establish the family at the nearby manor of Caister. Fastolf himself was born at Caister in 1380, and when his father died three years later he inherited the family's modest estate, with an income of a little less than £50 a year. In 1401, Fastolf entered the service of Henry IV's second son Thomas, Duke of Clarence, and travelled with him to Ireland when Clarence took up his appointment as the King's lieutenant there. After fourteen years in Clarence's household, Fastolf joined the army with which the Duke's elder brother Henry V invaded northern France in 1415, and he was knighted for his part in the spectacularly successful campaign in January of the following year. By the time he turned forty in 1420, Fastolf's record in royal service was solid but unexceptional. The most notable advance he had so far achieved in his own fortunes had come through his marriage in 1409 to Millicent Scrope, a wealthy widow twelve years his senior, whose lands were five times more valuable than his own.

It was in 1422 that Fastolf's career changed out of all recognition. The Duke of Clarence had been killed in battle at Baugé in 1421, and in the following year Fastolf was appointed master of the household of John, Duke of Bedford, the King's next oldest brother. After King Henry's sudden death in August 1422 – he succumbed to dysentery on campaign at the age of only thirty-five – Bedford was appointed Regent of the English lands in France during the minority of the infant Henry VI. Under Bedford's command, Fastolf quickly rose to an eminence far beyond anything he had experienced before. He was a member of the council in France over which Bedford presided, and in 1423 he was appointed governor of Anjou and Maine. At the Battle of Verneuil in August 1424 he was created a knight banneret, a mark of distinction awarded for bravery in combat, and two years later he was elected a knight of the Order of the Garter, an honour bestowed on only twenty-five men at any one time, most of them members of the nobility. However, his military commands brought him more than simply glory. Through a combination of wages, rewards, ransoms and plunder he amassed an extraordinary fortune. In recognition of his service to the crown he was granted lands in northern France, including the barony of Cilly-Guillaume, with an annual income of £400, but he was also able to send vast amounts of cash back to England via the secure hands of English and Italian financiers. There the trusted servants who managed his affairs in his absence invested the money, on his instructions, in the acquisition of a huge landed estate.

Fastolf spent nearly £14,000 buying properties in his native East Anglia and around his London base at Horselydown in Southwark, and thousands more building houses in both places of a size and grandeur befitting his new status. The construction of his moated townhouse at Southwark alone cost £1,100, but expenditure there was dwarfed by the money which Fastolf lavished on his birthplace at Caister. Over three decades he spent more than £6,000 on a new castle which combined defensive fortification with all the modern comforts money could buy. Built largely in brick, it had fifty rooms and, at one corner of the rectangular design, a tall and slender tower overlooking the moat. The house was furnished with an opulence to match the elegance of its architecture. The bedrooms contained featherbeds with woven or embroidered hangings which, in Fastolf's own room, were '*white and green with maple leaves*'; he also kept an astrolabe in his chamber and, in the room he used for bathing, part of his collection of books.[1] The walls were covered with fine tapestries: one, behind the dais at one end of the Winter Hall, showed a wild man of the woods carrying a child in his arms, while on the west wall hung a scene of the town of Falaise besieged by Henry V's forces in 1418. There were more than forty wall-hangings in all, of which two alone – '*a rich cloth of arras of imagery work of Justice administering, with another cloth of arras, containing every of the said cloths about sixteen yards long and five yards in breadth'* – cost Fastolf more than £220.[2] He also invested heavily in silver plate and fine jewels. He acquired three particularly exquisite pieces in pledge from the Duke of York as part of a loan agreement in 1452: '*a brooch of gold with a great pointed diamond set upon a rose enamelled white; a brooch of gold in fashion of a ragged staff, with two images of man and woman garnished with a ruby, a diamond and a great pearl; and a flower of gold, garnished with two rubies, a diamond, and three hanging pearls'.*[3] The spear-pointed diamond set in a white rose of York had cost the Duke more than £2,500 and was one of the most valuable jewels known to have existed in fifteenth-century England outside royal hands – but even the crucifix containing a fragment of the true cross which Fastolf wore around his neck every day was worth £200.

These sumptuous trappings of aristocratic living were not merely display for display's sake. Gems in elaborate settings and finely worked plate did not lose value over the years, and in times of need – which came even to noblemen as great as the Duke of York – they could be pledged out to raise ready cash. Fastolf had an astute financial brain, and his spending, however apparently ostentatious, was planned with care and meticulously supervised. His business interests included not only the profits of arable farming on his estates, but the wool which his flock of almost 8,000 sheep produced for the English and continental cloth markets, and a fleet of between eight and fourteen ships which, in the Fastolf family tradition, traded out of Yarmouth harbour. Even after Fastolf's French estates were lost in the disasters of 1450, his English lands brought him a net income of over £1,000 a year, and by the later 1450s his stock of cash and plate, not including his jewels, was worth more than £5,000, most of it deposited for safekeeping at the Norfolk abbey of St Benet of Hulme. There were a handful of noblemen whose wealth far outstripped even these riches, but very few men without a noble title who could afford to live in such style.

The price which Fastolf paid for his fortune was a personal one. His marriage to Millicent Scrope was financially advantageous, but her age – she was forty-one when they married – meant that it was always unlikely they would have children, even had Fastolf himself not spent most of the next thirty years abroad on campaign. When he retired from the war in 1439, his wife was already seventy-one, and she died seven years later. Fastolf was step-father to her son from her first marriage, Stephen Scrope, but the two men were never close, and their relationship deteriorated after Millicent's death because of Fastolf's determination to hold on to her estates rather than allowing Scrope, who was already approaching fifty, to take possession of his inheritance. By the early 1450s, Fastolf – now a widower in his seventies – was an isolated figure. He was living at Southwark while building work continued on his new house at Caister, but it was hard to say that either place was really his home. Most of his adult life had been spent away from England, first in Ireland and then in France. Without question, he thought of himself as a Norfolk man, but he had left East Anglia a long time ago, and in reality he was not, and had never been, an active participant in political life there. Back in London after his long years as a soldier, he was a fish out of water. The men in charge of government were a generation or more younger, and they were not listening as Fastolf thought they should to his voice of experience. The whole course of politics in the 1440s, culminating in the loss of the French lands which he had spent his life defending, was anathema to him. His sense of grievance was palpable, about the defeats in France, the personal losses he had sustained as a result, and the fact that, despite the wealth he had amassed, he believed he had not yet been paid all of what was due to him for half a century of service to the crown.

What made all this even worse in Fastolf's eyes was that the man who had presided over the regime of the 1440s, the Duke of Suffolk, had caused problems for him in England as well as France. Fastolf's programme of land purchase in East Anglia, where many of the Duke's lands also lay, was unusually ambitious, and, as the Pastons had discovered to their cost, estates which were bought rather than handed down through many generations often embroiled their buyers in complex disputes over ownership. Initially at least, Fastolf was lucky; his estates remained relatively untroubled when his spending on land was at its height during the 1430s and early 1440s, and his dealings with the Duke of Suffolk were not unfriendly during those years. Suffolk – who was short of money in the 1430s because he had been captured in France in 1429 and had to find a large ransom to secure his release – even sold Fastolf one of his own properties. As the 1440s went on, however, the relationship between the two men began to sour, whether because Fastolf opposed Suffolk's policy of trying to negotiate a peace with France, or because tensions at a local level brought their interests into conflict in East Anglia, or perhaps a combination of the two. In 1447 Suffolk seized Fastolf's estate at Dedham in Essex, which had belonged to the Duke's family three-quarters of a century earlier, and kept it until his fall from power three years later. In the same year a dispute also began between Fastolf and Suffolk's servant John Heydon over an old debt in the will of Joan, Lady Bardolf, of which Heydon was executor. At the same time, two courtiers, Sir Philip Wentworth and Sir Edward Hull, took the opportunity to challenge Fastolf over three of his estates in Norfolk and Suffolk. Hull was able to deprive Fastolf of the manor of Titchwell in Norfolk in 1448 on the grounds that his wife was the rightful heir to the property; Wentworth meanwhile claimed Beighton in Norfolk and Bradwell in Suffolk in the name of Thomas Fastolf of Cowhaugh, the young son of the distant relative from whom Fastolf had bought the manors.

It was never likely that Fastolf would be able to avoid having to fight for at least some of the estates he had bought. The scale of his newly acquired wealth made him a conspicuous target for such challenges, and his East Anglian estates were all the more vulnerable because he was not a powerful political presence there – or, in fact, a presence at all – to supervise and protect them. However, as the disputes over his lands multiplied in the increasingly unstable political atmosphere of the later 1440s, Fastolf himself had no hesitation in interpreting his troubles as a concerted campaign of harassment inspired by the malice of the Duke of Suffolk and his men. Always prone to see things in black and white rather than the murky shades of grey in which the political world operated, he nursed a growing conviction that he was the victim of a vendetta pursued by criminal means. His sense of persecution compounded his isolation: those who were not for him were against him, he believed, and some old friendships foundered as a result. A lengthy and fruitless dispute with the priory of Hickling over an annual rent of twenty-five marks cost him his friendship with Lord Scales, who as lord of the manor of Hickling was the priory's patron. Scales expressed regret about the falling-out, but Fastolf himself seems simply to have discounted any possibility of compromise.[4] Even the entire city corporation of Norwich could be cast from grace for being insufficiently supportive: '*there was no city in England that I loved and trusted more upon*', Fastolf remarked in the same year, '*till they did so unkindly to me and against truth in the Lady Bardolf's matter*'.[5]

Fastolf was not an easy man. He took good fortune for granted, but could not accept its opposite with any kind of equanimity. Every grievance, every perceived slight, was not only carefully noted but taken to heart, nourishing a sense of injustice and ill-treatment which expressed itself in the vehemence with which he spoke about those he believed had wronged him. William Dalling, the official responsible for the verdict in favour of Edward Hull's claim to Titchwell, for example, was a '*false harlot*', '*that old shrew Dalling*'; '*he is sore at my stomach*', Fastolf wrote in January 1451.[6]

Nevertheless, this difficult, demanding man did not find himself completely alone. Without close family, he relied instead, in both practical and (though he would not have admitted it) emotional terms, on a tightly knit circle of loyal servants. His chief representative at Caister in the years before he moved there himself was his chaplain Thomas Howes. Howes had his limitations – he could be garrulous to the point of indiscretion, and was not the most sophisticated political operator – but he was devoted to his master and tolerated a heavy and disparate workload without demur. His family also played a pivotal role in Fastolf's household: his sister Agnes was married to another of Sir John's servants, William Barker, and his niece Margaret was the wife of Fastolf's secretary William Worcester (or, when he chose to use his mother's maiden name, William Botoner).

Worcester was a remarkable man, and a complex one. Well educated and acutely intelligent, with a deep intellectual curiosity, he immersed himself in the study of astronomy, medicine, geography, natural history, philosophy, rhetoric and history. He compiled antiquarian and topographical collections, read widely in Latin and French, and was himself a prolific writer, although few of his works now survive. Somehow, he pursued these scholarly interests at the same time as serving a master who left him almost no time to himself. From the moment Worcester entered Fastolf's employment in the late 1430s as a young man not long out of Oxford, he became indispensable to the old knight, not only as his amanuensis but as the servant to whom Fastolf could entrust the detailed archival research necessitated by his increasingly convoluted legal affairs. Worcester travelled widely on Fastolf's business, in Normandy in the early 1440s (where, Worcester later noted, he was captured by the French at Dieppe and managed to escape only by bribing some sailors), and across England from Yorkshire to Devon in the attempt to elucidate the descents of the properties his master had bought.

His relationship with Fastolf was extremely close – he was probably a more constant companion to his elderly master than anyone else in the last two decades of Fastolf's life – but also extremely complicated. Worcester knew his limits as a man of business, and was particularly aware of his lack of legal expertise ('*I have said no word, for I cannot meddle in high matters that pass my wit*', he wrote on one occasion),[7] but this self-effacement was a little disingenuous. He also, with good reason, took himself seriously, and sometimes felt that he was both unappreciated and underpaid. In the early stages of their acquaintance, John Paston addressed him respectfully as '*Master Worcester*', but soon after the household moved to Caister in the summer of 1454 Worcester asked John pointedly to '*forget that name of mastership, for I am not amended by my "master" of a farthing in certainty*', whereas, he explained, as plain '*Worcester or Botoner*', servant of Sir John Fastolf, '*I have five shillings yearly, all costs borne, to help pay for bonnets that I lose*'. The point that he had neither independent means nor a decent salary was directed at Fastolf rather than John himself, but, when Worcester raised the matter with his employer, Fastolf said '*he wished me to have been a priest so I had been disposed, to have given me a living by reason of a benefice that another man must give it, as the Bishop*'. '*And so I endure*', Worcester went on, slipping briefly and discreetly into Latin, '*among the needy, as a serf at the plough*'. He tried to make light of it – '*Forgive me, I write to make you laugh*', he told John, '*and Our Lord bring my master in a better mood for others as for me*' – but it was clear that it was not, for him, a joking matter.[8] He had been sufficiently exercised by the issue that his request was repeated virtually word for word in another letter written to John on the same day by Thomas Howes ('*And where you call him master, he is displeased with that name, for he may spend five shillings yearly more by the name of Worcester or Botoner, and by his "master" not a farthing in certainty. He prays you forget it*').[9] But, difficult and tight-fisted though Fastolf was, Worcester's commitment to him was absolute. One of the projects on which he embarked in the little spare time he had was an attempt to write his master's life-story, and, although no manuscript now survives, it is clear that this was a labour not just of duty, but of love.

Worcester and Howes were the heart of the large household, but there were others, servants, friends and associates, on whom Fastolf relied heavily, among them his auditor Watkin Shipdam; his servant John Bocking; his legal advisers William and John Jenney and Judge William Yelverton; and his confessor Friar John Brackley, an aggressively opinionated and decidedly unlovely man who was, nevertheless, as loyal to Fastolf as the rest of his inner circle. It was among this close-knit group that John Paston began to make his mark once Fastolf finally arrived in Norfolk in 1454. The relationship between the two men was already well established by that point, and close enough for Fastolf to have become John's trustee in estates which included the disputed manor of Gresham. John's legal action against Lord Moleyns in 1450 was therefore taken in Fastolf's name; Fastolf had also sent crossbows to reinforce Margaret's defences there two years earlier. Sir John's willingness to respond to the Pastons' appeal for help was characteristic, but so was his servants' anxiety at the prospect of having to explain that the loaned weapons had been lost when Margaret was expelled from the manor.

'*Watkin Shipdam recommends him to you,*' she told her husband a month after the attack, '*and prays you that you will speak to Sir John Fastolf for the harness that you had of him, and tell him how it is that some thereof is gone*'.[10] Fastolf's assistance to the Pastons at Gresham can have done nothing to endear him to their enemy John Heydon, with whom Fastolf himself was already in dispute over the Bardolf will, and Heydon took the trouble to offer his help to others among Sir John's opponents, including Edward Hull and Philip Wentworth, and the priory of Hickling over the disputed rent. By 1450, therefore, Fastolf and John Paston were united in their loathing of Heydon, and worked closely together in their unsuccessful attempt to bring him down.

John saw Fastolf regularly during the late 1440s and early 1450s when the old knight was living at Southwark and John himself was in London for long periods dealing with his legal affairs. However, Fastolf's move to Caister, coinciding as it did with John's emergence from the worst of his struggles with Moleyns and Daniel, offered an opportunity for the relationship to develop under less stressful circumstances, for John at least. Fastolf himself still had legal battles to fight, principally his dispute with Philip Wentworth over the wardship of his young kinsman Thomas Fastolf of Cowhaugh. Not only that, but Sir John's chaplain Thomas Howes was in serious trouble as a result of the failed prosecutions of 1450–1. Howes had been his master's representative in Norfolk throughout the hearings, but he was out of his depth in the fight against Heydon and his associates, and made a tactical error in the legal proceedings which gave his enemies the opportunity to charge him with conspiracy and malicious indictment. Fastolf was annoyed at the prospect that his own good name might be dragged into a case which he saw as entirely Howes's responsibility ('*I commanded you not for to labour nor do thing that should be against the law, neither unlawfully against right and truth*'), and point-blank refused to pay any damages for which his chaplain might be found liable.[11] Nevertheless, he did agree, however grudgingly, to fund Howes's defence, and entrusted the management of the case not only to his lawyer William Jenney but also to John Paston, who of course had a legal training and, by now, a good deal of experience in handling complex and politically charged lawsuits. By November 1454 Fastolf had also asked John to help him in his own struggle with Philip Wentworth. '*I pray you heartily to take this matter tenderly to heart,*' he wrote, '*and that you like to seek a means, of such friends as you can best advise and may verily trust upon, to guide this matter in such wise as my intent might be sped*'.[12]

By the spring of 1455, after a few months during which John became increasingly busy in Fastolf's service, Howes reported that his master now valued his counsel more than that of either William Jenney or Judge Yelverton. '*I know verily,*' he wrote, '*your advice shall weigh deeper in my master's conceit than both theirs shall do*'. This might have been flattery on Howes's part – he was certainly desperate for John's continuing support in his own case ('*You have daily great labour for me, God reward you, and my poor prayer you shall have*')[13] – but his judgement was borne out by the growing extent to which Fastolf was relying on John's guidance. By May, Fastolf was prepared to trust John not only to carry out his wishes in pursuing his lawsuits, but to make strategic decisions on his behalf:

> And, cousin, methinks the matters concerning the ward, the suit against William Jenney and Sir Thomas, and other matters, be so strange and divers for me to understand, or to make any answer by me, that in good faith it lies not in my discretion. But if you might be at London yourself this term, if you tarried but three days there, it should speed much better than any writing from me; and so would heartily pray you, though I bear the costs. And in case be that you may in no wise, then I pray you, as my faithful trust is in you, to make answer of such matter upon the said letters as by your wisdom shall be thought most profitable and expedient; and I agree me to hold firm and stable that you write to my friends and servants there, which shall labour and execute this term as you shall advise or command them to do.'[14]

A month later Fastolf was taking it increasingly for granted that he could direct the activities of a man who clearly now played a central part in the management of his affairs. '*I desire that you will haste you to London,*' he told John on 11 June, '*for there is great labour against our intent.*' If John was now at Fastolf's beck and call, at least it was apparent that this was a result of Sir John's high opinion of him. '*I had rather you were at London two days too soon than two days too late,*' he wrote, '*for I trust no man's wit so well as your own*'.[15]

In a matter of little more than six months, John Paston had overtaken all of Fastolf's other advisers in his closeness to the old man and the trust with which Fastolf regarded him. It was becoming clear that John now occupied a unique role in the inner circle at Caister. He had a legal training, but he was not, like William and John Jenney or William Yelverton, a professional lawyer with other clients to attend to or a judicial career to pursue. Nor was he, like Thomas Howes or William Worcester, on Fastolf's staff; he was a '*squire of worship*', with political experience and political contacts of his own. His willingness to devote an increasing amount of his time to Fastolf's concerns was therefore both striking and extraordinarily valuable. Howes and Worcester were not resentful of John's influence, but grateful for his help with an employer who was always demanding, and sometimes unreasonably so. There was never a question of Fastolf being in any man's pocket – he was too tough-minded and fiercely independent for that; but he liked John and trusted him, and was convinced by his loyalty and commitment. The two men were temperamentally very similar, in their tendency to see the world in absolute terms of right and wrong, and their certainty in the justice of their own cause, a conviction verging on self-righteousness. If that meant they were often disappointed, it also brought them closer together. Fastolf's letters make it clear that his reliance on John was founded not only on respect for his abilities but also on genuine affection, perhaps almost for the son he never had. '*I feel well that I was never beholden so much to any kinsman of mine as I am to you, who tenders so much my worship and my profit*', he wrote at the end of 1455.[16] And, after all the difficulties he had faced over the previous decade, John had found an ally and a mentor – almost exactly the same age as his dead father – who valued his service and needed his help.

John was now thirty-four, and his life was more comfortable than it had been for a long time. He was still involved in complicated and protracted lawsuits, but the difference now was that they were not his own. For the first time in years, despite his trips to London on Fastolf's business, he was able to live mainly at home with his wife and family in Norwich. The baby, their fifth, to whom Margaret gave birth in 1454 turned out to be not a son named Henry but a daughter named Anne, and she was followed before the end of the decade by two more boys, Walter and William. In the autumn of 1454 John suggested to Fastolf that one of his daughters – Margery, now five or six, or Anne, the new baby – should in time marry Sir John's young cousin Thomas Fastolf of Cowhaugh, if his suit for the boy's wardship was successful. Fastolf was delighted at the suggestion: '*which motion I was right glad to hear of*', he wrote, '*and will be right well-willing and helping that your blood and mine might increase in alliance*'.[17] The match did not come off, but John's sister Elizabeth, for one, might have been forgiven for expressing some surprise at her brother's sudden interest in things matrimonial. She was still waiting for John and Agnes to find her a suitable marriage, a wait which dragged on until 1458. By that time she had at least escaped from under her mother's roof to board in the household of a family acquaintance, where, Agnes told her brusquely, '*she must use herself to work readily as other gentle-*

women do, and somewhat to help herself therewith'.[18] An arrangement which
would have been entirely normal as part of the education of a teenage girl
from a good family was rather less dignified for an unhappily unmarried
woman of twenty-eight, and it cannot have been anything but a huge relief
when a husband was finally found for her by the end of that year in the person of Robert Poynings, one of the twin younger sons of the Sussex
landowner Robert, Lord Poynings. It was not a love match, by the sound of
the letter Elizabeth sent to her mother shortly after the wedding, even if she
was hopeful that affection might grow between herself and her new husband
– '*my master, my best beloved that you call, and I must needs call him so now,
for I find no other cause, and as I trust to Jesu never shall, for he is full kind to
me'.* Nor had Agnes lost her reluctance to part with her daughter's dowry. '*I
beseech you, good mother,*' Elizabeth wrote anxiously, '*as our most singular
trust is in your good motherhood, that my master, my best beloved, fail not of
the 100 marks at the beginning of this term the which you promised him to his
marriage, with the remnant of the money of my father's will'.*[19] Nevertheless,
Elizabeth was at last free to begin an independent life as a married woman –
something for which she owed a debt of thanks to Fastolf's secretary
William Worcester, who travelled back and forth on John's behalf to negotiate the details of the agreement.

While John and Margaret were enjoying their new domesticity, however, the political world was again growing darker and more turbulent. After
seventeen months during which he '*knew not what was said to him, nor
knew not where he had been while he has been sick'*, King Henry finally woke
from his catatonic state at Christmas 1454. The King was overjoyed to see
his baby son, now more than a year old, and declared himself to be '*in
charity with all the world, and so he would all the lords were'.*[20] However
unwittingly, in those few words he revealed exactly what had always been
wrong with his kingship: vague benevolence was no substitute for the
assertive leadership which would have commanded the compliance of his
nobles. The Duke of York had done his best during Henry's illness to
impose impartial rule on the festering disorder in the country, but he was
not the King, and he could not sustain his fellow magnates' support for his
role as Protector now that Henry was well enough, at least in theory, to
take charge of his own government. The Duke of Somerset was still in
prison – York had tried and failed in the summer of 1454 to persuade the
rest of the nobility to try him for treason – but as soon as the King recovered his health it became clear that Somerset too would recover his position of influence. When York's Protectorate formally ended, early in

February 1455, Somerset was released from custody, and York had no choice but to withdraw from the court.

With his enemy Somerset back in power at the King's side, York's situation was now extremely perilous. However, he was no longer quite the isolated figure he had been during the previous period of Somerset's rule in the early 1450s. Violent conflict within the ranks of the nobility, unresolved after years of royal inertia, had deep roots by now in some parts of the country, and neither York nor Somerset had been able to put an end to the disorder. The great northern family of the Nevilles, led by York's brother-in-law Richard Neville, Earl of Salisbury, and his eldest son Richard, Earl of Warwick, had become convinced that the rule of Somerset and the court gave them no chance of securing justice in their vicious feud with their regional rivals the Percies. As a result, they were now prepared to join York in opposition to Somerset's reconstituted regime. Bolstered by the Nevilles' support, and fearing that Somerset would seek to destroy him, York decided that attack was the best form of defence. He and the Nevilles mustered their forces in the north and moved to intercept the King on his way to a great council which Somerset had summoned to meet at Leicester.

The confrontation which took place when the two sides met at St Albans in May 1455 demonstrated just how disastrously intractable political division among the nobility had become. For the majority of the lords, the sight of three great magnates marching at the head of an army against their anointed sovereign was a terrifying one which convinced them, whatever their attitude towards Somerset, that King Henry must be defended. York, Salisbury and Warwick, meanwhile, believed that they would never be safe while Somerset remained at the King's right hand; their call to arms was a last resort, designed to enforce the removal of '*our enemies of approved experience, such as abide and keep themselves under the wing of your Majesty Royal*'.[21] The attempt at negotiation which took place at St Albans did nothing to reassure them, since King Henry himself took no part in the discussions, and there were suspicions in York's camp that the letters which the Duke had sent to explain his grievances had not even reached the King's hands. Fighting began when York's forces entered St Albans at around ten in the morning on Thursday 22 May, and continued for several hours through the streets and houses of the town. York and the Nevilles rapidly secured the advantage, and there were probably fewer than a hundred casualties in all by the time their victory was apparent. Among the dead – probably deliberately hunted down and killed – were the Nevilles' chief enemy Henry Percy, Earl of Northumberland, and Somerset himself.

King Henry had been wounded in the neck by an arrow as he sat under his banner in the market square while his nobles fought in the streets around him. He was not seriously hurt, however, and, if any further demonstration were needed that he would endorse the views of whoever had most immediate access to him, it came later that day when York and the Nevilles formally submitted to his authority, '*and besought him of his Highness to take them as his true liegemen, saying that they never intended hurt to his own person*'. In response, it was reported, Henry '*took them to grace, and so desired them to cease their people, and that there should no more harm be done*'.[22] The Duke and his allies took the King back to London in ceremonial procession, amid tight security. This public display of unity was underlined by a service held at St Paul's Cathedral on Sunday 25 May during which York himself presented King Henry with his crown. That day a friend of John Paston's wrote from London to tell him what had happened at St Albans; '*and as for what rule we shall have*,' he said, '*yet I know never*'.[23]

Whatever the wider significance of the battle, Sir John Fastolf certainly believed that York's victory would help him in his lawsuit against the courtier Philip Wentworth, especially since Wentworth himself was in disgrace. He had carried the royal standard at St Albans, but once the fighting began to turn against the King's forces he '*cast it down and fled. My lord Norfolk says he shall be hanged therefore, and so is he worthy*', Fastolf's servant William Barker reported to William Worcester. '*He is in Suffolk now. He dares not come about the King*.'[24] John Paston shared Fastolf's optimism, and put out feelers about the prospects of getting himself elected as one of the Norfolk MPs for the parliament which was called to meet early in July. Fastolf's lawyer John Jenney thought this ill-advised, given the enormity of the events of the last month – '*Some men hold it right strange to be in this parliament*,' he told John, '*and methinks they be wise men that so do*'[25] – but John's plans were in any case thwarted by the Duke of Norfolk's determination to have his own choice of candidates returned. Norfolk had arrived at St Albans a day too late to take part in the fighting, but he was known to be sympathetic to York's cause and was therefore well placed to get his own way in the parliamentary election, although he made an elementary mistake in putting forward the name of his cousin Sir John Howard, a Suffolk landowner who held no estates in the county of Norfolk. As John Jenney pointed out, '*it is an evil precedent for the shire that a strange man should be chosen, and no worship to my lord of York nor to my lord of Norfolk to write for him*'. Once the Duke had been made aware of his misjudgement, he was willing to agree that '*the shire should have free election*,' so long as '*Sir Thomas*

Tuddenham were not, nor none that was towards the Duke of Suffolk[26] – an understandable stipulation, but one which revealed how much he was still struggling against the influence of a rival who had by now been dead for five years. Nevertheless, his authority in the wake of York's victory was such that Howard (who was said to have been *'mad as a wild bullock'* that his nomination had been challenged) was in the end elected, despite the misgivings of many gentlemen in the county.[27]

When parliament opened on 9 July, Fastolf took the opportunity to submit a petition detailing yet again his losses in France, the vast amounts of money he claimed he was owed by the crown, and his grievances against the late Duke of Suffolk's men. Another petitioner was Henry Woodhouse, the victim of Thomas Daniel's trickery over his engagement to Daniel's already-married sister, who at last secured restitution of his title to his own estates at Roydon. The judgement came too late to save his home there, however. Ten months earlier, desperate at his inability to defend himself more effectively, Woodhouse had arranged for the manor house to be demolished, rather than let it fall into Daniel's hands for good. Tension pervaded the parliamentary proceedings. '. . . *the King our sovereign lord and all his true lords stand in health of their bodies,*' it was reported, '*but not all at heart's ease*'. On 18 July, in an attempt to draw a line under the conflict, a bill was passed placing the blame for the fighting at St Albans on the dead Duke of Somerset, '*by the which bill all manner of actions that should grow to any person or persons for any offences at that journey done, in any manner of wise, should be extinct and void, affirming all thing done there well done, and nothing done there never after this time to be spoken of*'.[28] Despite the optimistic rhetoric, however, it hardly seemed likely that the battle could simply be expunged from public memory, and York, Salisbury and Warwick were taking no chances; London was full of heavily armed men wearing their colours. It took several more months of negotiation, during which violent disorder continued unchecked in Wales and the south-west, before York was once again installed as Protector in November.

In some respects, it seemed that York's task of trying to restore unity in government under his own leadership would be easier now that his rival Somerset was out of the way. On the other hand, the shocking fact of Somerset's death also brought a traumatic new dimension to the conflict. After years of fighting in France, the nobility were accustomed to war, but war fought overseas, in which it usually suited their enemies far better to capture the wealthy and powerful than to kill them; large ransoms could not, after all, be demanded for dead bodies. Now, noble blood had been shed on English soil by English hands, something which the heirs of those who had died would find it difficult either to forget or to forgive. At the same time, York's own role as Protector was much more problematic, and therefore more vulnerable, than it had been a year earlier. Then, the King had been ill, and explicitly unable to rule. Now, he was no less fit to govern than he had been for most of his reign. If that was not saying much, it still did not mean that it was a simple matter for York to claim the right to rule in his place. The Duke's position became all the more difficult to defend once it became clear that Queen Margaret, a powerful and fiercely partisan presence at King Henry's side, would not accept the Protectorate but intended to lead her husband's government herself. (*'The Queen is a great and strong laboured woman'*, John Bocking reported to Fastolf, *'for she spares no pain to sue her things to an intent and conclusion to her power.'*[29])York clung on, with increasing difficulty, for three months, but in February 1456 he resigned as Protector, and six months later Margaret moved the court up to Coventry in the heart of her own estates. With the Queen entrenched in the midlands, and York and the Nevilles still powerful in London, with backing both from their northern lands and from the garrison at Calais where the Earl of Warwick was now captain, the nobles who made up the royal council were left desperately searching for enough common ground to build some semblance of a workable government. The result was an uneasy impasse.

After a lifetime's involvement in war and politics, Sir John Fastolf heard of these disturbing events at second or third hand. At home at Caister, his mind was still sharp, but his health was no longer as robust as it had once been. His world was narrowing; he could no longer travel, and his interest even in the tumultuous course of politics was increasingly refracted through his obsessive quest for justice in his own legal battles. Even that, however, could be too much to cope with when he felt unwell. John Paston received an unusually abrupt response when he requested Fastolf's instructions on some business matters during one such period of illness. *'. . . you know how that I have put my trust in you both for my soul's health and also for the pursuit and defence of all worldly matters touching my person,'* Fastolf wrote, *'praying you heartily to do in your advertisements and all other matters as you, by the advice of my learned counsel when you be together, shall advise for my weal, worship and profit. For you know well I am so visited by the hand of God that I may not deal with such troublous matters without it should be too great hurt to my bodily welfare, which I trust you will not desire, etc.'*[30] That even John Paston, of whom Fastolf was normally so appreciative, could be told to get on with his job in such relatively direct terms is an indication of how onerous the demands were which the old knight was now making on his closest household servants. '*At reverence of God, be as soon as you may with my master, to ease his spirits*', the long-suffering William Worcester asked John some time later:

> *He questions and disputes with his servants here, and will not be answered nor satisfied some time but after his wilfulness, for it suffices not our simple wits to appease his soul. But when he speaks with Master Yelverton, you, or with William Jenney, and such others as be authorised in the law and with abundance of goods, he is content and holds him pleased with your answers and motions, as reason is that he be. So would Jesus one of you three, or some such other in your stead, might hang at his girdle daily to answer his matters.*[31]

By the spring of 1457, Worcester felt that Fastolf's control of his finances was beginning to slip, and appealed to John as an ally in the campaign to ensure that the household at least kept proper accounts. '*My master cannot know whether he goes backwards or forwards till this be done*', he told John on 20 April, and returned to the subject again ten days later: '*my master was wont to lay up money yearly at London and Caister*', he said, '*and now the contrary, from bad to worse*'.[32] Worcester was writing in confidence ('*I pray you and require you keep this matter to yourself*'), because he believed the problem stemmed from the failure of others in the household to do their jobs properly, while his own role as a mere secretary did not allow him to take command of the situation.[33] As Fastolf became less reliable and more irascible, his closest servants were all under increasing strain; the old man was so quick to criticise that some members of his household responded to the pressure by rounding on one another. '. . . *when my master commands such as of force by reason of their occupation must be near him to do a message to his fellow, or question of him, it shall be imagined amongst our fellowship that he does make matters to my master*', Worcester told John on another occasion, when questions were raised about accounts which William Barker had drawn up; '*and so it is imagined of me when I write letters to London to Bocking or Barker, that, in such matters as please them not, then it is my doing; if it take well to their intent, then it is their doing.*' Characteristically, having written heatedly, he tried to make light of his words – '*I am eased of my spirits now that I have expressed my lewd meaning because of my fellow Barker, as of such other barkers against the moon, to make wise men laugh at their folly*', he said. '*Forgive me of my lewd letter writing, and I pray you laugh at it.*'[34] But

Worcester could not so easily sweep away the fact that Fastolf's previously iron grip on his affairs was beginning to loosen. It was no coincidence that, by the end of 1457, the part John Paston played in Fastolf's business had expanded to include the supervision of his estate management. John travelled with Worcester around some of Fastolf's Suffolk manors in January 1458, and in May he went with Thomas Howes to check on Sir John's properties in Yorkshire, which he found in a state of some neglect.[35] John had become indispensable, in personal terms to Fastolf himself, and in practical terms to his household, a fact which did not go unnoticed in the world beyond Caister's walls. '*My master can do nothing the which shall come in open audience at these days but it shall be called your deed*', one correspondent told him.[36]

Fastolf was now in his late seventies. It was clear to everyone, including the old man himself, that he did not have much time left, and he was increasingly preoccupied with the question of what should happen to his spectacular wealth after he was gone. Whereas Judge William Paston, in the same situation, had had to weigh up the competing claims of his heir, his younger children, and the spiritual needs of his soul, the task confronting Fastolf was ostensibly much simpler, and certainly much lonelier. He had founded no dynasty; all he could hope for from his riches was to ensure some help for his soul on its way through purgatory, and to create some fitting earthly memorial to his name and family. That much was clear but it was a great deal less clear how it should be achieved, and in any case the contemplation of his own approaching death was not an agreeable pastime. Worcester was worried that his master was simply putting off matters which were too important and too complex to be left hanging: '*a great lack is in him*', he told John in 1456, '*he tarries so long to put all things of charge in a sure way*'.[37]

Worcester was an acute judge of character, and his concerns were well founded. Landowners could never be sure that their last wishes would be carried out promptly and to the letter; heirs were all too prone to prioritise their own worldly interests over the timely fulfilment of religious bequests, often waiting until they lay on their own deathbeds, for example, to stipulate that their parents' wills should be performed as well as their own. Fastolf himself, despite the huge scale of his disposable income, had still not arranged for memorial stones to be placed on his parents' tombs. However, Fastolf's childlessness made his own situation even more difficult. Without a son and heir, he would have to entrust the administration of his will to a group of executors. Some at least would need to be powerful men, if they were to have the influence to carry through whatever Fastolf's plans for his fortune might be; but powerful men were busy men, and the time they would be able to devote to the well-being of Fastolf's soul would be strictly limited. On the other hand, men such as Howes and Worcester, whose commitment to his interests was unquestionable, lacked political weight. Fastolf knew from personal experience what the consequences might be. He was one of the executors of his former lord, the Duke of Bedford, who had died without direct heirs in 1435, leaving a will which was nuncupative – that is, dictated on his deathbed rather than formally drafted – and unhelpfully vague. More than twenty years later, its terms had still not been completely fulfilled, and Fastolf, who was by now the only one of the Duke's seven original executors still alive, was struggling to locate the remainder of his dead master's possessions. Worcester was unhappily aware of the potential parallels, as he told John after Christmas 1456, when Fastolf refused him leave to visit Bristol, his home town, on the grounds that he was needed to help Sir John draft his will. '*God give him grace of wholesome counsel and of a good disposition,*' he wrote gloomily. '*It is not the work of a single day nor a single week. My lord Bedford's will was made in so brief and general terms that unto this day by the space of twenty years can never have end, but always new to construe and opineable; so a generality shall nor may be so good as a particular declaration. I write bluntly.*'[38]

The idea on which Fastolf eventually settled was the foundation of a religious college at Caister, to be made up of seven monks or priests and seven poor men – an institution which would simultaneously provide perpetual prayers for his soul and those of his family, and keep the Fastolf name alive for posterity.[39] It would be a complex project, requiring a licence from the King to allow the endowment of the college with a substantial part of Fastolf's estates. Sir John himself was, as usual, so convinced of the merits of his case that he saw no reason why he should not be granted the necessary licence '*without any great fine, in recompense of my long service continued and done unto the King and to his noble father, whom God assoil, and never yet guerdoned or rewarded*'. Warming to his theme, he added that, since he intended that his priests and poor men should also pray for the King himself, '*methinks I should not be denied of my desire, but the rather to be remembered and sped*'.[40] As so often, the finer points of the political circumstances had escaped him. Henry VI's government was not only profoundly unstable but chronically short of money, and it was not plausible that a man as wealthy as Fastolf would be allowed to pour his riches into a new religious foundation without the crown taking a cut of some sort. Sure enough, word came back in the summer of 1457 that '*it is too great a good that is asked of you for your licence*'.[41] The prospects of a more favourable response seemed limited in the extreme, given that the Lord Treasurer was John Talbot, Earl of Shrewsbury, whose father had fought in France with Fastolf thirty years earlier and had charged him with cowardice after he made a tactical retreat during the English defeat at Patay in 1429. Fastolf succeeded in clearing his name after a formal investigation, but relations between the two men never recovered, and there seemed little point in hoping that Shrewsbury's son might now be sympathetic to Fastolf's claims to a preferential rate for his licence on the grounds of his record in royal service. Fastolf himself was constitutionally incapable of agreeing to pay a sum he believed to be extortionate and unfair; he simply could not bring himself to do it, even if the needs of his immortal soul were at stake. He was therefore unable to secure formal permission to endow his college – something which only compounded his more general reluctance to commit his wishes to paper in any final form.

The other problem with Fastolf's plan was that his home at Caister was so conspicuously desirable. For Fastolf himself it was crucial that his lasting memorial should be at Caister itself, his birthplace, on which he had lavished so much money and care. It was already abundantly clear, however, that many covetous eyes were focused on a valuable house which was large, luxurious and defensible, and which would not, of course, pass in uninterrupted succession from father to son. In the early 1450s Thomas Daniel – never one to miss a potential trick – claimed to have been named Fastolf's heir, a '*slander*' which Fastolf complained was a '*noyous great vexation*' to him.[42] Not to be outdone, the Duke of Norfolk let it be known in 1451 that '*Sir John Fastolf has given him Caister, and he will have it plainly*'.[43] The Duke's own ancestral home was a 300-year-old castle in Suffolk, and the possibility of acquiring a comfortable and fashionable new house, strategically placed on the Norfolk coast, was too tempting to ignore. Others were a little more subtle in approach. Cecily Neville, Duchess of York, whose husband had estates in East Anglia but no residence there, visited Fastolf in the autumn of 1456 and '*sore moved me for the purchase of Caister*', he reported to John Paston once she had gone.[44] Rumour had it that other magnates interested in buying the property included the Duchess's nephew Richard, Earl of Warwick, as well as John, Viscount Beaumont, and, before his death, the Duke of Somerset. Fastolf did not entertain the offers for a moment, but they did make him all the more anxious about how to ensure that his wishes would be carried out. He had, first of all, to find a way of guaranteeing that his college would be founded at Caister as he wanted, and then to make sure that it could be protected from the acquisitive hands of powerful men.

Fastolf made a new trust for his estates in 1457, but he did not finally draft his will until the summer of 1459.[45] The long delay reflected his deep ambivalence, even at the age of seventy-nine, about setting down his last wishes. The text itself, however, was suffused with his desperate desire to bind the future, and his fear that he might not succeed in doing so. It was a lengthy and detailed document, in the course of which, with characteristic stubbornness, he required his executors to take over the disputes in which he was still engaged, and also warned them to beware of '*divers persons of divers descents*' who '*pretend . . . at this day to be next inheritor to me after my decease*', when in fact, he said, '*no creature has title or right to inherit*' anything he owned. The main business of the will, however, was the foundation of the college at Caister, which his executors were to establish with an endowment of £200 a year. If a licence for the foundation could not be obtained, then the endowment was to be given to the abbey of St Benet of Hulme, where Fastolf intended to be buried, to support his monks and poor men there instead, although it was abundantly clear that this option was an unhappy second best, raising questions in his mind about whether his wishes would be adequately fulfilled within an institution over which he could have little hold from beyond the grave. The rest of his lands were to be sold and the money disposed of for the good of his soul. Here his anxiety broke through the formality of the legal language. His executors, he said, '*shall so dispose my goods in effect faithfully that my soul, vexed in painful anguishes, with holy Job be not compelled to say, with great lamentation and mourning, "Have mercy on me, have mercy on me, namely you that my friends should be, for the hand of God's punishing has grievously touched me"*'.[46]

It was not hard to see why he was so uneasy. His difficulty in securing royal authorisation for the foundation had already brought into question the viability of his scheme. Even if the licence could be secured, the responsibilities which he proposed to entrust to his executors were so overwhelmingly complex and wide ranging that he could not be certain that they would have the time or the commitment to see them through with any urgency, or perhaps at all. It cannot have been lost on either Sir John himself or those closest to him that what he really needed was a man of political standing who would be prepared to devote himself totally to the realisation of Fastolf's designs. And an alternative proposal, along just those lines, did emerge in the last months of the old knight's life.

The exact course of events remains shrouded in uncertainty, not least

because, after Fastolf's death, the other main protagonists spent years arguing about what precisely had happened. John Paston later claimed that
Fastolf had been set on the new plan since the summer of 1457, but, if that
was the case, it was not reflected in the draft will of 14 June 1459. An oblique
reference in the surviving correspondence suggests both that the new
proposition came directly from John himself, and that it was not raised until
a few days after the will of June 1459 had been written. In a letter of 24 June
1459, William Barker told John that '*your matter that you have moved of to Sir
Thomas for the purchase, etc, my master is well agreed thereto, but first it was
taken strangely, etc.*'[47] The proposal – if this was indeed the '*matter*' to which
Barker alluded, with such tantalisingly elliptical *et ceteras* – was a radical
one. John suggested that he alone should take personal responsibility for the
foundation of Fastolf's college at Caister. In return (and this, it seems safe to
assume, was the part which might well be '*taken strangely*'), he should be
named sole heir to all Fastolf's estates in Norfolk and Suffolk, for which he
would pay a sum of 4,000 marks – a fraction of their market value – to Sir
John's executors for the performance of his will.[48]

This was a daring move. If John succeeded in persuading Fastolf to accept
him as his heir, he might effect a second transformation in his family's fortunes as astonishing as the one his father had achieved before him. On the
other hand, the risk he ran by raising the issue at all was that he might taint
himself in Fastolf's eyes by association with Daniel, Norfolk and all the others who had been circling around the inheritance, and thereby destroy the
relationship of trust between himself and his patron. The hard fact of the
matter was that John was both practical and unsentimental, and it must
have occurred to him almost from the beginning that he might one day be a
beneficiary of Fastolf's will in some form or other. Fastolf's childlessness
meant that there had been speculation for years about what would happen
to his estates, and Agnes Paston thought she had seen an opportunity for her
sons to profit from the family's association with him as early as 1451, when
Fastolf was rumoured to be selling some of his Norfolk properties. ('*I pray
you, as you will have my love and my blessing,*' she told John that November,
'*that you will help and do your devoir that something were purchased for your
two brothers. I suppose that Sir John Fastolf, if he were spoken to, would be
gladder to let his kinsmen have part than strange men.*')[49] But a moment's
reflection would have told Fastolf that, practical and unsentimental though
John might be, he was not a cynical man, and his sustained commitment to
Fastolf's concerns was too deep and full hearted to be written off now as a
mercenary act of self-interest. There were also powerful reasons why Fastolf

might conclude that the proposal would work to his advantage. He had trusted John implicitly in the handling of his affairs for a number of years, and had not been disappointed. If there was any gentleman of his acquaintance to whom he could confide responsibility for the welfare of his soul, it was surely John – and John would have an extraordinarily good reason, in the shape of Fastolf's estates, to do his utmost to carry out his patron's wishes. Once the college was safely established, Fastolf would be able to rest easy in his grave knowing that John would be on hand, living at Caister with his family, to make sure that the priests were fulfilling their duty of care for their founder's soul, and to protect the castle from the predatory interest of other landowners.

All the signs are that Fastolf did come round to John's suggestion. '*My master is well agreed thereto*,' William Barker said in June 1459, and a revised draft of the 14 June will exists in which the complex instructions to the executors about the founding of the college, and the frantic language which accompanied them, are replaced by the streamlined simplicity, expressed in cool legal prose, of John's scheme.[50] But, if this revision was carried out on Fastolf's instructions, the old man did not formally endorse the result; if he did indeed agree to make John Paston his heir, he never did so in writing. The absence of a sealed written will in John's favour cannot be taken as proof that Fastolf had rejected the idea of naming him his heir. He had taken years to come round to drafting one version of his will, and it was never likely that he might be prevailed upon to write another almost immediately. Apart from anything else, the very idea of settling once and for all on his final intentions came, for Fastolf, too uncomfortably close to acknowledging the proximity of death.[51] On top of this general unpredictability, Fastolf was also aware of the hold which the prospect of future reward gave him over his long-suffering servants, a hold which would remain useful only so long as they remained uncertain of what their reward would ultimately be. Over the years he had made promises to many, perhaps all of them, but the will of June 1459 made no specific bequests to any members of his household.[52] John Paston was not a servant to be kept dangling on a string, but the reward he hoped to receive was almost all of what Fastolf had to give, and the old man was never likely to give the decision official form either quickly or straightforwardly, however convinced he might be of the merits of the idea itself.

John's difficulty was that there was so little time left. Fastolf had been in remarkably good health in the early summer of 1459 – '*my master is as fresh as ever he was these two years, thanked be God*', William Barker reported to John in London[53] – but by the autumn he was seriously ill, and Friar

Brackley sent an urgent message summoning John to his bedside. '*It is high time,*' he wrote. '*He draws fast homeward, and is right low brought and sore weaked and feebled, etc.*' The question of the inheritance was clearly now urgent, but John was no nearer securing a written statement of his patron's wishes. Brackley was as oblique as Barker had been in mentioning John's proposal; neither he nor Howes, he said, had '*no more touched of the matter, etc, to my master, etc*'. At least it was clear that Fastolf's high opinion of John had not faltered. '*Every day these five days he says, "God send me soon my good cousin Paston, for I hold him a faithful man and ever one man"*', Brackley reported. '*To which I say, "That is truth", etc. And he, "Show me not the meat, show me the man". He repeats these words again and again with great feeling, etc.*'[54]

By the beginning of November, Fastolf was sinking fast. He was confined to his bed, '*so short in his breath, and so overcome with the pain of his sickness, that a man might not hear him speak but he laid his ear to his mouth*'.[55] For the second time, John Paston was about to lose a father. And, for the second time, John's claims on the estate which the old man would leave would be the subject of fierce controversy. His hopes now rested on the last whisperings of a frail and feverish invalid – and John, who had rejected his own father's dying requests so angrily on the grounds that he '*made no will of them in writing*', was about to find that the issue looked dramatically different from beside a second deathbed.

CHAPTER SEVEN

– *neither in trust nor favour* –

On 3 November 1459 the great house at Caister was full of activity. It was a Saturday – the day when the household's weekly provisions arrived from Yarmouth, usually brought by John Russe, a merchant and shipowner who had served Fastolf for years. As always, mass was celebrated in the chapel, and, as they did every morning, Fastolf's servants gathered in the hall for breakfast at eight. In the chamber where their master lay, however, it was clear that this was not a normal day. Fastolf was now close to death. Attendants came and went as the old man lay unmoving in his bed: Nicholas Newman, the most senior of his chamber-servants, brought him spiced wine to sip; his barber Harry Wynstall came to shave his beard; his doctor John Barnard looked in from time to time to check on his condition; and his chaplain Thomas Howes said mass at his bedside. Among them all, John Paston was a constant presence. He was there still the following afternoon, when Robert Inglose, the son of an old friend of Fastolf's, arrived at the house, intending to discuss some financial matters. John stepped in to protect his patron: Inglose could see Fastolf, he said, only on condition that he promised not to talk business. When Inglose was brought in to the bed-chamber, he understood why. Sir John was '*right weak and full feeble in his spirits*', he later recalled, '*as a man ready to die*'.[1] The old knight held on for twenty-four hours more, but on Monday 5 November, at around six o'clock in the evening – with John Paston still at his side – Fastolf died.

There seems no reason to doubt that this was a huge personal loss for John. The old man was not easy to deal with, particularly towards the end of his life, but he was capable of inspiring fierce loyalty in those around him. For John, who had been his closest confidant and friend for five years, Fastolf's trust and esteem must have meant a great deal, especially given how bereft of political support he had been in the aftermath of his own father's death. But, whatever the emotional consequences, it was also clear that this was a pivotal moment – perhaps *the* pivotal moment – in John's life. Before him lay two choices. The first was simple and uncontroversial: if the will to which Fastolf had put his seal four months earlier were allowed to stand,

John would go on being what he had always been – a safe pair of hands, not quite on the political inside track, but a determined champion of his family's interests and his father's legacy. There was nothing simple about the other choice. John could try to enforce what he believed to be his mentor's last wishes, despite the fact that the old knight had left no formal written statement of his intention to make John his heir. The scale of Fastolf's wealth, and the fact that he left no son of his own to inherit, meant that it was always likely that others would come forward to challenge for a share of the estate, even had John possessed incontrovertible evidence to support his claim. Because John could produce no such evidence, it was virtually certain that he would face a protracted and costly fight to secure the inheritance. If he succeeded, he would utterly transform his own position and that of his family: possession of Fastolf's lands would give him wealth and influence on a scale far beyond even his father's remarkable achievements. If he failed, the cost would not only be counted in the strain which years of struggle would inflict on himself and his family; he might also put everything his father had achieved at risk.

John did not hesitate. He announced that, on the Saturday morning before his death, Fastolf had dictated a new will superseding the one he had sealed nearly five months earlier. In it, he spoke of his '*very trust and love to his cousin John Paston*', and '*declared that the said John Paston was the best friend and helper and supporter to the said Sir John*'. The foundation of the college at Caister was to be entrusted to John alone, '*for which, and for other charges and labours that the said John Paston has done and taken upon him, to the ease and profit of the said Sir John Fastolf*', John should have all his lands in Norfolk and Suffolk for the sum of 4,000 marks, to be paid in instalments over the next decade. Ten executors were named – headed by William Wainfleet, the Bishop of Winchester, and including John himself, Judge William Yelverton, Fastolf's secretary William Worcester, his confessor Friar John Brackley and his chaplain Thomas Howes – but the administration of the will was to be committed to John Paston and Thomas Howes alone. Fastolf's fear that Caister might fall victim to the greed of great men was reflected in a contingency plan more drastic than anything he had previously specified: '*if the said John Paston, by force or might of any other desiring to have the said mansion, were letted to found the said college in the said mansion*', the document said, '*that then the said John Paston should do pull down the said mansion and every stone and stick thereof*', and support the seven priests or monks at religious institutions elsewhere instead. There was one more afterthought, apparently added when the whole text was read over to

Fastolf during that last weekend of his life: if John successfully founded the college as he had directed, then 'the said John Paston should be discharged of the payment of the said 4,000 marks, and naught pay thereof.'[2]

It is impossible to know whether Fastolf really did dictate this document word for word as John claimed, or whether John allowed himself some latitude in interpreting his patron's final, laboured attempts to make himself understood. Either way, it is certain both that this proposal had indeed been under discussion in the months before Sir John's death, and that John himself genuinely believed that the new will represented the old man's last instructions. His conviction that right was on his side was a constant in his life; in John's mind, there was nothing fraudulent about his claim to be Fastolf's heir. The question was whether others would agree – both Fastolf's friends and servants who would be involved in the execution of the will, and his enemies who would hope to find a way to get their own hands on the estates. All John could do now was stake his claim, and wait to confront whatever challenges lay ahead.

The first signs were encouraging. There was no immediate outcry from anyone in the household at Caister: no shocked protest that this was not what Fastolf had intended; no denunciation of the new will as a forgery. When John's younger brother William left for London on the day after Fastolf's death to take the first practical steps on his brother's behalf towards claiming the inheritance, William Worcester rode with him. By the following Monday, they had positive news to report. Bishop Wainfleet, the most senior of Fastolf's executors, and currently the Chancellor of England, was 'well disposed in all things'. William Paston had also spoken to John Stokes, another of the executors and a judge in the Archbishop of Canterbury's court where the will would have to be proved, as well as to the Archbishop himself, 'and I find them right well disposed both', he reported.[3] Some of Fastolf's valuables which had been left for safekeeping in London had been discreetly secured, and William had also retained a canon lawyer to represent the family in the probate hearing.

This was progress; but the two men also encountered the first stirrings of trouble. As soon as they reached London, they heard that the Duke of Exeter had his eye on Fastolf's townhouse at Southwark and was intending to take it by force. Paston and Worcester quickly arranged to meet the Duke's legal advisers, and together managed to persuade them instead to 'move my lord to sue by means of the law'. Exeter's claim was no more than an opportunistic attempt to acquire a desirable London residence by strong-arm tactics, and he retreated rapidly once it became clear that John would not be intim-

1 Peasant farmers at the plough, from the fourteenth-century Luttrell Psalter.

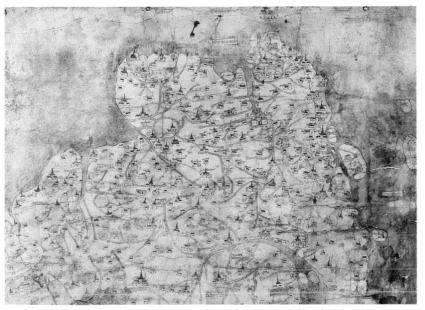

2 The south-east of England, from the Gough Map, dated 1360. North is to the left.

3 The court of Common Pleas in session. The judges, in red, sit on the bench; the serjeants-at-law, in white coifs and striped gowns, stand to plead their cases, while clerks at the table record the proceedings.

4 Westminster Hall, where the court of Common Pleas sat. The building dates back to the eleventh century, but was remodelled in the 1390s, when the magnificent roof – with a carved angel on each hammerbeam – was constructed.

Es nouuelles Dalbion
Sil vous en plaist escouter
Mon frere & mon copaignio
Achies qua mon retouner
Ly este sera sa mer
E ceu q iovruse chiere

5 Fifteenth-century London. The Tower is in the foreground, and London Bridge – the only bridge over the Thames in the capital in this period – can be seen in the background.

6 A medieval wedding.

7 The marriage of Henry VI and Margaret of Anjou.

8 and 9 Alice Chaucer, Duchess of Suffolk. Alabaster
effigy and tomb at Ewelme, Oxfordshire

10 From a fifteenth-century book of arms: the knight on the left is Sir John Fastolf.

11 The battle of Agincourt, 1415, where Sir John Fastolf served in Henry V's victorious army.

12 The ruins of Caister Castle.

13 Autograph letter from John Paston II to his mother Margaret, 20 November 1474. According to the modern editor of the correspondence, John II's handwriting is the most accomplished in the family, 'in a rather dashingly careless but fluent way'. The letter is signed, in the bottom right-hand corner, 'Yowre sone J Paston K (knight)'.

idated so easily. However, other possibilities were potentially more threatening. '*My lord Treasurer speaks fair*', William told his brother, '*but yet many
advise me to put no trust in him*'. As the most senior financial officer of a
regime with unremitting financial problems, the Earl of Wiltshire (who had
succeeded the Earl of Shrewsbury as Treasurer a year earlier) was only too
well aware of the significance of Fastolf's estate: '*there is laboured many
means to entitle the King in his good*', William reported.[4] It also transpired
that speculative claims on the inheritance might emerge from less grand
sources. One such, although the details remain obscure, was an attempt to
stake a claim to Caister itself by Elizabeth Heveningham, widow of the
Pastons' acquaintance Sir John Heveningham – a project in which she was
egged on by her newly acquired second husband, the Pastons' old enemy
John Wyndham.[5] Her claim, whatever its source, was clearly a non-starter,
and was dispatched within weeks, if not days. Wyndham, as usual, was full of
'*noiseful language, saying how he might have no law and that my lord
Chancellor was not made executor but for maintenance, with many other
words nothing profitable nor furthering his intent*' – but his bluster had no
effect, other than to confirm that '*my lord Chancellor is right good and tender
lord in all your matters*', as John Bocking reported early in December.[6]
Nevertheless, it was a reminder that nothing could be taken for granted in a
process which would be as much a matter of complex and unpredictable
politics as it was of legal technicalities.

In the meantime, Fastolf's burial had still to be organised. It took place, as
he had instructed, in the monastery of St Benet of Hulme, eight miles north-
west of Caister. His body was interred in the abbey church next to that of his
wife Millicent, in a new aisle on the south side of the chancel which had been
built by Fastolf himself at a cost of more than £600. William Worcester
worked tirelessly on the arrangements for the lavish funeral; he commissioned craftsmen in London to paint eighteen banners and more than fifty
pennants displaying Fastolf's arms and those of his parents, as well as
images of the Holy Trinity, the Virgin Mary, and Saints George and
Nicholas. Hundreds of pounds were spent on fine black gowns for the
mourners, including Judge William Yelverton, accompanied by his wife and
thirteen servants, and John Paston, who – in his concern to demonstrate
both his respect for his patron and his own standing as Fastolf's heir –
attended with an even larger entourage. Once the funeral was over,
Worcester continued to devote himself to his dead master's affairs, compil-
ing detailed inventories of Fastolf's possessions and distributing alms for the
good of his soul, while John left Caister for London to push ahead with

preparations for the probate hearing in the Archbishop of Canterbury's court. Pressure of business meant that, for the first time in years, he was unable to come home to spend Christmas with his family. '*I pray you that you will come as soon as you may*', Margaret wrote on Christmas Eve. '*I shall think myself half a widow because you shall not be at home*.'[7]

Neither Margaret nor John yet realised that a Christmas apart would be the very least of their worries in the months to come. However, there were already disturbing indications that progress might not be as smooth as they had hoped. Fastolf's servants at Caister had been under increasing strain during the last years of their master's life as the old man became ever more short-tempered and demanding, but it had not been clear until now quite how deep the rifts within his household had grown. His confessor John Brackley loathed William Worcester with a passion, and missed no opportunity to warn John against him in letters full of poisonous invective. '*For God's sake*,' he wrote within weeks of Fastolf's death, '*beware of trusting in that black Irishman*' – Worcester's home town of Bristol apparently being near enough to Ireland for the purposes of an abusive tirade. Worcester, he said, was '*half-blind and shifty-eyed; would that he were not still more shifty in heart, word and deed*'. Brackley was not simply letting off steam, but accusing Worcester of a serious breach of trust: he was conspiring, Brackley alleged, with Fastolf's valet Nicholas Newman (known in the household as Colin, and christened '*Colin the Frenchman*' by Brackley) to undermine John Paston's claim to their master's estate. '. . . *they shit out of the same arse*', he wrote, with characteristic elegance, in the colloquial Latin he habitually used in correspondence.[8] His hostility to Worcester must have been simmering for years to have reached such a pitch, but now that the restraining influence of his master's authority had disappeared he was free to express his feelings with a new degree of vituperation and malice.

There is no evidence that Brackley's specific accusations against Worcester and Newman had any foundation, and his obnoxiousness might have remained an irritation and nothing more, had it not been for the fact that trust – or the lack of it – was fast emerging as the most difficult and dangerous issue John Paston had to face in his quest for acceptance as Fastolf's heir. From Fastolf's point of view, the idea of bequeathing his estate to John made sense in terms of trying to ensure that one man had both the means and the commitment to carry through his wishes. However, the fact that he did not give this decision unchallengeable legal form before his death meant that John had to rely on others in Fastolf's circle to trust his word that the new will did indeed represent Sir John's final intentions. At the same time, neither the original will of June 1459 nor the new one of 3 November made any specific bequests to anyone else among Fastolf's servants and advisers. If they were to receive the reward they felt they deserved for years of devoted and often badly paid service – reward which many of them had been promised over the years by Fastolf himself – they in turn would now have to rely on John to give them their due. Their support for John's claim to the estate might therefore go hand in hand with an expectation that John would give their own claims similar recognition.

William Worcester, for example, had been away from Caister during the weekend when the new will had allegedly been dictated, and did not get back in time to see his master before he died. As a result, he was not in a position either to confirm or to deny John's story, although the fact that this conscientious man made no protest in the weeks immediately after Fastolf's death suggests both that the idea of John as Fastolf's heir did not come as a surprise to him, and that he saw nothing inherently improbable in John's version of his master's last days. Despite the fact that he could not testify to Sir John's final wishes, Worcester's closeness to Fastolf over the previous twenty years, and his detailed knowledge of the old knight's affairs, meant that he would be an invaluable ally in John's campaign to secure the inheritance. William Paston seized the opportunity of their journey to London together to sound him out on his brother's behalf, and reported back that Worcester would be loyal to John if he were confident that John would be loyal to him. '. . . *he trusts verily you should do for him and for his avail in reason*', William wrote, '*and I doubt not, if he may verily and faithfully understand you so disposed toward him, you shall find him faithful to you in like wise*'. Worcester had steadfastly tolerated years of high-handed treatment from an increasingly irascible old man, and what he now looked for was a settlement from Fastolf's will which would allow him to live independently in a modicum of comfort. William Paston believed his claims should be taken seriously. '*I understand by him he will never have other master but his old master*', he told his brother, '*and to my conceit it were pity unless he shall stand in such case by my master that he should never need service, considering how my master trusted him and the long years that he has been with him in, and many shrewd journeys for his sake*'.[9]

The very fact that William felt it necessary to point out to his brother that Worcester would be a deserving beneficiary suggests that there was some hesitation in his mind, only days after Fastolf's death, about whether John would give sufficient acknowledgement to other claims on the estate. Like Fastolf himself, John was not a natural politician; he had little instinctive understanding of other people's emotional reactions or of the motivations which drove their behaviour. His perception of the world was rooted in concepts of right and wrong which he understood as absolute values, making little allowance for the nuances and complexities of human interaction. Rather than seeing that a policy of trust and open-handedness might be the best way of sustaining a relationship of mutual support with his colleagues in Fastolf's service, John's overriding concern from the very beginning was to establish his own rights as Sir John's heir, and the uncertainty of his position made him immediately suspicious that others might try to challenge his claim to inherit. While he kept watch for signs of disaffection or disloyalty in those around him, they interpreted his behaviour as an indication that what they considered their rightful share in the will and its administration might be withheld. The result was a vicious circle of mistrust which spiralled out of control with remarkable speed.

Its corrosive effects were already apparent by the new year. In January 1460 William Paston and William Worcester were again in London, but this time neither travelling nor working together. Paston – this time accompanied by Thomas Playter, one of Fastolf's lawyers – was trying to find out whether Worcester was actively pursuing his own agenda in relation to the will, 'but we cannot espy openly that he makes any labour', William reported, 'nor privily neither, by no manner of hearkening nor by no manner of talking'. Playter had spoken to him face to face, 'and he says right not, saving that he will be rewarded for his long true service of my master's good, and like as my master promised him in his life'. Worcester was now presenting his demand for a share of the inheritance in such bald terms because his confidence that he would receive satisfaction from John Paston had been badly eroded – and his willingness to support John's claim to be Fastolf's heir was proportionately diminished. Playter tried to press him on the point: 'and ever more when I say unto him that it may not be gainsaid but, as touching to all my master's lands in Norfolk and Suffolk, it is his will and sufficient proof thereupon that you should have it, etc; and then he answers and prays me no more to speak of that matter'. The difficulty for John was that he still needed Worcester, even if he was no longer sure he could trust him. Worcester's intimate knowledge of Fastolf's finances meant that his participation in the administration of the estate might make a vast difference to its final value – the huge sum of 1,000 or even 2,000 marks, Worcester told Playter. Playter did not know whether or not to believe him, 'and to feel him whether he lied or said truth, I asked him whether he would take that which might not be saved without his help for his reward, and he said yes, with good will', a response which went a long way towards convincing him that Worcester was telling the truth.[10] It did not apparently occur to Playter, or to John, that it might be a political mistake to raise this possibility without any intention of seeing the offer through. From Worcester's point of view, it was a welcome suggestion which disappeared like smoke – a disappointment which could only re-inforce his conviction that he was not being treated fairly and honestly.

A week later, Worcester wrote a letter justifying his actions to another of Fastolf's servants, asking that '*such as you deem have misreported causelessly of me, I pray you that they see my letter as well as my friends*' – an instruction which was clearly carried out, since Margaret asked Richard Calle, the Pastons' estate manager, to copy it to send to her husband. Worcester's grievances were now multiplying, as the pervasive atmosphere of mistrust compounded his alienation from John. He had heard that his departure from Norfolk for London had been seen as deeply suspicious – '*that I should, by crafty counsel of some men, suddenly have departed into these parts, etc, and that I estranged me from certain persons too much, etc*' – a charge against which he indignantly defended himself. Far from being suborned by the Pastons' enemies, he had worked hard over the previous three months to do his part in the execution of the will, committing himself in the process to payments of more than £100 for the funeral and other expenses. He now needed to repay these debts in London, but John had not made it a priority to see that he was reimbursed from Fastolf's estate, with the result that he was now facing serious financial difficulties. More, he had been hurt and angered to find that, despite his closeness to Fastolf, he was not straightfor-wardly allowed to distribute money from the estate in alms:

> I was not put in trust among the said attorneys there to give one penny for my master's soul but I paid it of my own purse before; neither in trust nor favour to give an alms gown but that I prayed for it as a stranger should do, albeit my authority is as great as theirs, and rather more . . . And these precedents considered would discourage any man to abide but a little amongst them that so estranged themselves from me and mistrusted me without any cause.[11]

If Worcester felt that he had not been treated with proper confidence, he also believed that he had a specific claim on the inheritance which John and his co-executor Thomas Howes – Worcester's uncle by marriage – were try-ing to withhold from him. Fastolf, he said, had granted him a modest amount of land in return for his years of loyal service – '*a livelihood accord-ing to my degree, that I, my wife and my children should have cause to pray for him'.* Howes had even been there when the promise was made; *'this is truth, by the blessed sacrament',* Worcester protested in some agitation. *'And because I demanded my right and duty of my Master Paston, he is not pleased'.* For Worcester, the security of his family's future was at stake, but this was about more than money. It was also about respect, and proper acknowledgement of the role he had played in Fastolf's life. *'It is not universally known that I was one of the chief that kept both my Master Paston and my uncle in my master's favour and trust',* he wrote with bitter dignity; *'and if I would have laboured the contrary, by my soul – that is the greatest oath that I may swear of myself – they had never been nigh my master in that case they stand now. And if they will labour to damage or hinder me, all the world will misreport of them and little trust them, neither they shall not have worship or profit by it.'* However much John felt Worcester could not be trusted, in Worcester's eyes it was he who had been needlessly alienated and excluded by John. *'I would be to them as loving and as well-willing as I can',* he added, *'so I find cause'.*[12]

If it had been only Worcester who moved in a matter of weeks from working with John to a position of at best suspicion and at worst outright hostility, it might be tempting to give a little more credence to Friar Brackley's intemperate description of his duplicity. But it was not just Worcester: another relationship which broke down with astonishing rapidity, and even more serious consequences, was John's friendship with Judge William Yelverton. John and Yelverton went back a long way; they had worked closely together in the campaign against John Heydon and Thomas Tuddenham in 1450, and since then had been the two most senior figures in Fastolf's inner circle. Yelverton's co-operation would be crucial if the business of the will were to be settled quickly and peacefully. He was an ambitious man, and perhaps it would never have been easy for him to accept the idea of John as the main beneficiary of Fastolf's estate. What seems more certain is that John himself feared that Yelverton might resent his position, since the breach was precipitated only weeks after Fastolf's death when John accused Yelverton of betraying him.

The quarrel probably took place on the day of Fastolf's funeral; certainly, it happened at St Benet's Abbey on an occasion when John Brackley was also present, and it seems unlikely that John Paston, Yelverton and Brackley were together there more than once in the last weeks of 1459. The only surviving details come from a letter written by Brackley, who walked in when the argument was already in full flow – not in time to hear John's accusation, but just at the point when Yelverton exclaimed in response, *'Whosoever says that of me, he lies falsely in his head!'*[13] Being the fiercely partisan man that he was, Brackley did not stop to ask what the row was about, but it emerged in January that John suspected Yelverton of having instigated the claim to Caister made by Elizabeth Heveningham and her husband John Wyndham. Thomas Playter spoke to Yelverton towards the end of the month during his visit to London, and the judge denied it vehemently: '*as touching to the provoking that my lady Heveningham should sue forth for Caister, he says he never thought it, but the sending to my said lady was by a man of his . . . to know if she had any tidings from Coventry, and no other manner of language*'. Playter's judgement was that Yelverton was not yet completely alienated, nor irretrievably hostile to John's claim to the inheritance – but that his continued support and co-operation would depend on John's willingness to offer him trust and friendship. '*I understand he will not be strange to fall in with you again*', Playter wrote, '*and also that he will not hurt you in your bargain if you could be friendlily disposed toward him as you have been; for without a friendlihood of your part he seems he should not greatly help you in your bargain, so I feel him. He lives somewhat aloof, and not utterly malicious against you*.'[14]

Playter's advice, however, was too little, too late. By the time he recommended this course of action to John, he had already accompanied William Paston on a visit to John Stokes, the judge in the Archbishop's court who was advising them on their application for probate of the will, and '*informed him of Yelverton's needless wasting of my master's goods, and the mistrust that he had in them whom my master most earthly trusted, and how his desire was singularly to have had the keeping of Caister and all stuff within it, and there to have lodged himself; and also how he did move my lady Heveningham, etc*'. These were very serious allegations, and John was proposing very serious consequences: to remove Yelverton altogether from the will and its execution. '*We asked him*', Paston and Playter reported, '*that, if Yelverton would not be reformed, whether for the discharge of all your conscience a means might be found to avoid him out of the testament. And he said, if he be false to the dead, it is a cause reasonable, and perjury is another cause*'.[15] On this evidence, the chances of John trusting Yelverton enough to re-establish friendly relations with him were negligible. Meanwhile, should Yelverton hear a word about this consultation with Stokes, he would take it as no less than a declaration of war.

Just how badly the two men had fallen out was clear from a visit Yelverton and his wife paid to Friar Brackley's convent not long afterwards, in the early spring of 1460. After a good lunch and plenty of fine wine, the judge began to talk more unguardedly than usual, '*and held on so sore he could not cease*',

Brackley reported to William Paston, '. . . *and there was not forgotten none unkindness of my master J.P. your brother'*. Yelverton's acute sense of betrayal emerges powerfully despite the hostility of Brackley's account, and it was a sense compounded by what he felt was the indifference of his peers. When the Prior told him how shocked and how sorry he was that two such good friends should have argued in this way, Yelverton's retort was simply that *'there is no man busy to bring us together'*.[16] If the breach with William Worcester was a disastrous loss in terms of his comprehensive knowledge of Fastolf's affairs, the rift with Yelverton was even more so in terms of John's chances of making his claim good in the wider world. Yelverton was a judge in the court of King's Bench, with political clout and powerful connections, and he could make life very difficult for John if he chose. The practical consequences of these disintegrating friendships were already beginning to become apparent by the end of January 1460. When William Paston and Thomas Playter visited John Stokes to warn him against Yelverton, Stokes had already been informed – allegedly *'by one which he could not remember'* – that what was now being put forward as Fastolf's will was a forgery.[17]

Failing relationships with former friends were not the only problems John faced by the spring of 1460: his enemies were never likely to stand quietly by while he took possession of such a rich inheritance. Their first move was made on Tuesday 29 April, not quite five months after Fastolf's death, when an inquiry into Sir John's lands – officially known as an inquisition *post mortem*, designed to establish whether the King had any interest in the estate – was held at Buckenham in eastern Norfolk. The jurors declared that Fastolf's rightful heir was his distant relative Thomas Fastolf of Cowhaugh, over whose wardship the old knight had fought such a bitter battle with Philip Wentworth. There was much that was amiss with this inquisition – the jurors were so well informed, for example, that they gave the wrong date for Fastolf's death – but the principal error was that it had taken place at all: no royal commission had been granted to authorise it. The men who held the hearing were closely associated with John Heydon, the Pastons' chief enemy for many years now, and Philip Wentworth himself. The inquiry was not legal, and they could not hope to make its conclusions stand up in the long run, but it nevertheless served as a pre-emptive strike, designed to throw obstacles in John Paston's way by producing evidence which he would have to work hard to set aside.

This was worrying enough, but what made it worse was the possibility that some of John's former friends might now ally themselves with his opponents, a spectre which raised its head only three days after the bogus inquisition was held. On 2 May, William Paston told his brother that he had spoken with Fastolf's servant John Bocking, and the news was not good. '*He had but few words*', William wrote, '*but I felt by him he was right evil disposed to the parson*' – Thomas Howes – '*and you; but covert language he had. I think he is assented to the finding of this office taken at Buckenham*'. It had come to something if, knowing what had happened when his master was alive, Bocking was now prepared to fall in with Wentworth and Heydon – a development which was all the more threatening given Bocking's friendship with William Worcester. '*I understand that this Bocking and Worcester have great trust in their own lewd conceit*', William reported to his brother. '. . . *it is he that makes William Worcester so forward as he is.*'[18] Friar Brackley, meanwhile, was convinced that Judge Yelverton and his servants were, '*with their heady and fumous language*', fanning the flames of opposition to John by spreading '*lewd and shrewd*' allegations about his conduct.[19] In a terse postscript, William Paston made it clear what he believed lay behind the reverses they were now beginning to suffer. '*Omnia pro pecunia facta sunt*', he said: everything is done for money. In one sense, of course, he was right; but this reductive view of the motivation of those within Fastolf's circle who now opposed them took no account of the fact that the issue of money was inseparable from that of recognition for service given. '*Bocking told me this day that he stood as well in conceit with my master Fastolf four days before he died as any man in England*', William reported. It did John no good to dismiss such talk as window-dressing for unjustified claims on his patron's estate; it did not seem to cross his mind that greed might also appear, from the outside at least, to be the motive for his own actions. Whatever the rights and wrongs of the situation, its seriousness was now clear to William Paston. '*It is full necessary to make you strong by lordship and other means*', he warned his brother.[20]

The difficulty was that there could scarcely have been a worse time to be looking for help from powerful men. Political division at the highest levels of government was now sliding inexorably towards civil war. The stand-off between Queen Margaret and the Duke of York had persisted until the autumn of 1458, when the Queen brought her husband back to London and seized control of government. In the face of this self-assertion – and an attempt by members of the royal household to murder the Earl of Warwick – the Yorkist lords had little choice but to withdraw from the capital. Margaret sought to press home her advantage in the summer of 1459 by summoning the rest of the nobility to a great council at Coventry. In response, just as they had done four years earlier, York, Warwick and

Salisbury mustered their forces and set out to defend themselves. In September, at Blore Heath in Staffordshire, Salisbury succeeded in fending off an attempt to intercept him on his way to meet York at Ludlow Castle, a skirmish which cost a couple of thousand lives. Three weeks later, the main contingent of Queen Margaret's forces arrived to confront York and his allies just south of Ludlow at Ludford Bridge. This time the outcome was much less bloody, but much more damaging to the Yorkist cause. The soldiers whom the Earl of Warwick had brought with him from the garrison at Calais proved unwilling to fight against an army under the command – nominal though it was – of their King. Their defection undermined York's military position so severely that he was forced to flee under cover of darkness. He escaped to Ireland, accompanied by his sixteen-year-old son Edmund, Earl of Rutland, while his eldest son, seventeen-year-old Edward, Earl of March, took ship for Calais with the Earls of Salisbury and Warwick.

The Queen was determined to finish what she had started. A parliament was summoned to meet at Coventry, and in late November 1459 – a few weeks after Sir John Fastolf's death – a bill of attainder declared that the Yorkist lords were guilty of treason, and their lands forfeit to the crown. All hope of conciliation was now gone. Faced with an enemy as implacable as Queen Margaret had now shown herself to be, York and the Nevilles would have to fight not only for control of government, but for their own survival. In June 1460, after consultation with York in Dublin, the Earls of Warwick, Salisbury and March set sail from Calais for the Kent coast. They landed at Sandwich on 26 June, and a week later the citizens of London – who were deeply uneasy about the Queen's decision to base her government in the midlands and the north – opened the city gates to let their forces into the capital. On 5 July, a Yorkist army led by the Earls of Warwick and March left London to advance against Queen Margaret and her allies. While the Queen herself and her six-year-old son Prince Edward remained at Coventry, her forces in turn marched south under the command of the Duke of Buckingham and the Earl of Shrewsbury, taking King Henry with them. This time, the King's presence did nothing to rally his own troops or deter his opponents. On 10 July, in heavy rain, the two armies met just outside Northampton, and the Yorkists overran the field in little more than an hour as their enemies' guns sank into the mud. Buckingham and Shrewsbury were killed, and King Henry – who sat in his tent while the battle was fought – was captured. With the King in their custody, Warwick and March returned to join the Earl of Salisbury in London, where a detachment of Lancastrian forces was still holding out in the Tower under the command of

Lord Scales and Lord Moleyns, John Paston's old adversaries from the dispute over Gresham ten years earlier. Realising that their position was now hopeless, Scales and Moleyns tried to reach sanctuary at Westminster Abbey during the night of 19 July. Moleyns escaped, but Scales was recognised by boatmen on the Thames. He was murdered, and his naked body dumped in the churchyard of St Mary Overy in Southwark. It fell to the Earl of March – Scales's godson – to give him an honourable burial.

Nine months on from the rout at Ludford Bridge, the Yorkists' reversal of their political fortunes was complete. The Duke of York made preparations to return to England, and a parliament was called to meet at Westminster in October. The problem confronting him was what to do next. Publicly, York still maintained that he was a loyal subject of King Henry, seeking reform of government in the interests of the common good. In practice, however, there could be no lasting security for him while Henry remained on the throne, now that the Queen had made plain her determination to destroy him and all those who stood with him. With the King a prisoner, York was safe for the time being, but keeping the King in captivity would not in the long run enable the Duke either to reunite the political community or to establish a legitimate basis for his government. Meanwhile – with York and the rest of the nobility now playing for such terrifyingly high stakes – the normal cut and thrust of politics at a local level had been all but suspended. The fact that the entire framework of government was under threat meant that it was too dangerous for the gentry of Norfolk (or anywhere else) to indulge their competitive instincts to the full: it was in no one's interests to rock the boat when the waters around them were so treacherous. Even for a prize as valuable as the Fastolf inheritance, it was not worth taking risks which, in the absence of any effective royal authority, might precipitate the region into a state of anarchy. John Heydon and Philip Wentworth were not about to let John Paston's claim to be Fastolf's heir go unchallenged, and they had placed a stumbling-block in his way by staging a fraudulent inquiry into Fastolf's lands – but neither they nor anyone else simply helped themselves to any of the estates as Lord Moleyns had done at Gresham a decade earlier.

Queen Margaret had retreated into Wales with her remaining noble allies after the defeat at Northampton, and it was clear that the battle would not be the last confrontation of what was now, more clearly than ever before, all-out war. Nevertheless, for the time being at least, the Yorkist resurgence did seem to be good news for John Paston. His opponents' close connections with the royal household meant that it was always unlikely that he would find support from a regime under the leadership of the Queen. By the same token, Heydon and Wentworth could hope for little favour from the Duke of York – whose attainder Heydon had helped to draft at the Coventry parliament in November 1459 – whereas John was well placed to benefit from his restoration to power. By the autumn John had been elected as MP for Norfolk in the forthcoming parliament, and Friar Brackley was describing the Earl of Warwick in straightforward, if typically apocalyptic, terms as their saviour. '. . .*if aught come to my lord Warwick but good*,' he wrote, '*farewell you, farewell I, and all our friends, for by the way of my soul this land were utterly undone, as God forbid*.'[21] John also took the opportunity to offer the Duke a particular service: York's wife Cecily and their three youngest children, fourteen-year-old Margaret, George, who was ten, and Richard, seven, came to stay at Fastolf's house in Southwark in September to await the Duke's return from Ireland. The Duchess left after a few days to travel to meet her husband, but the children stayed on, visited every day by the Earl of March, their eldest brother.

If the political world seemed to be turning in John's favour, there was also reason to feel a little more positive about the practical business concerning Fastolf's will. Legitimate inquisitions *post mortem* into Sir John's estates were finally held in Norfolk and Suffolk in late October, and '*the matter is well sped after your intent, blessed be God, as you shall have knowledge of in haste*', Margaret reported to her husband after the Norfolk hearing.[22] What this meant, it transpired when Thomas Playter wrote with more detailed news, was that the jurors had confirmed what lands Fastolf had held, but had not committed themselves on the question of who should inherit them. While this gave no active support to John's case, at least it left the issue open and did not present him with further obstacles by registering another potential claimant. On the other hand, no progress had been made towards repairing the ruptured relationships within Fastolf's household. By the beginning of December, it was apparent that William Worcester was avoiding further contact with the Pastons; '*his wife says always that he is out when that I send for him*', Margaret told John in some frustration.[23] Not only that, but there were worrying signs that Thomas Howes might be developing grudges very similar to some of Worcester's. Howes had a vital role to play as the only one of Fastolf's executors appointed to share the administration of the estate with John under the terms of the new will. It had been clear from the outset, however, that John was the senior partner; Howes was politically a little naïve, and certainly not the most independent thinker among Fastolf's servants. All the more reason, perhaps, to have taken particular care to keep him on side – but

John seems simply to have taken his support for granted. By January 1461, when the Prior of Bromholm applied to Howes for a grant of alms from Fastolf's estate, the chaplain told him to speak to John instead, saying that he had recently given money to another monastery '*whereof, as he said to me*', the Prior told John, '*you grudged and were in manner displeased*'. It was John, Howes explained, who made the decisions, '*for he said to me you had much good of the dead to dispose, what of your father, God bless that soul . . . and what now of his good master Fastolf.*'[24] This was uncomfortably reminiscent of Friar Brackley's account of some of Worcester's complaints ('*he says that, whereas your father was a very rich judge, you did almost nothing for him in distributing alms for his soul, and since you did nothing for your own father, why should you do anything for Master Fastolf?*').[25]

If John even noticed the potential implications of Howes's words, he had little time to contemplate their significance. Political events were now moving at frightening speed. By the time the Duke of York arrived in London on 10 October 1460, he had decided that the only way out of the conflict was to cut through the whole question of who should rule in the name of the hapless King Henry by claiming the throne for himself. He rode into the capital under banners displaying the royal arms of England rather than the ducal ones of York, and on his arrival at Westminster Hall, where the lords of the realm were assembled for the parliament, he walked immediately to the marble throne as if to take up his rightful place as king. He had hoped for acclamation: instead, he was met with consternation and confusion. York's position as the next in line to the throne after King Henry and his son was undeniable, but his claim to supersede them – based on his mother's descent from Lionel of Clarence, the second son of Edward III – was controversial in the extreme. Even had it been unequivocally established that the crown could pass through the female line, which it was not, the legitimacy of the Lancastrian dynasty had been put beyond question almost half a century earlier by Henry V's victories in France – triumphs which demonstrated that his kingship was sanctioned by God. Since then, of course, Henry VI's personal inadequacies had gone a long way towards undermining the security of his crown, but it was not a straightforward matter to argue that he had forfeited his right to rule. Two fourteenth-century kings, Edward II and Richard II, had been overthrown as a result of their tyrannical behaviour, but the grounds which were used to justify their depositions could not easily be applied to Henry VI: he had not actively threatened the interests of his realm and his subjects, even if only because he had not actively done anything at all.

For York, his claim to the throne seemed to offer a means of establishing his own rule on a foundation which would give Queen Margaret no foothold from which to regain power. For his peers, however, the idea of York as king compounded the problem rather than solved it. They desperately needed to find some way to reunite the political community as a whole under a workable government – and, after a decade of conflict, York was too divisive a figure to achieve that. Apart from anything else, in his enemies' eyes he had just vindicated the charges of treason which the Queen had laid against him. On 31 October, after three weeks of urgent negotiation, a formal settlement was announced: King Henry would remain on the throne, but the Duke of York was named as his heir – a compromise which served the immediate purpose of acknowledging York's claims while allowing his regime to function in King Henry's name. It also meant that a renewal of war was inevitable, since Queen Margaret would never accept the disinheritance of her son.

By December the Queen had travelled north to seek support for her cause at the Scottish court, leaving her forces in Wales under the command of Jasper Tudor, Earl of Pembroke, her husband's half-brother.[26] Other nobles loyal to the Queen, including the heirs of the Duke of Somerset and the Earl of Northumberland who had been killed at St Albans five years earlier, were mustering men in the north of England. York dispatched his eldest son, the Earl of March, to head off the Lancastrian threat in Wales, and marched north himself with his brother-in-law the Earl of Salisbury. The resistance he met was much greater than he had foreseen. On 30 December 1460, in a vicious battle fought just south of Wakefield in Yorkshire, the Duke of York was defeated and killed. His seventeen-year-old son Edmund, Earl of Rutland, died with him; so too did Salisbury's son Thomas Neville. Salisbury himself was captured and executed once the fighting was over. A few days later, the severed heads of the four men – the Duke's festooned with a paper crown – were impaled on spikes on the gates of the city of York by their jubilant enemies.

As soon as she heard the news, Queen Margaret left Scotland to rejoin her army, and immediately pushed south towards London, where Salisbury's eldest son, the Earl of Warwick, had been left in command. There was already deep suspicion in the capital, and more widely in the south of the country, about the Queen's intentions, and it was compounded by the fact that she allowed her troops – who included French and Scottish mercenaries – to loot the towns through which they marched. '*In this country every man is willing to go with my lords here*', John Paston was told by his youngest brother Clement, a student in London, on 23 January; '*and I hope God shall help them, for the people in the north rob and steal and are appointed to pillage all this country, and give away men's goods and livelihoods in the south country, and that will ask a mischief.*'[27] Warwick gathered his forces and moved north to St Albans, taking the captive King Henry with him. Despite having several days to prepare his defences, the Earl misjudged his enemies' movements and was taken by surprise when the Lancastrian army attacked on 17 February. For the second time in six years, a running battle was fought through the streets of the town; this time, it was the Yorkists who lost both the battle and the person of the King to the Lancastrians. Henry was found sitting quietly under a tree, and taken to St Albans Abbey to be reunited with his wife and son. Warwick was forced to retreat northwards from the scene of his first military defeat, leaving the way clear for the Queen to advance on London.

Only five months after York's return from Ireland to take control of government, the Duke was dead and his cause seemed lost. The last remaining hopes of his supporters rested on the shoulders of his son and heir Edward, Earl of March, who, at eighteen, was now Duke of York in his father's place. Edward's sortie into Wales had provided the only good news in two miserable months for York's allies: on 2 February, at Mortimer's Cross near Wigmore, he inflicted a crushing defeat on the Lancastrian contingent in the west under the command of the Earl of Pembroke. When he learned what had happened at St Albans, Edward turned his troops eastwards as quickly as he could, joining forces with the retreating army of the Earl of Warwick in the Cotswolds on 22 February. Their only hope, it seemed, was to race south in an attempt to take the capital before the Queen could do so – although it scarcely seemed possible that this was a race they could win, given that London was at least four days' march away, and the Lancastrian army had already reached Barnet, only ten miles from the city. It was nevertheless a chance they had to take. As they drew nearer to London, the extraordinary news reached them that Queen Margaret had not advanced into the city, but instead retreated twenty miles from Barnet to Dunstable. She was now paying the price for identifying herself too closely with a regional interest rather than a national one, and for failing to keep her troops on a tight leash: the Londoners – fearing the devastation of their city by a northern rabble – had closed the gates against her. As she hesitated, word came of the Yorkist advance. Margaret turned away northwards, her men still looting as they went, leaving Edward and Warwick to sweep into the capital on Thursday 26 February.

Edward now had no choice but to show his hand. The attempt to construct a Yorkist regime under the nominal authority of King Henry had ceased to be an option once the King himself was recaptured by Lancastrian forces. In any case, it was striking that Henry's presence at the Queen's side had not made his subjects in London any more inclined to admit her army to their city. With the authority of the Lancastrian crown now so profoundly compromised, the way was finally open for Edward to claim the throne for himself. It was, of course, only five months since his father's attempt to do the same thing had been rebuffed by his peers – but Edward's position in the spring of 1461 was significantly different from his father's in the autumn of 1460. For what it was worth, Edward could argue that his claim was technically justified by the terms of the formal settlement which had named the Duke of York as King Henry's heir. In theory at least, the King had endorsed the agreement; he could therefore be said – through his 'decision' to rejoin his wife at St Albans – to have reneged on his oath and, in effect, resigned his crown. More importantly, Edward himself was a young, charismatic and commanding leader who offered the political community the chance of a fresh start – something which his father, tainted by his central role in ten years of bitter and bloody conflict, could never have provided. On Wednesday 4 March, Edward took his seat on the throne in the Great Hall at Westminster, and was formally acclaimed as King Edward IV.

The cautious welcome which the new King received in London was echoed by many of the East Anglian gentry, including the Pastons, whose interests clearly now lay with the restoration of effective government under a Yorkist crown. For one member of the family, however, Edward's accession had already come at too great a price. John's sister Elizabeth had endured a long and unhappy wait before her mother and brother had found her a suitable marriage. Just two years after her wedding, and only three months after giving birth to her first baby – a son named Edward – she was left a widow when her husband Robert Poynings was killed fighting for the Earl of Warwick at St Albans. John himself was already well aware of the dangers of the battlefield: his friend Osbert Mundford had died in the summer of 1460, executed for his part in the unsuccessful Lancastrian defence of Sandwich against the invasion of the Yorkist earls. However relieved he was at the accession of a Yorkist king, John was deeply reluctant to commit either himself or his teenage sons to take up arms on Edward's behalf – and, with the Queen's forces regrouping in the north, it was clear that more fighting was inevitable if the new regime were ever to be securely established. In January, before the battle at St Albans, his brother Clement had suggested that John should respond to Warwick's call to arms in London, '*for it lies more upon your worship and touches you more near than other men of that country, and also you are more had in favour with my lords here*'[28] – advice which John must have been heartily glad he chose to ignore when news came of the Earl's defeat. By March – in a letter so cagily drafted that he referred to himself in the third person – John was protesting that the situation was too dangerous to allow him to leave Norfolk, '*for he would have his own men about him if need were here*', although he was prepared to send one of his household men to join King Edward if it became clear that '*other men of worship of this country*' were doing the same.[29] It was not only the obvious hazards of combat against which he was trying to protect himself. Just as John was hoping for the final defeat of the Queen and her allies by the new Yorkist government, his enemy John Heydon was banking on the reverse, and had laid plans '*to bring you to the presence of such a lord in the north as shall not be for your ease*', Margaret warned her husband, '*but to jeopardy of your life, or great and importable loss of your goods*'. The world was so deeply uncertain that Margaret did not dare refer to Heydon by name in case her letter fell into the wrong hands; the threat came, she told John carefully, '*by the means of the son of William Baxter that lies buried in the Grey Friars*'.[30]

King Edward left London on 13 March – without John Paston in his company – to advance against the Queen's army, which was massing in the north under the command of the Duke of Somerset and the Earl of Northumberland. The Earl of Warwick had gone ahead a week earlier to muster his men in the midlands; he and Edward joined forces at Notting ham before pressing on to Pontefract. On Palm Sunday, 29 March 1461, Edward and Warwick took up position just outside the village of Towton in Yorkshire for one last assault on their enemies. Both sides ordered their troops that quarter should neither be asked nor given once battle was joined. In driving snow, the fighting lasted more than eight hours. The slaughter was so great that the two sides had to draw back from time to time while the bodies of the dead were dragged out of their way. In the middle of the afternoon, the arrival of the Duke of Norfolk with reinforcements for the Yorkist army gave Edward's men fresh impetus; even then, it was another couple of hours before the Lancastrian line finally broke. The Yorkist surge became a rout in which thousands more died, cut down as they tried to flee, or drowned in the attempt to cross the freezing waters of the river which blocked their retreat. When the news reached the city of York, where Queen Margaret was waiting with her husband and son, the King, Queen and Prince fled first to Newcastle, and then to Scotland. For Edward and

Warwick – after years of conflict which had claimed the lives of their fathers and brothers as well as thousands of their men – it was an overwhelming victory. Edward of March was now, in fact as well as in name, King of England.

CHAPTER EIGHT

– *the infinite process* –

Edward IV was crowned in Westminster Abbey on Sunday, 28 June 1461. After the ceremony, as he walked under a canopy of cloth of gold to Westminster Hall for the coronation feast, the contrast between the new King and the shabby and distracted figure of his predecessor could not have been more arresting. At nineteen, Edward was unusually tall, standing almost six foot four, and strikingly handsome; '*I cannot remember ever having seen a finer-looking man*', Philippe de Commines, a Burgundian diplomat who met him several times, later wrote.[1] The lavish ceremonial could not, however, disguise the fact that Edward's authority remained precarious in many parts of the country, especially the north, where there was still significant support for the Lancastrian cause. The Lancastrian royal family were still in Scotland, and there were already worrying signs that the Scots and the French would make the most of the opportunity to destabilise the new government in England by offering Henry and Margaret their help. Nevertheless, it was also clear that the young King intended to impose his rule throughout his kingdom as quickly and decisively as possible; the date of the coronation itself had been brought forward by two weeks to allow him to leave London all the sooner to deal with the threats he faced. For the first time in years, a framework of government was in place in which the landed classes could feel a substantial degree of confidence.

As a result, Edward's accession to the throne broke the spell which had held Norfolk politics virtually in a state of suspended animation. Landowners were once again free to pursue their own interests as aggressively as they could without fearing that conflict might escalate into uncontainable disorder. In fact, they had every incentive to do so, in the attempt to secure their position to the best possible advantage while the new regime was still in the process of taking shape. Of course, the turbulent and frightening events of the past months had not prevented gentlemen such as John Paston from continuing to worry about their private concerns. Even in January 1461, with Queen Margaret's army advancing on the capital, John was still sending instructions for the prosecution of his own business to his brother Clement in London, but Clement – who had a wise head on his young shoulders – reminded him that it was a complicated time to be asking lords for favours. '. . . *if you do well*', he wrote, '*remember these lords have many matters to think on, and if it be forgotten the harm is yours*'.[2] Now that King Edward's victory was clear, John had a fresh opportunity to press his claim to the Fastolf inheritance while his enemy Heydon was otherwise occupied trying to scramble to safety. However, he was not the only one who saw the chance to profit from the change of government. The nobility as well as the gentry had everything to play for in the establishment of a new local order – and, amid the frantic jostling for position, it was not John's search for support that caught the attention of great lords, but the conspicuous attractions of the Fastolf estates themselves.

John's old unreliable patron the Duke of Norfolk was one of the few magnates who had been prepared to associate himself with the Yorkist cause at a relatively early stage in the conflict, and he could claim an important part in Edward's victory through his timely arrival on the battlefield at Towton. After years of struggling against the local influence of the Duke of Suffolk, it seemed that Norfolk at last had a chance to emerge as the leading power in East Anglia under the new Yorkist regime. Unfortunately for John, the Duke had also had an acquisitive eye on the castle at Caister for a very long time. He had tried to persuade Fastolf to sell it to him on a number of occasions, most recently only two months before the old man's death. Now, the combination of Norfolk's new-found influence with the uncertainty of John's claim to be Fastolf's heir gave the Duke the perfect opportunity to intervene in the matter of the inheritance – and it was no longer the case that direct action was too risky a strategy for landowners keen to assert their rights to disputed properties. By the beginning of June, Norfolk had sent his men to take Caister for himself.

The new King's government was only two months old, and already John's hopes that he would find it easier to secure his position in this new Yorkist world than in the old Lancastrian one had been shattered. Edward had not yet even returned to the capital; he had moved north from Towton to impress his personal authority on the north-east with visits to Durham and Newcastle, and was now making his way slowly back to London for his coronation, via Queen Margaret's former strongholds in the north-west and the midlands. John immediately set out northwards to petition the King for help, and sent his estate manager Richard Calle to Framlingham to make representations to the Duke himself. The response was not encouraging. Norfolk refused even to see Calle, but messages were passed backwards and forwards by the Pastons' acquaintance Richard Southwell, a leading member of the Duke's household. Norfolk sent to ask why John had not come to see him in person, '*and I told him you were with the King*', Calle wrote, '*and so he sent me word that an answer should be made by Southwell to the King, saying that two or three heirs had been with my lord and showed their evidence and delivered it to my lord, saying they have had great wrong, beseeching my lord that it might be reformed; wherefore he commanded me that I should go home, for other answer could I none have*'. The Duke had no intention of ordering his men to leave Caister; '*he trusts to God to show such evidence to the King and to the lords that he should have best right and title thereto*', Calle reported. He advised his master to wait with the King until Norfolk's letter arrived and it was clear exactly what claims the Duke was making, but then to take his own evidence to London as quickly as possible to prove his case in the courts. Calle also, very circumspectly, let John know that more direct steps could be taken to reclaim the castle, if he felt it necessary: '*there be but two or three men within the place, and if you think it best to etc, send word and I suppose a remedy should be had*'.[3] However, attempting to eject a Duke from a valuable house by force would not necessarily be either wise or easy. Norfolk's men were still in control there by 21 June when John arrived home.

The loss of Caister was devastating. It was the heart of the inheritance, the place where Fastolf was born and where he died, and the site of the college which John was to found in the old knight's name and for the good of his soul. It was not, however, the only property to be snatched from John's hands during the summer of 1461. The valuable manor of Dedham lay just over the Suffolk border in Essex, and had been the subject of an ill-tempered dispute between Fastolf and the late Duke of Suffolk, who had seized the estate in 1447. The Duke's fall from power in 1450 ended the dispute in Fastolf's favour, but Suffolk's widow had not forgotten her husband's claim in the decade since his death. Alice Chaucer, now dowager Duchess of Suffolk, could scarcely have been more closely associated with the Lancastrian court in the 1440s and 1450s, and it therefore seemed highly unlikely that she would be in any position to benefit from the Yorkist victory. It was not for nothing, however, that her husband had appointed her sole executor of his will, declaring that, '*above all the earth, my singular trust is most in her*'.[4] With characteristic foresight, she took the opportunity before the autumn of 1460 to arrange a marriage alliance between her son John, the young Duke of Suffolk, and the Duke of York's daughter Elizabeth. Her political agility was such that in October of that year, with the conflict almost at its height, she seemed to be in favour with both sides. When she wanted to lobby for her own choice of sheriff in Norfolk and Suffolk, she was able to send her son to petition his new father-in-law York; at the same time, Friar Brackley was telling John Paston that the Duchess was '*in great favour with the Queen and Prince*', and suggesting pointedly that the loyalty of her son to the Yorkist cause should be tried in battle.[5]

Four months later, the eighteen-year-old Duke passed Brackley's test with flying colours, and impeccable timing. He fought alongside the Earl of Warwick at St Albans in February, and then commanded the Yorkist vanguard for his brother-in-law King Edward on the advance towards Towton. As a result, he found himself well placed in the spring of 1461 at the heart of the new regime. The Duke himself had three more years to wait before taking formal possession of his inheritance at the age of twenty-one, but in any case his formidable mother had a controlling interest in his estates for her lifetime, since they had all been settled on her as her jointure when she married. It seems likely, therefore, that it was Duchess Alice who was behind the decision to seize Dedham again that summer, fourteen years after her husband had first taken it from John Fastolf. This was bad enough for John Paston, already bruised by the loss of Caister, but the risk was that it might be only the beginning of the Duchess's ambitions where the Fastolf estates were concerned. Her husband had also challenged Sir John's possession of Drayton and Hellesdon, two adjoining manors near Norwich which lay on the doorstep of Suffolk's own property at Costessey, only a mile away. Also potentially vulnerable was the manor of Cotton in Suffolk – the late Duke's birthplace – which he had sold to Fastolf in 1434 when he needed money urgently to pay the ransom demanded by his French captors. The Duchess might well decide that an enforced sale of this kind should not override her son's birthright, and that Cotton too should be restored to the de la Pole inheritance. Mustering some kind of resistance to the loss of Dedham was therefore all the more urgent to deter any further possible incursions.

In August, John sent his eldest son John Paston II, who was now nineteen, to travel with the royal household in the hope that he would find some opportunity to lobby King Edward for redress. It took some time, but when John II did finally succeed in getting a message to the King, Edward said only that '*he would be your good lord therein as he would be to the poorest man in England*' – in other words, that no special royal intervention would be forthcoming. The new King's priority in his public pronouncements was to establish himself unequivocally as a credible and impartial lawgiver; '*as for favour*,' John II was told, '*he will not be understood that he shall show favour more to one man than to another, not to one in England*'.[6] However, it was much less clear what that should mean in the specific context of the Fastolf estates; after all, John's right to the inheritance had not yet been formally confirmed. In the meantime, the King's attention was principally occupied by the campaign to suppress continued rumblings of unrest in the south and to defeat the Lancastrian loyalists holding out in Wales and the north, a process in which he needed the support of his brother-in-law the Duke of Suffolk, as well as that of the Duke of Norfolk. In John Paston's mind, it was obvious that he was the victim rather than the perpetrator of injustice, but from the King's perspective his troubles appeared to be one of many messy disputes which would take time to sort out once the turbulence which Edward's accession had precipitated at a local level had begun to subside.

The frenzied atmosphere in which Norfolk politics were still operating was all too evident from the attempt to select the county's two MPs for the parliament which was called to meet in July. Parliamentary elections were organised by the sheriff – this year the Duke of Norfolk's cousin Sir John Howard – and all local landholders with an annual income of forty shillings or more were qualified to participate. It was usually possible, sometimes with a nudge in a particular direction from an influential magnate, to find a consensus in support of two politically appropriate names. On this occasion, however, there was '*much to-do*', according to the deputy sheriff William Price, who conducted the election on his master's behalf. Price's interpretation of the wishes of the meeting was that John Paston and another gentleman named Henry Grey had been chosen as the shire's representatives, but the third-placed candidate, a distant relative of Margaret's named John Berney of Witchingham, challenged his decision. When news of the altercation was relayed to the sheriff, Howard refused to confirm the nomination of Paston and Grey, instead returning a report alleging that Berney and his supporters had intimidated the meeting with their riotous behaviour. There clearly had been trouble, but John was adamant that he at least had been duly elected. With the airy confidence of the first-placed candidate, and his usual failure to appreciate that what seemed to him to be logically correct might not be politically acceptable, John pointed out that the solution was simple: Berney and Grey should each produce the names of those who had voted for them at the election, '*which of them that had fewest to give it up as reason would*'.[7] However, neither Berney nor Grey showed any inclination to fall on his sword, and the political temperature continued to run very high. '. . . *the world is right wild*', a friend told John on 6 July, and three days later Margaret, who was staying at the Fastolf manor of Hellesdon just outside Norwich, warned her husband in London to '*beware how you ride or go, for naughty and evil disposed fellowships. I am put in fear daily for abiding here, and counselled by my mother and by other good friends that I should not abide here unless the world were in more quiet than it is*.[8] Amid all the pushing and shoving, the controversy over the disputed election would not go away, and by the end of July – with the parliament postponed until November because of continuing Lancastrian resistance in the north and west – a new election had been called for 10 August.

Margaret was right to fear that John faced real danger, both political and personal. John himself sounded sanguine about the prospect of the reconvened election when he wrote home from London at the beginning of the month; his main concern was the reliability of Price, the sheriff's deputy, who had initially seemed keen to confirm the result of the original meeting. '. . . *the undersheriff was somewhat flickering while he was here*,' he told Margaret, '*for he informed the King that the last election was not peaceable, but the people were . . . riotously disposed, and put him in fear of his life*'.[9] However, it was John's life that proved to be at risk when the new election was held, and Sir John Howard, the sheriff, about whom he should have been worrying. Howard had several potential reasons, both current and historical, for hostility to Paston interests: he was a leading supporter of his cousin the Duke of Norfolk, who had seized Caister Castle only weeks earlier; his sister was married to Thomas Daniel, John's patron-turned-antagonist of the early 1450s; and his wife Catherine was aunt to Lord Moleyns's wife Eleanor, through whom Moleyns had acquired his claim to Gresham. When the gentlemen of the shire gathered at Norwich on 10 August, tempers were frayed, as they had been all summer. John and Howard argued; the quarrel got out of hand, and one of Howard's men lashed out at John with his dagger. A thick doublet saved him from serious injury, but the incident left his family and friends deeply shaken.

What made it worse was that the repercussions of the confrontation seemed likely to play out against him. By early October King Edward was back at Greenwich, attended by both John Howard, who was a member of the new royal household, and the Duke of Norfolk. Clement Paston wrote to warn his brother that the Duke '*has made a great complaint of you to the King*' – probably because by this stage John had made a move to reclaim Caister, although information is frustratingly scarce. Howard added his voice to Norfolk's accusations, and the Duke of Suffolk too was helping to '*call upon the King against you*'. Royal letters were dispatched to summon John to answer the charges laid against him, but John – preoccupied, it seems likely, with events at Caister – did not respond, and the King was furious. For Edward, the most important thing at this early stage in his reign – more important than the rights and wrongs of any particular situation – was that he should be obeyed without question. His ability to impose effective rule on his kingdom depended on convincing his subjects that his authority was incontestable – not an easy task when an alternative king was still at large, with a number of English nobles and foreign powers willing to offer him their support. Under those circumstances, John's failure to comply with a direct royal command was making Edward dangerously angry, and doing no good at all to the Paston cause. '*We have sent two privy seals to Paston by two yeomen of our chamber, and he disobeys them,*' the King declared; '*but we will send him another tomorrow, and by God's mercy and if he comes not then, he shall die for it. We will make all other men beware by him how they shall disobey our writing.*' Clement was told that the King meant what he said, and that John should show his face at court as soon as was humanly possible, even though it might seem a risky prospect for other reasons. '. . . *if you do well, come right strong*', Clement advised, '*for Howard's wife made her boast that, if any of her husband's men might come to you, there should go no penny for your life, and Howard has with the King a great fellowship*'.[10]

The hopeful prospect of a new Yorkist regime had turned into a chaotic nightmare for John Paston. Dedham was lost to the Duke of Suffolk; Caister was under continuing threat from the Duke of Norfolk; and his dispute with John Howard had involved him first in a dangerous fight, and now in serious trouble with the King. He left for London as soon as he could, and, on his arrival, found himself committed immediately to the Fleet Prison. It was adding insult to injury to learn that he had managed to offend his brother as well. '*I spoke to my brother William as you bade me*', Margaret wrote at the beginning of November, '*and he told me, so God him help, that he hired two horses two days before that you rode, that he might have ridden forth with you; and, because that you spoke not to him to ride with you, he said that he thought you would not have had him with you*'.[11]

It came as an overwhelming relief to discover that good luck could arrive as unexpectedly as bad in this unpredictable new world. John's stay in prison lasted no more than a few days. King Edward would not tolerate disobedience, but he also knew that the credibility of his justice would play an important part in his ability to maintain order in the longer term. Having brought John to heel, he therefore took the trouble to investigate the substance of the allegations against him, and, as a result, John was released from the Fleet. Not only that, but John Howard was arrested instead '*for divers great complaints that were made to the King of him*', Margaret was told on

Monday 2 November.[12] Four days later, the Duke of Norfolk died suddenly at the age of only forty-six. His son and heir had just turned seventeen, four years away from his majority, and any ambitions he had to pursue his father's claim to Caister would have to wait until he was in charge of his inheritance and could flex the political muscle it represented. If there seemed little that could be done about the loss of Dedham to the Duchess of Suffolk and her son, at least John now had a breathing-space in which to consolidate his hold on Caister and the rest of the Fastolf lands.

It was crucial that John should use it well. The summer's events were a warning that Fastolf's fears about the vulnerability of his estates had been well founded. Even though the change of regime meant that John's old enemy John Heydon was unlikely to be in a position to trouble him for some time, there would clearly be no shortage of new opponents keen to take advantage of the insecurity of his claim to the inheritance. John therefore needed to obtain a grant of probate on the revised will as soon as possible to give him a firm legal basis from which to repel any further attacks. He stayed on in London, lodging at the Inner Temple where he had once been a student, and Margaret had no choice but to accept that yet again he would not be at home for Christmas. This time she responded not with affectionate reproaches but with real apprehension about what his absence might mean. '*I fear me that it is not well with you that you are from home at this good time*', she wrote on 29 December.[13] By the end of the first week in January she was deeply uneasy at his failure even to write or send news. '*I had no tidings nor letter of you since the week before Christmas, whereof I marvel sore*', she told him. '*I pray you heartily that you will vouchsafe to send me word how you do as hastily as you may, for my heart shall never be in ease till I have tidings from you*'. The disorder in Norfolk seemed to be getting worse rather than better. Many who had hoped that King Edward would act swiftly to address their grievances were becoming frustrated by the lack of response from a government which was still occupied in defending its very existence. Others were exploiting the political uncertainty in the region to take matters into their own hands. Margaret was not easily unnerved, but even she was becoming frightened. '*People of this country begin to wax wild*', she wrote on 7 January. '*. . . God for his holy mercy give grace that there may be set a good rule and a sad in this country in haste, for I heard never say of so much robbery and manslaughter in this country as is now within a little time.*'[14]

John's lengthy absence from home at such an uncertain time reflected the urgency of the legal matters with which he was dealing, but he showed little sign of recognising that his chances of securing his possession of Fastolf's estates depended just as much on the personal politics of his situation. John's mishandling of his colleagues in Fastolf's service in the wake of the old man's death meant that he was facing opposition from within Fastolf's circle as well as outside it, and in the months since the establishment of the Yorkist regime he had made no progress in repairing his fractured relationships with former friends such as William Yelverton and William Worcester. Judge Yelverton's local influence had been much bolstered by the change of government; he had even hoped that King Edward might promote him to the rank of chief justice in the court of King's Bench, but had to settle for a knighthood instead. However, his increasing political clout did not inspire John to make any more concerted effort to heal the rift between them. '*Yelverton is a good threadbare friend for you and for other in this country, as it is told me*', Margaret reported from Norfolk in January 1462.[15] A month earlier, it had seemed that the news of William Worcester might be a little more positive. With encouragement from Thomas Howes, Worcester spoke to John several times in London during the autumn, and paid a visit to Margaret at Hellesdon that Christmas. '. . . *he told me that he hoped you would be his good master*', she told her husband, '*and said he hoped you should have none other cause but for to be his good master. I hope*', she added, '*. . . that he will do well enough, so that he be fair fared with*'.[16] What exactly that meant, however, remained an insuperable sticking point. Worcester was still demanding the lands he believed Fastolf had granted him before his death, '*and I feel by him utterly that he will not appoint in other form*', Thomas Howes told John in February.[17] By that stage, doubts were again beginning to surface about the reliability of Howes himself. Since coming home from a trip to London he had neither spoken to Margaret nor sent any word to her, she reported at the end of January, but he had found the time for two meetings with Judge Yelverton, and '*what they have talked I cannot say*', Thomas Playter told John.[18]

The possibility that Howes might now be wavering in his support for John's claim was all the more alarming given the first indications that there was yet another name to be added to the list of those with grievances about John's handling of the estate since Fastolf's death. In January, Fastolf's lawyer William Jenney appeared at his old master's manor of Nacton, near Ipswich in Suffolk, '*saying that he was one of the feoffees of the same manor and that he was feed with Sir John Fastolf, of which fee he was behind for two years*'. The tenants should therefore pay their rents to him, he said, and to no one else, so that '*he might be paid of his said fee, like as the will of the dead was*'. As a result, when Richard Calle arrived to collect rents on John's behalf at the end of the month, he was forced to leave empty-handed. '*I can get no money of them unto the time they have knowledge how it stands between your mastership and Master Jenney*', he told John; '*. . . wherefore that it please your mastership to remember to speak to Master Jenney*'.[19] Yet again, this was an apparently small issue which became a serious problem because, despite Calle's advice, John did not address its root cause soon enough or carefully enough to prevent it from escalating. The surviving correspondence from 1462 is patchy, but there is no sign that John made any effort to stay in direct or even indirect touch with Jenney, a colleague with whom he had worked closely throughout the 1450s. Instead, by the end of the summer, Jenney had joined forces with William Yelverton to launch an open challenge to John's claim to the inheritance.

On Friday, 3 September 1462, Yelverton and Jenney rode to Fastolf's manor of Cotton in central Suffolk and instructed the tenants there to withhold their rents from John Paston and to pay them instead to Judge Yelverton. If they refused to comply, the villagers were told, they would be subject to distraint: in other words, their property – usually farm animals, which were both valuable and easy to move – would be seized in lieu of payment. The following day Yelverton and Jenney moved on to Nacton, where they made the same claims and issued the same threats. John dispatched a Paston servant, John Pamping, to find out exactly what had happened, but the news he sent back was profoundly discouraging. Pamping tracked down Yelverton and Jenney at church in Ipswich on Sunday morning, '*and there I spoke to them*', he reported later that day, '*and told them you marvelled that they would take any distress or warn any of your tenants that they should pay you no money*'. Judge Yelverton's response was hostile and aggressive: '*he said that he would do in like wise in all manors that were Sir John Fastolf's in Norfolk as they have begun, and other language as I shall tell you*'. On Yelverton's orders, Pamping was then unceremoniously arrested. '*And so I am with the gaoler, with a clog upon my heel, for surety of the peace*', he wrote – adding, with remarkable forbearance, '*wherefore please your mastership to send me your advice*'.[20]

Yelverton and Jenney had made their intentions plain, and they had done so in disturbing company. They were accompanied on their visit to Cotton by John Andrew, a close friend of John Heydon and servant of the Duchess of Suffolk, who had taken a leading role in the prosecution by which Thomas Howes had been so harassed in the years after 1450. In church two days later, Pamping saw them talking to the Pastons' old enemy John Wyndham, and also to Gilbert Debenham, a gentleman in the Duke of

Norfolk's household who had repeatedly challenged Fastolf's ownership of the manor of Caldecott Hall, less than ten miles south of Caister, a dispute which he was now threatening to resuscitate. There could be no clearer demonstration than this of John's failure to sustain Fastolf's circle as a group bound together by mutual interests and shared loyalties. If Jenney and Yelverton – whom Fastolf had called *'brother'* – were now prepared to ally themselves with their patron's enemies, then the battle over his will was no longer a dispute about the exact form of the old man's last wishes: it had become a fight to prevent John Paston from inheriting the estate, to be pursued by any means necessary.

Word of the weekend's events spread quickly. Three weeks later the Pastons' chaplain James Gloys warned John that *'there is great noise of this revel that was done in Suffolk by Yelverton and Jenney, and your wellwillers think that, if they might prevail in this, they would attempt you in others'.*[21] John decided to strike back before they had a chance to extend their activities further. He sent instructions from London that his second son, John Paston III, should go with Richard Calle and as much support as they could muster to reassert his authority at Cotton by holding a court there and collecting rent from the tenants. The Paston contingent arrived at the manor on Friday 8 October; the next day John III rode on with thirty men towards William Jenney's home at Leiston, twenty-five miles east. At six o'clock on Sunday morning he raided Jenney's estate, seizing three dozen of his cattle in retaliation for distraints taken from the tenants at Cotton. Meanwhile, Calle, whom John III had left at Cotton with twelve of their men, had heard that their opponents were threatening *'if we abode there two days we should be pulled out by the heads'.*[22] As a public gesture of defiance Calle stayed for five, and took care to speak personally to all the tenants. They were well disposed, he told John, but worried about what would happen once the Pastons' men were gone.

The villagers were right to be frightened. A few days after Calle left, Jenney's men moved into Cotton. Seven or eight of them took over the manor house; *'they melt lead and break down your bridge'*, John was told, *'and make that no man may go into the place but on a ladder'.*[23] The occupation did not last – it was not sufficiently well organised to have been intended as a long-term enterprise – but it had served its purpose: the Pastons' possession of the manor and their ability to collect any revenue there were now extremely insecure. Not only that, but Yelverton and Jenney brought felony charges against Richard Calle, alleging that his conduct at Cotton had been riotous and unlawful. Calle was an experienced and usually imperturbable man, but he was shaken by the prospect of facing a criminal trial, especially because he had heard from the sheriff that John thought he was somehow complicit in his own arrest.

And God knows it was never my will nor my intent, as I might be saved at the dreadful Day of Doom, for there is no man so sore hurt as I am by the taking, both in loss and also in reproof of my own person and of my friends, without that my master be my good master, as I trust he will be, or else I am deceived. He has my true service, and shall have while that I live, whatsoever his mastership do to me; but I can think he has been informed by my enemies that would make him displeased with me and to be my heavy master . . .[24]

Calle's distress emphasised yet again the deficiencies in John's handling of the people around him. If it was true that he suspected Calle of conspiring with his enemies, it was a groundless and implausible accusation against a servant who had proved his loyalty repeatedly, most recently at significant personal cost. John's inability to see the world from any perspective but his own – something which compromised his political judgement, and made him capable of great tactlessness – was becoming more marked in his dealings from the lowest to the highest social levels. At the beginning of December, Margaret had to remind him to write to the townspeople who had stood bail for John Pamping when he was arrested at Ipswich in September. '*. . . saving your better advice*', she wrote, '*. . . it were well done that you sent a letter to Ipswich . . . thanking them for their good will, letting them know that they shall be saved harmless; for, as I heard say, they marvel that they hear no word from you*'.[25] He was no more diplomatic with great men. Earlier in the year, his brother Clement had decided against delivering a letter which John had written to the Chancellor; '*methought your letter was not most pleasantly written to take to such a lord*', he said.[26] John was under stress – and when he was stressed he was more and more likely to revert to the refrain of what he believed to be legally right, while at the same time becoming less and less adept at managing the relationships which might have allowed him to achieve what he saw as justice.

Margaret and Clement were not the only ones attempting to persuade John to conduct himself in a more politic fashion. The vicar of Caister, a priest named Robert Cutler, tried to alert him to the urgent need to pay more attention to Thomas Howes, whose support John was still taking for granted despite repeated intimations that his loyalties were now deeply divided. At the very least he was not reliably discreet; '*for Our Lady's love, beware what you utter unto him but only in matters that he needs must know*',

Cutler wrote in the spring of 1463, '*for he is not secure in the bite*'. Howes was a good-hearted but impressionable man whose career had been defined by his devotion to his master – and the more bitter the conflict over the will became, the harder it was for him to know what he should do in order to remain loyal to Fastolf's legacy. Now that battle lines were drawn, it was not realistic for John to assume that Howes would simply sever all ties with those members of the Caister household who were opposing his claim. '. . . *in truth*', Cutler told John, '*he works much by William Worcester*' – who was, of course, Howes's nephew by marriage as well as a friend and colleague of many years' standing. John had given too little thought to the need to sustain Howes's trust and confidence, and it seemed that he might now be paying the price. Howes had reportedly agreed to accept William Jenney and John Heydon as arbitrators in his long-standing legal battle with John Andrew, '*and methought, if he were as he should be in all matters,*' Cutler pointed out, '*all these should not be his good friends but rather his enemies*'.[27]

Despite this explicit and timely warning, John's relations with Howes deteriorated still further by the end of the year. '*I understood by him that he is disposed to excuse Yelverton in all matters rather than you*', the vicar reported in December. A date for the probate hearing had finally been set witnesses were called to appear in the Archbishop of Canterbury's court in January 1464 – which should have been good news for John, had it not been for the fact that the estrangement of his co-executor Howes was now threatening to undermine his entire case. Cutler desperately tried to persuade John of the need to tread carefully: '*make good cheer to the parson as though you understood that he were your friend, till time you have your intent*', he wrote, '*but beware and trust him not, but make you so strong in lordship and in the law that you reck not much whether he be good or bad*'. The obvious risk was that John would take a characteristically narrow and technical approach to the legal proceedings. Cutler was an astute man who recognised only too well the intensely political nature of the process, and he pleaded with John to be pragmatic in the attempt to keep key players on side. '. . . *for Our Lord's love, go through with William Worcester,*' he urged, '*and also please shrews as you think in your heart best for to do; for it is a common proverb, "A man must some time set a candle before the Devil", and therefore, though it be not most rewarding and profitable of all, yet of two harms the least is to be taken*'.[28]

Four years earlier, John Stokes, the judge in the Archbishop's court who advised John on the business of the will, had been optimistic about the likely outcome of the hearing. John would need no witnesses to testify in support of his claim to the inheritance, Stokes said, unless someone contradicted his account of Fastolf's final intentions; '*and, if there be a contradiction, three or four witnesses is enough*'.[29] If that had ever been true, it was no longer the case by January 1464, when Judge Yelverton and William Worcester mounted a formal challenge to John's application for probate on the revised will. John had already secured written statements from a number of people who could testify that Fastolf had spoken of his plans to make John his heir in the months before his death, but the critical question was what had happened in Fastolf's bedchamber on the morning of Saturday 3 November when the new will had allegedly been dictated. On that issue, John had the support of Friar John Brackley and the vicar Robert Cutler, as well as John Russe, the Yarmouth merchant who was responsible for provisioning the household at Caister. All three men claimed to have been in Fastolf's room that Saturday morning, and to have heard him make his last wishes known.

In response to John's evidence, Yelverton and Worcester produced a succession of witnesses who were examined by the court during the spring, summer and autumn of 1464. Their strategy was a simple one: to challenge and undermine as many aspects of John's case as they could. The details of his claims were raked over and any vulnerable points picked out for particular scrutiny. One stipulation in the revised will – that John should be excused the payment of 4,000 marks to Fastolf's executors if he succeeded in founding the college according to his patron's wishes – appeared to be a last-minute addition to the deal even by John's own account, and Fastolf's servant John Bocking, who testified for Yelverton and Worcester in May, declared that he, for one, did not believe it, on the grounds that '*in his whole life he had not known such generosity in the said lord John Fastolf*'.[30] The character of John's witnesses came under sustained attack: Robert Cutler, they said, was an unreliable man with little moral judgement and a history of perjury. The merchant John Russe had provided crucial evidence for the Paston case, and Yelverton and Worcester made a great effort to discredit him in particular. Those called upon to testify that he had not been present in Fastolf's chamber on the Saturday morning in question included Sir John's barber Harry Wynstall, and his manservant Nicholas Newman – Friar Brackley's much-loathed '*Colin the Frenchman*' – who was now working as an usher of the chamber to the dowager Duchess of Norfolk. Yet more witnesses were called in an attempt to demonstrate that Russe had been at Yarmouth rather than Caister that morning, buying food for the household as he usually did on Saturdays.

Amid the claims and counter-claims, one piece of testimony mattered a great deal: that of Thomas Howes, with whom John Paston maintained he was to share the administration of the estate. Howes was called to appear before the court in April 1464. John made a last-ditch attempt to put pressure on him before the hearing, sending his brother Clement to see him at his inn when he arrived in London, but Howes pretended to be out rather than face the conversation. Clement resorted to writing him a letter to remind him of his responsibilities – '*to remember what his witnesses had said for his sake*', Clement told John, '*and what shame it should be to him to say the contrary, and also if he said the contrary you would hereafter prove the truth and contrary to his saying, and prove him in a perjury*'. There was no response from Howes, but a few days later Clement bumped into him in the street. '*I found him passing strangely disposed*,' he reported, '*and sore moved with conscience that you should have the land and found the college but with 100 marks, notwithstanding he might find in his conscience right well that the college should be founded in another place but with 100 marks, and the remnant of the livelihood sold so that he might purse the money*'. This issue – in less loaded terms, whether John would recognise the validity of claims on the estate other than his own – was the crux of the matter. '*I felt by him that all his strangeness from you is for that he deems that you would part from nothing*'. Clement denied it – '*I told him the contrary thereof to be true*' – but words could do nothing at this late stage to repair the calamitous breakdown of trust between John and his former colleagues.[31] If there remained any doubt that Howes was now lost to the Pastons, it was dispelled when he gave his evidence. He declared under oath that he had seen neither John Russe nor Robert Cutler, John's key witnesses, in Fastolf's chamber on the Saturday morning before his death.

John's problems were mounting. The opposition of Yelverton, Worcester and now Howes meant that there was no prospect of the probate case being resolved quickly. Given the trouble John was facing on so many fronts, it was, if anything, in his opponents' interests to ratchet up the pressure by spinning out the proceedings for as long as they could. Apart from anything else, the Pastons were beginning to run short of money. The cost of defending the Fastolf estates in both physical and legal terms was multiplying, while at the same time the persistent harassment of their tenants at a growing number of manors was making it increasingly difficult to collect rents and other income. Already in February 1464 the legal fees which John owed in the court of King's Bench were in arrears, '*and that makes the clerks and your attorney weary*', Clement told him.[32] Meanwhile, further threats were still emerging. In the summer, news came that the Duchess of Suffolk was intending to seize the manor of Caldecott Hall, of which Yelverton's new ally Gilbert Debenham claimed to be the rightful owner, and to keep it until the dispute could be resolved. John's sons managed to avert the danger, at least temporarily, by moving into the manor themselves, but their father had more trouble dealing with charges brought against him by William Jenney as a result of the conflict at Cotton. Jenney succeeded in having John outlawed in the autumn of 1464, and he spent another couple of days in the Fleet Prison in November before the decision was finally overruled at the end of the month.

The difficulty was that he was having to work increasingly hard simply to maintain his position. As his opponents forced him into ever more frantic defence on a succession of fronts, his hopes of securing the inheritance in the foreseeable future – or perhaps at all – grew fainter. Margaret was becoming very concerned. '. . . *at the reverence of God, arm yourself as mightily as you can against your enemies*', she told her husband in June 1464, '*for I know verily that they will do against you as mightily as they can with all their power*'.[33] She was not alone in her fears. John Russe was John's staunch supporter, but he was not afraid to speak his mind in plain terms. '*Men say you will neither follow the advice of your own kindred nor of your counsel*', he wrote in July, '*but only your own wilfulness, which, but grace, shall be your destruction. It is my part to inform your mastership as the common voice is.*' John was not a stupid man, but he was extremely stubborn. He could not see, and would not accept, that his tactics were misguided. He persisted in his belief that the case would be lost or won in a court of law in London, despite Russe's warning that his presence was urgently required to defend his interests in person in Norfolk ('*the longer you continue there, the more hurt grows to you*').[34] Of course, as John was well aware, his father had always opted to use the courts as his battleground of choice – but that was because the courts were home territory for a vastly experienced lawyer and judge like William Paston, whereas John could find no advantage there over Judge Yelverton and William Jenney. William Paston had also had political connections at the highest levels of government to back up his legal manoeuvres. John, on the other hand, was still struggling to attract any influential support for his cause.

The toll that years of conflict were now taking was clear by the beginning of 1465. John's mood was not improved at Christmas 1464 by an acrimonious falling-out with his eldest son – something which had threatened to happen for years – as a result of which he threw John II out of the house. By the middle of January, John was back in London, and furious with the world. He was very short of money, and convinced himself that Margaret and Richard Calle were mismanaging his affairs in his absence.

> *Remember you, before ever I had ado with Fastolf's livelihood, while I took heed to my livelihood myself it both served my expenses at home and at London and all other charges, and you laid up money in my coffers every year, as you know. And I know well that the payment of my priests and other charges that I have for Fastolf's livelihood is not so great as the livelihood is, though part thereof be in trouble. And then consider that I had nothing of my livelihood for my expenses at London this twelvemonth day. You may verily understand that it is not guided wittily or discreetly, and therefore I pray you heartily put all your wits together and see for the reformation of it.*

They were inept with money, he said, whether because they were incompetent at collecting it or foolish in spending it ('*either you gather shrewdly or else you spend lewdly*').[35] Not only that, but their failure to take their responsibilities more seriously showed that they cared little about his welfare: '*you may remember by this how you should do if this were yours alone*', he wrote, '*and so do now*'.[36] It was an angry diatribe, both offensive and unfair to a devoted wife and a loyal servant who had defended his interests with remarkable tenacity. It was also totally unrealistic in its assessment of the strain which the conflict was putting on the family's resources, both personal and financial. Evident in every word was the distress of a man under intense pressure – and, if the situation in which John found himself was largely self-created, that only compounded his problems, since he was simply incapable of modifying his behaviour.

John Russe tried again to talk him round in May 1465. His advice was that John should negotiate, and by Russe's account Yelverton and Jenney were more than willing to talk: '*they many times have moved a treaty*', he said, '*and never it takes to no conclusion*'. At the very least, he suggested, if John agreed to a meeting, he would have a chance to discover what his opponents wanted, and for what they might settle. He pressed the point despite the fact that he knew his advice was likely to fall on deaf ears: '*I conceive well your mastership has a conceit that, if a man of goodwill moves you or remembers you to treat, that that man, whatsoever he be, should be moved by your adversaries to move you in that matter*'. More than anyone else, Russe was prepared to tell John to his face that he was his own worst enemy. The letter itself was torn at both sides at some point after it was written, making it impossible now to reconstruct everything Russe wrote, but the force of his comments is unmistakable:

> *Sir, at the reverence of Jesu consider how many years it is past that my good lord and master deceased, and how little is done for . . . of the great substance that he had; it is heavy to remember. You say the default is not in you, after your conceit; but I can hear no . . . in that of your opinion, for this I know for certain, if it had pleased you to have ended by the means of treaty you had made . . . peace to the great well of the dead with the fourth part of the money that has been spent, and as men say only of very wilfulness . . . own person. For the mercy of God, remember the unstableness of this world, how it is not a minute's space in comparison to ever . . . leave wilfulness, which men say you occupy too excessively.*

He had no hesitation, either, in telling John that his reputation was suffering. '*It grieves me to hear that you stand in no favour with gentlemen nor in no great awe with the commons*', Russe said bluntly. '. . . *It is a death to me to remember in what prosperity and in what degree you might stand in Norfolk and Suffolk if you had peace and were in heart's ease*'.[37]

By the time John received Russe's letter, however, peace was a more remote prospect than ever. The pressure on John and Margaret intensified sharply in February 1465 when the young Duke of Suffolk decided – as it had always seemed likely that he would – to revive his father's claim to the manors of Drayton and Hellesdon near Norwich. Suffolk sent a small force under the command of a priest named Philip Lipyate to take possession of Drayton on his behalf, and Lipyate let it be known that he intended shortly to do the same at Hellesdon. John, who was still in London, believed that this was a diversionary tactic to distract him from his continuing fight to reclaim Dedham, and he sent word to Margaret that she should reassure their tenants. '. . . *if they will be so steadfast to me, and keep them strange and forward from the Duke's council*', he said, '*all this matter shall turn to a jape and not hurt them near*'.[38] It was not quite that easy, however, for the tenants to take comfort from John's assurances. They were now caught in the middle of a war of attrition, as Suffolk and the Pastons competed to assert their authority over the manors by demanding rents from the villagers and distraining the property of those who would not pay. And, given John's continued refusal to countenance any kind of negotiation, it seemed inevitable that competition of this kind would lead to an escalation of hostilities.

By the spring, Margaret at least had a little more help in Norfolk, since she finally succeeded in persuading her husband, after a four-month stand-off, that their eldest son should be allowed to return home. However, as soon as one family rift was patched over, another opened up. The tensions between John and his mother Agnes, which went back twenty years to their disagreement over the terms of his father's will, were bubbling to the surface again, something about which Margaret sounded despairing. '*In good faith, I hear much language of the demeaning between you and her*', she told her husband in May. '*I would right fain, and so would many more of your friends, that it were otherwise between you than it is, and if it were I hope you should have the better speed in all other matters*'. Margaret was now approaching a point of exhaustion. The inescapable consequence of John's determination to focus on their legal battles in London was that she was left in the front line in Norfolk, dealing with their enemies face-to-face at Hellesdon just as she had done almost twenty years earlier at Gresham. She coped, as she always did, and remained uncomplaining even when he vented his frustration at her, but the strain was beginning to show. '*I pray God be your good speed in all your matters and give you grace to have a good conclusion of them in haste*,' she wrote on 10 May, '*for this is too weary a life to abide for you and all yours*'.[39]

Nevertheless, despite her weariness, she had not lost her resourcefulness. She continued to search for help where she could, appealing – as John had done thirteen years earlier when he was struggling against the aggression of Thomas Daniel – to Walter Lyhert, the Bishop of Norwich, in the hope that he might exert a restraining episcopal influence on the Duke of Suffolk's priest Philip Lipyate. The Bishop seemed sympathetic – '*My lord of Norwich said to me that he would not have abided the sorrow and trouble that you have abided to win all Sir John Fastolf's good*', Margaret reported in May – but his advice, like John Russe's, was that John himself should return from London. He '*would right fain that you were come home*', she told her husband, '*and said to me that it should be a great comfort to your friends and neighbours, and that your presence should do more amongst them than a hundred of your men should do in your absence, and more your enemies would fear to do against you if you might be at home and steering amongst them*'.[40]

However, any faint hope that John might be persuaded to leave his lawsuits for long enough to take the Bishop's advice disappeared completely at the beginning of June, when he was again committed to the Fleet Prison. He had been there twice before, but for no more than a couple of days on each occasion. This time, it was much more serious. Out of nowhere, the accusation which John Wyndham had hurled at Margaret in the street in

Norwich years earlier – that '*the Pastons and all their kin were churls of Gimingham*' – had come back to haunt them. If it was true that John had unfree blood in his veins, then he had no right to own manorial land or exercise manorial lordship, and King Edward ordered that he be kept in custody while the charge was formally investigated. It is not clear who raised the allegation, but it seems likely that it had something to do with Anthony Woodville, the new Lord Scales, possibly acting at Judge Yelverton's instigation. Certainly Woodville, who had married the Scales heiress after her father's murder, was involved in trying to confiscate some of John's property in Norfolk as a result of his imprisonment. Whoever was responsible – and, after all, there was no shortage of possible candidates – John's arrest was a crippling blow which put renewed heart into their enemies. '*Great boast they make that the Duke should have Drayton in peace, and after this Hellesdon, and that within short time*', Margaret reported. '*They are much the bolder, I suppose, because that you be where as you be. At the reverence of God, if you may by any worshipful or reasonable means, come out thereof as soon as you may, and come home among your friends and tenants, and that should be to them the greatest comfort that they might have, and the contrary to your enemies*'. John hardly needed telling that prison was not the ideal situation in which to find himself, but there was nothing he could yet do to secure his freedom. He did what he could to encourage Margaret to hold fast in Norfolk, and she did her best to respond in kind – '*I would fain do well if I could, and as I can I will do to your pleasure and profit*' – but the effort it took to sound positive was now visible: she signed herself, in an uncharacteristic moment of vulnerability, '*your faint housewife at this time*'.[41]

In public, however, there was no room for faintness. The Duke of Suffolk's hold over the tenants at Drayton was now established so firmly that an advance on Hellesdon could not be long in coming. With John under lock and key in London, it was left to Margaret and her sons, together with Richard Calle and John Daubeney – the younger son of a local gentleman, who had joined the Pastons' household some years earlier and was now one of their most trusted servants – to organise the defence of the manor. The expected assault materialised on Monday 8 July when the Duke's priest Philip Lipyate rode to Hellesdon at the head of a large company of Suffolk's men. Margaret and John II were there to meet them with sixty men of their own, '*and guns and such ordnance so that if they had set upon us they had been destroyed*', Calle reported. Lipyate was taken by surprise; he was prepared for a confrontation, but not for a pitched battle. After some hasty negotiations conducted by two priests sent by the Bishop of Norwich, both sides agreed to disperse their forces, and Lipyate and his men retreated. However, the respite lasted barely a matter of hours. Suffolk's men made their presence felt in Norwich instead, '*and face us and fray upon us daily*', Calle told John two days later. The sheriff had already had to rescue him from one attack, '*and they make their avaunt where that I may be gotten I shall die, and so they lie in await for to mischief me*'. He asked John urgently for advice, '*for you must seek some other remedy than you do, or else in my conceit it shall go to the Devil and be destroyed, and that in right short time*'. It was not like Calle to write to his master in such forthright terms, but it was bluntness borne of desperation: '*I beseech you to pardon me of my writing, for I have pity to see the tribulation that my mistress has here, and all your friends, etc.*'[42]

His message was echoed on 12 July by Margaret herself – '*praying you heartily*', she wrote, '*that you will seek a means that your servants may be in peace, for they be daily in fear of their lives*'. She had refused to be intimidated at Hellesdon, but in private she was suffering. '. . . *what with sickness and trouble that I have had, I am brought right low and weak*', she told her husband, '*but to my power I will do as I can or may in your matters*'.[43] On its way to London, her letter crossed with one travelling in the opposite direction from John himself. News of her illness had already reached him, '*which I like not to hear*', he said, '*praying you heartily that you take what may do you ease and spare not, and in any wise take no thought nor too much labour for these matters, nor set it not so to your heart that you fare the worse for it*'. His concern was welcome – as was the fact that he was no longer accusing her of neglecting his business while he was away – but it was hard to avoid the conclusion that his lengthy, and now enforced, absence in London had left him unable to comprehend the reality of Margaret's situation in Norfolk or the scale of the problems she was facing. Much of his letter was taken up with recounting details of the deficiencies in the Duke of Suffolk's claim to Drayton – but, however right he was, in practice Drayton was already lost. Margaret now had to find a way of protecting Hellesdon against the same fate, and John's suggestion that she should lecture the Bishop of Norwich on the subject – '*let my lord of Norwich know that it is not profitable nor becoming well of gentlemen that any gentleman should be compelled by an entry of a lord to show his evidence or title to his land*' – was not likely to be the answer.[44]

Margaret tried again in August to emphasise the need for John to come home as soon as he could – '*men cut large thongs here of other men's leather*', she told him – but there seemed to be little he could do about his captivity, and it was clear that he too was sometimes in need of consolation and encouragement; 'trust verily by the grace of God,' Margaret told him, 'that you shall overcome your enemies and your troublous matters right well, if you will be of good comfort and not take your matters too heavily'.[45] At least his situation was not physically unpleasant, since the Fleet was probably the most comfortable prison in London, at least for those who had money to spend. Lying just outside the city walls, near Ludgate, the prison itself was bounded on one side by the river Fleet and on the other three by a moat, which had originally been navigable but was now so choked with sewage and refuse – including animal waste dumped by the butchers who rented a wharf on the riverfront nearby – that it was possible to walk across the filthy water. Inside the walls, shielded a little from the stench, stood what was by contemporary standards a genteel establishment, which typically housed prisoners condemned in civil rather than criminal cases. Comfort and gentility, however, came at a price. Inmates had to pay for their board and lodging; they were also expected to contribute tips for the servants, and were charged one-off fees when they entered the prison and when they left it – a regime so costly that those imprisoned for debt could find themselves trapped behind bars by their spiralling expenditure. All the charges were calculated on a sliding scale to reflect the range of accommodation within the prison buildings, from luxurious private rooms reserved for the wealthy to dormitories where the less well-off slept two to a bed. Those who were destitute paid nothing for their lodging but received nothing in return; they were allowed to beg through a grate in the prison wall for money to pay for food, but even they had somehow to find more than two shillings as a discharge fee once the order came for their release. The huge profits to be made from the running of the prison meant that the warden-ship of the Fleet was a covetable position. It was a hereditary office which in the 1460s, unusually, was held by a woman, Elizabeth Venour – 'my fair mistress of the Fleet', as John Paston III called her when he sent his regards from Norfolk in September.[46]

As a gentleman of means, John Paston had a private room to himself, and he kept his servant John Pamping to wait on him. Within the prison close he had a fair measure of freedom, and spent time with other well-to-do prisoners, including Sir Henry Percy, the sixteen-year-old heir to the earldom of Northumberland, whose father had been killed fighting for the Lancastrians at Towton. John was still able to supervise his legal business, and gave his own statement about Fastolf's will to the ongoing probate hearing at a deposition held within the Fleet, at Elizabeth Venour's house, that summer. He was also allowed to receive visitors. In September Margaret left her sons to protect Hellesdon for a few days, and rode to London to see him. John and Margaret had not met for a long time, possibly as much as nine months. They were both stoical, practical characters for whom personal pleasure would never come before duty, but it was nevertheless clear quite how much this brief meeting meant after such a long separation. Its effects suffused the letter John sent while Margaret was still travelling on her way back to Norfolk – the most openly affectionate and playful letter he ever wrote to her. He was suddenly almost unrecognisable as the dour, critical and humourless man he had so often seemed in the last few years. His letters usually began with a succinct and functional '*I recommend me to you*', but this one was addressed to '*mine own dear sovereign lady*'; '*I recommend me to you and thank you of the great cheer that you made me here*', he continued – adding teasingly, '*to my great cost and charge and labour*'. The bulk of the note was, inevitably, taken up with business, much of it dealt with in characteristic style; his sons, for example, had written to ask for money to help with the defence of Cotton, a request about which he was scathing ('*remember them that they have divers times had money thitherward and do right naught, and my adversaries sent thither men without money and had their intent*'). At the end of all the reminders and the advice, however, he launched into a cheerfully dreadful piece of self-penned poetry. He could not resist devoting his first twelve lines to the supposed inadequacies of Richard Calle's financial management, but his intention was clearly to make Margaret smile:

> And look you be merry and take no thought,
> For this rhyme is cunningly wrought.
> My lord Percy and all this house
> Recommend them to you, dog, cat and mouse,
> And wish you had been here still,
> For they say you are a good Jill.
> No more to you at this time,
> But God him save who made this rhyme.
>
> Written the vigil of St Matthew
> by your true and trusty husband, J.P.[47]

Margaret too showed the benefits of the visit, if in rather more subdued fashion. '*Right worshipful husband, I recommend me to you*', she wrote a week later, '*desiring heartily to hear of your welfare, thanking you of your great cheer that you made me, and of the cost that you did on me. You did more cost than my will was that you should do but that it pleased you to do so. God give me grace to do that may please you.'* It was harder for Margaret to remain buoyed up by their meeting, given that she was plunged back into the maelstrom of their affairs the minute she set foot in East Anglia, although the lingering effects of her trip were perhaps visible in her unusually light-hearted account of a threatening incident at Caldecott Hall on 24 September: *'you will laugh for to hear all the process of the demeaning there',* she told John, a reaction which would hardly have seemed plausible two weeks earlier.[48]

The pressure, however, was mounting. The confrontation at Caldecott Hall had been precipitated by William Jenney's attempt to hold a court there, and John Daubeney was forced to muster sixty men from Hellesdon and Caister to ward him off. Only a week later, John Paston III had to gather more men at short notice and use all his political skills to keep Jenney and Gilbert Debenham out of Cotton. No one in the family was now thinking in terms of positive advances for their cause; their successes were measured in terms of averting the threats which came thicker and faster with each passing month – and the risk in moving men around from manor to manor was always that, in protecting one front, they might leave themselves exposed on another. As Richard Calle had warned John three months earlier, it was Hellesdon which was their most vulnerable point. There they faced their most powerful opponent, the Duke of Suffolk, whose own property at Costessey lay only a mile away, close to the manor of Drayton which his men had already overrun. On the other side of Hellesdon from Drayton and Costessey lay the city of Norwich, where the mayor, Margaret believed, was in the Duke's pocket; he had been at Drayton in May, and said *'that if my lord of Suffolk needs a hundred men he would purvey him thereof, and if any men of the town would go to Paston he would do lay them fast in prison'.*[49] Despite the mayor's hostility, the Pastons were not completely bereft of support among the townspeople, but no amount of sympathy there would have enabled them to resist the Duke when he arrived in the city on the morning of Tuesday 15 October – accompanied, Margaret told John, by 500 men. Even allowing for a degree of error or exaggeration, this was a menacing show of strength, and their old enemies within Suffolk's household were helping to ensure that the Duke and his mother remained implacable in their determination to wrest Hellesdon from the Pastons' hands: *'the old lady and the Duke is set fervently against us',* Margaret reported.[50]

The final attack came later that day. When it was over, Hellesdon was not only lost, but destroyed. *'The Duke's men ransacked the church and bore away* all the goods that were left there, both of ours and of the tenants', Margaret wrote, 'and left not so much but that they stood upon the high altar and ransacked the images and took away such as they might find, and put away the parson out of the church till they had done, and ransacked every man's house in the town five or six times.' When she saw what had been done to the house which had been a home to her during the last six years, she was deeply distressed: '. . . in good faith there will no creature think how foully and horribly it is arrayed unless they see it. There come much people daily to wonder thereupon both of Norwich and of other places, and they speak shamefully thereof. The Duke had been better than £1,000 that it had never been done, and you have the more goodwill of the people that it is so foully done.' It was already clear, however, that goodwill could not protect them. '. . . they made your tenants of Hellesdon and Drayton, with others, to help to break down the walls of the place and the lodge both, God knows full evil against their wills, but that they dared no otherwise do for fear.' She urged her husband to arrange that 'some men of worship might be sent from the King to see how it is both there and at the lodge, before that any snows come, that they may make report of the truth; else it shall not more be seen so plainly as it may now'.[51] But the unpalatable truth was that the Duke of Suffolk was a powerful man, who was married to the King's sister. The Pastons' own right to Hellesdon was no clearer than it had been six years earlier – less so, in fact, given how fiercely John's claims were now being contested by Yelverton and Worcester – and, while that remained the case, they stood little chance of persuading the King to intervene in the dispute in their favour.

Margaret retreated to Caister, keeping with her a garrison of thirty men 'for salvation of us and the place,' she told John, 'for in very truth, if the place had not been kept strong, the Duke would have come hither'.[52] She drew up an inventory of the possessions they had lost at Hellesdon – among them featherbeds, kitchenware, clothes, a 'book of French' belonging to her eldest son, and 'a great comb of ivory' of her daughter Margery's – and begged John to renew his efforts to find a solution to their problems: 'at the reverence of God, speed your matters now, for it is too horrible a cost and trouble that we have now daily, and must have till it be otherwise'.[53] Over the winter, John did at last manage to obtain his release from prison – probably by 10 December, when he again testified at the probate hearing, but this time not within the walls of the Fleet. However, he was unable to achieve anything more. The charge that he was a bondman still hung over him; Lord Scales used it as justification for an attempt to confiscate Paston property in Norwich in the new year. Worse, his hopes of securing the Fastolf inheritance for his family were in shreds. Six years on from the old man's death, Dedham and Drayton were gone; Hellesdon was destroyed; Cotton and Caldecott Hall were under constant threat; Caister was under armed guard; Fastolf's college was not yet founded there; and John's relationship with his closest colleagues in his patron's service had broken down irretrievably. Along the way, he had ignored every piece of good advice he had been given, and it was hard to see where help might now come from.

In May 1465, in his most blunt and critical letter, John Russe told John that persisting in his fight was making Margaret ill. '... *by my troth*', he wrote, '*the continuance of this trouble shall shorten the days of my mistress, and it shall cause you to great loss; for certain she is in great heaviness*'.[54] Russe was almost right. It was not Margaret but John himself whose life was cut short. He had marked his forty-fourth birthday in prison, five days before Hellesdon was destroyed by the Duke of Suffolk's men. Seven months later, on 22 May 1466, he died suddenly in London. Margaret's worst fears had been realised: John's health had given out under the protracted strain of conflict and imprisonment. No record survives of his mother's reaction to his death, but Agnes too seems to have had a premonition that all might not be well. Her last surviving letter, written to her first-born in his quarters in the Fleet, makes haunting reading:

> *By my counsel, dispose yourself as much as you may to have less to do in the world. Your father said, 'In little business lies much rest'. This world is but a thoroughfare and full of woe; and when we depart therefrom, right naught we bear with us but our good deeds and ill. And there knows no man how soon God will call him, and therefore it is good for every creature to be ready.*[55]

It was William Worcester – who understood far more about what had happened to them all since his master's death than John ever gave him credit for – who found a telling epitaph for his former friend. Worcester made careful notes in his copy of a book of philosophical maxims translated by Fastolf's stepson Stephen Scrope. Where the text said, '*a man should not enforce him in this world to make great buildings nor great gettings the which after his death is left to serve others*', Worcester wrote: '*for John Fastolf, the very rich knight who acted against this advice*'.[56] Next to the saying that '*heaviness is a passion touching things past, and sorrow is a fear of things for to come*', he wrote his own name. But it was by a dictum on the subject of trust – or, rather, the lack of it – that Worcester wrote the initials '*J.P.*': '*to be suspicious makes man to be evil conditioned and to live evil*'.[57] Only a man who felt betrayed, as Worcester did, could think of John Paston as evil – and perhaps Fastolf's extraordinary wealth would always, in the end, have come between those he left behind. Certainly, though, John's inability to see that he could not demand the trust of those around him without giving trust in return turned his friends into enemies. In the process, it helped to destroy his life.

CHAPTER NINE

– *a drone among bees* –

John Paston was buried in splendour. A priest and twelve poor men bearing torches walked beside his coffin as it was carried from his lodgings at the Inner Temple in London to his parish church of St Peter Hungate in Norwich. There, with thirty-eight priests in attendance, the Office of the Dead was sung. As the cortège rested briefly in the city, intensive preparations were under way at Bromholm Priory for the burial and the funeral feast. Richard Calle, James Gloys and John Daubeney threw themselves into the massive task of securing the necessary provisions. So many animals were slaughtered – 49 pigs, 49 calves, 10 cows, 34 lambs and 22 sheep – that two men worked for three days to flay them. More than ninety servants were paid to wait on the guests; a barber was hired for five days; and fourteen bell-ringers were employed at a cost of half a shilling each. When John's body arrived at the priory, it was laid on a hearse draped in fine grey linen fringed with silk, lit with candles which alone had cost more than £22. In the first week of June, the elaborate arrangements complete, John was laid to rest. The church was so ablaze with torches that afterwards the stench of tallow was overwhelming; two panes of glass had to be removed '*for to let out the reek*', and soldered back into place once the air had cleared.[1]

Margaret kept precise notes of the funeral expenses, down to the twenty pence it cost to replace eight pieces of the Prior's pewter which had some-how been mislaid. The final total, including black gowns for the mourners and a new robe for the Prior, came to almost £250 – a vast sum which represented more than a year's income from John and Margaret's estates. It was a defiant display, as though the strain of her husband's last years, and the stain of his imprisonment, could be wiped away in death by the dignity of his burial. The Pastons' determination to hold their heads high is evident, but the grief and shock of a husband and father dying so young and so sudden-ly are harder to recapture; there are no surviving letters written by Margaret or by anyone else in the family for five months after the funeral. In any case, Margaret herself was not prone either to emotional introspection or to self-pity, but she and John had been married for more than twenty-five years, and his death could not be anything but a devastating blow. Their relationship had never been one of high romance, but from the beginning it was a real partnership based on mutual respect and deep affection. At forty-four, she was left a widow with five children still to care for, as well as her two grown-up sons. Her loss was unequivocal – but the reaction of her eldest son to his father's death was almost certainly more ambivalent.

John Paston II was twenty-four when his father died, just two years older than John himself had been when Judge William's death left him at the head of the family. The similarities between father and son, however, ended there. John Paston at twenty-two had been a married man with two small children; he was serious, careful, even careworn, from his first moments in charge of his inheritance. John II at twenty-four was unmarried, and showed no sign of any inclination to settle down. Not only was he not following in his father's footsteps, but he had gone far enough in the other direction to precipitate a period of complete estrangement. Temperamentally, John II was his father's polar opposite: this son of a man who had never been young in some ways never grew up. He was, of course, intelligent and well educated; the son of John and Margaret and grandson of William would be nothing less. However, he was also impulsive, irrepressibly optimistic, and impatient with the minutiae of managing business and finance – all of which made him, in his father's eyes, careless and irresponsible. It was not that John II deliberately set out to defy his father – after his own fashion, he made huge efforts to please him – but in outlook on the world they were so fundamentally at odds that they never came close to understanding each other.

John II and his younger brother John Paston III were educated first in Norfolk, and then in Cambridge and London. It seems likely that they were given some basic schooling in the law, but not the specialist training provided by the Inns of Court; at least, if they were members of an Inn, they never took advantage of its London lodgings as their father had done at the Inner Temple. It is possible that plans for their further education were disrupted by the upheaval in the family caused by Fastolf's death in November 1459 and the demands of John's campaign to secure the inheritance. Certainly, the two boys were back at home not long after the old knight's funeral. Margaret was preoccupied in December of that year with making sure that her arrangements for the festive season were appropriately sombre, and sent her sons to ask advice from two distinguished local households – seventeen-year-old John II to Lady Morley, and fifteen-year-old John III to Lady Stapleton – about what Christmas entertainments should be allowed, given the constraints of public mourning. Isabella, Lady Morley, who had lost her husband shortly before Christmas seventeen years earlier, confirmed that in her house '*there were no disguisings nor harping nor luting nor singing, nor no loud disports, but playing at the tables*' – backgammon – '*and chess and cards, such disports she gave her folks leave to play, and none other*'. Margaret passed the information on to her husband in London, but was just as concerned to tell him that '*your son did his errand right well, as you shall hear after this*'.[2] Perhaps this was simply an expression of maternal pride, but – given that she took the trouble to point out the success of John II's mission, while that of his younger brother attracted no comment – it seems likely that their eldest son's conduct and reliability had already come into question. The pattern of maternal defence against paternal criticism was one which would play itself out repeatedly in John II's relationship with his parents.

It was appropriate that this first semi-political errand should concern Sir John Fastolf. The battle for Fastolf's estates, which consumed John Paston's last six years, dominated his eldest son's life from the moment he reached adulthood. In the summer of 1461, at the age of nineteen, John II was sent to join the new Yorkist court in the hope that he would find chances there to further his father's cause. John Paston himself, travelling between his estates in Norfolk and his legal business in London, could not hope to stay in close personal touch with those around the King, especially since Edward spent the first months of his reign almost constantly on the move around his disordered kingdom. However, if his eldest son succeeded in securing a place within the royal household, John would have a permanent representative near the heart of government to give him first-hand information about political developments, and to foster influential connections on the family's behalf. A great weight of expectation lay on John II's shoulders – but the task he faced was not an easy one. As the Yorkist regime began to take shape, the political world was intensely volatile, and the court was a complex, subtle, even dangerous place. The Pastons had one immediate contact there – a friend and distant relative named John Wykes, an usher of the King's chamber – but John II would need to work hard to secure the lordship of more powerful men. It would take social poise to cultivate friendships among those close to the King, and political skill to use such personal contacts to his family's advantage; he would also require a good deal of money to enable him to live in a style appropriate to a gentleman in royal service. He had not been at court long before it became clear that he was running into difficulties on all three fronts.

John Paston II and the young King were almost exactly the same age – John II was older by just a few weeks – but the contrast between them made

that fact difficult to remember. At nineteen, King Edward was a commanding figure who had won his throne on the battlefield, and was now stamp-
ing his personal authority on a country which had not experienced strong
royal leadership for the past forty years. John II seemed like a child in comparison, floundering out of his depth in the competitive world of Edward's
new court. In August 1461, his uncle Clement – John Paston's youngest
brother, who was only a little older than John II, and studying in London –
sent word that what he had heard of his nephew's activities was not reassuring. John II was travelling with the royal household, but had not yet
succeeded in finding himself a place within its establishment, even to the
extent of securing his board and lodging. '. . . *my nephew is not yet verily
acquainted in the King's house*', Clement wrote, '*nor with the officers of the
King's house. He is not taken as none of that house, for the cooks are not
charged to serve him*'. Nor had he so far been able to capitalise on the
Pastons' one contact within the household itself: '*he is not acquainted with
nobody but with Wykes*,' Clement reported, '*and Wykes had told him that he
would bring him to the King, but he has not yet done so*'.[3]

If John II was socially too reticent to make friends easily among the new
King's entourage, he was also too naïve for the fine art of political lobbying.
His instructions from his father were to bring the Duchess of Suffolk's
seizure of Dedham to the King's attention, and – in his anxiety to pre-empt
suggestions that he was not trying his hardest – he wrote home with an
exhaustive account of the representations he had made to the Lord
Treasurer, the Earl of Essex:

> *I laboured daily my lord of Essex . . . every morning before he went to the
> King, and often times inquired of him if he had moved the King in these
> matters. He answered me nay, saying it was no time, and said he would it
> were as fain sped as I myself, so often delaying me that in truth I thought to
> have sent you word that I felt by him that he was not willing to move the
> King therein. Nevertheless, I laboured to him continually, and prayed
> Baronners, his man, to remember him of it.*

John II's desperation to convince his father that no one could have done
more to press the Paston case was rapidly becoming part of his problem. The
Earl of Essex might well have been trying to fob him off, but his message –
that timing was crucial in presenting petitions to great men – was no less
true for that; and what applied to the Earl's conversations with the King
should also have applied to John II's dealings with the Earl, since increasingly insistent daily reminders were more likely to amount to pestering than

effective lobbying. Even worse, when these constant enquiries produced no immediate results, John II redoubled his efforts. '*I told often times to my said lord that I had a man tarrying in town that I should have sent to you for other sundry matters*', he told his father, '*and he tarried for nothing but that I might send you by him an answer of the said matters; other times beseeching him to speed me in those matters for this cause that you should think no default in me for remembering*.'[4] The hope that one of the most influential noblemen in England might be swayed by the prospect either of a Paston messenger kicking his heels, or of a teenager getting into trouble with his father for forgetfulness, demonstrated an alarming degree of political gaucheness.

Whatever the deficiencies in John II's political judgement, it became clear when he did finally manage to get a response from the King on the subject of Dedham – '*as for favour, he will not be understood that he shall show favour more to one man than to another, not to one in England*' – that there could be no realistic expectation of imminent royal intervention in what, seen from Edward's perspective, was a dispute of minimal significance.[5] If no immediate help for the family was likely to be forthcoming, the question was whether John II's continuing presence at court would prove beneficial in other ways. Clement Paston initially thought that it would be better for his nephew to leave the royal household rather than to persevere there as an unsuccessful hanger-on: '*it were best for him to take his leave, and come home till you had spoken with somebody to help him forth*', he told John, '*for he is not bold enough to put forth himself*'. However, that strategy had its own disadvantages, since John II's departure from the fringes of the court would not now go unnoticed. '*But then I considered*', Clement went on, '*that, if he should now come home, the King would think that when he should do him any service somewhere, that then you would have him home, the which would cause him not to be had in favour; and also men would think that he were put out of service*.' His conclusion, on balance, was that John II should stay – but that would require more funds, '*for the costs are greater in the King's house when he rides than you thought it had been*'.[6] That message was hammered home in typically forthright terms by the merchant John Russe, who had heard from an acquaintance at court about John II's progress, or lack of it. '. . . *he said there shall nothing hurt him but your straitness of money to him*', Russe wrote, '*for without he has money in his purse so as he may reasonably spend amongst them, else they will not set by him; and there are gentlemen's sons of less reputation that have money more liberal ten times than he has*'.[7]

It was decided that John II should stay, for the time being at least, but, as so often, his father proved stubbornly resistant to good advice. He chose to interpret his son's shortness of money as the result of his extravagance rather than an inevitable reflection of the costs of court life, and as a result John II's financial difficulties were, if anything, worse by the following spring. In March 1462 the King was in Lincolnshire, on his way north to reinforce a campaign led by the Earl of Warwick against Lancastrian loyalists still holding out in Northumberland. John II, riding with the royal household, was in desperate need of funds, and wrote to his father to ask for help. His letter makes clear how distant their relationship now was; he sounded at once formal, ostentatiously respectful, and plaintive in trying to convince his father that his need was genuine. '*Please it you to understand the great expense that I have daily travelling with the King*', he wrote, '... *beseeching you to consider these causes and so to remember me that I may have such things as I may do my master service with and pleasure, trusting in God it shall be to your worship and to my avail. In especial, I beseech you that I may be sure where to have money somewhat before Easter* ...'[8]

By the beginning of 1463 John II was back at home, and Margaret pointedly reported to his father that he had made a positive impression on Agnes and others in Norfolk. '*My mother and many other folks make much of your son John the older*', she said, '*and right glad of his coming home, and like right well his demeaning*'.[9] His time at court did finally seem to be paying some dividends by the spring of that year when he was knighted, probably to mark his formal coming of age on his twenty-first birthday. Knighthood was an honour, but it made no practical difference to the complex problems with which his father was struggling, and the new title seems to have had no effect on John's estimation of his son's abilities. By May, the tense relationship between the two was beginning to cause gossip. '*And of one matter, at reverence of God, take heed*', John was warned by Robert Cutler, the vicar of Caister, '*for in truth I hear much talking thereof, and that is both in Norfolk, Suffolk and Norwich among all men of worship, as well that love you as other; and that is of my master your son Sir John, because he is so at home and no other wise set for.*' None of the speculation about the reasons for John II's presence in Norfolk was flattering – '*some say that you and he both stand out of the King's good grace, and some say that you keep him at home for niggardliness and will nothing spend upon him*' – while the vicar's attempts to explain the situation for public consumption were unconvincing at best: '*I have answered and said the most cause is in part for cause you are so much out that he is the rather at home for the safeguard of the coast* ...' His advice was that, '*for eschewing of common language*', John II should '*worshipfully be set for, either in the King's service or marriage*'.[10] John had tried the first, and felt that

the costs he had incurred had produced insufficient return; the second –
which would, of course, have been even more expensive – does not seem to
have been under active consideration by anyone in the family.

John II was therefore left to kick his heels in Norfolk. In the end, he lost
patience, and left home in the autumn of 1463, without his parents' knowledge or permission, to rejoin the King's household. His father was furious,
and this time Margaret too was incensed. John already thought her overly
indulgent, and John II's impetuous departure merely served to rob her of
credibility in her attempts to act as his advocate. '*I let you know I was right evil
paid with you*', Margaret told her son on 15 November. '*Your father thought,
and thinks yet, that I was assented to your departing, and that has caused me to
have great heaviness.*' Most of her letter was taken up – clearly not for the first
time – with advice about how to repair his relationship with his father. John
II should write to him '*as lowly as you can, beseeching him to be your good
father*', and sending news from where he was with the King; it was also an
absolute necessity to be careful with his money – '*that you be ware of your
expense better than you have been before this time, and be your own purse-
bearer. I trow you shall find it most profitable to you*'. However, she found it difficult to stay angry for long. Above all, she wanted news of John II himself,
however much trouble it might end up causing with her husband. '*I would
you should send me word how you do*', she wrote, '*and how you have managed
for yourself since you departed hence, by some trusty man, and that your father
have no knowledge thereof. I dared not let him know of the last letter that you
wrote to me because he was so sore displeased with me at that time.*'[11]

Despite the seriousness of John II's misjudgement in leaving, Margaret
had some success in her role as intermediary by the following spring, when
John allowed their son to return home, even if under a heavy cloud. On 6
May, Margaret sent her husband a careful report of his behaviour. '*As for his
demeaning since you departed*', she wrote, '*in good faith it has been right good
and lowly, and diligent in oversight of your servants and other things the which
I hope you would have been pleased with if you had been at home . . . I beseech
you heartily that you vouchsafe to be his good father*', she added, '*for I hope he
is chastised and will be the warier hereafter.*'[12] John II remained in Norfolk
over the summer, attempting to prove that he deserved his father's trust by
helping his younger brother to defend the Fastolf estates against incursions
by their enemies. However, the pressure on John's possession of the inheritance, and therefore on John himself, increased markedly during the second
half of 1464. Quite apart from the threat to the manors themselves, Thomas
Howes had now defected to the opposing camp in the dispute over the will;

the family's finances were increasingly precarious; and in the autumn John was outlawed and spent a couple of days in the Fleet Prison as a result.

Perhaps unsurprisingly, given the unpropitious circumstances, the chilly reconciliation between father and son broke down completely that Christmas. By January 1465 John had barred John II from home and was refusing to have anything more to do with him. Their surviving correspondence gives no clue about what particular episode precipitated the breach, but the tension between them was now so deep-rooted that it need not even have been a major incident. Certainly, there was a familiar litany of complaint – if unfamiliar in its intensity – in John's letters to Margaret in the first two months of the new year. The long, detailed and angry letter he wrote on 15 January was mainly concerned with the inadequacies he perceived in her management of the household in his absence, but the vehemence of his anger was fuelled by deep frustration with his son. What infuriated him more than anything was John II's failure to subscribe to his own profound sense of duty. For John himself, life was serious, effortful, and laden with responsibility for the security and advancement of his family. '*Also, remember you in any household, fellowship or company that will be of good rule,*' he told Margaret, '*purveyance must be had that every person of it be helping and furthering after his discretion and power, and he that will not do so, without he be kept of alms, should be put out of the household or fellowship*'. If it was not already abundantly clear of whom he was thinking, the next paragraph put it beyond doubt. Margaret had yet again attempted to intercede on their son's behalf, and this provoked her husband to what was for him practical, prosaic John – an emotional and finely expressive outburst:

> *howbeit that in his presumptuous and indiscreet demeaning he gave both me and you cause of displeasure, and to other of my servants ill example, and that also guided him to all men's understanding that he was weary of biding in my house, and he not ensured of help in any other place, yet that grieves me not so evil as does that I never could feel nor understand him politic nor diligent in helping himself, but as a drone among bees which labour for gathering honey in the fields, and the drone does nothing but takes his part of it.*[13]

John's patience was exhausted; so too, after years of disappointment, was his hope that his son might one day live up to his expectations:

> *And if this might make him to know the better himself, and put him in remembrance what time he has lost and how he has lived in idleness, and*

that he could for this eschew to do so hereafter, it might fortune for his best. But I hear never yet from no place that he has been in of any politic demeaning or occupation of him; and in the King's house he could not put himself forth to be in favour or trust with any men of substance that might further him.

His decision was made, and he was unmoved by Margaret's pleas for forgiveness. '. . . *as for your house and mine*', John told her, '*I purpose not he shall come there, nor by my will none other, but if he can do more than look forth and make a face and countenance.*'[14] They were now going round in circles, Margaret refusing to give up her attempts to reconcile her husband and son, and John reiterating the principles on which he was judging John II and finding him wanting. '*Item, as for your son*', he wrote on 21 February,

I let you know I would he did well, but I understand in him no disposition of policy nor of governance as man of the world ought to do, but only lives, and ever has, as man dissolute, without any provision, nor that he busies him nothing to understand such matters as a man of livelihood must needs understand. Nor I understand nothing of what disposition he purposes to be, but only I can think he would dwell again in your house and mine, and there eat and drink and sleep.

Amid all his other problems, the idea that his own son was adding to his troubles was too much to bear:

Every poor man that has brought up his children to the age of twelve years waits then to be helped and profited by his children, and every gentleman that has discretion waits that his kin and servants that live by him and at his cost should help him forward. As for your son, you know well he never stood you nor me in profit, ease or help to value of one groat, saving at Caldecott Hall when he and his brother kept it one day against Debenham, and yet was it at three times the cost that ever Debenham's sons put him to . . .

John was determined that, this time, his son should have to prove himself – his character, his intentions and his reliability – before he would be re-admitted to the family. '. . . *give him no favour*', he told Margaret, '*till you feel what he is and will be.*'[15]

Twelve days later, on 5 March – undoubtedly at Margaret's prompting – John II wrote to beg his father's forgiveness. '*Might it please your fatherhood*', he said, '*to remember and consider the pain and heaviness that it has been to me since your departing out of this country, here abiding till the time it pleases*

*you to show me grace, and till the time that by report my demeaning has been
to your pleasing'.* He could not quite conceal the subtext that John was
impossible to please – how, after all, could he demonstrate his trustworthi-
ness to his father's exacting standards if he were excluded from the family
and all its activities? – but wisely, or under maternal pressure, ended on a
note of abject supplication: *'I beseech you of your fatherly pity to tender the
more this simple writing, as I shall out of doubt hereafter do that shall please
you to the uttermost of my power and labour. And if there be any service that I
may do, if it please you to command me or if I may understand it, I will be as
glad to do it as anything earthly, if it were anything that might be to your pleasing.'*[16] Despite this appeal, or perhaps because it was all too familiar, John
remained implacable. A month later, Margaret sent her husband a letter full
of practical business: developments relating to the Duke of Suffolk's seizure
of Drayton, the price of malt, the need for repairs to the tenants' houses at
Mautby. She left the subject of their son until last, but tackled it in the same
direct and businesslike tone. It was an issue they had discussed many times
before, but Margaret was no less stubborn than her husband, and it was clear
in every word that she would not let the matter drop until his answer was the
one she wanted. *'Item'*, she wrote, *'I understand by John Pamping that you will
not that your son be taken into your house nor helped by you till such time of
year as he was put out thereof* – December, eight months away, which
Margaret plainly felt was far too long.[17] *'For God's sake, sir,'* she continued,
*'have pity on him and remember you it has been a long season since he had
anything of you to help him with, and he has obeyed him to you and will do at
all times, and will do that he can or may to have your good fatherhood. And, at
the reverence of God, be his good father and have a fatherly heart to him.'*[18]

For all John's determination that his son should be taught his lesson, it
was Margaret who got her way. Perhaps John's anger had blown itself out;
perhaps the indignity of being the subject of local gossip became harder to
bear in the face of the battles they were fighting on so many fronts; perhaps
the need for an extra pair of hands to help fight those battles became more
pressing; perhaps, simply, Margaret's resolve proved impossible to resist
indefinitely. If there were fireworks in the course of the discussions leading
to John II's return home, they have left no surviving trace. Nor was the
prodigal welcomed back with open arms – or not, at any rate, when his
father was looking. On 3 May Margaret once again tackled the subject as
one among many items of business, and reassured her husband that she
understood the conditions on which John II was being permitted to return.
'Your son shall come home tomorrow, as I trow', she wrote, *'and as he demeans*

him hereafter I shall let you have knowledge; and I pray you think not in me that I will support him nor favour him in no lewdness, for I will not. As I find him hereafter so I will let you have knowledge.'[19] John II spent most of the rest of the summer in Norfolk helping to defend the Fastolf estates, first taking charge at Caister, and then, in July, at Hellesdon, where he stayed until the Duke of Suffolk's men launched their final destructive assault in October. He was, at last, applying himself as his father wanted to the family's business, even if John himself – who was in London, and from the beginning of June imprisoned in the Fleet – was not there to see it. The whole household, though, now shared Margaret's habit of making sure that any successes were relayed in full to his father. '*. . . my master Sir John . . . has gotten him as great worship for that day as any gentleman might do, and so it is reported of their party and in all Norwich,'* Richard Calle reported after a confrontation with Suffolk's priest Philip Lipyate in July.[20] Communications between father and son remained formal and distant, but at least the bitterness of the early months of the year did not resurface, even when John II joined John in London after his release from prison at the beginning of 1466.

Four months later, not long after John II's twenty-fourth birthday, his father died. The sudden bereavement was as much of a shock for John II as it was for the rest of the family, but for him it was a liberation as well as a loss. At last, he was free from the oppressive weight of his father's negative expectations. This was his chance to prove that John had been wrong – that he could, after all, be trusted to shoulder the responsibility of the family's interests – and to do so on his own terms. Admittedly, the position in which he found himself was in many ways unenviable: his inheritance included all of the crippling problems which had driven his father into an early grave. On the other hand, John's own misjudgements had played a significant part in creating those difficulties in the first place, and the fact that John II was instinctively a more flexible character might now stand him in good stead. John II also had one major political advantage over his father: after five years, he had finally succeeded in establishing some personal connections within Edward IV's household.

The benefits of this access at court became apparent almost at once. In July 1466, only two months after John's death, John II appeared before the King to refute the '*surmise of great charge*' – the allegation that his father was a bondman – which had resulted in John's imprisonment. John himself had struggled for six months even to secure his freedom, but John II immediately won a sympathetic hearing for the family's case, arguing that the Pastons were '*gentlemen descended lineally of worshipful blood since the Conquest hither*', when '*their first ancestor Wulstan came out of France*'. The many documents he produced attested to a lengthy and complex family tree descended from this Norman lord; the leap of faith – or, rather, of fiction – was the assertion that '*Sir John Paston was heir to all those, for they died sans issue*'. However, it was a fiction which King Edward was now prepared to accept as '*openly proved and affirmed, without contradiction or proof to the contrary*'.[21] With the dismissal of the charge came formal restitution of the family's property. Royal letters were issued ordering that '*our trusty and wellbeloved knight Sir John Paston*' should have full possession of his lands, including Caister and the other Fastolf estates, '*like as the said John Paston deceased had in any time of his days*'.[22] This was not a verdict which had implications for the family's battles with Yelverton and Worcester, and the Duke of Suffolk and his mother – possession '*like as the said John Paston deceased had*' was, after all, contested possession – but, whatever else happened, John II was now safe from the imprisonment which had blighted the last year of his father's life.

However, despite this success, John II was still not free from fretful parental advice. Now that there was no longer any need to defend him against his father's criticisms, Margaret found it impossible to contain her own reservations about her eldest son's conduct and judgement. She had no confidence in his common sense over even the most elementary things. '. . . *in all wise I advise you for to beware that you keep wisely your writings that be of charge*', she told him in the autumn, '*that it comes not in their hands that may hurt you hereafter. Your father . . . in his trouble season set more by his writings and evidence than he did by any of his moveable goods.*' Money was short, as ever these days, and she was tired and worried. '. . . *at the reverence of God, speed your matters so this term that we may be in rest hereafter*', she wrote, '. . . *and remember the great cost and charge that we have had hithertoward, and think verily it may not long endure.*' When John was alive, it had always been clear that Margaret's duty was to support him and represent him wherever he needed her to be, and she had never once baulked at it; but the responsibility of mother to son was less clear cut, and signs were beginning to emerge that John II could not simply rely on her to be at his beck and call. Her letter ended with a pointed reminder that it was '*written at Caister . . . where as I would not be at this time but for your sake*'.[23]

In one important respect, for which Margaret in the course of her strictures made no allowance whatsoever, John II's situation was even worse than his father's had been. John himself had not inherited all of the Paston estates, partly because a substantial proportion of them were in the hands of his mother Agnes – who was still hale and well in her mid-sixties – and partly as a result of his father's bequests to his younger siblings. Nevertheless, the Paston lands he did receive, together with Margaret's Mautby inheritance, gave him an income of probably £200 a year, and it was from this annual sum that Margaret and all their children had to be provided for after his death. Margaret's share was clear: she retained possession both of her own valuable Mautby lands and of Gresham, the jointure she had received when she married – estates which together accounted for more than half of John's landed revenue. The problem which John faced on his deathbed, just as Judge William had done before him, was how to distribute the rest of his properties between his heir and his younger children. Extraordinarily, for a man who had fallen out with his mother over the ambiguities of his father's will and was embroiled in a ferocious dispute over that of his patron, John left no written will of his own, probably because his final illness was so sudden and unexpected. Nevertheless, it seems that he did have time to express his last wishes, and, looking at the dilemma now from the other side, John made exactly the same decision as his father: that he was not prepared to risk impoverishing his younger sons, even if it meant leaving his eldest with perilously little. One manor – Swainsthorpe, near Norwich – was to go to John III; other lands, worth a few pounds a year in each case, were earmarked for Edmund, now in his mid-teens, and ten-year-old Walter; while the youngest, seven-year-old William, was to receive an annuity of 10 marks from the manor of Sporle. With characteristic generosity – or what his father might in other circumstances have called negligent disregard of his own interests – John II made no protest at these arrangements, despite the fact that, if his mother and grandmother were still alive when his brothers all came of age, his share of the Paston lands would amount to no more than two manors: Sporle in western Norfolk, from which he would have to pay his brother William's annuity, and Snailwell in Cambridgeshire. It was not until seven years later, under financial pressure more intense than any his father had experienced, that John II was driven to point out explicitly to his mother that '*my father, God have his soul, left me scant £40 land in rest, and you leave me as pleases you, and my grandam at her pleasure. Thus may I have little hope of the world.*'[24] If John Paston had staked his career and reputation on his claim to the Fastolf inheritance, the fight to secure at least some of those estates was, for John II, a matter of financial survival.

Margaret was not completely unwilling to help, but, in the midst of reproving her son for his profligate habits, seems barely to have noticed that his income was only a fraction of the revenues her husband had had at his disposal. Luckily for John II, his mother was not his only lieutenant in Norfolk; he had a more cheerful and much less critical ally in his brother John III. Before their father's death, while John II spent time – with permission and without – in the royal household, John III had stayed mostly at home in Norfolk, quietly and efficiently becoming indispensable to the running of the family's affairs. At fifteen, he was acting as his mother's secretary, and by 1461, at the age of seventeen, he was closely involved in the management of the family's estates in his father's absence. Such responsibility was perhaps unexceptional in a country ruled by a nineteen-year-old king, but, within a family where his older brother was struggling to find his feet as an adult in the wider world, John III's competence was striking. By the following autumn, at eighteen, he was working with Richard Calle not only to supervise the running of the Paston and Fastolf estates, but in the politically sensitive and sometimes dangerous task of defending them against his father's rivals. Calle, an older, more experienced and extremely able man, took John III seriously as an ally and – however respectfully, given the relationship between employer and employee – a friend. He was not the only one to appreciate John III's abilities. John and Margaret's approbation is harder to demonstrate, but the fact that their letters barely mention their younger son speaks volumes by contrast with the heated prose generated by his older brother. As the second son, John III was of course under less pressure and less scrutiny than his brother, but in any case it is clear how capable and likeable he was; he shouldered his responsibilities lightly, rather than taking them lightly, as his father believed John II did.

John III's talents were social as well as practical. In the spring of 1462, he made a great success of entertaining John Wykes, the usher of the King's chamber who had been his brother's first contact at court, on a visit to Norwich. He made an equally positive impression on the young Duke of Norfolk. At eighteen, six months or so younger than John III himself, the Duke had not yet taken possession of his inheritance, and his political influence was still therefore limited – but that did not mean his lordship was worthless. Any positive contact at this early stage in Norfolk's career might help to dissuade him from reviving his father's designs on Caister, or perhaps even convince him to champion the Pastons' cause against his rival, the Duke of Suffolk. In the autumn of 1462, John III was sent by his father to appeal for Norfolk's support against their opponents at Cotton – a meeting which had little effect in terms of the dispute, but produced immediate results for John III himself. By December, he had entered the Duke's service, and travelled with him to Northumberland to join the Earl of Warwick's campaign to retrieve the castles of Alnwick, Dunstanburgh and Bamburgh from forces loyal to King Henry. He spent another few months with Norfolk in the winter of 1463–4 at his castle of Holt in north Wales, helping to subdue pro-Lancastrian disturbances in the west. Nevertheless, the main focus of his activities remained at home, working with his mother, with Richard Calle, and, when relations with their father allowed, with his brother, to defend the Fastolf estates. It was a campaign in which his relationship with Norfolk added another string to his bow, and he was sent as an envoy to the Duke on a number of occasions in 1464 and 1465. For the time being, his visits achieved little, but there was every reason to hope that Norfolk's influence would grow; he was still a very young man, coming of age only in October 1465 – and it was a mark of the favour in which he now held John III that the latter was summoned to attend the ceremony by which the Duke received possession of his estates.

In May 1466, when John Paston died, a division of labour between his two eldest sons was so natural as to seem inevitable. John II, now head of the family, spent most of his time in London, at his lodgings in Fleet Street. In the light of his protracted absences, and his lack of either the inclination or the skills needed to do the job well, it made sense that John III should take the leading role in managing the family's interests in Norfolk. On the whole, the system worked. The brothers got on well, with an easy banter, and kept their spirits up more successfully than their beleaguered father had ever managed. Unsurprisingly, however, there were also moments of tension. Always practical and focused on the task in hand, John III tried in March 1467 to secure money for repairs to the fabric of the buildings at Caister:

> *Sir, etc, it is so that, without you have hasty reparation done at Caister, you are like to have double cost in haste, for the rain has so moisted the walls in many places that they may not tile the houses till the walls are repaired, or else you shall have double cost for to untile your houses again at such time as you shall amend the walls; and if it be not done this year many of the walls will lie in the moat before long . . .*

His difficulty was that John II controlled the family purse-strings, and it was not easy to persuade him of the urgency of domestic concerns from which his metropolitan life left him semi-detached. '*Pamping and I shall clout up your houses as we may with the money that we have till more comes*', John III continued in some exasperation, '*but you should do better yourself. I pray, read this bill once a day till you have sped these matters written herein*'.[25]

In response, John II was heroically vague. '*Right worshipful and verily wellbeloved brother*,' he wrote, '*I heartily commend me to you, thanking you of your labour and diligence that you have in keeping of my place at Caister so surely, both with your heart and mind, to your great business and trouble; and I againward have had so little leisure that I have not sped but few of your errands, nor cannot before this time.*' Despite his lack of leisure, he devoted the rest of the letter to advising his brother on how best to go about wooing Alice Boleyn, a potential bride ('*bear yourself as lowly to the mother as you list, but to the maid not too lowly, nor that you be too glad to speed nor too sorry to fail . . .*').[26] Another letter arrived in Norfolk soon afterwards, this time full of excitement about a tournament at the King's palace of Eltham, a few miles south-east of London, in which John II had fought. He had hurt his hand, but '*I would that you had been there and seen it*', he told his brother, '*for it was the goodliest sight that was seen in England these forty years*'.[27] All in all, he accorded the difficulties with which John III was dealing no more than a cursory postscript: '*I suppose if you call upon R. Calle he shall purvey you money. I have written to him enough*'.[28] John III could not suppress his irritation:

> *whereas it pleases you for to wish me at Eltham at the tourney for the good sight that was there, by troth I had rather see you once in Caister Hall than to see as many King's tourneys as might be between Eltham and London. And, sir, whereas it likes you to desire to have knowledge how that I have done with the Lady Boleyn, by my faith I have done nor spoken naught in that matter, nor not will do till time that you come home, if you come not these seven years.*

If John II had been cursory, John III was more than prepared to be curt: '*as for R. Calle*,' he went on, '*we cannot get half a quarter the money that we pay for the bare household, beside men's wages. Daube nor I may no more without money.*'[29]

In many ways, it was a characteristic exchange. John II, the inexperienced teenager who had been too shy to make his mark in Edward IV's household, had become something of a courtier, an accomplished fighter with a passion for books and an eye for female company – '*the best chooser of a gentle-woman that I know*', according to a friend in London.[30] He had never had the patience or the commitment to devote himself to the day-to-day mundanities of estate management, and at a distance it was easy for him to forget how draining they could be. His brother, to whom patience and commitment were second nature, was having to shoulder heavy responsibilities for an inheritance which was not his own. Characteristics can all too easily become caricatures, however, and the brothers had more in common than their different circumstances sometimes suggested. John III – prudent and practical though he was – cared enormously about his appearance, and often sent to London for finer clothes than were available in Norwich. He took the opportunity of his mother's visit to see his father in the Fleet in the autumn of 1465, for example, to ask her to pick up two pairs of hose for him, one black and one rose-pink. '*I beseech you that this gear be not forgot*', he wrote, '*for I have not a whole hose to do on*'.[31] And despite his brother's vaunted expertise with women, it was John III who seems first to have fathered an illegitimate child. '. . . *mother, I beseech you that you will be good mistress to my little man*', he asked Margaret during a trip away from home in 1468, '*and to see that he goes to school*'. There are few other mentions of his '*little Jack*' in the letters – and no clue about the identity of the boy's mother – but enough all the same to suggest that some of his more po-faced asides to his brother ('*God keep you this Lent from lollardy of flesh*') were written with tongue firmly in cheek.[32]

John III's impatience with his brother was at times heartfelt, but so, always, was his affection. In the end, too, John II was doing more in London than merely gadding about. The Eltham tournament – however irritating from the point of view of his younger brother, trying to hold back the spreading damp at Caister – was far more significant than simply a chance to enjoy himself in glamorous surroundings. With hard-won experience under his belt, and liberated at last from his father's disapproval, John II was proving that he could be as charming and at ease in powerful company as his brother. The fact that he was chosen as one of only three knights to fight with King Edward himself, against a team led by the King's best friend, William, Lord Hastings, showed not only his physical prowess but the political progress he had made – and such marks of royal favour could only improve his chances of securing influential support in his fight to save the Fastolf inheritance.

It had to be said, however, that there was little reason otherwise to feel cheerful about the progress of the dispute. The probate hearings continued in London during the course of 1466, uninterrupted either by the death of John Paston, or by that of Friar John Brackley a little earlier in the year. Whatever his faults, Brackley's loyalty to the Paston cause had been absolute, and he protested the justice of John's claim to the very end. '*I desire you that you will report after my death that I took it upon my soul at my dying that that will that John Paston put in to be proved was Sir John Fastolf's will'*, he told his confessor hours before he died.[33] Nevertheless, twenty more witnesses appeared to testify for Yelverton and Worcester in May and June, most of them alleging that the evidence produced to support John's claim was false and, in some cases, procured by bribery. The judges found most of these depositions unconvincing, but so much mud had already been thrown by both sides that the facts of the case now seemed more obscure than they had done when the hearings started. Meanwhile, Judge Yelverton's men were extending their campaign of harassment from Fastolf's Suffolk estates to two of his Norfolk manors, Saxthorpe and Guton Hall in Brandiston, north-west of Norwich. *'There dare no poor man displease them'*, John III told his brother in January 1467, *'for whatsoever they do with their swords they make it law, and they take distresses out of men's houses, horse or cattle or what they will'.*[34]

If the legal deadlock were to be broken in the Pastons' favour, John II would have to exploit all his political contacts to secure more powerful backing for his cause. In 1467, it seemed as though he had found the answer to his prayers in the person of the Earl of Warwick's younger brother, George Neville, Archbishop of York, who held office as Lord Chancellor in King Edward's government. There had been indications that he was well disposed towards the family even before John Paston's death – in February 1466, he was reported to be the Pastons' *'singular good lord'*[35] – and John II took pains to cultivate the relationship. His uncle William Paston, who was carving out a profitable career for himself in London as a lawyer and administrator, knew Archbishop Neville well, and worked hard in the summer of 1467 to secure his help for his nephew. William arranged, for example, for John II to lend the Archbishop the huge sum of 1,000 marks. In view of John II's chronic financial problems, and the difficulty of enforcing repayment from such a powerful man, this was clearly a political investment rather than a business deal, but it was one which soon seemed to be producing results. Archbishop Neville declared himself ready to arbitrate in the dispute with Yelverton and Worcester over Fastolf's will, and set about brokering a deal with the dowager Duchess of Suffolk by which she and her son would abandon their claim to Hellesdon in return for a payment of 100 marks. It did not seem beyond the bounds of possibility that the Archbishop's support, combined with John II's more flexible approach to the family's problems, might at last offer hope of negotiating a settlement to the conflict.

It took only a few weeks for that hope to be dashed. At the end of July it emerged that Duchess Alice and Judge Yelverton had been in secret contact, and an agreement made that, in their capacity as Fastolf's executors, Yelverton and Worcester would sell Hellesdon to the Duchess and her son. The prospect of an alliance of this kind between the Pastons' opponents was profoundly alarming. Suffolk's claim to Hellesdon would be much reinforced by what he would argue was a legitimate purchase from Fastolf's estate, and Yelverton and Worcester would in turn be able to draw on the Duke's influence to strengthen their position in the probate case. John II could at least console himself with the knowledge that Archbishop Neville was not wavering in his support. '. . . *my lord will in any wise that you keep well all the livelihood that you have of Sir John Fastolf*', John Daubeney reported, '*and that you suffer no man to enter no land nor place, lord nor other persons whatsoever they be. You may verily think he is your special good lord, and that you shall know in time coming*.'[36] On the other hand, it was also becoming disconcertingly apparent that the Archbishop was too sure of himself, even blasé, for the intricate work of unravelling the knot of disputes into which the Pastons were now wound. He was initially unable to believe that Duchess Alice had double-crossed him over Hellesdon – '*I dare swear upon a book that the Duchess of Suffolk has no knowledge thereof*', he exclaimed – and, when presented with incontrovertible evidence, '*he marvelled sore of her disposition*', Daubeney told John II, but '*bade me not care, you should do well enough*'.[37] That was certainly what John II wanted to hear, but, given the Duchess's steely intelligence and vast political experience, it was a far from adequate response.

More worrying even than this were indications that the structure of power within which they were all manoeuvring was itself beginning to undergo major convulsions. By the mid-1460s, King Edward had made huge strides in securing his rule throughout England. Lancastrian resistance in the north had been all but wiped out by the late summer of 1464, and a year later the fugitive ex-King Henry VI was captured in Lancashire and imprisoned in the Tower of London. Queen Margaret had escaped to France with their nine-year-old son in 1463, but, in the absence of significant Lancastrian support among the nobility in England, her chances of mounting another challenge to Edward's hold on the throne were slim. One problem, however, remained for the King to face: his relationship with his cousin Richard Neville, Earl of Warwick. The fact that Warwick had played such a key part in Edward's victory in 1461 meant that the Earl now saw his leading role in government as one held by right rather than royal command, and he acted accordingly. In England, '*they have but two rulers*', an observer reported archly to the King of France, '*Monsieur de Warwick and another, whose name*

I have forgotten'.[38] It was clear to Edward that he could not continue to tolerate his cousin's pretensions – effectively, the supervision of his rule by one of his subjects – if he were ever to exercise the untrammelled authority of a legitimate king.

Signs that all was not well between Edward and Warwick were apparent as early as the spring of 1464, when the twenty-two-year-old King made the extraordinary decision to marry in secret, without either consulting or informing his nobles and advisers. Equally extraordinary was his choice of bride. His new wife was Lord Scales's sister Elizabeth Woodville, a widow with two young sons whose husband had been killed fighting in the Lancastrian army at St Albans in 1461. The motive behind this impetuous and politically inappropriate match was probably entirely personal: Elizabeth was an extremely beautiful woman, who allegedly refused Edward's advances unless he married her. However, when news of the wedding finally emerged four months later, it had the added effect of proclaiming the King's independence from Warwick, who was in the midst of negotiating a match for Edward with the French King's sister-in-law. Warwick had no choice but to accept the marriage as a *fait accompli*, but by 1466 the tensions between the two men were developing into a major rift over the direction of foreign policy. Warwick continued to press for an alliance with France, while Edward increasingly favoured France's enemy Philip of Burgundy, the ruler of the Netherlands. In the summer of 1467, the divergence of opinion between King and Earl became embarrassingly public. Warwick left England to lead an embassy to France, and in his absence Edward entertained Duke Philip's illegitimate son Anthony, Bastard of Burgundy, with great ceremony when he visited London to joust with the King's brother-in-law Lord Scales. If the glittering welcome accorded to the Bastard was a clear statement of Edward's intent to direct his own diplomacy, the King was no less determined to be master of his own government within England. On 8 June 1467, three days before the lavish tournament was held at Smithfield, Archbishop Neville of York – Warwick's brother – was abruptly dismissed from the Chancellorship, which he had held since the beginning of Edward's reign.

From the Pastons' point of view, the timing of the Archbishop's loss of office could not have been more disheartening. His sudden sacking probably explains why the Duchess of Suffolk and Judge Yelverton felt able to go behind his back a month later to agree the sale of Hellesdon from under the Pastons' noses. They were not the only ones to see the opportunity presented by the discomfiture of the family's new patron. Word reached Margaret at

Norwich in July that Thomas Fastolf of Cowhaugh, Sir John's distant relative, was preparing to claim Caister by force. '*It is said that he has five score
men ready*', she told her eldest son, '*and sends daily spies to understand what
fellowship keep the place. By whose power or favour or supportation he will do
this I know not, but you know well that I have been affrayed there before this
time when that I had other comfort than I have now*'.[39] Margaret may not have
known for certain who was behind Thomas Fastolf's plans, but her mention
of previous threats to the castle – together with the fact that Thomas had
supported the old Duke of Norfolk when he seized Caister briefly in 1461 –
suggests that the new Duke was the prime suspect. This was a disastrous
turn of events. Norfolk had represented the Pastons' best prospect of local
support against Suffolk and his mother, and John III's success in securing
the personal favour of the young Duke had seemed to make that hope realistic. All things being equal, John III's service – and the prospect of bloody-
ing Suffolk's nose – should have disposed the Duke well towards the Pastons'
cause. All things were not equal, however, when properties as desirable as
Fastolf's were at stake. In the end, it seemed, Caister was too great a prize for
Norfolk to resist.

Confronted with this renewed danger, Margaret sounded deeply weary.
She had faced attack before – long ago at Gresham, and much more recently at Hellesdon – but that had been in partnership with her husband, '*when
that I had other comfort than I have now*'. Now John was dead, and Margaret,
having to make a new life for herself as a widow, was no longer willing to
stand in the front line. '*And I cannot well guide nor rule soldiers*', she told
John II, '*and also they set not by a woman as they should set by a man.
Therefore I would you should send home your brother or else Daubeney to
have a rule and to take in such men as were necessary for the safeguard of the
place*'. She had other business to attend to – her own estates to run – and she
wanted her son to know that he could not simply take her presence for
granted. '*I have been about my livelihood to set a rule therein as I have written to you*', she said, '*which is not yet all performed after my desire, and I
would not go to Caister till I had done.*' She was not completely unwilling to
help, but she was not prepared to be her son's right hand as she had been
her husband's. At the same time, she did not find it easy to let go – nor was
she confident that John II could be trusted to deal with the dangers which
the family faced. Her letter pulled in two directions at once, resisting the
demands being placed on her, but at the same time insisting that her son
follow the advice she offered. '*I marvel greatly that you send me no word how
that you do*', she told him, '*for your enemies begin to wax right bold, and that*

*puts your friends both in great fear and doubt. Therefore purvey that they may
have some comfort that they be no more discouraged, for if we lose our friends
it shall be hard in this troublous world to get them again.'*[40] As it turned out,
the threat from Thomas Fastolf came to nothing, but there could be no
guarantee that the ambitions of the Duke of Norfolk would be so easy to
shake off.

Nor was that the last of the shocks which the summer of 1467 had in store.
On 26 August, nearly eight years after Fastolf's death, the legal battle over the
administration of his will at last came to judgement. The court's ruling
awarded probate jointly to John Paston II and Thomas Howes. This was a
decision which should straightforwardly have been a victory for the Pastons'
cause; after all, it had been John Paston's version of events which named
himself and Howes as Fastolf's sole executors. It was a long time, however,
since anything to do with Fastolf's will had been straightforward. More
specifically, it was years since the family had been able to rely on Thomas
Howes for any kind of support, and John II now had to face the fact that,
after all their struggles, this was not victory, but at best another move in the
game. Only two months earlier, John II had formally accused Yelverton and
Worcester of bribing witnesses to testify against the Pastons' version of the
will, and Howes had responded by giving a lengthy statement repudiating
the allegations. He had asked the witnesses to come forward himself, Howes
declared, *'for great remorse I have in my soul of the untrue forging and con-
triving certain testaments and last will by naked words in my said Master
Fastolf's name after he was deceased'.*[41] He went on to give a detailed rebuttal
of the Pastons' claims – for the first time not only denying that their key witnesses had been present in Fastolf's chamber when the new will had allegedly been made, but explicitly accusing John Paston of forgery and deception.
If John II could now argue that he had the court's sanction to administer
what he believed to be Fastolf's last will, then Yelverton and Worcester could
– through Thomas Howes – maintain exactly the same thing. There was no
disguising the fact that, little by little, the Pastons' hold on the Fastolf lands
was becoming more tenuous. They had no option but to keep up their
defences as best they could, and watch and wait for a new opportunity to
seek powerful help.

The new year brought with it, if not a new opportunity, then at least a
fillip for John II and John III in the form of a diversion from their troubles.
In the course of the negotiations with the Duke of Burgundy which King
Edward had pursued, much to the Earl of Warwick's irritation, in 1467, a
marriage was proposed between Edward's twenty-year-old sister Margaret –

the girl who had stayed at Fastolf's Southwark house with her mother and younger brothers almost seven years earlier – and Duke Philip's son and heir Charles. John II, now every inch the worldly courtier, wagered half the price of '*an ambling horse*' that Warwick's pro-French policy would prevail and the marriage would not take place.[42] He lost the bet, but won a place in the Princess's huge entourage when she travelled to Flanders for her sumptuous wedding in June 1468. Chief among the ladies who attended her was Elizabeth, the young Duchess of Norfolk. The Duchess seems to have taken a liking to John III during the time he spent in her husband's service, and, despite the previous year's tensions over Caister, she invited him to travel with the wedding party in her own retinue. Both brothers therefore witnessed Princess Margaret's ceremonial entry into Bruges, carried on a litter of crimson cloth of gold, to be greeted by pageants, tournaments and feasts which continued for more than a week. John III was dazzled:

> As for the guiding here in this country, it is as worshipful as all the world can devise it, and there were never Englishmen had so good cheer out of England that ever I heard of . . . And as for the Duke's court, as of lords, ladies and gentlewomen, knights, squires and gentlemen, I heard never of none like to it save King Arthur's court. By my troth, I have no wit nor remembrance to write to you half the worship that is here . . .[43]

The respite was brief. Only a couple of months after their return from Flanders, the Duke of Norfolk's speculative interest in Caister suddenly took more concrete and much more threatening form when Yelverton, Worcester and Howes agreed to sell the castle and a number of other Fastolf properties to the Duke for 500 marks. Thomas Howes explained their decision by arguing that the Paston claim to the estates was '*not just nor true*', and that he and Fastolf's other executors needed money '*to dispose in charityful deeds to do for his soul*'.[44] It seems more likely that Yelverton and his allies were seeking to win the dispute by proxy, or at least, after nine exhausting years, to end their own involvement and their liability. By selling the estates they could indeed secure the means to make some sort of provision for Fastolf's soul, but also pay off their own obligations and reward themselves as they believed the old knight had wanted, while passing on the battle against the Pastons to more powerful men. In fact, it seems that Norfolk's purchase of Caister was one part of a more comprehensive projected sale of Fastolf's lands: the Archbishop of Canterbury had his eye on the manor of Guton Hall, while the Duchess of Suffolk, to no one's surprise, was circling acquisitively around her husband's birthplace of Cotton.

Whatever the arguments over the Paston claim to the inheritance, Caister in the hands of the Duke of Norfolk, and the rest of the estates carved up between other great lords, clearly did not satisfy any version of Fastolf's last wishes. Nine years into the dispute, that was a price which Yelverton at least was prepared to pay, although Thomas Howes seems to have been less certain about the deal. An anonymous but well-informed correspondent urged John II to arrange for pressure to be brought to bear on Howes, the last to join the anti-Paston alliance, and always potentially its weakest link. If he were *'made believe and put in hope of the moon shone in the water and I know not what'*, John II was told, *'that such labour were made that either he should be a pope, or else in despair to be deprived of every ecclesiastical benefice for simony, lechery, perjury and double variable peevishness, and for administering without authority'* – if all of this were impressed upon him *'half in game and half in earnest, it should make him to depart, for Yelverton and he are half at variance now'*.[45] However, even if it was true that Howes and Yelverton were on the brink of falling out, the Pastons' opportunity to exploit the differences between the two men was snatched away almost immediately. Howes died on 4 February 1469, too soon to see what would become of the legacy of a master to whom he remained devoted to the very end. All hope of undermining Yelverton's position by regaining Howes's support died with him.[46]

At least Caister itself was still in Paston hands. The Duke had paid only 300 marks, a fraction of the estate's real value, because what he was buying was a disputed title, not possession of the property itself. However, he could – and did – send his men to harass the tenants there, and the possibility that he might make some move to seize the castle was sufficiently serious that in November 1468 John II engaged four professional soldiers to help his brother protect it. *'. . . they are proved men and cunning in the war and in feats of arms'*, he told John III, *'and they can well shoot both guns and crossbows, and amend and string them, and devise bulwarks or any things that should be a strength to the place; and they will, as need is, keep watch and ward.'* He was concerned that the local men on whom his brother could call might be too afraid for their own property to be reliable beyond question in the face of attack; these men-at-arms would provide leadership and expertise to shore up Caister's defences – albeit that John II's efforts at recruitment had characteristic drawbacks. *'They are sad and well advised men'*, he wrote, *'saving one of them which is bald and called William Penny, which is as good a man as goes on the earth, saving a little he will, as I understand, be a little cupshotten'* – in other words, too fond of his drink.[47] Despite its small size and potential deficiencies, the new garrison provided reassurance in case the worst should happen, and in the meantime acted as a deterrent by making clear to Norfolk that the castle could be taken only with a degree of force to which the King was unlikely to turn a blind eye. However, it also represented a significant new drain on resources, which could not easily be met. In May 1469, only six months after the soldiers had been retained, Richard Calle wrote from Caister to tell John II that money was needed urgently '*that men's wages might be paid, for they complain grievously*', he said; ' . . . *there is like to grow right an evil noise of it if it should endure any while*'. The family's finances were now so precarious that, as Calle pointed out, his job was costing him money; he had spent forty shillings out of his own funds, '*and of all this twelvemonth I have not had one penny for my wages*'.[48] John II and his brother were caught in a vicious circle: without money, they would struggle to protect their tenants from their enemies' demands, but the attempt to secure money from their harassed estates risked alienating or ruining the tenants altogether. '*And labour hastily a remedy for these premises*', Margaret warned her eldest son, '*or else Sir John Fastolf's livelihood, though you enter it peaceably, shall not be worth to you a groat this year without you will undo your tenants*'.[49]

Exactly what that remedy should be, however, was not at all clear. John II could still count on support from Archbishop Neville, who reacted with fury when he heard of the Duke of Norfolk's deal with Yelverton and Worcester. '. . . *it is open in every man's mouth in this country the language that my lord of York and my lord of Warwick had to my lord of Norfolk in the King's chamber*', John II was told in October 1468, '*and that my lord of York said, rather than the land should go so, he would come dwell there himself*'. Norfolk was unprepared for the vehemence of this attack, and responded limply by implying that it was his wife rather than himself who was set on the purchase of Caister ('*he would speak to my lady his wife and entreat her*').[50] However, it was difficult to feel confident that the Archbishop's outrage would produce tangible results for the Pastons' cause, since the Nevilles' relationship with the King had not improved since the tensions of the previous year. Edward was hoping that Warwick could gradually be brought to accept participation in government rather than the controlling share he wanted; to that end, the King had not turned a completely cold shoulder to his cousin, but had been careful to offer him continuing marks of trust and favour. Nevertheless, Edward's determination to rule independently of Warwick's influence was unmistakable. The Earl was no longer the irresistible force he had once been, and, as a result, there was more room for manoeuvre in the power structures around the King than had been the case for some years. Apart from anything else, a new element had been introduced into the political dynamics of Edward's regime by his marriage to Elizabeth Woodville four years earlier. Leading members of the nobility scrambled to ally themselves with the new Queen's many relatives, a process in which the King's need to provide for his wife's two sons, five brothers and seven sisters coincided with his magnates' concern to position themselves advantageously at the reconfigured court. The rapid series of betrothals included, in 1465, a startling match between Catherine, dowager Duchess of Norfolk, the young Duke's grandmother, who was in her late sixties and had already survived three husbands, and the Queen's brother Sir John Woodville, who was only just out of his teens. John Paston II could not hope to compete in this stampede for the members of the Queen's immediate family, but it was with some political nous that he realised a more distant Woodville connection might not be beyond his reach. He had never before shown any inclination to find himself a wife, but at the beginning of 1469 he sought the hand in marriage of one of the Queen's cousins, a gentlewoman named Anne Haute. By the end of February he was engaged.

The benefits of his strategy were immediately apparent. The King and Queen for the first time showed an interest in the Pastons' troubles. News reached John II via one of Anne Haute's brothers that King Edward had sent a letter to the Duke of Norfolk ordering him to put '*all manner of matters*' into abeyance until the King '*shall take a direction therein*'. Queen Elizabeth, meanwhile – well aware that there were powerful female influences behind the young Dukes of Norfolk and Suffolk – wrote to '*my lady of Norfolk and another letter unto my lady of Suffolk the elder, desiring them to commune with my lords that all such matters as the King wrote unto them for may be kept so that no default be found in them*'.[51] The dowager Duchess of Suffolk, than whom there were few more canny political operators, was straightaway prepared to soften her previously aggressive stance to one of gracious friendship – '*it is told me that my lady of Suffolk has promised you her goodwill if your bargain of the marriage holds*', Margaret reported in March – before retreating to her home at Ewelme in Oxfordshire, '*that she might be far and out of the way, and the rather feign excuse because of age or sickness, if that the King would send for her for your matters*'.[52] There was reason to hope that these expressions of royal concern might at least curb the two Dukes' ambitions in relation to the Fastolf estates, but John II also secured more explicitly partisan support from the Queen's brother Anthony Woodville, Lord Scales. Although Scales's only previous intervention in the family's affairs had been predatory – he seems to have been involved in pressing the charge of villeinage against John Paston in the last year of his life – he responded to his cousin's engagement by offering John II his protection. This was not simply a matter of charity on Scales's part: his marriage to the Scales heiress had brought him estates in western Norfolk along with his title, and he saw in the Pastons' predicament an appealing opportunity to assert his own authority in the region at the Duke of Norfolk's expense. It was with some relish, therefore, that Scales wrote to one of Norfolk's counsellors in April requiring that, '*forasmuch as marriage is fully concluded between the said Sir John Paston and one of my nearest kinswomen*', and that '*nature must compel me the rather to show my goodwill, assistance and favour unto the said Sir John in such things as concern his inheritance*', the Duke should end his harassment of the tenants at Caister until a settlement could be found, '*to the saving of the right title of the said Sir John Paston*'.[53]

Margaret, who was scarcely able to believe that help was at last on the horizon, could not stop herself from telling her son that Scales's support was more than he merited. '*You are beholden to my lord of his good report of you in this country*', she wrote, '*for he reported better of you than I trow you deserve.*' She was pleased about John II's engagement – '*I pray God send you joy and worship together*' – although she was also, as ever, worried, partly about whether he would commit himself to the costs of married life before he was sure enough of his lands, and partly about whether he was temperamentally ready for the commitment. '. . . *before God*', she told him, '*you are as greatly bound to her as you were married; and therefore I charge you upon my blessing that you be as true to her as she were married unto you in all degrees*'.[54] John III, on the other hand, sounded amused at the prospect: '*I pray you send me word whether you shall be made a Christian man before you come home or not*'.[55] He was under a great deal of pressure at Caister, both because money was so short and as a result of Norfolk's aggression, but he still managed flashes of his usual resilient humour. '. . . *whoever sends you word that I have spent you any money since you went hence*', he told his brother, '*they must give you another reckoning, saving in meat and drink, for I eat like a horse of purpose to eat you out at the doors; but that needs not, for you come not within them, wherefore, so God help me, the fellowship here think that you have forgotten us all.*'[56] However, strain and frustration were beginning to show through the familiar banter. He knew the Duke and Duchess of Norfolk better than anyone in the family, and was convinced that John II was mishandling the situation by not petitioning them directly. '. . . *by God that redeemed me, the best Earl in England would not deal so with my lord and my lady as you do without making of some means to them',* he wrote; *'so God help me, whosoever advises you to do so, he is not your friend.'*[57] Still, if he was miserable, he would not let it show in public. He asked his brother to send him a hat and a bonnet from London – the messenger, by John III's specific instruction, to wear the stiffened hat rather than carry it, to save it from being squashed out of shape in transit. *'I have need to both',* he said, *'for I may not ride nor go out at the doors with none that I have, they be so lewd; a mulberry bonnet, and a black or a tawny hat.'* It took two months, but John II got them for him – *'To begin, God yield you for my hats',* John III wrote in June.[58]

It was fortunate that the hats arrived when they did, since John III was required to make a good showing when King Edward visited Norfolk that same month, on his way north to deal with an outbreak of disorder in Yorkshire. After several years during which Edward had succeeded in bringing much-needed stability to his realm, the political world was again becoming more uncertain. The unsettling effects of the growing tension between the King and the Earl of Warwick were compounded in 1468 by an attempted Lancastrian invasion of Wales led by Henry VI's half-brother Jasper Tudor, with assistance from the King of France. Tudor's small force was repelled before it could do any serious damage, but the threat which further French support for the Lancastrian cause might pose was underlined by fresh fears of pro-Lancastrian conspiracies within England. One of those who came under suspicion was the Earl of Oxford, Warwick's brother-in-law, who was arrested in November 1468 and imprisoned in the Tower. His father and brother had been executed for treason in the first year of Edward's reign, but Oxford managed to avoid following them to the scaffold, even if it was at the cost of sending others to their deaths: *'he has confessed much things',* it was reported in December, and was pardoned and released early in 1469.[59] Meanwhile, for the first time there were serious rumblings of popular discontent with Edward's government, largely because he had demanded a grant of taxation from his subjects to pay for an invasion of France which failed to materialise once the money had been collected. In April 1469 risings erupted in Yorkshire and Lancashire, led by men calling themselves Robin of Redesdale and Robin of Holderness. Both rebellions were suppressed easily enough, but by the beginning of June news reached London that the Redesdale rising was reanimating itself. This time, King Edward intended to deal personally with what he saw as no more than a little local difficulty, but decided on his leisurely way north to make pilgrimages to Bury St Edmunds in Suffolk and Walsingham in Norfolk, stopping at Norwich en route.

John II hoped to travel from London with the King, even though it would mean decking out twenty servants in new livery. He proposed that Margaret should take charge at Caister, '*as there shall be no doubt for the keeping of the place while the King is in that country*', leaving his brother, he thought, with the possibility of rejoining the Duke of Norfolk's household. '. . . *whether you will offer yourself to wait upon my lord of Norfolk or not, I would you did that best were to do*', he wrote.[60] In the event, the idea that John III could move seamlessly from defending Caister against the Duke to serving in his retinue proved a bridge too far, and he was not offered Norfolk's blue-and-tawny livery for the royal visit. However, a substantial Woodville contingent accompanied the King to Norwich, and in John II's absence, delayed yet again by legal business in London, John III busied himself in discussions with the family's new patrons about how best to take advantage of the King's presence to press the Paston case. Scales and his brother Sir John Woodville, whom John III entertained to lunch with a number of other gentlemen from the royal household, were particularly reassuring. '*And when that I prayed them at any time to show their favour to your matter*,' he reported back to John II, '*they answered that it was their matter as well as yours, considering the alliance between you*', and '*bade me that I should cast no doubts but that you should have your intent*'. However, concrete action proved harder to come by than comforting words. Scales's father, Earl Rivers, promised to ask the King to speak to the Dukes of Norfolk and Suffolk on the Pastons' behalf, but John III could not be sure whether he had done so before his departure, and when he checked with Scales himself the response he received was worthy of Archbishop Neville in its airiness: '*he gave me this answer, that, whether he had spoken to the King or not, that the matter should do well enough*'.[61]

From King Edward himself there were conflicting signals. William Brandon, one of the Duke of Norfolk's men and no friend to the Pastons, asked the King to favour the Duke in his claim to Caister, and the King took the request very badly. '*Brandon*', he said, '*though thou can beguile the Duke of Norfolk, and bring him about the thumb as thou list, I let thee know thou shall not do me so, for I understand thy false dealing well enough*.' If this was cheering news, John III was quick to warn his brother against any complacency. An acquaintance in the King's household had promised to draw Edward's attention to the ruined lodge at Hellesdon when the royal party rode past the manor on the way out of Norwich towards Walsingham, but the sight of their damaged property did not have the effect for which the Pastons were hoping. '... *my uncle William says that the King told him his own mouth when he had ridden forby the lodge in Hellesdon warren that he supposed as well that it might fall down by the self as be plucked down*', John III reported.

> ... *And then my uncle says how that he answered the King that you trusted to his good grace that he should set you through with both the Dukes by means of treaty, and he says that the King answered him that he would neither treat nor speak for you but for to let the law proceed.*[62]

It was a disingenuous response. The Pastons' difficulty was yet again one of timing: in 1469, as had been the case in 1461 when John II sought the King's help at Dedham on his first stay at court, Edward was under pressure. Until the Earl of Warwick had been conclusively brought to heel, the threat of a Lancastrian resurgence averted, and the unrest in the country stamped out, the King would not risk alienating magnates as powerful as the Dukes of Norfolk and Suffolk, even had the justice of the Pastons' case been clear beyond doubt, which of course it was not. In these circumstances, the command to '*let the law proceed*' allowed Edward to opt out of engaging with the politics of the dispute and the niceties (or otherwise) of his lords' behaviour. He would not condone the Duke of Norfolk's actions, but nor would he slap him down, which in practice meant that the Duke could continue to make the Pastons' lives extremely difficult at Caister, just as the Duke of Suffolk had already done at Hellesdon. Despite the Woodvilles' fine speeches, John III was concerned. '... *labour your matters effectually, for by my troth it is need*', he told his brother, '*for, for all their words of pleasure, I cannot understand what their labour in this country has done good; wherefore be not over-swift till you be sure of your land, but labour sore the law, for by my troth, till that be passed with you, you get but easy help, as I can understand.*'[63]

The great opportunity of the King's visit to Norfolk had come and gone, and the brothers had little to show for it, other than that John III had made his customary good impression, personal and political, on those he had met. Lord Scales had spoken to him about the possibility of entering the King's service for the coming campaign to suppress the northern rising, but, as ever, John III put his family responsibilities first. '*I made no promise so to be*', he told John II, '*for I told him that I was not worth a groat without you, and therefore I would make no promise to nobody till they had your goodwill first; and so we departed.*' He was unwilling to leave his post at Caister, but also aware that apparent signs of favour might not always be what they seemed; he had heard a rumour that royal letters had been issued summoning his brother to attend on the King, but *'if it be so I think verily it is done to have you from London by craft, that you shall not labour your matters to a conclusion this term but put them in delay'.*[64]

John III could not have known it, but the difficulty of being away from London turned out to be the least of the Pastons' – or the country's – problems stemming from the King's journey to the north. All still seemed well when Edward left Walsingham for Lincolnshire, and then spent a week with Queen Elizabeth, who had recently given birth to their third daughter, at Fotheringhay in Northamptonshire. From Fotheringhay he moved on to Grantham, and then to Newark. There, at the beginning of the second week in July, he received devastating news. The second wave of the Redesdale rising was no local disturbance: it was a full-scale revolt fomented and orchestrated by the Earl of Warwick. Edward had hoped that his cousin would come to accept that he could no longer dictate royal policy, and was prepared to allow Warwick an influential – if no longer dominant – role within his government if he did so. The inescapable and horrifying conclusion in July 1469 was that his strategy had failed. In the end, it seemed, Warwick could not tolerate his royal protégé's determination to rule for himself. The northern rebels were no peasant rabble, but a well-equipped and well-organised force bigger than Edward's own. Rather than press on to meet them, the King retreated to Nottingham to await reinforcements.

Warwick himself had spent most of June in Kent, ostensibly supervising the refitting of one of his ships. His brother the Archbishop of York joined him there. So, too, did King Edward's twenty-year-old brother George, Duke of Clarence – who, until such time as Queen Elizabeth should produce a son, was also the next male heir to Edward's throne. Two years earlier, Warwick had planned that Clarence should marry Isabel, the elder of his two daughters. With so many noble heirs snapped up by the swarm of Woodville brides, the Earl was convinced that the King's brothers were the only fitting husbands for his daughters, while Clarence was understandably attracted by a match with one of the wealthiest heiresses in the country. However, the King was seeking to restrain Warwick's ambition rather than encourage it with a royal marriage, and he refused permission for the wedding to take place. Unfortunately for Edward, Clarence – who was vain, ambitious and profoundly immature – took the refusal as badly as his prospective father-in-law, to such an extent that he was now, extraordinarily, prepared to join Warwick in rebellion against his own brother. On 6 July,

Warwick, Clarence and Archbishop Neville sailed to Calais where, less than a week later, in open defiance of the King's command, Clarence married Isabel Neville. Also present at the ceremony was the Nevilles' brother-in-law, the Earl of Oxford, whom Edward had released from the Tower only months earlier.

In the middle of July, Warwick and his allies arrived back in England. They sent ahead a manifesto claiming they wanted only to remedy the ills of Edward's government by freeing the King from '*the deceivable covetous rule and guiding of certain seditious persons*' – in other words, those, including the Woodvilles, who Warwick believed had supplanted his rightful role in government.[65] Edward – still hoping to avert the crisis, or at least to buy himself some time – had written on 9 July in temperate terms to Warwick, Clarence and the Archbishop, requesting that they should come to him '*as soon as you goodly may*'. '*We trust not*', he told Warwick, '*that you should be of any such disposition towards us as the rumour here runs, considering the trust and affection we bear in you . . . And cousin*', he added as a postscript, '*think not but you shall be to us welcome.*'[66] The damage, however, was far too deep to be repaired by warm words. Warwick ignored Edward's summons, and armed confrontation now seemed inevitable. With his recent patron Archbishop Neville on one side, and his new lords the Woodvilles on the other, John Paston II was caught in the middle. The Archbishop's brother-in-law Oxford, with whom John II had had friendly dealings over the past couple of years, wrote on 18 July to ask him to procure some horse armour – a letter which the Earl addressed to '*my especial true-hearted friend*', adding, '*I trust to God we shall do right well*'.[67] However, if Oxford expected John II's support, so too did King Edward. A few days later, John II received a summons to join the King's forces at Doncaster on 3 August, '*with as many men defensible in array as you can bring to us*', to resist '*the malice of our enemies, traitors and rebels*'.[68]

Edward himself never arrived at Doncaster. On 26 July, at Edgecote in Northamptonshire, a division of his army on its way to his muster was defeated by the Earl of Warwick's northern supporters. Three days later, the King – who had not yet received news of the battle – set out from Nottingham to join reinforcements which no longer existed. Edward was captured on the road outside Northampton, and taken under guard to his cousin's castle at Warwick. The King had already sent those members of the Woodville family who had attended him in Norfolk away for their own safety: Lord Scales escaped, but his father, Earl Rivers, and his young brother, Sir John Woodville, were caught and beheaded – the latter leaving his elderly bride, the dowager Duchess of Norfolk, a widow for the fourth time. With King Edward a prisoner, the normal rules of government were effectively suspended. If the Pastons had any doubts about what the chaos would mean for them, they were quickly dispelled. On 21 August, the Duke of Norfolk sent an army to lay siege to Caister Castle.

John Paston II, the gawky teenager turned cultured courtier, had come a long way since his father's death, but he had arrived precisely nowhere. Or worse than nowhere: the fabric of politics had been ripped to shreds for the second time in a decade, and this time his family could not choose to lie low until the fighting was over. This time, the battle had come to them.

CHAPTER TEN

– *till better peace be* –

The Pastons' garrison at Caister, under the command of John III, numbered about thirty men. John Daubeney and John Pamping were there, as was Margaret's cousin Osbert Berney, the illegitimate son of her maternal uncle, who had served the family for some years. The rest of the castle's defenders ranged in experience and expertise from the four professional soldiers hired by John II eight months earlier, to the indomitable figure of Thomas Stumps, so called because he had no hands, who nevertheless insisted he could shoot a crossbow. Between them, they had twenty guns of various sizes, and had taken their training so seriously over the summer that they had broken three steel bows practising their shots. The castle – complete with its moat, tower and crenellations – was designed to be defensible, and they had hoped that their presence would be enough to convince the Duke of Norfolk that he could not take it without breaching the peace spectacularly enough for King Edward's fury to be unavoidable. By August 1469, however, the peace had been shattered by the Earl of Warwick's rebellion, and the King was no longer in a position to object to anything Norfolk cared to do. As a result, the thirty men of the Caister garrison found themselves facing an army hundreds strong, with field artillery deployed in three positions around the castle walls.

If it seemed unlikely that the Duke would risk wholesale damage to a house he wanted for himself, that did not mean the siege was a sham. The feast of St Bartholomew, which fell three days after the army first arrived at Caister, '*was a cruel day*', William Worcester recorded in one of his notebooks, '*with guns fired at the castle*'.[1] Rather than an all-out assault, the plan seemed to be to prevent food and supplies reaching John III and his men, and in the meantime to intensify the pressure on them as much as possible by making clear that their lives would be at risk for as long as they refused to surrender the castle into Norfolk's hands. John III, meanwhile, was determined to hold out until his brother could muster help. What form that help might take, however, was far from obvious. The difficulty was that the circumstances which had allowed the Duke to act in the first place – the disintegration of political order at the highest level – also made responding to his attack deeply problematic. Control of government now lay in the hands of the Earl of Warwick, who was attempting to rule in his cousin's name by taking control of the royal council with support from his brother Archbishop Neville, his brother-in-law the Earl of Oxford, and his new son-in-law the Duke of Clarence. Warwick, Oxford and the Archbishop had been sympathetic to the Pastons' cause in the recent past, but their new eminence did not straightforwardly bode well for the family's interests. In his determination to regain what he saw as his rightful place at the heart of government, Warwick had overlooked the fact that trying to rule on King Edward's behalf, when Edward was clearly neither incapable of ruling for himself nor happy to be sidelined in this way, left Warwick himself bereft of authority. The council of lords was just that – a council of lords – rather than an anointed sovereign, and their ability to command the Duke of Norfolk, their peer rather than their subject, was therefore extremely limited.

The prospect of negotiating a resolution to the siege was difficult even in the practical terms of how talks should be conducted, let alone their substance. The Duke of Norfolk's men would allow no messages to pass in or out of Caister's walls. John II, frantically searching for support in London, was therefore attempting to negotiate without any clear sense of exactly how long his brother might be able to hold out, while John III was trying to hold out without any clear sense of the progress of negotiations. Margaret, staying at her mother-in-law Agnes's house in Norwich, was stuck in the middle – closer to the military action at Caister, about which she was desperately worried, but further away from the political manoeuvres in which her eldest son was engaged. Predictably enough, she had little confidence either that he understood the gravity of the situation, or that he would respond with sufficient urgency or judgement. Ten days after the siege began, the Duke of Norfolk – who was directing operations at Caister from a base a couple of miles away at Great Yarmouth – sent an envoy to Margaret with an offer for John II: if he would allow the Duke to take possession of Caister peacefully, Norfolk would agree to pay compensation for all wrongs done to the Pastons if the courts subsequently found in the family's favour. This was so bad a deal as to be no deal at all. If possession was nine-tenths of the law – and more than nine-tenths, if the person in possession were a duke at a time when there was no higher authority in the land to overrule him – then this would be not compromise but capitulation. Margaret had an alternative proposal, suggested, she told John II, by 'a faithful friend of ours': that a neutral party should hold the castle and take

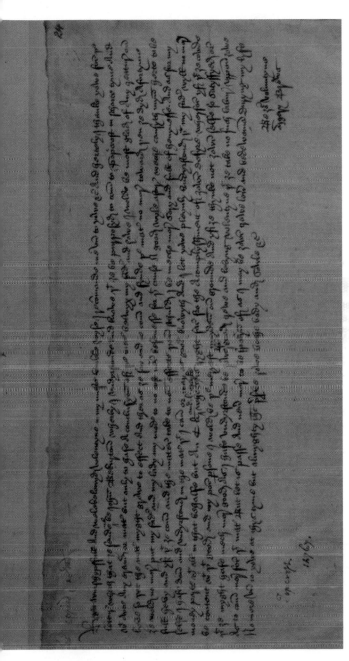

14 Letter written by a clerk for Margery Brews, addressed to her 'Ryg* r*ur*chypfull and welebelouyd volentyne' ('Right worshipful and well-beloved valentine'), John Paston III, February 1477.

15 The Neville family. George Neville, Archbishop of York, wears a mitre at the back of the group.

16 The battle of Mortimer's Cross, 2 February 1461. On the morning of the battle three suns were seen in the sky, a phenomenon claimed as a portent of his victory by eighteen-year-old Edward, Earl of March, the future Edward IV. In this illuminated manuscript of scenes from Edward's life, crowns descend towards him with the suns' rays. Edward later adopted the 'sun in splendour' as his personal badge.

17 The Office of the Dead. Mourners hold torches around a coffin as the funeral mass is sung.

18 The ruins of Bromholm Priory, near Paston on the Norfolk coast, where John Paston was buried in 1466.

19 Queen Elizabeth Woodville. By an unknown artist.

20 A fifteenth-century tournament. The knights display heraldic crests on their helmets; the ladies wear steeple headdresses, with hairlines plucked to achieve a fashionably high forehead.

21 The court of Charles the Bold, Duke of Burgundy.

22 The figure on the left is Richard Neville, Earl of Warwick, the 'Kingmaker'. In the centre is his elder daughter Isabel, and on the right her husband George, Duke of Clarence, younger brother of Edward IV. From the Rous Roll, a history of the Earls of Warwick compiled in the 1480s.

23 Edward IV enthroned on the wheel of Fortune. Illumination by an English artist before 1465.

24 The battle of Barnet, 14 April 1471, at which both John Paston II and John Paston III fought in the Lancastrian army under the command of the Earl of Oxford.

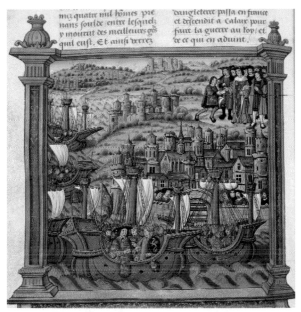

25 Edward IV and his fleet arriving at Calais in preparation for the invasion of France in 1475. John II, John III and their brother Edmund were among the English forces.

RICARDVS · III · ANG · REX ·

26 Richard III. By an unknown artist, sixteenth century.

27 Henry VII. Painted terracotta bust by Pietro Torrigiano, early sixteenth century.

the profits until the title to the estate could be determined in the courts. Margaret thought this a good idea – or, at the very least, preferable to the current situation. '*Of all these premises send word how you will be demeaned by as good advice as you can get, and make no longer delay*', she told her eldest son;

> for they must needs have hasty succour that be in the place, for they be sore hurt and have no help. And if they have hasty help it shall be the greatest worship that ever you had, and if they be not helped it shall be to you a great disworship, and look never to have favour of your neighbours and friends but if this speed well. Therefore take it in your mind and purvey therefor in haste.

Her tendency since her husband's death to think the worst of John II's good sense, or lack of it, was compounded by the fact that he was such a bad correspondent. '*Robin came home yester evening*', she wrote, '*and he brought me neither writing from you nor good answer of this matter, which grieves me right ill that I have sent you so many messengers and have so feeble answer again.*'[2]

John II *was* a bad correspondent, it was true – but in this instance he could perhaps be excused for feeling that writing to his mother was not his first priority. By the beginning of September – having revived the association with Archbishop Neville which had taken second place in recent months to his Woodville connections – John II had secured some assistance from the lords of the council in the person of Walter Writtle, a gentleman in the service of the Duke of Clarence. Writtle was dispatched from London to Caister, armed with the authority of the lords, such as it was, to broker an end to the siege. Whatever Margaret believed, John II's letters to Writtle make clear how desperately concerned he was, and how deeply he was torn between, on the one hand, the need to ensure that his brother and his men were safe, and, on the other, the fear – after everything his family had been through – of losing Caister completely. Always, incorrigibly, the optimist, he was hoping that the intervention of the lords in the name of the King might convince the Duke of Norfolk to withdraw, and in the meantime urged Writtle not to cut a deal on the Duke's terms if John III could continue to hold out against the siege:

> For, as God help me, I had liefer the place were burned, my brother and servants saved, than the best appointment that ever you and I communed of should by my goodwill be taken, if this message from the King may rescue it . . . For in good faith this matter sticks more nigh my heart and me than I

can write unto you, and to my brother and servants more near than, as
God knows, they know of. Wherefore, Master Writtle, all our welfare rests
in you, beseeching you to remember it, for this matter is to all us either
making or marring.[3]

The proposal which Writtle took with him to Yarmouth was that the
Duke should lift the siege while the dispute was adjudicated by the lords of
the council. Several days passed without news, which John II took to be a
good sign: '*my lord Archbishop and other of my lords and I deemed because of*
your long tarrying that by your sad discretion all had been set through', he told
Writtle. They were wrong. When a message finally arrived, it was to say that
the Duke preferred not to accept the lords' suggestion. Instead, he was insisting that Caister should be handed over to him until the question of title was
determined by law. As John II pointed out, this was exactly the deal which
the Duke had proposed to Margaret at the end of August, and Norfolk and
his advisers had therefore moved not an inch in response to the council's
intervention. '*I cannot understand what regard my lord's counsel takes to my*
lords' letter and to your labour in this behalf', he wrote, '*but that they offered as*
largely before'. Writtle's advice, nevertheless, was that the Duke's proposal
should be accepted, as much as anything to rescue John III and his men, who
were beginning to run out of supplies. John II – under a different kind of
pressure in London, and unable because of the siege to communicate directly with his brother – was incredulous that it could yet be a question of safeguarding their lives, '*which you think doubtful if so be that they lack stuff, shot*
and victuals; marvelling sore and think it impossible in this short season, or in
four times the season hithertowards, that they should lack, either without it so
be that my lord's men have entered out the place and so had the stuff from
them, which I cannot think.'[4]

Writtle had achieved nothing, but felt that he could do no more, protesting that he dared not exceed the authority he had been given. John II, with
as much respect as he could muster given his shock and frustration, told him
he protested too much:

You write in your letter that you dare not pass your credence. Please you to
remember, that said your credence before the lords was right large, and as
large as might well be in this matter both to my lord's counsel of Norfolk to
withdraw the siege, with more other matter as you know, and to the justice
of the peace and to the sheriff and his officers – your authority was great
enough to each of them. Wherefore, Master Writtle, I never for this nor yet
will take appointment in this matter but as my lords will and my lord

> Archbishop, which as well as I myself have wholly put our trust to your dis-
> creet direction.

The problem was that, however great the goodwill of Archbishop Neville and his allies, their attention and their interests were principally focused elsewhere, on their attempt to govern in the name of a king whom they had imprisoned; and the very nature of their regime meant that they simply did not have the authority to compel the co-operation of the Duke of Norfolk. As a result, Writtle's lack of progress left John II chasing his own tail:

> ... if it be so that, through recklessness, my brother and servants be in such
> jeopardy as you have written to me – which should be half impossible in my
> mind that they should misuse so much stuff in four times the space – and
> that you have evident knowledge by my said brother himself thereof, I
> would pray you to see him and them in surety of their lives, whatsoever
> should fall of the livelihood. Howbeit, I would not that my brother and ser-
> vants should give up the place, not for £1,000, if they might in any wise
> keep it and save their lives . . .[5]

If John II was sure that the situation could not yet be so grave, he was about to be disabused of that certainty. On Tuesday 12 September, Margaret wrote to her son in London with appalling news:

> ... your brother and his fellowship stand in great jeopardy at Caister, and
> lack victuals; and Dauboney and Berney are dead and others greatly hurt,
> and they fail gunpowder and arrows, and the place sore broken with guns
> of the other part; so that, but they have hasty help, they are like to lose both
> their lives and the place, to the greatest rebuke to you that ever came to any
> gentleman, for every man in this country marvels greatly that you suffer
> them to be so long in so great jeopardy without help or other remedy.

Margaret was at the end of her tether. The situation at Caister was parlous, and the loss of two such valuable servants and loyal friends as John Daubeney and Osbert Berney utterly devastating. Her usual manner of writing to John II was weary and critical, but this was different: she was sick with worry, and desperate that he should do something – anything – to rescue the men at Caister from the Duke of Norfolk's guns. Writtle, she was convinced, had done more harm than good – 'The Duke has been more fervently set thereupon, and more cruel, since that Writtle, my lord of Clarence's man, was there than he was before' – and Norfolk had summoned more men and more ordnance to gather at the castle for a 'great assault' planned for the following

Thursday morning. Her advice was to accept Norfolk's terms – to let him have the castle until the law should determine title – but she was even afraid that this arrangement would not now be acceptable to the Duke, given that it had already been refused twice. In that case, she said, the Duke of Clarence or the Archbishop should send instructions to the Earl of Oxford to rescue the Caister garrison, even if it meant giving the castle itself to Oxford for his lifetime in return. She barely had time for reproaches in her urgency: '*Spare not this to be done in haste if you will have their lives and be set by in Norfolk*', she said, '*though you should lose the best manor of all for the rescue. I had liefer you lost the livelihood than their lives.*'[6]

For John II, Margaret's letter was the last straw. His customary mode with his mother was deferential and placating – the product of a lifetime's practice of fending off parental criticism. This time, though, he was angry. Margaret was neither at Caister with his brother, nor in London with him in the attempt to find a solution; she was misinformed and she was panicking, and he was having to find time amid everything else to write to tell her so. For once, the reply he sent on Friday 15 September observed none of the niceties of formal and respectful greeting:

> *Mother, upon Saturday last was, Daubeney and Berney were alive and merry, and I suppose there came no man out of the place to you since that time that could have ascertained to you of their deaths. And as touching the fierceness of the Duke or of his people showed since that time Writtle departed, I trow it was concluded that truce and abstinence of war should be had since he departed, which shall endure till Monday next coming. And by that time I trow that truce shall be taken till that day seven night after, by which time I hope of a good direction shall be had.*

Not only were Daubeney and Berney alive rather than dead, and hostilities temporarily stopped rather than spiralling out of control, but there were other flaws in her proposals. '*And whereas you write to me that I should sue for letters from my lords of Clarence and York*', he said, '*they are not here; and if they wrote to him, as they have done two times, I trow it would not avail*'. John II had been told since his teens that he was irresponsible and lazy, and now – when he was trying his hardest both to protect the family's interests and to rescue his brother and his men from mortal danger – he had had enough:

> *But, mother, I feel by your writing that you deem in me I should not do my devoir without you wrote to me some heavy tidings; and, mother, if I had need to be quickened with a letter in this need I were of myself too slow a*

*fellow. But, mother, I assure you that I have heard ten times worse tidings
since the siege began than any letter that you wrote to me, and some time I
have heard right good tidings both. But this I assure you, that they that be
within have no worse rest than I have, nor cast more jeopardy. But whether
I had good tidings or ill, I take God to witness that I have done my devoir
as I would be done for in case like, and shall do till there be an end of it.*

He had answered back to his mother for the first and only time in his life.
Once he had let off steam, his good nature and his optimism, irrepressible
even under these bleak circumstances, began to reassert themselves. He
could see, after all, that anxiety and fear lay behind Margaret's criticisms,
and he did what he could to reassure her. '*And with God's grace it shall be
remedied well enough*', he wrote; '*for by my troth I had liefer lose the manor of
Caister than the simplest man's life therein, if that may be his salvation.*'[7]

However, the awful truth was that, whatever he did, he was not in a position to guarantee his men's safety. Margaret was not right that Daubeney
and Berney were both dead, but neither was John II right to say that they
were both alive. John Daubeney – loyal 'Daube', who had given devoted service to the Pastons for the best part of ten years – had been killed by a crossbow bolt, probably on Saturday 9 September. In response, the Caister
garrison was returning fire: two men among the Duke of Norfolk's forces
had already been killed by gunshots from the castle. John II wrote to his
brother on Monday 18 September, hoping that the letter would get through
and that his words of comfort would be believed:

*. . . they that are about you are in obloquy of all men, and moreover they
have been written to by as special writing as might be after the world that
now is, and I promise you that the Duke's counsel would that they had
never begun it. And moreover they are charged in pain of their lives that,
though they get the place, they should not hurt one of you. There is neither
you nor none with you but, if he knew what is generally reported of him, he
or you – and God fortune you well – may think him four times better in
reputation of all folk than ever he was.*[8]

Even this attempt at reassurance could not conceal the difficulties of their
situation. John II had certainly acquired '*as special writing as might be after
the world that now is*', but it was not special enough. However violent the
events at Caister, they were not enough to distract attention from the continuing upheavals in national government. King Edward had been moved
from Warwick Castle late in August to another Neville stronghold,

Middleham Castle in Yorkshire. While the King was kept securely out of the way, the Earl of Warwick's attempt to rule in his stead was falling apart. East Anglia was not the only region in which serious disorder had erupted, and it was not only private disputes which were threatening to get out of hand: at the end of August Lancastrian sympathisers began to organise themselves in the far north, and Warwick discovered that no one would answer a call for troops to suppress the revolt on his own questionable authority while the King remained a prisoner. As a result, he had no option but to release Edward from custody. As soon as the King showed himself in public at York – which he did during the week after John Daubeney's death at Caister – forces rallied in his name to defeat the Lancastrian rebels. Having taken the genie out of the bottle, however, Warwick found that he could not put it back. Edward was not about to submit to imprisonment for a second time, and he summoned a number of his nobles from London to join him in Yorkshire.

At Caister, meanwhile, hope was fading. The council under Warwick had already tried and failed to persuade the Duke of Norfolk to back down. If King Edward – preoccupied as he was with the battle for supremacy in his own government – even gave Caister a second thought, it was probably to note that Norfolk's violent self-aggrandisement had, if anything, helped Edward's cause by demonstrating that Warwick could not keep order without him. Moreover, the King's immediate concern was to gather as much noble support as he could to reinforce his newly regained freedom of action; for the time being at least, conciliating Norfolk was likely to take priority over disciplining him. It was becoming chillingly clear that there was no one to whom the Pastons could appeal who had both the will and the authority to help them.

By the third week in September, almost five weeks into the siege, there was no avoiding the conclusion that negotiations would now have to focus on terms for surrender. The objective had been reduced to the bare minimum: to get John III and his remaining men out of the castle in safety. The message was relayed to Norfolk's headquarters at Yarmouth, and on 26 September 1469 formal letters were drawn up under the Duke's seal. Noting that John Paston III and his small garrison had, *against the peace, kept the manor of Caister with force against the will and intent of us the Duke of Norfolk, to our great displeasure*, the Duke nevertheless graciously agreed – at the request of the lords of the council, *and also at the great labour and instance of our most dear and singular beloved wife* – to allow John III and his men to give up the castle, and depart under his safe-conduct.[9]

It was over. John III – of whose feelings during the siege no record exists, since he had no means of communicating with the world beyond his attackers – wrote immediately to let his brother know what had happened: *'we were, for lack of victuals, gunpowder, men's hearts, lack of surety of rescue, driven thereto to take appointment'*. Despite the ordeal he had endured, he was calm, collected, and full of praise for the four men-at-arms who had helped him to lead the castle's defence – *'I pray you give them their thanks'*, he told John II, *'for by my troth they have as well deserved it as any men that ever bare life'*. Unbelievably, he even tried to lift his brother's spirits. *'God preserve you, and I pray you be of good cheer till I speak with you'*, he wrote, *'and I trust to God to ease your heart in some things'*.[10] But there was little comfort to be found. Almost exactly ten years after Fastolf's death, the family's prospects had never looked bleaker. After a decade of struggle, Caister – Fastolf's home, and the greatest prize of the inheritance – was gone. John Daubeney had been killed in the attempt to keep it, and Norfolk's servants were still issuing threats against the remaining members of the garrison, despite the Duke's safeguard, which, in any case, John III had not accepted for himself – *'it were shame to take it'*, he told his brother.[11] Meanwhile, in what increasingly seemed to be a looking-glass world, John II found himself under threat of arrest for his riotous and disorderly conduct in ordering his men to resist the Duke of Norfolk's army.

Yet there was no question but that they would cope. From the beginning of October, John II, John III and Margaret slipped quietly back into their familiar routines, John II in London doing what he could to push their cases forward in the courts, while John III handled the family business in Norfolk. The effect of his recent experiences was evident in John III's concern to ensure that the men who had served under his command at Caister were properly looked after, even though the household of which they had been a part no longer existed. Margaret had promised to give them a month's board, and John III urged his brother to help find other employment for those he could not afford to retain. *'If I were of power to keep them'*, he said feelingly, *'. . . they should never depart from me while I lived'*.[12] He was also determined to ensure that John Daubeney's will was properly fulfilled as his friend had wanted. Otherwise – superficially, at least – he showed remarkably little sign of the trauma of the last two months. There even seemed to be a possibility that he might re-enter the Duke of Norfolk's service; the conflict, after all, had never been personal. John II and Margaret, too, soon settled back into normality after the outbursts which the siege had precipitated. Margaret, of course, had to have the last word with her eldest son: '... *you think that I should write to you fables and imaginations*', she said, '*but I do not so; I have written as it has been informed me, and will do*'. However, when her lectures resumed, they were in relatively subdued mode. '*God visits you as it pleases him in sundry wises*', she wrote. '*He would you should know him and serve him better than you have done before this time, and then he will send you the more grace to do well in all other things*'.[13] For his part, John II was keen to make amends, and made sure to offer an elaborate olive branch at the start of his next letter ('*Right worshipful mother, I commend me to you and beseech you of your blessing, and God thank you for your tenderness and help both to me, my brother and servants*').[14]

It was vital that their differences should be forgotten as quickly as possible, since the project now was bare survival. Money was desperately tight. John III, visiting his brother in London in October, wrote to tell their mother that, '*so God help me, he has at this season not a penny in his purse, nor knows not where to get any*'.[15] They also now had to handle their affairs without John Daubeney, whose death was not only a grievous personal loss but a blow to the management of the family's business. They could ill afford to lose his experience – particularly since, with appalling timing, they had also lost the service of Richard Calle, the man who knew more about the running of their estates than anyone else. He had been in the family's employment for fifteen years; his family were shopkeepers in Framlingham, close by the Duke of Norfolk's castle, and Calle himself had originally been recommended to John Paston by the Duke's father. But it was not the conflict with Norfolk, nor anything so violent as a crossbow bolt, which parted Calle from the Pastons. Instead, it was a marriage proposal.

The first hint that something was amiss in Margaret's household had come six months earlier, when Margaret asked her eldest son to find alternative accommodation for his sister Margery. '*I would you should purvey for your sister to be with my lady of Oxford or with my lady of Bedford, or in some other worshipful place where as you think best*', she told John II, '... *for we be either of us weary of other. I shall tell you more when I speak with you. I pray you do your devoir herein as you will my comfort and welfare and your worship, for divers causes which you shall understand afterward, etc.*'[16] Margaret's reasons for writing in such guarded terms – and for wanting her daughter out of the house – became clear a month later. Margery, at not much more than twenty, had fallen in love with Richard Calle. Not only that, but her feelings were reciprocated. The relationship had begun in secret two years earlier, but the couple were now so committed to one another that they had decided to brave the family's displeasure by seeking permission to marry.

Their request was met with horror. Surprisingly, the most extreme reaction came from John III. '*I conceive by your letter . . . that you have heard of R.C.'s labour which he makes by our ungracious sister's assent*', he wrote to his brother in May; '*but whereas they write that they have my goodwill therein, saving your reverence they falsely lie of it, for they never spoke to me of that matter, nor none other body in their name.*' The only person who had approached him on the subject was a family friend, but '*I can think that it was by Calle's means*', he said, '*for when I asked him whether C. desired him to move me that question or not, he would have got it away by hums and by hays*'. John III's response was implacable. '*I answered him that if my father, whom God assoil, were alive and had consented thereto, and my mother and you both*', he told John II, '*he should never have my goodwill for to make my sister to sell candle and mustard in Framlingham*'.[17]

The family felt they had good reason to be outraged. Their objections were not to Calle in person: he was an intelligent, capable and likeable man, on whom they had relied heavily for years. He was much older than Margery – probably in his late thirties – but that hardly mattered. What did matter was that he was a servant. The Pastons' gentility was so recently acquired, and potentially still so fragile, that the idea of Margery wilfully throwing away her status by marrying into a family of shopkeepers was appalling and distressing in equal measure. If John III's reaction sounds like small-minded snobbery – which comes as a shock by contrast with the easy generosity, warmth and humanity which characterised most of his dealings – it is at least comprehensible in terms of the damage Margery could do to the family's good name. His bitterness may also speak of personal hurt, perhaps less at Margery's conduct than at Calle's. He had worked closely with Calle since his teens, a relationship which had always been one of trust, camaraderie and respect. But Calle had not spoken to him about his intentions towards Margery – probably, of course, because he feared exactly this response. Margery and Calle were left in no doubt that they could not hope to secure the family's blessing for their plans.

However, in the late summer of 1469 – at the worst possible moment, given that Caister was besieged by the Duke of Norfolk's men on 21 August – it became clear that the couple were not prepared to take no for an answer. They married in secret. When Margaret discovered what had happened, Margery – who was evidently too like her strong-willed mother for either's comfort – refused to acquiesce in the face of the family's demands that she renounce her new husband. They were kept apart, Calle in London and Margery under watch in her mother's household. One letter from Calle survives from this period, despite the fact that he urged Margery to burn it as soon as she had read it. Perhaps it was intercepted before it reached her, or perhaps she could not bring herself to destroy it, only for it to be discovered subsequently by her mother. Either way, it is apparent how much pressure the couple were under, and how difficult it was to cope with a situation where they were each being told that the other was betraying them. Calle was suffering, not least because the separation from Margery was almost more than he could bear:

> My own lady and mistress, and before God very true wife, I with heart full sorrowful recommend me unto you as he that cannot be merry, nor naught shall be, till it be otherwise with us than it is yet; for this life that we lead now is neither pleasure to God nor to the world, considering the great bond of matrimony that is made between us, and also the great love that has been, and as I trust yet is, between us, and as on my part never greater . . . it seems a thousand years ago since that I spoke with you.

He could not tolerate the thought of what Margery was enduring for his sake. 'I understand, lady, you have had as much sorrow for me as any gentlewoman has had in the world', he told her; 'as would God all that sorrow that you have had had rested upon me, so that you had been discharged of it . . . it is to me a death to hear that you be entreated otherwise than you ought to be.' All the same, he felt justified in what they had done: they loved each other, and had acted honourably by marrying. Calle must have known exactly what he was jeopardising – his career, his friends, his standing – and was prepared to risk it all; but he was also a proud man, who would not accept that Margery was ruining herself by becoming his wife. 'I marvel much,' he said, 'that they should take this matter so heedfully as I understand they do, remembering it is in such case as it cannot be remedied, and my desert, upon every behalf it is for to be thought there should be none obstacle against it'. Isolated as he was, his mood swung between despair, resignation, defiance and hope. 'I suppose', he wrote, 'if you tell them sadly the truth, they will not damn their souls for us. Though I tell them the truth, they will not believe me as well as they will do you. And therefore, good lady, at the reverence of God be plain to them and tell the truth, and if they will in no wise agree thereto, between God, the Devil and them be it.'[18]

The difficulty for the family was that no witnesses were required to make wedding vows binding: the couple's promises to each other, and the consummation of the relationship, were enough to make the union irrevocable. That had meant that Margaret and her sons were powerless to prevent the marriage, but it also left them a loophole. If Margery could be brought to deny that such promises had been made, escape would be possible. By the end of the first week in September – with John III defending Caister against the Duke of Norfolk's forces, and John II urgently searching for help in London – Margaret and Agnes were grappling with the problem of Margery's wilfulness and determination. The question of whether the marriage had in fact taken place had been referred to the Bishop of Norwich for judgement, and Margaret and Agnes were trying to hold off his investigation until the situation at Caister had been resolved and Margery's brothers could participate in the discussions. The Bishop was sympathetic – '*he knew well that her demeaning had staked sore at our hearts*', Margaret reported – but '*said plainly that he had been required so often for to examine her that he might not, nor would, no longer delay it*'. Margaret and Agnes, meanwhile, were indulging in some wishful thinking on the subject. '*. . . my mother and I informed him*', Margaret said, '*that we could never understand by her saying, by no language that ever she had to him, that neither of them were bound to other*'. They sustained their hopes as best they could until Friday 8 September, when Margery was brought before the Bishop. He did his utmost to remind her what was at stake:

> *how she was born, what kin and friends that she had, and should have more if she were ruled and guided after them; and, if she did not, what rebuke and shame and loss it should be to her , , , and said that he had heard say that she loved such one that her friends were not pleased with that she should have, and therefore he bade her be right well advised how she did, and said that he would understand the words that she had said to him, whether it made matrimony or not.*

In response, Margery did not hesitate for an instant. '*. . . she rehearsed what she had said, and said, if those words made it not sure, she said boldly that she would make it surer before that she went thence; for she said she thought in her conscience she was bound, whatsoever the words were.*' This defiance was the last straw for her mother. '*These lewd words grieve me and her grandam as much as all the remnant*', Margaret told John II.[19]

The investigation proceeded. Bishop Lyhert questioned Calle separately, asking when and where they had married and exactly what words they had used, to see whether his story matched Margery's. Clearly, it did. The Bishop said '*he would not be too hasty to give sentence thereupon*', on the grounds that something else might emerge to stand in the way of the marriage, and postponed his decision for a month. Margery and Calle both protested; '*they would have had their will performed in haste'*, Margaret reported, *'but the Bishop said he would no otherwise than he had said'*. In the meantime, Margaret refused to receive Margery back into her house, and sent messages to friends that they too should refuse to take her in. *'I had given her warning'*, she said; *'she might have been ware before if she had been gracious.'* For all that, she did care where her daughter went. At the Bishop's request, Margery was given temporary lodging in the household of Roger Best, a prominent citizen and former mayor of Norwich. *'I am sorry they are encumbered with her'*, Margaret wrote, *'but yet I am better paid that she is there for the while than she had been in other place, because of the sadness and good disposition of himself and his wife, for she shall not be suffered there to play the brothel.'* The situation was deeply painful, but she was determined to stand firm; no compromise was possible given the extent to which, in Margaret's eyes, her daughter had betrayed the family by her duplicity and disobedience. *'I pray you and require you that you take it not pensively'*, she told John II sternly, perhaps as much to convince herself as him, *'for I know well it goes right near your heart, and so does it to mine and to other; but remember you, and so do I, that we have lost of her but a brothel, and set it the less to heart; for if she had been good, whatsoever she had been it should not have been as it is, for if he were dead at this hour she should never be at my heart as she was.'* John II had suggested they might find other ways to undo the damage, but, as Calle had predicted, Margaret would not countenance the idea that they should *'damn their souls for us'* by seeking to annul a marriage which – however objectionable it might be – was nevertheless lawful in the eyes of God:

> . . . *as for the divorce that you wrote to me of, I suppose what you meant, but I charge you upon my blessing that you do not, nor cause no other to do, that should offend God and your conscience; for if you do, or cause for to be done, God will take vengeance thereupon, and you should put yourself and other in great jeopardy. For know well, she shall full sore repent her lewdness hereafter, and I pray God she must so.*[20]

Despite Margaret's confidence, there is no sign that Margery did repent. The couple's resolve held, in spite of all the pressures on them and the fact that their future – Margery with no prospect now of any inheritance, and Calle without employment – was uncertain at best. Neither would give up on what was clearly, however great the difference in their ages and their status, true love.

In the end, there was nothing the family could do. For Margery's mother and brothers, the trauma caused by her headstrong behaviour was compounded by the disastrous timing of the breach with Calle. The loss of his expertise while the battle for Caister was in the process of being fought – at the very point when the death of John Daubeney deprived them of another of their most trusted servants – could hardly have been worse. The complications of his sudden departure from their employment took weeks to resolve. Calle was doing all he could not to alienate the family further, but he also needed to protect himself in terms of the large sums of money for which his business dealings on their behalf had left him liable. For their part, the Pastons had to be careful to retrieve all the valuable documents – property deeds and financial accounts – which Calle had in his keeping. Margaret initially handled the negotiations, since John III – fresh from the siege – was still too angry to deal with him. '. . . *as for me, I had liefer he were hanged than to be bound to him*', he wrote on 5 October.[21] Once Calle had delivered the documents, however, John III seemed to be softening a little; even he had to admit that – unsurprisingly – Calle was behaving well. Margaret was not prepared to say the same of her daughter. '. . . *as for your sister, I can send you no good tidings of her*', she wrote to John II on 28 October. '*God make her a good woman.*'[22] Despite his best efforts, Bishop Lyhert had been unable to find any impediment to the marriage, and Margery and Calle had now been reunited. '. . . *as for his abiding*', John III told his brother, '*it is in Blackborough nunnery a little from Lynn, and our unhappy sister's also; and as for his service, there shall no man have it before you, if you will.*'[23] Calle had never wanted to leave the Pastons' household, and by his own lights he had done nothing wrong. He also knew his own worth, and realised that, given time, deep-rooted Paston pragmatism might come to the fore. The damage to Margery's status and reputation could not now be avoided, but the same was not true of the harm to the family's affairs that the loss of his experience would entail. The rift was too deep to be smoothed over immediately, and in the meantime he would have to take employment wherever he could find it – but, with humility and patience, Calle made it clear that his service would be at the family's disposal whenever they might choose to call on it.

In the meantime, there was plenty to occupy the Pastons' attention while they considered Calle's offer. The political situation remained in turmoil. King Edward returned from Yorkshire to London in mid-October, '*accompanied in all people with a thousand horse*', John II told his mother. Among the noblemen who rushed to join him were the Dukes of Suffolk and Norfolk. If the Pastons' enemies were welcome at the King's side, their recent patrons had less reason to feel confident now that Edward was his own master again. Archbishop Neville had accompanied him on his journey south, and the Earl of Oxford rode out from London to greet the royal party on their arrival, but John II heard that Edward had ordered both men to stay away when he entered the capital: '*the King sent them a messenger that they should come when that he sent for them*'. John II was as confused as anyone else about what it all meant. '*I know not what to suppose therein*', he wrote. '*The King himself has good language of the lords of Clarence, of Warwick, and of my lords of York, of Oxford, saying they be his best friends. But his household men have other language, so what shall hastily fall I cannot say.*'[24] The '*other language*' circulating privately in the royal household was much more plausible than the idea that Edward might be best friends again with the brother and cousins who had imprisoned him, but the King had decided for the time being to take no reprisals against them. Instead, he sought to maintain at least a front of unity while he rebuilt his government, rather than risk further confrontation before he was ready to deal with it. As a result, it was difficult for John II to know which way to turn. He was still in touch with Archbishop Neville, but Lord Scales (who had now, after his father's execution, inherited the title of Earl Rivers) was also back at court. Woodville connections had temporarily become a liability rather than an asset under the Earl of Warwick's regime, and John II had therefore been very quiet for a number of months on the subject of his engagement to Scales's cousin, but, with his usual optimism, he was hoping now to revive the relationship. '*As for my good speed, I hope well I am offered yet to have Mistress Anne Haute*', he told his brother brightly in the new year, '*and I shall have help enough, as some say.*'[25]

Despite John II's cheerfulness, there was little sign of any practical improvement in the Pastons' situation. The Duke of Norfolk was attempting to reinforce his possession of Caister by keeping up the pressure on the family; at the end of 1469 he threatened to seize the Fastolf manor of Guton Hall, and to procure the widows of the two men killed by gunfire at Caister to bring charges against John III for the murder of their husbands. '. . . *the cause is this*', John III told his brother, '*as it is told me by divers, that you make no more suit to my lord for yourself than you do, and therefore they do the worse to me for your sake*'. If John II was wondering why he should contemplate going cap in hand to a man who had forced him out of what he considered to be rightfully his own property, his younger brother – who was more diplomatic, and more philosophical about the ways of great lords – knew that they had little alternative. For once, John III sounded weary, asking his brother to make enquiries for him about the possibility of serving as a soldier in the English garrison at Calais, since he had no other service in Norfolk and was out of money. As always, though, he managed to find a stoical word or two. '*Item,*' he wrote, '*you must purvey a new attorney in this country as for me, for our matters and clamour is too great and our purse and wit too slender; but I will rub on as long as I may, both with my own and other men's that will do for me, till better peace be.*'[26] Discretion dictated that John III should try to make his peace with the Duke and Duchess of Norfolk, but they were not yet willing to receive him, even though the Duchess's fondness for him was undiminished; '*every man tells me that my lady says passingly well of me always*', he told John II. To add insult to injury, the Duke had done nothing with Caister other than shut it up. '*There is now but three men in it*', John III reported, '*and the bridges always drawn*'.[27]

There was, however, one flicker of hope. John II, the flexible pragmatist, had finally reached the conclusion that his father had never come close to accepting: that the only prospect of securing even a part of the Fastolf inheritance lay in agreeing a compromise. Caister had been lost to the Duke of Norfolk because those among Fastolf's executors who opposed the Pastons' claim, represented principally by Judge Yelverton, had been willing to sell their putative title to the Duke. The Pastons' only chance of loosening Norfolk's hold on Caister now was to make their peace with Yelverton, get him to ratify their claim, and thereby undermine the Duke's legal position. Peace with Yelverton would undoubtedly come at a price – but, whatever it cost, failing to accept that would mean losing everything. The family desperately needed powerful help to broker such a deal, and not just the benevolence of a patron such as Archbishop Neville who had far too much else to do. What they needed was the support of a lord with his own stake in seeing that their claims were pursued – a possibility which finally appeared on the horizon at the beginning of 1470.

William Wainfleet, the Bishop of Winchester, had a long-standing interest in Fastolf's affairs as one of the old knight's trustees, and as the most senior of the executors named in the revised will of November 1459. He also, like everybody else involved in the dispute, had his own agenda: in his case, it was his foundation of a new college, dedicated to St Mary Magdalen, at Oxford. Building had begun there three years earlier, and substantial further funding would be required if the project were ever to be completed. Meanwhile, Fastolf's plan for a college at Caister had not yet come to fruition, and might never do so if the Duke of Norfolk's seizure of the castle proved to be permanent. Wainfleet's suggestion was that the needs of Fastolf's soul might be better served by committing his lands to pay for prayers at Wainfleet's own college rather than at a foundation at Caister which did not yet exist – a proposal, he must have thought, of conveniently mutual benefit. Not only that, but the Bishop was also an ideal person to act as an intermediary between William Yelverton and the Pastons, since his relationship with both sides went back years, to the days when John Paston had been Yelverton's colleague in Fastolf's service. Two conditions would have to be met before the negotiations could move forward: Wainfleet needed to secure some kind of formal authority over the disposition of Fastolf's estate to underpin his position as a potential arbiter in the dispute; and the proposed displacement of Fastolf's college from Caister to Oxford required approval from the Pope. The Bishop tackled both issues in the first months of 1470. In January, he sent a servant to Rome to seek papal dispensation for the move to Oxford. In the following month, despite the fact that the probate hearings in the Archbishop of Canterbury's court had come to judgement more than two years earlier, Wainfleet secured the intervention of the Archbishop himself in the case, on the grounds that the two executors appointed by the terms of the revised will to take charge of its administration – John Paston and Thomas Howes – were both now dead. On 13 February, sole administration of Fastolf's estate was awarded to Bishop Wainfleet.

Only a week or so later, discussions between the various parties were already well advanced. '*Item, there is a way moved by the means of my lord of Winchester between Sir William Yelverton and me*', John II told his brother, '*and both Sir William Yelverton and I agreed to abide his award.*' Wainfleet had so far played his hand with enough skill that both sides believed he looked favourably on their claims. '*I hope this next term there shall be a way taken and an end*', John II went on, '*and, in counsel be it, I fear not the award.*'[28] At almost exactly the same time, William Worcester was telling Margaret that '*he thinks that the Bishop will be against you*', John III reported back to his brother from Norwich.[29] The fact that Worcester had renewed contact with Margaret – after the long years of hostility provoked by her husband's refusal to countenance his claims on their old master's estate – was itself an encouraging sign. Worcester, like his ally Yelverton, was now co-operating with Bishop Wainfleet's attempt to find a solution to the conflict. He was still holding fast to his claim that Fastolf had promised him a modest living from his estates, and complained to the Bishop that a decade of conflict had utterly impoverished him:

> *Item, my lord, the costs and charges that I have borne these ten years day in London and in ridings when I awaited upon the infinite process of the*

deciding of my Master Fastolf's testaments in the Court of Audience, that I am so indebted and so unpurveyed of goods to live that I may not ride nor continue in London, but am fain to withdraw me for my poor solace to Cambridge, that is but a day journey from my poor friends, and to eschew greater costs to abide me there till I may be purveyed of a competent living.[30]

Nevertheless, Worcester's personal and financial exhaustion was likely, if anything, to encourage him to sign up to a settlement, if the Bishop could find some basis for agreement.

The deal which Wainfleet hammered out over the following months was this. John II would be confirmed in his right to Caister – which of course he no longer held – and one other Fastolf manor, at Herringby, four miles east. Bishop Wainfleet would then do everything he could to help the Pastons retrieve the castle from the Duke of Norfolk. The Bishop also promised to help John II recover the manors of Hellesdon and Drayton, on condition that those properties would then be shared between them. Of the remaining Fastolf estates, John II would receive as much as, with Caister and Herringby, would provide an income of £50 per year. Everything else would go to the Bishop, to be used to endow his college in Oxford for the good of Fastolf's soul, and John II would therefore be relieved of his obligation to found and fund Fastolf's college at Caister. If Wainfleet could not reclaim Caister for the Pastons within a fixed period, John II would have the right to the manor of Guton instead, or to receive financial compensation. John II would also be released from any obligation to pay the sum of 4,000 marks which had originally been specified in his father's bargain with Fastolf. Details of Wainfleet's negotiations with Yelverton, Worcester and Fastolf's lawyer William Jenney do not survive, but it is clear that the settlement made some provision for their interests; Worcester, for example, did eventually receive the lands he claimed Fastolf had promised him. Certainly, the Bishop succeeded in securing their assent to the agreement. Once John II's deal with Wainfleet was concluded, it was formally set out in legal documents to which both parties put their seal on 14 July 1470.

John Fastolf and John Paston would have been outraged. This, after all, was what Fastolf had been afraid of all along: that, once he was gone, his executors' commitment to realising his plans for the college at Caister would falter in the face of the complexities of dealing with his estate. Fastolf's soul would now be remembered at Magdalen College in Oxford, but Magdalen was not Caister, and Wainfleet's foundation was a long way in nature and purpose from Fastolf's vision of seven priests and seven poor men living and praying together at his birthplace. Fastolf's college – the scheme which had been at the heart of his will, and therefore of the whole dispute – was now abandoned. It was exactly the outcome which the old man had hoped to avoid by giving John Paston a personal investment in its foundation, but his reluctance to give his intentions legal form in good time before his death had left what proved to be an open invitation for his wishes to be challenged. John Paston, meanwhile, would surely have seen the agreement as one more example of his eldest son's lack of responsibility. The castle at Caister and lands worth an annual sum of £50 represented a small fraction of the prize which had once been within his grasp. Nor would he have accepted the language in which the agreement was framed, referring as it did to a bargain '*alleged to be made*' between himself and Fastolf.[31] Nevertheless, his own misjudgements had gone a long way towards undermining his case and leaving his son in a position which had turned out to be indefensible. Of the properties to which John II's title was confirmed by the terms of the deal with Wainfleet, he was in possession of hardly any – but that was part of the point: he now had a claim to Caister, and to Hellesdon and Drayton, which was uncontested by any of Fastolf's executors, and he had the Bishop's backing in his attempt to enforce it. It was a gamble, but it was also the only chance he had left to retrieve anything from the debacle which his father's claim to Fastolf's lands had now become.

Or so it seemed. What he could not know in July 1470 was that all political certainties were about to be swept away with terrifying speed. The uneasy reconciliation between King Edward and the Earl of Warwick at the end of the previous year had lasted only until March. By then, disorder had erupted again in Lincolnshire. Warwick and his son-in-law Clarence – knowing now that their ambitions would never be fulfilled while Edward remained in power, and fearing that it could only be a matter of time before the King took decisive action to punish them for their disloyalty – seized the opportunity of the unrest to instigate a second rebellion against him. They covered their tracks well enough that their intentions were not clear for some weeks. '*I cannot tell you what will fall of the world, for the King verily is disposed to go into Lincolnshire and men know not what will fall thereof nor thereafter*', John II told his brother late in February. '*. . . my lord of Warwick, as it is supposed, shall go with the King,*' he reported. '*. . . Some men say that his going shall do good, and some say that it does harm.*'[32] Edward himself found it particularly difficult to believe that his own brother – vapid and totally self-centred though Clarence was – would betray him for a second time. However, the King had little choice but to come to that unpalatable conclusion after his decisive defeat of the Lincolnshire rebels near Stamford on 12 March. So many of the rebel soldiers dropped their jackets as they fled the rout that the battle was named 'Losecoat Field' – and it turned out that a number of those who discarded items of clothing had been wearing the livery of Clarence and Warwick. Not only that, but among the dead was one of Clarence's servants, in whose possession were found incriminating letters from the Duke and the Earl. Interrogations carried out after the battle suggested that the plan – for which there could be no public justification whatsoever, driven as it was purely by Warwick and Clarence's self-interest – had been to depose Edward and install Clarence on the throne in his place.

The King set out in force after his brother and cousin; '*it was said that were never seen in England so many goodly men and so well arrayed*', John III was told.[33] Warwick and Clarence continued to protest their willingness to co-operate with Edward, but dared not confront him in person. When they found that they could command no support among the wider political community, they fled. The King pursued them as fast as he could, only to discover when he arrived at Exeter on 14 April that Warwick and Clarence had already reached the coast and set sail for Calais – of which Warwick, who had held the captaincy there for more than a decade, was still officially in command. However, the Calais garrison refused them entry, leaving Clarence's wife, Warwick's eighteen-year-old daughter Isabel, to give birth to her first child on board ship. The young Duchess survived the experience, but the baby died shortly afterwards. They sailed on – the small fleet reinforced by Warwick's capture in the Channel of a number of ships belonging to the Duke of Burgundy – and, at the beginning of May, landed at Honfleur in Normandy. Warwick had decided that his best hope now lay in seeking help from the King of France, Louis XI, who would be only too pleased to see the downfall of King Edward and the end of the English alliance with Burgundy.

Also in France, living in a château in Bar belonging to her father the Duke of Anjou, were Henry VI's wife Margaret and their sixteen-year-old son Prince Edward. She had never given up on her husband's cause, but its apparent hopelessness – with Henry himself still a prisoner in the Tower of London, and no more capable of leadership than he had ever been – meant that she had made limited headway in recent years in securing any significant international interest in her family's plight. Her situation changed dramatically, however, with the Earl of Warwick's arrival on French soil.

Warwick's attempt to rule in King Edward's name while keeping his cousin under lock and key had proved unworkable, and since then it had become clear that the Earl's idea of replacing Edward with his more malleable brother Clarence was too implausible and unpopular to be viable. Warwick therefore decided to try his hand at kingmaking yet again, but this time with a more convincing candidate – convincing, that is, not in terms of his personal qualities, but by virtue of the fact that he had held the crown once already. In late July, a meeting was convened by the French King at Angers, at which Warwick came face to face with Queen Margaret. The Earl offered his renewed allegiance to King Henry VI, and agreed to lead an invasion of England to restore him to the throne. In return, Margaret gave her consent to the betrothal of her son Edward to Anne, the younger of Warwick's two daughters. Given that King Henry was manifestly incapable of ruling, it was agreed that Prince Edward should act as Regent on his father's behalf, and his father-in-law Warwick would stand at his right hand in the new Lancastrian government.

It was an extraordinary and profoundly unlikely alliance. Warwick had been one of the greatest enemies of the Lancastrian cause ever since he had first fought for the Duke of York at St Albans in 1455, and his own father and brother had lost their lives at Lancastrian hands. After so much blood had been spilled to resolve the conflict in favour of his own side, his defection was an astonishing step in personal, as well as political, terms. However, Warwick clearly believed that the role he had played in bringing down the Lancastrian regime entitled him to more power than King Edward was now prepared to allow him, and he was resolved to go to any lengths to achieve what he felt was rightfully his – even if it meant re-establishing the regime he had fought so hard to topple, and compromising his own integrity in the process. His was not the only spectacular *volte-face*. Queen Margaret had been furious at the very suggestion that she should have anything to do with the man she saw as '*the greatest causer of the fall of King Henry, of her, and of her son*'. It took King Louis several weeks of hard work – '*His Majesty has spent and still spends every day in long discussions with the Queen*', it was reported at the end of June – but he eventually convinced her that the potential benefits of Warwick's help outweighed her distaste at the alliance.[34] Nevertheless, when the Earl knelt before her at Angers to ask her forgiveness and pledge his loyalty, Margaret kept him on his knees for more than fifteen minutes. She consented to the marriage between her son and Warwick's daughter only with the greatest reluctance, and could not be persuaded that Prince Edward should accompany Warwick when he invaded England in her husband's name; instead, the Prince would remain safely with her in France until King Edward had been defeated. It was abundantly clear that the animosity between the Queen and the Earl had not been dispelled by a deal based on expediency rather than trust. The agreement also had the disadvantage of undermining the whole basis on which the Duke of Clarence had offered Warwick his support. Vanity and ambition had led the Duke to betray his brother in the hope of securing the crown for himself, but his father-in-law's decision to throw in his lot with the Lancastrian cause cut adrift Clarence's personal pretensions. For the time being, it seemed as though he could be placated with a promise that he would be granted the Duchy of York under the new regime. However, Clarence's usefulness to Warwick had been based from the beginning on the fact that he was both self-centred and impressionable, and the risk was that he would no longer be a dependable ally if asked to fight in someone else's cause.

Whatever doubts remained, the deal was done. With help from the French King, Warwick gathered his fleet and set sail for England on 9 September, accompanied by his son-in-law Clarence, his brother-in-law the Earl of Oxford – who had fled the country soon after Warwick and Clarence to join them in France – and Henry VI's half-brother Jasper Tudor. They landed in the south-west four days later, declaring that they had come in the name of '*our most dread sovereign lord, King Henry the Sixth*' to resist '*his great rebel and enemy Edward, late Earl of March, usurper, oppressor, and destroyer of our said sovereign lord and of the noble blood of all the realm of England and of the good, true commons of the same*'.[35] King Edward himself was in Yorkshire, where he had gone a month earlier to deal with yet more unrest, and now began to move south, giving every appearance of confidence in his ability to resist Warwick's attack. However, as he paused at Doncaster to await reinforcements, he received the shocking news that one of his most trusted lieutenants had defected to join the rebellion against him. John Neville, another of the Earl of Warwick's many siblings, had demonstrated impeccable loyalty to Edward throughout his reign – loyalty which had not wavered even in recent months when it meant taking the field against his own brother. He had played a key role in the early 1460s in the suppression of Lancastrian resistance in the north-east, and Edward had rewarded him with the earldom of Northumberland, of which the Percy family had been deprived because of their adherence to Henry VI. However, the problem of disorder in the north had now grown so acute, and had played such a significant part in Warwick's capacity to undermine Edward's rule, that the King had been forced to reconsider his strategy there. In March 1470 Edward restored

Henry Percy – formerly John Paston's fellow-prisoner in the Fleet – as Earl of Northumberland, believing that only the Percies had the depth of support along the eastern border with Scotland to hold the region securely, and seeking through this policy of reconciliation to attach the family to his own cause. He did not ignore the need to provide John Neville with compensation for his lost title: Neville himself became Marquis Montagu, and his ten-year-old son was created Duke of Bedford and betrothed to King Edward's eldest daughter. However, Neville was deeply unimpressed with the way he had been treated. Despite his immaculate record in Edward's service, one of the greatest estates in England had been taken from him, and he saw the reparation he had received as wholly inadequate. '. . . *he had many fair words and no lordships*', he was later reported to have claimed; his new title was all very well, but the King had given him no more than '*a magpie's nest to maintain his estate with*'.[36] The extent of Neville's unhappiness and Edward's miscalculation became clear only in September, as Neville and his troops advanced towards the King at Doncaster. They were within six or seven miles of Edward's position by the time the King learned that Neville had declared for Henry VI, and was coming not to help but to capture him.

Neville's defection was a crippling blow. Edward was now caught between two hostile armies: Neville approaching from the north and Warwick from the south. The King's own troops, dispersed in billets to await Neville's arrival, were not ready to fight. Rather than face battle against overwhelming odds, or submit to imprisonment for a second time – especially given that his personal safety would be less than assured now that Warwick had discarded all pretence of loyalty and declared him a usurper – Edward decided to run. Accompanied by his youngest brother Richard, Duke of Gloucester, his friend Lord Hastings, and his wife's brother Earl Rivers, he fled east. He nearly drowned crossing the Wash, but managed to reach King's Lynn, where, on 2 October, he and his small company took ship for the Netherlands to seek refuge and support from his brother-in-law the Duke of Burgundy. Amid riots in London, Queen Elizabeth, who was eight months pregnant, fled the royal apartments in the Tower in the middle of the night to take sanctuary at Westminster Abbey with her three small daughters. As Warwick and his army approached the capital, the Earl's brother Archbishop Neville seized control of the Tower. Bishop Wainfleet of Winchester was among those who conveyed the hapless figure of Henry VI from his prison quarters there to the royal chambers which the Queen had so recently been forced to abandon. On 6 October the Earl of Warwick arrived in London, and immediately went to kneel at King

Henry's feet to offer his allegiance. Five years earlier, Henry had been in Warwick's charge when he was brought into London as a captive, his feet tied to the stirrups of his horse. Now, on Saturday 13 October, the Earl carried his train when Henry was crowned for a second time in St Paul's Cathedral.

The course of politics had been chaotic and unpredictable ever since Warwick had taken up arms against Edward fifteen months earlier, but this was different: the world had been turned upside down in a matter of weeks. John Paston II had made his career at the Yorkist court, but the Yorkist court was now irrevocably split in two, and John II found himself with a foot in each camp. His Woodville connections – he was, after all, still engaged to Queen Elizabeth's cousin – had suddenly become dangerous, with the Queen herself sheltering in the Westminster sanctuary, and her brother, Earl Rivers, a fugitive with King Edward in the Netherlands. However, John II could also call on his association with Archbishop Neville, who had just been appointed Chancellor in the new Lancastrian government. Whatever the Pastons' feelings about the deposition of King Edward – thoughts which, prudence dictated, should not be committed to paper – it was clear that the Nevilles now represented their best hope of retrieving Calster from the Duke of Norfolk. As it turned out, it was not Archbishop Neville himself but his brother-in-law the Earl of Oxford – the new Constable of England – who emerged as the Pastons' principal champion. John II and John III had enjoyed a good relationship with the Earl and members of his household for years, but Oxford's political influence had been limited as he slowly rebuilt his family's position after the execution of his father and brother in 1462. At last, he had a chance to demonstrate the benefits of his lordship. Oxford had estates of his own in Norfolk, and he savoured the opportunity to exercise his authority there – especially at the expense of the Duke of Norfolk, whose identification with Yorkist interests was sufficiently close that he was placed under arrest on Warwick's orders. By Friday 12 October – only a week after Warwick's arrival in the capital, and the day before Henry VI's second coronation – John II and John III were in London, and full of excitement at what Oxford's help might mean. '*I trust that we shall do right well in all our matters hastily*', John III told Margaret, '*for my lady of Norfolk has promised to be ruled by my lord of Oxford in all such matters as belong to my brother and to me.*' He sounded exhilarated; after a deeply traumatic year, they could never have imagined such a dramatic transformation in their prospects. '*And as for my lord of Oxford, he is better lord to me, by my troth, than I can wish him in many mat ters'*, he wrote, *'for he sent to my lady of Norfolk . . . only for my matter and for none other cause, my unwitting or without any prayer of me, for when he sent to her I was at London and he was at Colchester, and that is a likelihood he remembers me.'* The idea of a lord who would help without even being reminded to do so seemed almost too good to be true – as was the effect on the Duke of Norfolk and his wife. *'The Duke and the Duchess sue to him as humbly as ever I did to them'*, John III reported, *'in so much that my lord of Oxford shall have the rule of them and theirs by their own desires and great means.'*[37]

Margaret was not so easily impressed. The day after her son's letter was written, Norfolk's men at Caister had stolen sixteen sheep from her manor of Mautby a mile away, and had taken pot-shots at her farmer there as he rode past the castle on his way home from Yarmouth. *'They stuff and victual sore the place, and it is reported here that my lady of Norfolk says she will not lose it in no wise,'* she told John III.[38] Margaret had a point. The authority of the new government was precarious in the extreme – not least because, to achieve any kind of lasting stability, it would have to find some way to reconcile competing noble interests divided by bitter personal enmities: Lancastrian lords returning from exile; Yorkist lords newly reborn as Lancastrians under the Earl of Warwick's leadership; and those Yorkist lords – such as the Duke of Norfolk – who had not supported Warwick's rebellion, but who might now be prevailed upon to accept the restoration of King Henry. In the attempt to secure the broadest possible support for his rule, Warwick could not afford to take too hard a line with former opponents, and the Duke of Norfolk was freed from prison after only a few days. If the Duke's release came as a disappointment to the Pastons, they also had to contend with the possibility that the return of a Lancastrian government might mean the return of those who had been powerful when Henry VI was last on the throne – including, among others, their old enemy John Heydon. Heydon had retreated almost entirely from the political arena since the fall of the regime under which he had built his career. Years earlier, in his darkest moments, John Paston had suspected that he might somehow be pulling strings behind the scenes in his conflict with the Duke of Suffolk at Drayton and Hellesdon, but it seems more likely that Heydon had merely enjoyed the spectacle of Fastolf's executors squabbling among themselves and the resulting devastation of the Pastons' hopes; *'he has a great while laughed at us both'*, John II told Judge Yelverton during the negotiations brokered by Bishop Wainfleet earlier in the year.[39] However, Heydon's renewed capacity for dirty tricks became a matter of concern when the Earl of Oxford visited Norwich in late November. John II had hoped to attend on the Earl himself, but was unable to travel after a fortnight's illness; '*I have gone with a staff as a ghost, as men said*', he told his brother, '*more like that I rose out of the earth than out of a fair lady's bed*'. John III was to represent the family in his stead, but '*then must you beware of one pain*', John II warned him, '*and that is this: Heydon will of craft send among you perchance six or more with harness for to slander your fellowship with saying that they be riotous people and not of substance*'. Not only should John III take precautions against the possibility of such misrepresentation, John II wrote anxiously, but he should '*cause the mayor in my lord's ear to tell him, though he should bind my lord to counsel, that the love of the country and city rests on our side, and that other folks be not beloved nor never were*'.[40]

Margaret had never been convinced by her sons' confidence in the new political order, but she was left frantic by reports of John II's illness – about which sinister rumours reached Norfolk – and an attack on John III by unknown assailants. '. . . *it was told me this day that you were hurt by affray that was made upon you by fellows disguised*', she wrote to her younger son on 1 December. '*Therefore in any wise send me word in haste how your brother does, and you both, for I shall not be well at ease till I know how that you do. And for God's love let your brother and you beware how that you walk and with what fellowship you eat or drink, and in what place; for it was said here plainly that your brother was poisoned.*' She already blamed the conflict over Fastolf's estates for the premature death of her husband, and could not bear the idea that she might now lose a son in the same cause. '*I had liefer you had never known the land*', she told John III. '*Remember it was the destruction of your father.*' She certainly had no faith in the stability or the integrity of the new Lancastrian world. '*Trust not much upon promises of lords nowadays, that you should be the surer of the favour of such men*', she wrote. '. . . *A man's death is little set by nowadays. Therefore beware of simulation, for they will speak right fair to you that would you fared right evil.*'[41]

Despite her misgivings, only ten days later her sons' greatest hopes were realised at last. The combined support of the Earl of Oxford, Archbishop Neville and Bishop Wainfleet proved enough to persuade the Duke of Norfolk that the surrender of Caister would be a price worth paying to secure his position under the new regime. On 11 December 1470 the Duke put his seal to a document which declared, with wide-eyed sincerity, that new information had come to light about his purchase of the castle from Judge Yelverton and his allies two years earlier:

... forasmuch as by our dear uncle and cousin the Archbishops of Canterbury and York and the Bishop of Winchester we be informed that the said bargain was made contrary to the last will of Sir John Fastolf, to whose behalf the said William Yelverton etc were enfeoffed, therefore at the especial request of the aforesaid reverend fathers in God and to accomplish the said Sir John's last will, and in discharging of our conscience, we agree ... to depart from all the said manors etc unto the said bishop of Winchester, who has taken upon him to execute the will.[42]

In return, Bishop Wainfleet graciously agreed to repay the Duke the purchase price of 500 marks. Just over a year since John III had led his men, defeated, from the castle gates, the Pastons were able once again to take possession of Caister.

In two short months their situation had been completely transformed. Thanks to the unforeseeably tortuous process of national politics, the deal with Wainfleet had paid off spectacularly. The Duke of Norfolk had been forced to relinquish Caister, and the Pastons now held the castle with the support of all Fastolf's executors. '*I am right glad that Caister is and shall be at your commandment, and yours in especial*', William Worcester told Margaret that Christmas. He wrote warmly, even though the passage of the years had done nothing to ease his bitterness at the way he had been treated. '*Would Jesu, mistress,*' he wrote, '*that my good master that was sometime your husband ... could have found in his heart to have trusted and loved me as my master Fastolf did, and that he would not have given credence to the malicious contrived tales that Friar Brackley, W. Barker and others imagined untruly, saving your reverence, of me.*' However, he was now willing to accept a reconciliation, so long as his integrity and his honesty were recognised. '*And now you may openly understand the truth*', he went on, '*and your son Sir John also. And yet for all that I put never my master Fastolf's livelihood in trouble, for all the unkindness and covetise that was showed me*'.[43] More than ten years after the old knight's death, the rift which had torn apart the formerly close-knit circle of his friends and servants was finally beginning to heal.

But the Pastons had little time to enjoy their good fortune. The Earl of Warwick was not finding it easy to establish secure foundations for his rule. He could not restore the estates of returning Lancastrian exiles without depriving those – himself included – who had benefited from their forfeitures. The position of the Duke of Clarence, who was not the most reliable ally under the best of circumstances, was becoming increasingly invidious; quite apart from the fact that Warwick's conversion to the Lancastrian cause had deprived him of all hope of achieving the crown for himself, Clarence was said to be '*held in great suspicion, despite, disdain and hatred with all the lords . . . that were adherents and full partakers with Henry*'.[44] The impending arrival from France of Queen Margaret and her son promised to introduce a forceful and unpredictable new element into a government which was already acutely unstable. Meanwhile, King Edward was not about to give up on the throne from which he had been ousted so suddenly. He had not been met with an effusive welcome on his arrival in Holland; his brother-in-law the Duke of Burgundy had no wish to be drawn into all-out war on Edward's behalf, and refused to meet him for almost three months, at the same time sending conciliatory messages to the Lancastrian regime in England. However, Warwick had secured French backing for his coup on the basis of his commitment to an Anglo-French alliance against Burgundy. He therefore rebuffed the Duke's overtures, and made clear his intention to support King Louis when he declared war on Burgundy in December. Duke Charles's response to this aggression was to offer Edward his help, in the form of money and ships. On 11 March 1471, after an agonising nine-day wait for favourable winds, Edward set sail to reclaim his kingdom.

He aimed for the Norfolk coast in the hope of joining forces with the Dukes of Norfolk and Suffolk, but found that the Duke of Norfolk had been placed under arrest for a second time as soon as news reached England that Edward's arrival was imminent. Instead, the Earl of Oxford was raising men in East Anglia in King Henry's name. Edward's small fleet therefore turned away north. On 14 March – having survived a violent storm at sea – he landed at Ravenspur in Yorkshire. The situation in which he found himself was intensely dangerous. He had only a thousand or so soldiers under his command in what proved to be hostile territory; the city of Hull barred its gates against him, and scarcely any local men rallied to his cause. However, the fragility of Warwick's regime was equally apparent. Two northern lords could have taken decisive action against Edward in the first few days after his landing: John Neville, whose defection had precipitated Edward's deposition six months earlier; and Henry Percy, whose restoration to the earldom of Northumberland had provoked Neville's discontent. Neither made any move, either to stop Edward or to join him. Edward was therefore able to forge southwards, gathering support at last as he moved through the midlands. He marched on Coventry, where his enemy Warwick was waiting for the Duke of Clarence to arrive with reinforcements. Warwick shut himself within the city walls and refused to respond to Edward's challenges – a strategy which proved to be a costly mistake when word finally came that Clarence and his troops were approaching. On 3 April, Edward rode out to meet the brother who had betrayed him. Clarence – who had for months been under concerted pressure from his mother and sisters to abandon Warwick, and was looking now to save his own skin – threw himself on his brother's mercy; in response, Edward embraced him with *'right kind and loving language'*.[45] With his army swelled by Clarence's forces, and Warwick still refusing to fight, Edward turned south to London. News of the approaching Yorkist army threw the city into a panic; the mayor had already taken to his bed, claiming he was too ill to make any decisions. Archbishop Neville paraded King Henry through the streets in a last attempt to rally the Londoners, but Henry now cut such a frail and pathetic figure that the sight of him had the opposite effect. On 11 April Edward encountered no resistance when he entered the capital. He rode to Westminster Abbey, where the crown was ceremonially placed on his head once more. He was then reunited with his wife and daughters, and saw for the first time the baby boy – his son and heir Edward, Prince of Wales – to whom Elizabeth had given birth in the Abbey's sanctuary five months earlier. On Edward's orders, King Henry was returned to the Tower under guard; Archbishop Neville and Bishop Wainfleet were imprisoned with him.

It seemed scarcely credible that another reversal of power could be possible so soon – and certainly Edward's victory was not yet assured. Warwick was now advancing on London, with his brother John Neville and his brother-in-law Oxford in his company, and Queen Margaret – whose departure from France had been repeatedly delayed by bad weather – was expected to land on the Dorset coast any day. It was clear that the rule of England would yet again be contested on the battlefield. Until now, John Paston and his sons had kept their heads down when political division gave way to open warfare; wherever their sympathies lay, they had always known that they had nothing tangible to gain by committing themselves in battle, and potentially everything to lose if they backed the wrong side. Now, it was different. The restoration of Lancastrian government had meant the restoration of Caister to the Pastons, and had brought them for the first time, in the person of the Earl of Oxford, a truly powerful lord who welcomed their service and went out of his way to further their interests. They had spent most of their adult lives under the rule of Edward of York, but a victory for him now would be a victory for the Duke of Norfolk, and all the family's achievements of the past few months would disappear without trace. It was not a question of being 'Lancastrian' or 'Yorkist': the relationship between the two sides was in any case more complex than that, now that the Yorkist Earl of Warwick had seized power in the name of the Lancastrian Henry VI. The Paston brothers had no option but to follow the lords – the Earl of Oxford, Archbishop Neville and Bishop Wainfleet – who had championed their interests and offered hope for the future.

By the time Edward took control of London on 11 April, therefore, John II and John III had already left to serve under the command of the Earl of Oxford in the Earl of Warwick's army, now marching south from the midlands. On 12 April – Good Friday – Warwick's forces reached St Albans, and the next day he pressed on as far as Barnet, where he drew up his troops on a ridge of high ground just north of the town. That same afternoon Edward moved north from London, accompanied by his brothers Clarence and Gloucester, his brother-in-law Rivers, and his friend Hastings. As night fell, the Yorkist army advanced through Barnet itself, and, under cover of darkness, took up position immediately opposite Warwick's troops. A few hours later, at around four in the morning on Easter Sunday, Edward gave the order to attack. When the fighting began, in semi-darkness and thick fog, it gradually became clear that the positions of the two armies had not, after all, been exactly aligned. The right flank of Warwick's army – commanded by the Earl of Oxford, and including among its number John Paston II and John Paston III – extended beyond the left flank of Edward's forces by some distance, giving Oxford an advantage which he was quick to exploit. But, as the Yorkist left crumbled, the opposite situation was playing itself out on the other side of the battlefield. There, the right flank of Edward's army reached beyond the left flank of Warwick's, which in turn began to buckle under the pressure. As a result, the two lines wheeled round until they faced east–west rather than north–south. At the same time, the vicious mêlée, and the disorientating effects of the fog, made it difficult for the commanders on either side to see or hear exactly what was happening. Oxford's men, who had now routed the Yorkist left, pursued their fleeing opponents as far as Barnet, and it was a while before the Earl could regroup his forces and return to the field. By the time he did so, the battle lines had swung so far from their original position that, without realising what they were doing, Oxford's troops launched an assault on their own side. They were not the only ones confused by the appalling conditions. Warwick's men mistook the livery their attackers were wearing – emblazoned as it was with Oxford's badge of the Enrayed Star – for the Sun in Splendour, the personal emblem of King Edward. They opened fire, and Oxford and his soldiers fled in disarray. Amid the chaos, cries of treason began to spread among Warwick's army. The Earl's brother John Neville died in the fighting, and Warwick himself – seeing that Edward had now decisively secured the upper hand – tried to escape. He was cut down and killed by Yorkist soldiers before Edward could reach him.

It was the best part of a week later before Margaret received word that her sons were safe. '... *blessed be God, my brother John is alive and fares well, and in no peril of death*', John II wrote from London on 18 April. '*Nevertheless he is hurt with an arrow on his right arm beneath the elbow, and I have sent him a surgeon which has dressed him, and he tells me that he trusts that he shall be all whole within right short time.*' He was doing what he could to reassure her; despite the catastrophic reversal in their fortunes, they were at least alive, and John III's wound was not serious. Their situation – with Warwick dead, Oxford on his way to seek shelter in Scotland, and Archbishop Neville and Bishop Wainfleet incarcerated in the Tower – was far from good. On the other hand, Lancastrian hopes had not been completely obliterated by Edward's victory. With dreadful irony, Queen Margaret – who had refused to bring her son back to England until the country was safely in Warwick's hands – finally landed at Weymouth on the day the Earl died at Barnet. With the help of the Duke of Somerset, recently returned from exile, she was now raising forces in the south-west in King Henry's name.[46] Edward responded to news of Margaret's advance by mustering fresh troops – and, until the two armies met, all conclusions were provisional and all political activity dangerous: '*the world, I assure you, is right queasy*', John II told his mother. Nevertheless, his instinctive optimism shone through, even if he had to choose his words with extreme care. '*God has showed himself marvellously, like him that made all and can undo again when he pleases*', he wrote, '*and I can think that by all likelihood shall show himself as marvellous again, and that in short time ... Be you not doubted of the world, for I trust all shall be well. If it thus continue I am not all undone, nor none of us; and if otherwise, then, etc.*'[47]

By the end of the month John III had almost recovered, and added his voice to his brother's attempt to set their mother's mind at rest. '*If it please you to have knowledge of our royal person*', he wrote with deliberate cheerfulness, '*I thank God I am whole of my sickness, and trust to be clean whole of all my hurts within a sevennight at the furthest*'. He was also so desperately short of money – '*in my greatest need that ever I was in*' – that he found himself forced to ask Margaret for help: '*I have neither meat, drink, clothes, leechcraft nor money but upon borrowing*'. However, he was convinced – or perhaps doing his utmost to convince his mother – that it would be only days before Queen Margaret's forces delivered the news for which they had been waiting. '... *with God's grace it shall not be long before that my wrongs and other men's shall be redressed'*, he wrote, *'for the world was never so like to be ours as it is now'*.[48]

He was right that it would be a matter of days, but wrong about the outcome. On 4 May 1471, Queen Margaret's army met Edward's at Tewkesbury in Gloucestershire. It proved to be the final disaster for the Lancastrian cause. The Queen herself was captured, and her seventeen-year-old son – the Lancastrian heir to the throne, fighting in his first battle – was killed in combat. The events of the past two years had warned Edward about the dangers of being over-merciful, and, on the night he arrived back in London, Henry VI – now an ex-king twice over, and once again a prisoner in the Tower – was murdered. With him died all the Pastons' hopes. The heady experience of powerful patronage had persuaded them to fight against the Yorkist King to whom they had offered loyal service for a decade, but getting too close to powerful men in dangerous times meant that the risks, as well as the rewards, were great. It was a gamble they had been forced to take, but they had lost in spectacular fashion. The Duke of Norfolk was quick to seek his revenge. On 23 June 1471 he seized Caister Castle again, and this time the Pastons – all hope of protection gone – dared offer no resistance.

CHAPTER ELEVEN

– *the matter of Caister* –

King Edward had won his throne on the battlefield for the second time in ten years. He was determined that he would not lose it again. The Lancastrian line had been wiped out: Henry VI and his son were dead, and Edward ordered that Henry's body should be publicly displayed on a bier at St Paul's Cathedral, its face uncovered, to forestall rumours that the former King might still be alive. Queen Margaret remained a prisoner, at first at Windsor Castle and later in the Tower. As Edward yet again set about the task of reimposing his authority on the country, the Pastons were left to contemplate what might have been. Power had changed hands so often and so rapidly during the past two years that the topsy-turvy course of politics might have seemed almost farcical, had it not been for the fact that the rule of England, and thousands of lives, were at stake. At stake for the Pastons, of course, was Caister. The family had sacrificed a great deal, and John Daubeney had died, in the attempt to keep hold of the castle. Now it was gone. More than a decade after John Paston had first claimed the Fastolf inheritance, scarcely any of the old knight's estates were left in Paston hands.

John II and John III lay low during the summer of 1471, doing what they could to secure formal pardons for having taken up arms against King Edward at Barnet. They were in no immediate danger, since the King's concern – which he was pursuing with remarkable magnanimity – was to reunite his subjects under his rule, not to engage in a witch-hunt. Much more powerful men than the Paston brothers had already been forgiven, officially at least: their patrons Archbishop Neville and Bishop Wainfleet, for example, were pardoned and freed in the months after Edward's final victory at Tewkesbury. Nevertheless, the Pastons' situation would remain uncomfortably vulnerable until they could obtain royal documents absolving them of any possible charges of treason. '*I pray you beware of your guiding, and in chief of your language*', John II warned his brother that autumn, '*so that from henceforth by your language no man perceive that you favour any person contrary to the King's pleasure*'. The threat was not an idle one; word had reached John II from Norfolk that dangerous accusations had been made in public against John III. '*I heard yesterday*', he wrote, '*that at Norwich one should have had large language to you and called you traitor, and picked many quarrels to you. Send me word thereof. It were well done that you were a little surer of your pardon than you be.*'[1]

It did not help the Pastons that, although Archbishop Neville and Bishop Wainfleet were now at liberty, neither was in a position of sufficient trust with the King to intercede with him on their behalf. Even more disappointingly, their one former patron who had fought at King Edward's side throughout the conflict proved to be no more use than the two prelates. The Queen's brother Earl Rivers – or Lord Scales, as he was still better known in Norfolk – had declared his intention to go to Portugal on crusade against the Moors, '*and because he thinks that I would go with him*', John III told his mother in July, '*. . . this is the cause that he will be my good lord and help to get the pardon*'. However, Edward was unimpressed by his brother-in-law's plan to leave the country so soon. '*The King is not best pleased with him*', John III reported, '*. . . in so much that the King has said of him that, whensoever he has most to do, then the Lord Scales will soonest ask leave to depart, and thinks that it is most because of cowardice*'.[2] Rivers, who prided himself on his chivalric reputation, can hardly have been pleased by this disparaging interpretation of his motives, especially when Edward responded by dismissing him from the lieutenancy of Calais and appointing Lord Hastings captain there instead. It was perhaps because Rivers was under such a cloud at court that John II made no urgent attempt to revive his relationship with the Earl's cousin Anne Haute, to whom he was still formally engaged – a match, it had to be said, for which he had never shown any particular personal enthusiasm. The young woman herself seemed equally ambivalent, and the couple were considering the possibility of seeking an annulment of their betrothal, something which would require a papal dispensation. '*I had almost spoken with Mistress Anne Haute*', John II told his brother in September, '*but I did not. Nevertheless, this next term I hope to take one way with her or other. She is agreed to speak with me, and she hopes to do me ease, as she says.*'[3] However, when they did finally meet in February 1472, both parties seem to have surprised themselves by agreeing that the marriage should go ahead after all. '*. . . as for tidings*', John II reported cheerfully to John III, '*I have spoken with Mistress Anne Haute at a pretty leisure and, blessed be God, we be as far forth as we were heretofore, and so I hope we shall continue; and I promised her that at the next leisure that I could find thereto that I would come again and see her*'.[4]

John II had other reasons too for his good spirits in the early months of

1472. Despite their political miscalculations, the brothers had not lost all their friends among the gentlemen of King Edward's household. John II and John III were not, after all, full-blooded Lancastrians, but renegade Yorkists who were now keen to demonstrate their repentance of their misdeeds. As a result, they both finally succeeded in securing official pardons, John III in February and his brother two months earlier, '*for comfort whereof I have been the merrier this Christmas*', John II told Margaret at the beginning of January.[5] He was still spending most of his time in London, often staying at the Black Swan Inn, where he became so friendly with the landlady, Elizabeth Higgins, that he took the trouble to send news of her family back to his brother in Norwich ('*Mistress Elizabeth has a son, and was delivered within two days after St Bartholomew, and her daughter A.H. was the next day after delivered of another son, as she says eleven weeks before her time. It was christened John, and is dead. God save all*').[6] However, he spent Christmas itself in Surrey with his aunt Elizabeth Paston and her recently acquired second husband, a gentleman named Sir George Browne, before moving on to celebrate Twelfth Night with Archbishop Neville at his magnificent house in Hertfordshire, '*where I have had as great cheer, and been as welcome, as I could devise*', he reported to Margaret. He signed off with a solicitous attempt to transmit his positive mood to his mother: '*I beseech God send you good health and more joy in one year than you have had these seven*'.[7]

However, as so often, Margaret was not convinced by his optimism. The months since King Edward had reclaimed his throne had been difficult for her as well as for her two oldest sons. Apart from anything else, there had been a frightening outbreak of plague in the autumn of 1471 – '*the most universal death that ever I knew in England*', John II called it. '*Wherefore, for God's sake*,' he told his brother, '*let my mother take heed to my young brethren, that they be not in no place where that sickness is reigning, nor that they disport not with no other young people which resort where any sickness is*.'[8] In November Margaret reported four deaths among their acquaintances in Norwich, although she and the children had so far escaped. '*All this household and this parish are safe, blessed be God*', she wrote on 5 November. '*We live in fear, but we know not whither to flee for to be better than we are here*.'[9]

Not that the younger Pastons were all still children. William, the baby of the family, was eleven, and Walter and Anne were both teenagers. Edmund was twenty and had completed his education, but his further prospects had so far been blighted by the fact that his mother and older brothers had been too preoccupied with the family's difficulties at Caister to help find him some honourable and remunerative position, perhaps in the service of a great lord. '*Also my brother Edmund is not yet remembered*', John II had noted as an afterthought at the end of a letter to John III more than a year earlier. '*He has not to live with; think on him, etc.*'[10] Nothing had been done by November 1471, when Edmund himself asked John III if he could secure him '*any profitable service*'; '*I would have right an easy service till I were out of debt*', he added. He still owed money to Staple Inn in London, where he had spent some time as a student learning the basics of the law, but he did not allow his financial straits to compromise his exuberant taste in clothes. He included a lengthy shopping list in his letter to John III, who was staying in the capital for a few weeks: three yards of purple camlet – a lightweight cloth – at four shillings a yard; a '*bonnet of deep mulberry*' for two shillings and fourpence; woollen cloth, in yellow, to make a pair of hose; a belt made out of ribbon in a grey-blue colour known as '*plunket*'; three dozen '*points*' – laces by which hose were tied on to other garments at the waist to prevent them falling down – in white, red and yellow; and three pairs of pattens, wooden overshoes worn to raise the wearer's feet above the mud and refuse in the streets.[11] He, too, sent his regards to Elizabeth Higgins at the Black Swan, and was clearly chafing at the restrictions of life at home in Norfolk.

Edmund was made particularly unhappy in the spring of 1472 by his mother's insistence that he dismiss his manservant Gregory, whom Margaret held responsible for the fact that a prostitute had recently spent the night in the stables of her manor house at Mautby. Gregory had availed himself of the woman's services in the close of the rabbit-warren there when two ploughmen saw what was happening, '*and desired him to have part*'. It was with the ploughmen that she stayed overnight in the stable, '*and Gregory was clean delivered of her*', Edmund pointed out indignantly, '*and, as he swears, had not ado with her in my mother's place*'. He blamed the loss of a man from whom he was '*as sorry to depart . . . as any man alive from his servant*' on the growing influence of his mother's chaplain James Gloys, on whom Margaret had come to rely heavily in recent years.[12] Gloys was no longer the hot-head he had been in his twenties when he fought in the street with John Wyndham, although, from the point of view of the Paston brothers, it seemed that his arrogance was undiminished. He was of their mother's generation – Margaret was now fifty, and Gloys cannot have been much less – and was asserting his authority in the household to an extent which Edmund thought excessive and profoundly irritating. He was not the only one. In July, John III reported to his older brother that he too had argued with '*the proud, peevish and evil disposed priest*'; '*we fell out before my* mother with "*Thou proud priest*" and "*Thou proud squire*"', he told John II gloomily, '*my mother taking his part*'. That was the heart of the problem. Margaret had coped with the traumas of the past three years with her usual fortitude, but she had also found them exhausting; and, while she leaned on her chaplain for practical and emotional support, she was less appreciative of her sons' continued presence in her household. '*Many quarrels are picked to get my brother E. and me out of her house*', John III wrote. '*We go not to bed unchidden lightly. All that we do is ill done, and all that Sir James and Pecock do*' – Pecock being a Mautby man who had been in Paston service for years – '*is well done*'. The difficulty for both John III and Edmund was that they had nowhere else to go until they succeeded in finding themselves a position in noble service which would give them an income on which to live independently. There seemed to be no possibility that they might receive the lands which had been allotted to them in their father's will while they were still unmarried and had no household of their own to support. In the meantime, friction with their mother was doing their prospects no good at all. Margaret had recently declared her intention to draw up her own will, '*and, in this anger between Sir James and me, she has promised me that my part shall be naught*', John III told John II; '*what yours shall be, I cannot say*'.[13] There was some consolation in the fact that one older breach within the family had begun to be mended. As Richard Calle had hoped – and thanks, perhaps, to the disastrous turn the family's affairs had taken, which made competent and loyal service all the more valuable, whatever its source – Margaret's hostility to her unwanted son-in-law had now subsided far enough that he was back in the Pastons' employment. He was not yet accorded the same level of responsibility that he had once enjoyed, and Margaret's forgiveness may not have extended as far as her wayward daughter, since she made no mention of Margery in her letters. Nevertheless, Calle's experience and his capabilities were such that his return could only be a relief, in practical terms at least – although Edmund quickly managed to fall out with him too.

However trying she found the squabbles within her household, Margaret was preoccupied above all with the need to find some kind of answer to the reverses the family had suffered. So far, there was no sign of any improvement in their fortunes. In the autumn of 1471, John II had suggested to John III that he should sound out the Duchess of Norfolk and other members of the Duke's household to see '*whether it be possible to have Caister again, and their goodwills, or not*'.[14] Even by John II's standards, this seemed wildly over-optimistic. After everything that had happened, it was hardly likely that

Norfolk could simply be persuaded to accept a deal which involved him giving up the castle, let alone to do so with good humour. It was far from clear even by what means the Pastons might succeed in bringing the Duke to the negotiating table. Certainly, Norfolk's claim to Caister was technically weak, if not non-existent. His purchase of the estate had been legally questionable from the outset, and his position was undermined still further when Yelverton and Worcester subsequently disavowed the sale by agreeing terms with Bishop Wainfleet – a settlement which had also, at last, established John II's title to Caister on a sound legal footing. On the other hand, the fact of the matter was that the castle was now in Norfolk's possession. Even if King Edward could be persuaded of the justice of the Pastons' cause, his principal preoccupation for the moment at least was the consolidation of his hold on power after the chaos of the past few years – a process in which the support of the Duke of Norfolk weighed more heavily than the claims of a gentleman who had forfeited Edward's goodwill when he took the field against him at Barnet. There was no sign that the King had any immediate intention to discipline the Duke over his actions at Caister; instead, on St George's Day, 23 April 1472, Norfolk was created a knight of the Order of the Garter in a splendid ceremony at Windsor Castle. Two days later, any hope that Archbishop Neville might eventually recover enough influence to press the Pastons' case suddenly vanished when he was once again placed under arrest. '. . . *my lord Archbishop was brought to the Tower on Saturday at night*', John II told his brother, '*and on Monday at midnight he was conveyed to a ship and so into the sea, and as yet I cannot understand whither he is sent nor what is befallen of him.*'[15] The news, when it came, was not good. The Archbishop was a prisoner in Hammes Castle, one of the forts within the Calais Pale, on suspicion of conspiracy with the Earl of Oxford, who had fled via Scotland to France after the disaster at Barnet and was now launching raids on Calais with the support of the French King. John II and John III had to face the fact that none of their former patrons was in any position to help them.

By the beginning of June, not much more than a month after the Archbishop's arrest, Margaret sounded depressed about how little they had to show for all their years of labour, and how bleak their prospects now were. She had heard that Bishop Wainfleet – under pressures of his own – had agreed to sell two manors from his share of the Fastolf inheritance to John Heydon's son Henry. The idea that some of the property for which her husband had fought so hard should go to the family of his oldest rival was almost heartbreaking. '*We beat the bushes, and have the loss and the diswor-*

ship, and other men have the birds', she told John II. *'My lord has false counsel and simple that advises him thereto . . . What shall fall of the remnant, God knows; I trow as evil or worse. We have the loss among us.'* Not only that, but the Duke of Norfolk's men were now threatening her own manor of Mautby, which lay too close to Caister for comfort when the castle was in hostile hands. She took the opportunity to tell her son what needed to be done: John II should quickly find a way to retrieve Caister itself, she said, for *'if we lose that, we lose the fairest flower of our garland. And therefore help that he may be out of possession thereof in haste, by my advice, whatsoever fortune hereafter.'*[16]

John II's reply to his mother's letter does not survive, but – whatever Margaret thought – he hardly needed reminding of the obvious need to recover Caister. In practice, there was little that he and his brother could do but be patient, be careful, cope as best they could with the little money they had, and take what few political opportunities came their way. However, Margaret's confidence in her eldest son's handling of the family's affairs had been badly eroded over the previous year, as their relationship deteriorated under the strain of their increasingly desperate financial difficulties. Seven months earlier, in the autumn of 1471, Margaret had been thrown into panic when her friend Elizabeth Clere suddenly found that she needed to reclaim a loan of 100 marks, a sum which Margaret had borrowed in order to pass the money on to John II. Loans between friends were commonplace – helping to ease the cash shortages which landowners inevitably suffered from time to time, given that their incomes were seasonal – but in the family's current circumstances Margaret did not have the means to make good what she owed. *'And I know not how to do therefor, by my troth',* she wrote to John III during his trip to London that November, *'for I have it not, nor I cannot make shift therefor'* – not even *'if I should go to prison'.* She sounded agitated and overwrought: she could raise money by selling the timber from her woods, she said, but there was a glut on the market in Norfolk and she would not get a good price; and in any case such a sale would devalue her lands in the longer term. Her anxieties were compounded by the prospect of public humiliation, since gentlemen and gentlewomen of standing were expected to be responsible financial managers; borrowing against future income was one thing, but it was not worshipful to extend one's credit to a point where valuable assets might have to be sold to raise cash for repayments. The only solution she could see was that John II himself would have to find the money – but she no longer had any faith that she could rely on him to help her. *'And when I remember it, it is to my heart a very spear',* she wrote, *'con-*

sidering that he never gave me comfort therein, nor of all the money that he has received will never make shift therefor. If he had yet before this time have sent me fifty marks thereof yet, I would have thought that he had had some consideration of my danger that I have put me in for him.'[17]

She was so unhappy with her eldest son's behaviour that she was now communicating with him only through his younger brother. '*Methinks by your brother that he is weary to write to me*', she told John III three weeks later, '*and therefore I will not encumber him with writing to him. You may tell him as I write to you.*'[18] John III's role as go-between was an unenviable one. His mother's messages were increasingly angry and censorious, while his brother was simply unable to raise the money she needed. John II's failure to repay the loan was hardly a surprise, given how limited his resources now were. While Margaret and his grandmother Agnes were still alive, he held only a small proportion of his Paston inheritance, and virtually all of the Fastolf estates to which he still had a claim had now been taken from him. Margaret, however, persisted in believing that extravagance lay at the root of his financial problems. '*He writes to me also that he has spent this term £40*', she told John III. '*It is a great thing. Methinks by good discretion there might much thereof have been saved. Your father, God bless his soul, has had as great matters to do as I trow he has had this term, and has not spent half the money upon them in so little time, and has done right well.*' The comparison with his dead father – against whose criticisms she had once defended John II so tenaciously – was deeply unfair, not least because it involved a substantial rewriting of history: John Paston could hardly be said to have '*done right well*' in his handling of the Fastolf dispute, however economical his methods had been. Nevertheless, unfair though they were, her reproaches were an expression of genuine distress. '*So may I answer before God, I know not how to do for the said money . . .*', she wrote; '*it is a death to me to think upon it.*'[19] They also served to demonstrate how estranged she now felt from a son who spent so little time at home in Norfolk that she scarcely had a chance even to try to see things from his point of view.

John II sought to rebuild bridges with his mother with his cheerful message from Archbishop Neville's house that Christmas, adding some good intentions to accompany the good wishes he sent her. If all went well, he said, '*I purpose me to come home and see you this Lent, and set my land in better rule than it has been heretofore*'.[20] He also renewed his efforts to lay his hands on some money. Over the past few years, he had already been forced to supplement his landed income by pawning a substantial amount of the family's silver plate – ninety pounds' worth in a single week in July 1470, for example. Now, although Margaret was unwilling to contemplate selling valuable timber to raise the cash they needed, John II saw no alternative but to do so on his own estates, and he set about finding a buyer for the wood at his manor of Sporle. John III thought the proposal unwise: the short-term gain was obvious, but fine trees would take years to grow again, and while they did so the annual value of the whole manor would suffer. '. . . *by God, if I were as you, I would not sell it for a hundred marks more than it is worth*', he told his brother.[21] Despite his objections, there was little else John II could do if he were serious about securing a lump sum with which to settle his debts, especially once all hope of further help from Archbishop Neville had been dashed by his arrest in the spring of 1472. John II found a purchaser and agreed the sale by the end of that summer, all the while making every effort to keep the deal secret from his mother. In the end, however, his subterfuge was exposed by the Norfolk rumour-mill. Word of his plans reached Margaret in October. She was distraught – '*my mother weeps and takes on marvellously*', John III reported – and threatened to cut her eldest son out of her will altogether: '*she says that she will purvey for her land that you shall none sell of it, for she thinks you would if it came to your hand*'.[22] When Margaret herself wrote to John II, it was to speak her mind in no uncertain terms. If what she had heard was true, she told him,

> . . . *it should cause both your enemies and your friends to think that you did it for right great need, or else that you should be a waster and would waste your livelihood . . . Wherefore, in eschewing of the great slander and inconvenience that may grow thereof, I require you and moreover charge you upon my blessing, and as you will have my goodwill, that if any such sale or bargain be made . . . that you restrain it.*

It was abundantly clear that she meant what she said. '. . . *whosoever will counsel you the contrary*', she wrote, '*do as I advise you in this behalf or else trust never to have comfort of me*.'[23]

John II could have been forgiven for feeling that, whatever he did, he could not win. On the other hand, Margaret was undoubtedly right that it would damage him politically to expose his financial problems to public view by going ahead with the deal. She got her way, and the trees at Sporle remained unfelled. As a result, it became all the more urgent that John II should make some progress in the attempt to put pressure on the Duke of Norfolk over his continuing occupation of Caister. A month earlier, in September 1472, John II had written to Norfolk's council to propose a settlement by which he would reclaim the castle from the Duke in return for some token financial compensation – perhaps as little as £40 – and the promise of his own future service. John III took the letter to Framlingham on his brother's behalf, and received a surprisingly encouraging response. Norfolk's councillors referred him to the Duchess, who was not willing to broach the subject with her husband herself, but '*this she promised, to be helping so it were first moved by the council*'. When John III returned to the council, '*they answered me your offer was more than reasonable*', he told John II, '*and, if the matter were theirs, they said they knew what conscience would drive them to*'. It seemed that the Duke's advisers were beginning to feel that the best way of dealing with the transparent frailty of his claim to Caister was to settle the dispute on his own authority, rather than wait for the undesirable possibility that the King might intervene to take the castle from him. Meanwhile, the Duchess had other priorities: after years of childlessness, she was now pregnant for the first time. Against all the odds, the signs seemed positive – but within days it became depressingly clear why the Duchess and the council had each suggested that the other should be the one to raise the issue with the Duke. His councillors finally agreed to '*move my lord with it, and so they did*', John III reported; '*but then the tempest arose, and he gave them such answer that none of them all would tell it me*'.[24]

Even though the Duke had dismissed the petition – and had done so in terms too intemperate to be repeated – John III remained hopeful. Apart from anything else, the fact that the Duchess still showed a particular liking for him was one of the strongest cards in the family's hand. A month later, however, it seemed that John II might have undone all his brother's good work when he bumped into the Duchess in the street on a visit to Yarmouth. She was now almost eight months into her pregnancy, and John II made an elaborate attempt to pay her a gallant compliment. '*I should have said that my lady was of stature good, and had sides long and large*', he told his brother, '*so that I was in good hope she should bear a fair child; he was not laced nor braced in to his pain, but that she left him room to play him in.*' John II was usually confident and charming in the company of women – at least, women who were not his mother – but it became clear when gossip began circulating shortly after their encounter that on this occasion he had miscalculated badly. '*They say that I said my lady was large and great, and that it should have room enough to go out at . . .*' He was aghast at the idea that he might have caused offence on the inevitably sensitive subject of the Duchess's size – '*I meant well, by my troth, to her and to that she is with, as any he that owes her best will in England*' – and appealed to John III to find out how much harm had been done.[25] The faux pas knocked his usual cheery self-assurance to such an extent that four days later he was still trying to find the right form of words with which to convey his respects to the Duchess, but this time with unmistakable courtesy. John III was about to attend the ceremony which would accompany her formal retreat into confinement – the period of a month before the birth which she would spend entirely in female company – '*and where you go to my lady of Norfolk's and will be there at the taking of her chamber*', John II wrote, '*I pray God speed you, and Our Lady her to her pleasure, with as easy labour . . . as ever had any lady or gentlewoman save Our Lady herself. And so I hope she shall to her great joy and all ours, and I pray God it may be like her in worship, wit, gentleness, and every thing except the very very thing*' – in other words, that the baby should be the much-desired son and heir, but resemble its mother in every way other than its sex.[26]

However, John II's preoccupation with restoring the Duchess's good opinion of him did not prevent him from achieving what appeared to be a major breakthrough in the fight for Caister. In late November, for the first time, he secured an expression of concern from King Edward that the castle was being kept from its rightful owner, in the form of royal letters addressed to the Duke and Duchess. '*The King has specially done for me in this case*', John II told his brother in some excitement, '*and has put me, and so have the lords, in right great comfort that, if this fail, that I shall have undelayed justice.*'[27] John III suggested he should bring the letters to Framlingham himself, '*as hastily as you may, so that you may be at the christening of the child that my lady is with. It shall cause you great thank, and a great advantage in your matter*'.[28] John II did not take his brother's advice, but when the Duchess gave birth on 10 December – to a daughter named Anne – it was the Pastons' good luck that Bishop Wainfleet of Winchester was invited to stand godfather and baptise the baby. It was a fleeting visit: the Bishop arrived on the evening of Wednesday 17 December and left the following lunchtime after a morning christening. However, he did find time to speak to the Duchess about Caister, '*as well as he could imagine to say it considering the little leisure that he had with her*'. It seemed to be the perfect opportunity to lobby the Duchess on the subject, but Wainfleet proved disconcertingly evasive about her response. '. . . *he told me that he had right an agreeable answer of her*', John III wrote, '*but what his answer was he would not tell me*'. However, when more details emerged of the Duchess's conversations with the Bishop and his servants, it became clear quite how far the Pastons still were from any prospect that Norfolk might agree to relinquish the castle. The Duchess had explained that she and her husband were planning soon to visit London, '*at which time she herself would devise to my lord of Winchester such a way to break in to my lord of that matter, that he should speed of his intent*'. If no one had yet dared even to broach the subject of the Paston claim to Caister with the Duke himself since his furious outburst in September, then all their efforts of the last two months had achieved nothing. Not only that, but John III's foothold in Norfolk's household again seemed to be becoming less secure. '*I let you plainly know I am not the man I was, for I was never so rough in my master's conceit as I am now*', he reported miserably, '*and that he told me himself before Richard Southwell, Timperley, Sir W. Brandon and twenty more, so that they that lowered now laugh upon me.*'[29]

As if that were not enough, it was also becoming painfully apparent that the King's promise of '*undelayed justice*' was not about to materialise. King Edward does not appear to have been particularly impressed by Norfolk's political talents; certainly – the grant of the Order of the Garter aside – the Duke was not given major rewards or assigned significant responsibilities as the King rebuilt his regime, unlike many of the other noblemen who had supported Edward during the conflict of 1470–1. Nevertheless, even if Norfolk was not high in the King's esteem, that was all the more reason for Edward not to risk alienating him by insisting that he restore Caister to a family whose own title to the castle had been in dispute for a decade, and who had temporarily abandoned their Yorkist allegiance to support the restoration of Henry VI. The King had written to the Duke to ask him to attend to the Pastons' complaints, but it was far from clear that Edward would contemplate any more forceful intervention. It also remained the case that the King had other, more pressing concerns of much greater significance for the security of the realm. The Earl of Oxford was still at large, and made an attempt with French help to land on the Essex coast in the spring of 1473. Although he was quickly repulsed, he and his small fleet spent the summer harrying and robbing English ships in the Channel. Meanwhile, Edward was also having to deal with a vicious dispute between his two younger brothers, the Dukes of Clarence and Gloucester, over the rich inheritance of the earldom of Warwick. Clarence was married to Isabel Neville, the elder of the dead Earl's two daughters, and early in 1472 Gloucester married her sister Anne, who had previously been betrothed to the Lancastrian Prince of Wales under the terms of her father's alliance with Queen Margaret. Isabel and Anne were each entitled to inherit half of the Warwick estate, but Clarence – who seemed to have no inkling of how fortunate he had been to escape punishment for his rebellion against his brother – objected furiously to the idea that the lands should be split between himself and Gloucester, insisting that he should keep his father-in-law's property in its entirety.[30] The King brokered a compromise in the spring of 1472, but the ill feeling between the two Dukes continued to simmer, and in 1473 whispers were beginning to spread that Clarence might yet again be involved in treasonable correspondence with his old ally the Earl of Oxford, and, through him, with the King of France. Under the circumstances – and despite the hopes inevitably raised by the arrival of King Edward's letters at Framlingham in December 1472 – it would have been foolish to expect a speedy settlement at Caister by royal means.

John II and John III were therefore left to pursue their own petitions to the Duke and Duchess as best they could. Their efforts were not helped by the fact that relations between John II and Margaret remained tense and distant, not least because the business of Sporle wood was still rumbling on. By the time John II halted the sale of his timber there, at his mother's insistence, in the autumn of 1472, Margaret's own finances seemed to have recovered a little, since he agreed not to sell the wood on the understanding that in return she would lend him £100, to be repaid from the manor's revenues over the next five years. However, by the spring of 1473 Margaret was utterly refusing to advance him the money, whether because she had changed her mind or because the promise had never been made in the first place. John II believed the former and Margaret the latter – a mix-up which had only been made possible by the fact that, yet again, they were not in direct contact with one another; instead, increasingly frosty messages were passing back and forth via John III and the family's lawyer Thomas Playter. '*My mother does me more harm than good*', John II told his brother with uncharacteristic bitterness in April, by which time he had defiantly embarked on another attempt to find a buyer for the wood at Sporle.[31]

There were other issues too on which their exchanges were becoming more barbed, among them the question of John Paston's tomb at Bromholm. The place where John had been buried in the priory church had been covered with a cloth after the funeral, but, more than six years after his death, no monument to mark the grave had yet been commissioned. In September 1471 John II had got as far as asking his brother to measure the dimensions of the site, but he had done nothing further by the end of November, when Margaret added pointed reproaches on the subject to her recriminations over John II's financial mismanagement. '*It is a shame*', she wrote, '*and a thing that is much spoken of in this country, that your father's gravestone is not made. For God's love, let it be remembered and purveyed for in haste – there has been much more spent in waste than should have made that.'*[32] By April 1473, after six months of unrelieved tension over Sporle, John II's patience was exhausted, and he threw the criticism back. *'I pray you remember her for my father's tomb at Bromholm'*, he told John III. *'She does right not; I am afeared of her that she shall not do well.'*[33] Margaret's point was that the grave was John II's responsibility as head of the family; John II's was the not unreasonable one that his mother's income was larger than his own, and that she herself might therefore bear the cost of his father's memorial. Both were under pressure, and each felt let down by the other. It was John II who finally made an attempt to make peace – *'I heard not from you of long time, which causes me to be right heavy'*, he wrote in July 1473 – although his letter was noticeably short on apologies and long on self-justification.[34]

That summer he was at least enjoying a few pleasant distractions from his financial troubles and his mother's rebukes. His letter to Margaret was written not from London but Calais – the great port which was the last surviving English foothold on the continent after the disastrous defeats of Henry VI's reign – where he had contracted to serve in the English garrison under the command of Lord Hastings. For John II, the prospect of spending time at Calais had multiple attractions. By offering military service to King Edward's government, he might help to expunge Barnet from his record and speed up his political rehabilitation. At the same time, he would have the chance to renew his acquaintance with Hastings, one of the King's most trusted friends, whom he had known at court in the 1460s and who might now be a powerful ally in his campaign to reclaim Caister. It also gave him something adventurous to do in congenial company which would help to pay his expenses and take him away, physically at least, from the stresses he faced at home. The idea had occurred to him as early as the summer of 1472, but his plans made slow progress during the autumn, preoccupied as he was with his unsuccessful attempt to petition the Duke and Duchess of Norfolk about Caister. As a result, he did not arrive at Calais until January 1473, and then only for an initial visit of a month or so. By June of that year he was impatient to return, but delayed by the fact that he was having trouble persuading likely members of the Paston household to serve as the archers he had contracted to bring with him. *'I hoped to have been very merry at Calais this Whitsuntide'*, he told his brother in some exasperation, *'and am well apparelled and appointed save that these folks fail me so'.*[35] Nevertheless, he was using his enforced stay in London to free himself from other potential ties to domestic life in England. The attempt to renew his relationship with Anne Haute had not, after all, proved a success, and he was now negotiating the terms on which her family would agree to seek an annulment of the betrothal. The discussions went well enough that arrangements to apply for a papal dispensation were in place by the autumn – '*I have answer again from Rome that there is the well of grace and salve sufficient for such a sore*', John II told his brother somewhat ungallantly in November – although the process was expensive, and threatened to become yet another alarming drain on his resources.[36]

However fragile his financial position, the good sense of John II's decision to join the Calais garrison was confirmed by political developments at the end of the year. The Earl of Oxford's piracy in the Channel, together with the increasing uncertainty about the intentions of the Duke of Clarence, had made the capital a tense place to be in the spring and summer of 1473; '*there be in London many flying tales*', John II reported.[37] On 30 September, the threat from Oxford suddenly crystallised – albeit on a much smaller scale than many had feared – when he seized the fortress of St Michael's Mount off the coast of Cornwall. Having failed to persuade the Kings of France and Scotland to back a full-scale invasion, the Earl had decided to do what he could with his own tiny force of about eighty men. Once taken, the castle on its towering rock was all but impregnable in the hands of determined defenders, but the problem facing Oxford was what to do next, especially when the King sent troops and ships to besiege the fortress and stop supplies getting through to the rebels. In February 1474, after four months of resistance, Oxford was left with little choice but to capitulate. Edward spared his life, but he was imprisoned in Hammes Castle without hope of release. With the lord for whom the Paston brothers had fought at Barnet, and from whom they had once hoped so much, now under lock and key, John II's decision to busy himself in the service of Lord Hastings at Calais was a diplomatic one. As he had remarked to his brother the previous summer, '*some men think it wisdom and profit to be there now, well out of the way*'.[38]

Life at Calais suited John II. Within its massive fortifications lay a cultured town made wealthy by the lucrative trade in English wool, and the gentlemen of the garrison had plenty of free time – at least while England remained at peace – in which to amuse themselves, or even to spend a few days travelling in the Low Countries. On his first trip to Calais in January 1473, John II took the opportunity to return to some old haunts in Flanders, which he had last visited with his brother in the entourage of King Edward's sister Margaret when she married the Duke of Burgundy in 1468. He sent back news of mutual friends in Ghent to John III in Norfolk:

Peter Metteney fares well and mistress Gretkin both, and Babkin recommends her to you. She has been very sick, but it has done her good, for she is fairer and slenderer than she was. And she could make me no cheer, but always my sauce was, 'How fares Master John your brother?', wherewith I was wroth and spoke a jealous word or two, disdaining that she should care so much for you when that I was present.[39]

The brothers had slipped back into their familiar banter along with their old division of labour – John II living the glamorous life of the cosmopolitan gentleman (albeit at the moment an impecunious one), while John III stayed in Norfolk taking care of the family's business. In the autumn of 1472, John III complained with mock despair that Norwich offered so little in the way of entertainment that he was in urgent need of a hawk with which he could at least go hunting. '*Now think on me, good lord*', he told his brother reproachfully, '*for if I have not a hawk I shall wax fat for default of labour and dead for default of company*'.[40] He asked John II to buy one for him in London or Calais, and they spent two months in half-joking correspondence on the subject, partly because it took John II that long to make any progress with his brother's errand. '*I thought to have had one . . . before this time; but far from eye, far from heart*', John III observed caustically in October.[41] A bird finally arrived in Norfolk in November – '*as for the hawk that I sent you, thank me for it, God save it*', John II wrote – but it proved to be a poor specimen; '*she shall never serve but to lay eggs*', John III reported with a mixture of regret and exasperation, before taking his brother to task for his indolence. '*Now, if you have as many ladies as you were wont to have, I require you for her sake that you best love of them all, once trouble yourself for me in this matter, and be out of my clamour.*'[42]

However sharp the teasing became, it was full of affection, and for John III perhaps went some way towards alleviating the frustrations of life at home. His difficult relationship with his mother's chaplain James Gloys had not improved: '*Sir James is ever chopping at me when my mother is present*', he wrote in October 1472, '*with such words as he thinks wroth me and also cause my mother to be displeased with me . . . And when he has most unsitting words to me, I smile a little and tell him it is good hearing of these old tales.*'[43] This annoyance, it turned out, was one he had to tolerate for only another year, since Gloys died in November 1473 – a painful loss for Margaret, but a relief for her sons, and one which offered John III an opportunity to reclaim a position of greater trust and responsibility in his mother's household. '*I am right glad that she will now do somewhat by your advice*', John II told his brother; '*wherefore beware from henceforth that no such fellow creep in between her and you, and if you like to take a little labour you may live right well, and she pleased. It is as good that you ride with a couple of horse at her cost as Sir James or Richard Calle.*'[44] It seems that John III had at least managed to escape briefly from Norfolk earlier that year by travelling on pilgrimage to the great shrine of St James at Santiago de Compostela in north-western Spain. None of John III's surviving letters mention this journey, far removed as it was from his daily life in Norwich; the only references to the trip can be found in letters written before the event by John II, who was looking forward to seeing his brother when he visited Calais on the way home. As a result, it is impossible to know exactly what the experience – if indeed he did take ship for Spain as planned – meant to John III. However, he had also made a pilgrimage on foot to the shrine of St Thomas Becket at Canterbury in the summer of 1470, and it may not be stretching interpretation too far to see these journeys as an attempt to make some sort of reparation for the death of John Daubeney under his command at Caister in the autumn of 1469. There was nothing intrinsically unusual in John III's decision to visit two of the most famous holy places in Europe, both of which attracted thousands of pilgrims each year, but the specific timing of his travels perhaps indicates that his emotional recovery from the ordeal of the siege may not have been as untroubled as his outwardly calm and collected letters suggested.[45]

Memories of the siege would not fade easily, of course, while Caister was in the hands of the Duke of Norfolk. The brothers did not give up their efforts to pursue their claim to the castle, but while the Duke himself remained so fiercely intransigent they had little prospect of success. John II's customary optimism was beginning to sound more like blind faith than anything grounded in a realistic assessment of their chances. '*Item, as touching Caister, I trust to God that you shall be in it to my use before Christmas be past*', he told John III in November 1473.[46] Three months later he assured his mother that, '*as for the having again of Caister, I trust to have good tidings thereof hastily*'.[47] By the autumn of 1474, however, nothing had changed, and even John II was becoming defensive on the subject. '*Item, as for Caister, it needs not to spur nor prick me to do aught therein*', he told Margaret in November. '*I do that I can with good will, and somewhat I hope to do hastily therein that shall do good.*'[48] Whatever it was that he was planning – if, indeed, he had anything in mind other than the need to convince his mother that he was on top of the situation – had no effect. Norfolk's men still held Caister at the beginning of 1475, with John II and John III still going through the motions of trying to find influential support for their cause. Their old patron Archbishop Neville had at last been freed and allowed to return to England in November 1474, but he could offer the Pastons no help: at forty-one, he was a broken man, who took no further part in political life, and died less than two years after his release. Meanwhile, John II's service at Calais had earned Lord Hastings's benevolence in general terms – '*if there be anything that I can and may do for you, I shall with right good will perform it to my power*', Hastings wrote in a genial note in the autumn of 1473 – but it was apparent that it would take a great deal more than that to force Norfolk to reconsider his position.[49]

However, one thing at least had changed by the beginning of 1475: Margaret and John II had finally found a way out of the spiralling recriminations which had threatened to overwhelm them. The turning point seems to have come in the autumn of 1474, when John II was taken ill on a rare visit to Norfolk. On his return to his lodgings in London – now at the George Inn, near Lord Hastings's house on St Paul's Wharf – he thanked his mother for '*the great cost and the great cheer that you did to me . . . at my last being with you, which cheer also has made me perfectly whole, I thank God and you*'. He had been worried, '*so green recovered of my sickness*' as he was, that the journey back would be too much for him, '*but, God thank you, I took so my crumbs while I was with you . . . that God and you had made me stronger than I thought*', he told her.[50] It is impossible to know from their surviving letters exactly what had happened when they met, but the effect was a startling transformation in Margaret's feelings – whether because she had at last had a chance to spend time with the son she now hardly saw, or because his illness conjured up the threat of losing him completely. Their increasingly acerbic exchanges of the last three years – usually conducted via the long-suffering John III – were suddenly replaced by correspondence full of solicitous affection. Previously, Margaret's letters to her sons had invariably begun with an unadorned and functional '*I greet you well*', but when she wrote to John II, by this time back at Calais, in January 1475 she addressed him in markedly different style: '*Right wellbeloved son, I greet you well and send you God's blessing and mine, letting you know that I marvel that I have had no writing from you*'.[51] For once, it was not a reproof, but an expression of genuine eagerness to hear from him.

The contents of Margaret's letter were even more extraordinary. John II's financial woes continued, but for the first time his mother was taking them in her stride, offering constructive advice and concrete help, and sounding sanguine and cheerful as she did so. Not only had she agreed to stand surety for him for another loan, but she was now, after all the months of misery the subject had provoked, calmly organising the sale of some of the timber at Sporle on his behalf. *'I shall be as good a housewife for you as I can'*, she told him, *'and as I would be for myself.'*[52] It seemed suddenly obvious that money had been a symptom of her unhappiness with her eldest son, not its root cause. She had always expended more energy worrying about him than about any of her other children, and, perhaps as a result, found it all too easy to fall back on her husband's conviction that John II was irredeemably unreliable when her son was not there in person to reassure her. However, it is hard to avoid the conclusion that – although she probably would not have admitted it – John II was her favourite child, or at least the one with whom she was most closely emotionally involved. Whatever it was that had happened on his visit in October, it had at last succeeded in reminding her of his good nature and convincing her of his good intentions, and in response she became as protective of him as she had once been in defending him against his father. For his part, John II was keen to let her know that he was – and always had been – appreciative of everything she was doing for him. *'I have put you to cost, charge and loss enough, God thank you of it . . .'*, he told her in February; *'wherefore, if Sporle wood spring any silver or gold, it is my will that first of all you be your own payer of all that is behind'.*[53] He also had to cope with the fact that her renewed affection was manifesting itself in ways which, for John II, probably verged on the alarming. *'Send me word how you do of your sickness that you had on your eye and your leg'*, she told him in January, *'and, if God will not suffer you to have health, thank him thereof and take it patiently, and come home again to me, and we shall live together as God will give us grace to do.'*[54] It took all John II's charm and courtesy to side-step the suggestion while simultaneously assuring her of his devotion. *'God thank you of your large proffer,'* he wrote, *'whereof I would be right glad if I might'* – but the military commitments he had taken on for the coming months made it impossible for him to return to Norfolk. However, *'that journey with God's grace once done'*, he said, *'I purpose verily with God's grace thereafter to dance attendance most about your pleasure and ease.'*[55]

It was perhaps lucky for John II that he could claim the pressing excuse of duty to his sovereign. It had not taken King Edward long after he regained the throne to consider the possibility of renewing war against France – a project which offered the dual attraction of recapturing the English territories which had been so humiliatingly lost during the previous thirty years, and of moving the arena of Anglo-French conflict back into the domains of the French King, whose support for the Earl of Warwick had cost Edward his crown, however briefly, in 1470–1. Three years had gone by while he levied taxes to pay for a major campaign and tried to persuade his potential allies, the Dukes of Burgundy and Brittany, to commit themselves to his plans. By the beginning of 1475, however, preparations were well under way. Edward's army numbered almost 15,000 men, as well as hundreds of others recruited for their technical expertise, among them armourers, smiths, tent-makers, saddlers, bowyers, fletchers, carters for the artillery train, and miners to dig tunnels and trenches. The King was determined to ensure that his forces were well supplied with provisions and ammunition – 779 stone cannon balls and more than 10,000 sheaves of arrows were shipped across the Channel – and that he would lead his army in appropriately sumptuous style: campaign expenses included more than £400 spent on cloth of gold, and Edward ordered a portable house made of wood and covered with leather for his use in the field. Almost all of his nobles agreed to serve in person on the expedition, each bringing with him men-at-arms and archers to join the '*finest, largest and best appointed force that has ever left England*', an Italian observer reported from Bruges.[56]

Among the soldiers were John II, John III and their younger brother Edmund. John II probably took his place in Lord Hastings's retinue, and John III may have joined him, although it is difficult to be sure, given that Earl Rivers and the Duke of Norfolk – both of whom he had previously served – were also recruiting men for their contingents. Edmund, meanwhile, was retained by King Edward's youngest brother, the Duke of Gloucester. There may even have been four Pastons among the King's forces, if Walter, who was still not quite twenty, accompanied his brothers to France. It seems unlikely that he did so, given that he was now studying at Oxford and intended for the priesthood, but on the other hand it is otherwise hard to explain the letter Margaret wrote to her eldest son at Calais in May 1475, while the newly recruited forces which included his brothers were gathering at Canterbury in readiness for the crossing to France. '*For God's love*', she wrote, '*if your brothers go over the sea, advise them as you think best for their safeguard, for some of them be but young soldiers and know full little what it means to be a soldier, nor for to endure to do as a soldier should do.*'[57] John II and John III, now in their early thirties, had both been in battle before under the Earl of Oxford's command at Barnet, and Edmund had already gained some relevant experience by joining John II at Calais in the summer of 1473 – although admittedly life in the garrison there could not be said to be active service in the sense which Margaret had in mind, and it is possible that Edmund rather than Walter was the '*young soldier*' of whom she was thinking. Nevertheless, however many of her sons travelled to France that summer, it is clear that she was troubled at the prospect of any of them going to war.

As it turned out, she had little to fear. Even before Edward's army began to move slowly out of Calais in mid-July, it had become apparent that the support of the Dukes of Brittany and Burgundy would not, after all, be forthcoming. The Duke of Brittany had committed himself to Edward's cause so much at the eleventh hour that their treaty of alliance had not yet been formally ratified by the time the King embarked for France, and, in the end, the Duke made no move to assist the English invasion. Meanwhile, the Duke of Burgundy was preoccupied with his own interests in the Rhineland, in particular his attempt to secure control of the city of Neuss, to which he had laid siege in July 1474. The Duke persisted in his campaign throughout the winter; John II had hoped to see the besieged city for himself in January 1475 on a trip into Flanders to buy himself a horse and armour for the coming English expedition. '... *perchance I shall see the siege at Neuss before I come again if I have time*', he told his brother cheerfully; '*I think that I should be sick unless I see it*'.[58] Duke Charles did not finally admit defeat there until the middle of June, by which time he had neither the troops nor the money to help Edward against the French. Under the circumstances, Edward made the pragmatic decision to use the presence of his army on French soil to press his advantage in negotiating a settlement with King Louis, who was anxious to see off the English threat before the Anglo-Burgundian alliance could resurrect itself. The two kings met on 29 August at the village of Picquigny near Amiens, where a bridge over the River Somme had been hurriedly built with a wooden screen across the middle through which Edward and Louis could talk without fear of assassination. Terms had already been agreed by delegates from both sides, and the treaty was rapidly concluded: England and France were to observe a truce for the next seven years; and the King of England would receive a sum of £15,000 from the King of France before his departure, to be followed by a pension of £10,000 each year. In effect, Louis was paying Edward handsomely to take his army home.

The end of the campaign meant the safe return of all Margaret's sons. '... *blessed be God, this voyage of the King's is finished for this time*', John II wrote from Calais on 11 September, the same day that his brothers took ship back to England. Margaret should perhaps have been more worried about the climate at Calais than the French King's guns, since both John II and John III fell ill on their return there. '*I ... mislike somewhat the air here*', John II told her, '*for by my troth I was in good health when I came hither, and all whole, and to my knowledge I had never a better stomach in my life, and now within eight days I am crazed again.*'[59] John III blamed the temperature: '*all my sickness that I had at Calais, and since I came over also, came but of cold*', he reported to his brother from Norwich a month later; '*but I was never so well armed for the war as I have now armed me for cold*'.[60] Despite his precautions, he was still ill a fortnight later. '*It will not out of my stomach by no means*', he wrote miserably. '*I may not eat half enough when I have most hunger. I am so well dieted, and yet it will not be. God send you health, for I have none three days together, do the best I can.*'[61] Margaret, meanwhile, remained unnervingly keen to have her eldest son at home in Norfolk: '*. . . she would fain have you at home with her*', John III wrote, '*and if you be once met she tells me you shall not lightly depart till death depart you*'.[62]

The brothers themselves were preoccupied with the urgent need to make one more attempt on Caister. By gathering the great men of England in one place, the abortive invasion had offered an unparalleled opportunity to seek powerful help, and it seemed at last that King Edward might be prepared to put pressure on the Duke of Norfolk. '*I was in good hope to have had Caister again*', John II told Margaret on his return. '*The King spoke to my lord of Norfolk for it, and it was full like to have come, but in conclusion it is delayed till this next term, by which time the King has commanded him to take advice of his council and to be sure that his title be good, or else the King has ascertained him that for any favour he must do me right and justice*'.[63] It was not yet the result they wanted, but even the Duke's acceptance that there was a case to answer represented substantial progress, and in the meantime they still had the advantage of the Duchess's support. In early October, John III visited her at Norwich, where she was staying during her second pregnancy; '*she would as fain you had it as anybody*', he told his brother.[64]

Two weeks later, he wrote again to John II – but this time with shattering news. He had seen the Duchess of Norfolk for a second time, '*and she told me that the King had no such words to my lord for Caister as you told me*', he said. Instead, a startling scene of defiance had unfolded at Calais as King Edward and the Duke were preparing to leave for England. '*. . . the King asked my lord at his departing from Calais how he would deal with Caister*', John III reported, '*and my lord answered never a word*'. While Norfolk maintained a mulish silence, Edward forced an answer out of one of his retainers, Sir William Brandon. According to Brandon, the Duke had declared '*that the King should as soon have his life as that place*' – and when Edward asked Norfolk '*whether he said so or not*', the Duke confirmed that he had. '*And the King said not a word again, but turned his back and went his way*',

John III went on. '*But my lady told me if the King had spoken any word in the world after that to my lord, my lord would not have said him nay.*'[65] Perhaps the Duchess was right; or perhaps she was trying to put a positive spin on her husband's intransigence. Either way, Norfolk's brinkmanship confronted Edward with an uncomfortable dilemma. Insisting on the Duke's compliance, but that would risk precipitating serious political conflict with a magnate who, despite his questionable judgement, had at least been consistently loyal. Edward was determined to be master in his own kingdom, but, as the French expedition had just demonstrated in no uncertain terms, he was a pragmatist who knew that he had to pick which battles to fight. In the end, there was no reason for him to stake his authority on the Pastons' claim to Caister. As always, the Pastons' problem was that they were not important enough – either in their own right or in the service of anyone more influential – to force concessions from a vastly more powerful opponent. As a result, it suited the King better to let it be known that he had commanded Norfolk '*to take advice of his council*', and then to walk away, than to make an issue of the Duke's recalcitrance.

At least it was now clear that there was no point in continuing to petition the Duke in the hope that he might one day relent. John III immediately told the Duchess that, under the circumstances, he could not serve her husband any longer. She was so sorry to see him go that she made him promise to talk to her again before committing himself to the service of any other lord. John II, meanwhile, for the first time drafted a formal petition to the King detailing the losses he had suffered as a result of Norfolk's seizure of Caister – a total, he said, of more than £1,300 – and setting out his grievances, '*for redress whereof your said supplicant has, this said space of four years, sued to my said lord and his council*', he wrote, '*and of all that time . . . my lord would never suffer him to come in his presence nor hear him, nor none other for him, to declare or show his grief*'.[66] However, there was little chance that a public complaint would succeed where private manoeuvres had failed. There was nothing more they could do except wait and hope for a miracle.

They did not have to wait long. On Tuesday, 16 January 1476 the Duke of Norfolk was suddenly taken ill at Norwich. He died the same night, at around midnight, at the age of thirty-one.[67] John II managed to compose himself well enough the next morning to cast his letter reporting the news to his mother in appropriately respectful terms: '*it is for all that loved him to do and help now that which may be to his honour and weal to his soul*'. However, he was already – only hours after the Duke's death – deep in plans to take full advantage of an opportunity which was so momentous and so fortuitous that it seemed scarcely credible. The Duke's heir was his three-year-old daughter Anne, the baby who had indirectly caused John II such embarrassment with the Duchess in the winter of 1472. The Duchess herself was pregnant again and might yet have a son, but, even if she did, the political power of the dukedom would be in abeyance, or at least much reduced, for many years. It had been the Duke himself – not his wife or his council – who had been immovable on the subject of Caister, and if the Pastons were ever to have a chance to make their claim good, this was surely it. John II immediately threw himself into action on two fronts. First, he sought to do what service he could to the newly widowed Duchess and her shocked household. '. . . *it is so that this country is not well purveyed of cloth of gold for the covering of his body and hearse*', he told his mother, '*wherefore, every man helping to his power, I put the council of my lord in comfort that I hoped to get one for that day*'. As luck would have it, he had bought some '*cloth of tissue*' for his father's uncompleted tomb, and he now offered it for use instead at the Duke's funeral. The purchase had clearly been made some time before, since he was not certain '*if it be not broken or put to any other use*', but he asked Margaret to send it, and promised that '*it shall be saved again for you unhurt at my peril. I deem hereby to get great thank and great assistance in time to come*'.[68]

The second step he took was less likely to be received with favour by the Duchess and her advisers. Three days after the Duke's death, John II left Norwich for London to present his claim to Caister to the King, and sent a servant to assert his rights at the castle itself. John III – who was temperamentally more cautious than his brother, and personally much closer to the Duchess – was convinced the move was ham-fisted and premature. '*I assure you your sending to Caister is evil taken among my lord's folk*', he wrote a few days later, '*in so much that some say that you tendered little my lord's death, in as much as you would so soon enter upon him after his decease without advice and assent of my lord's council.*'[69] John II was stung by the criticism, but rejected out of hand the suggestion that he had acted without courtesy or judgement. He had been patient for more than six years since Norfolk had first seized the castle, and during that time diplomacy had got him nowhere. His reply was defiant and angry:

> . . . *where that some towards my lady of Norfolk noise that I did unkindly to send so hastily to Caister as I did, there is no discreet person that so thinks; for if my lord had been as kind to me as he might have been, and according to such heart and service as my grandfather, my father, yourself*

*and I have owed and done to my lords of Norfolk that dead be – and yet if I
had wedded his daughter – yet must I have done as I did.*

He was certain that his tactics were necessary if they were to succeed in
recovering Caister, but he had also been rattled by the emergence of yet
another potential threat to their hopes. If the Duke's small daughter did in
the end inherit her father's estates, the King had proposed that she should
marry his second son, two-year-old Richard, Duke of York, and John II
feared that Edward might therefore have an acquisitive eye of his own on the
castle, along with the rest of the Norfolk inheritance. It was clear that a little
more patience would be required, since the Pastons could not be sure what
attitude the King and the widowed Duchess would adopt towards their
claim until the fate of the dukedom itself was decided by the birth of her
baby. '. . . *let us all pray God send my lady of Norfolk a son*', John II told his
brother, '*for upon that rests much matter*'.[70]

As winter gave way to spring, John II continued to press his case as force-
fully as he could – '*I pray you send me some word if you think likely that I may
enter Caister when I will, by the next messenger*', he asked his brother in
March – while John III still tried to restrain him ('*take not that way if there
be any other*').[71] John III himself was back in the service of the Duchess, and
it seemed a hopeful sign for the family's prospects that she had asked
Margaret to attend on her when she went into labour. '. . . *if it were your ease
to be here I would be right glad*', John III told his mother, '*for I think your
being here should do great good to my brother's matters that he has to speed
with her*'.[72] If Margaret did join the Duchess's attendants, her help could not
secure a happy outcome for the birth, either for the expectant mother or for
Margaret's own family. The baby did not survive, and the King therefore
pursued his plans for the marriage of the three-year-old heiress to his toddler son – exactly the course of events which the Pastons had feared.
However, John II's irrepressible optimism – which he had somehow maintained despite the crushing setbacks of the previous ten years – was about to
be vindicated at last. He worked hard to avert the possibility that Caister
might be swept into the King's hands by playing down the castle's charms –
King Edward '*was informed of the truth and that it was not for a prince*', John
II reported – and playing up the financial compensation he would demand
in return for relinquishing his own title to the estate.[73] Whether or not the
King was convinced by these protestations, Edward was a shrewd politician
who knew that the Duke of Norfolk's death offered a chance to settle once
and for all a dispute which had festered, in one form or another, for as long

as he had ruled England. He secured the dukedom for his son, but graciously allowed the Pastons' claim to Caister to be heard without challenge from the crown.

By the end of May, John II was at last sounding genuinely confident, if also more than a little weary. '. . . *as for my matters,*' he told his mother and brother, '. . . *they do, blessed be God, as well as I would they did, save that it shall cost me great money and it has cost me great labour*'.[74] It took one more month, but on 30 June 1476 – almost seventeen years since the death of Sir John Fastolf, and more than ten since that of their father – John II was able to send his brother the good news for which they had been waiting so long. '*Item, blessed be God, I have Caister at my will*', he wrote. '*God hold it better than it was done heretofore.*'[75]

CHAPTER TWELVE

– *I pray get us a wife somewhere* –

John Paston II turned thirty-five in the spring of 1477. The battle for the Fastolf inheritance had overshadowed his entire adult life, but at last it was over. He was left exhausted rather than triumphant: the human cost of the struggle – in lives cut short, friendships broken and opportunities missed – had been high, and the prize itself was not what it had once been. Most of Fastolf's estates were now helping to pay for the construction of the hall, chapel and cloisters at Magdalen College in Oxford under Bishop Wainfleet's direction. Meanwhile, Caister was no longer quite the elegant and luxurious home of Fastolf's original design. John III had thought a number of repairs necessary ten years earlier, but since then the buildings had been damaged during the siege, and, for all the Duke of Norfolk's insistence that it was his property, he had shown little inclination to spend either time or money there. Now that it was back in Paston hands, none of the family took up permanent residence in the castle. Margaret's household was already well established a mile away at her own manor of Mautby, from where she and her servants could at least keep a close eye on the estate, but there was no sign that her eldest son had any imminent intention of making Caister his home.

Apart from anything else, the fact that the castle was back in John II's possession did not mean that he was suddenly freed from legal entanglements in the London courts. Even after the Duchess of Norfolk's men had left Caister in the summer of 1476, it took more than a year to secure formal ratification of John II's title. Not only that, but in the early months of 1478 he was precipitated into further litigation over the manors of Drayton and Hellesdon, which had been lost to the Duke of Suffolk for more than a decade, apparently without hope of recovery. The Duke's redoubtable mother, Duchess Alice, had died in 1475 at the age of seventy-one, and was buried under an exquisite alabaster monument in the church near her home at Ewelme in Oxfordshire. Three years after her death, it appeared that the Pastons might at last stand a chance of retrieving the manors when the Duke – who seems to have inherited the political talents of neither of his formidable parents – ran short of money. Despite their own financial worries, John III urged his brother to seize the opportunity which the Duke's difficulties presented: *'a hundred marks will do more now . . . than you shall peradventure do with two hundred marks in time coming if this season be not taken'*, he wrote.[1] John III believed that their best hope lay in petitioning the Duke's wife, King Edward's sister Elizabeth; it seemed that, yet again, they might find more favour with a pragmatic duchess than with her stubborn husband. However, the parallel with their dealings with the Duke of Norfolk proved all too exact. Suffolk reacted to his need for cash not by agreeing to part with Drayton and Hellesdon, but by selling timber there, and taking the opportunity to reassert his ownership of the estates by visiting them in person. Despite the fact that he was ill and, on a hot May afternoon, needed two men to keep him on his feet, the Duke made great show of being as implacable as Norfolk had been at Caister. *'. . . he would meet you with a spear and have none other amends for the trouble that you have put him to but your heart's blood, and that will he get with his own hands'*, John II's servant John Wheatley reported back to his master in London; *'for if you have Hellesdon and Drayton you shall have his life with it.'* Wheatley was distinctly unimpressed with the Duke's behaviour – *'there was never no man that played Herod in Corpus Christi play better and more agreeable to his pageant than he did'*, he said – not least because John III and Wheatley himself were now facing threats and harassment from Suffolk's servants in Norwich.[2] In the attempt to protect his men and what he considered to be his property – which was rapidly being devalued as the trees at Drayton were cut down – from such ostentatious aggression, John II was left with little option but to start new legal proceedings to challenge the Duke's hold on the manors.

He had continued to divide his time between London and Calais over the past couple of years, although life in the garrison seemed to have lost some of its excitement along with its novelty. He had been ill there again in the spring of 1476; *'in truth I am somewhat crazed, what with the sea and what with this diet here'*, he told his brother.[3] His reluctance to return was more marked by February 1477, when Lord Hastings was planning a personal visit to Calais, and John II thought – rightly, as it turned out – that his own presence would be required in his lord's retinue for the trip. *'I fear that I cannot be excused'*, he reported to John III, *'but . . . if I go, I hope not to tarry long'.*[4] However jaded he felt, it remained the case that his attachment to Hastings was too valuable to put at risk. Hastings had known the King since childhood, and was now one of the most powerful and prominent members of

Edward's inner circle, entrusted with wide-ranging responsibilities not only at Calais, but within the royal household as Lord Chamberlain, and as the leading magnate across a huge swath of the north and east midlands. Service to Hastings, potentially at least, offered political access of a kind which John II's old patron, the Queen's brother Earl Rivers, could not have provided. Since the controversy over his crusading plans in 1471, Rivers's relationship with the King had recovered enough for him to be put in charge of the household of the young Prince of Wales, an appointment which brought him substantial authority in the Welsh borders. However, he was not even a constant presence in England, let alone at the heart of government; he spent much of 1476 travelling in Italy on an expedition which was part pilgrimage, part sight-seeing tour – a trip marred only by an encounter with thieves on the road outside Rome who relieved him of plate and jewels worth more than 1,000 marks. If Rivers had proved little help in John II's attempt to rehabilitate himself after the traumas of 1470–1, the Paston brothers had other contacts from those years which they were even more keen to leave behind. The Duke of Clarence – whose servant Walter Writtle had tried to broker an end to the siege at Caister in 1469 – had learned no lessons whatsoever as a result of his lucky escape from the consequences of his own treason. Rumours persisted in England and on the continent of Clarence's continuing disloyalty, while at the same time the Duke's public behaviour remained provocative and confrontational. Every attempt Edward made to curb his brother's excesses was met with petulant defiance, and by the summer of 1477 the King's patience was finally exhausted. Clarence was arrested and held in the Tower until January 1478, when he was found guilty of high treason at a specially convened meeting of parliament. He was put to death privately in the Tower a month later. A few months after his execution, the Earl of Oxford – Clarence's former ally and the Pastons' former lord – evaded his guards at Hammes Castle for long enough to jump from the battlements into the moat; '*he leapt the walls and went to the dyke and into the dyke to the chin*', John II reported to his brother, '*to what intent I cannot tell – some say to steal away, and some think he would have drowned himself.*'[5] Whether the Earl had intended escape or suicide, he achieved neither, but was caught and returned to his prison quarters. For John II, who heard the news in London, it was a reminder that, whatever trials he had faced over the past seven years, he was fortunate to have found the chance in Lord Hastings's service to resuscitate a political career which might have ended on the field at Barnet.

By the end of 1477 John II had also secured his freedom from his long-drawn-out betrothal to Anne Haute. They had been engaged for nearly nine years, the last six of which had been spent trying to obtain official sanction for their separation. The delay in procuring a dispensation from Rome had prevented him from embarking on other matrimonial plans, but that fact appeared to trouble him little. His engagement had been a matter of political advantage rather than personal inclination, and the idea of settling down seemed to hold no greater appeal for him at the age of thirty-five than it had done ten years earlier. He was not short of female company: in the summer of 1473, for example, he had asked his brother Edmund to send news from Calais of one of his conquests there (*'I pray you send me word . . . of her welfare, and whether I were out and other in, or not'*).[6] Letters he received from a friend in London when he was back in Calais himself in the spring of 1477 were full of laboured innuendo on the subject (*'we have heard say that the fraus of Bruges with their high caps have given some of you great claps, and that the feat of their arms doing is such that they smite all at the mouth and at the great end of the thigh . . .'*).[7] Meanwhile, a liaison in England with a woman named Constance Reynforth produced at least one illegitimate child, a daughter, also named Constance. But it is clear that, tired though he was after the years of struggle over Caister, the prospect of a more permanent relationship and greater domesticity was not enticing. Instead, as a gentleman in London and a soldier at Calais, he preferred to live the courtly life, or at least whatever version of it he could afford. He indulged his love of books, collecting not only fine manuscript volumes but a copy of *The Game and Play of the Chess*, one of the first books produced by William Caxton's new printing-press at Bruges. He also pursued his enthusiasm for knightly feats of arms. The two passions were combined in the *'Great Book'* he had commissioned several years earlier from a scrivener named William Ebesham, which contained copies of treatises on war, knighthood, tournaments and chivalry.[8] John II enjoyed music, masques, hunting and good company, both male and female, and it was sufficiently clear to his mother that he was unlikely to change his ways that she was deeply sceptical when she heard rumours of another engagement in the spring of 1478. Whatever the possible advantages of the match, she said, he should contemplate marriage only *'if you can find in your heart to love her, so that she be such one as you can think to have issue by; or else, by my troth, I had rather that you never married in your life'*.[9]

On the face of it, Margaret's lack of enthusiasm at the prospect of seeing her eldest son settled at last was surprising, but by now her hopes that he would come home for good had given way to the bitter realisation that, whatever he might say, it was unlikely to happen. At the end of 1475 she had still expected his imminent return. '. . . *my mother would fain have you at Mautby*', John III told his brother in October. '*She rode thither out of Norwich on Saturday last past to purvey your lodging ready against your coming*.'[10] The prospect of the recovery of Caister after the Duke of Norfolk's death may have raised her hopes further, particularly given John II's increasing disenchantment with life at Calais. He sent profuse apologies for a lengthy stay there in the spring of 1476, claiming that it was driven solely by political necessity ('*mother, I beseech you to take no displeasure with me for my long tarrying, for I dare do none otherwise for displeasing of my lord. I was nothing glad of this journey if I might goodly have chosen*').[11] However, by the summer of 1477, as he continued to make excuses for his absence, the warmth and optimism of Margaret's earlier letters were replaced by weary resignation, and she gave up asking when he would come back to Norfolk. As so often before, her distress manifested itself in her husband's old complaints, unfair though they were: her son was negligent, extravagant and unreliable; he paid little attention to her advice, and cared less about her welfare. Inevitably, given the circumstances, his financial troubles again became a source of conflict. John II owed money to a man named Cockett, a debt which he was struggling to repay, and he was hoping for help from his mother. Two years earlier the request might have elicited a positive response, but now it merely served to make Margaret angry. '*I put you in certain that I will never pay him penny of that duty that is owing to him though he sue me for it*', she declared, '*not of my own purse, for I will not be compelled to pay your debts against my weal*'.[12] John II insisted that he was doing his best, but his attempts to raise cash had already forced him to mortgage the manor of Sporle, a tactic with which Margaret was so unhappy that she made scarcely veiled threats to withhold his inheritance as a result:

> *I marvel much that you have dealt again so simply with Sporle . . . It causes me to be in great doubt of you what your disposition will be hereafter for such livelihood as I have been disposed before this time to leave you after my decease, for I think verily that you would be disposed hereafter to sell or set to mortgage the land that you should have after me, your mother, as gladly and rather than that livelihood that you have after your father. It grieves me to think upon your guiding . . .*

Acute though their money problems were, the emotional charge of Margaret's reproaches was clearer than ever. '*I think you set but little by my* blessing', she told him, '*and if you did you would have desired it in your writing to me. God make you a good man*'.[13]

If John II would not come home, Margaret was all the more adamant that he should not escape what she saw as his responsibilities. His father's tomb had still not been constructed, and in 1476 word came from Bromholm that '*the cloth that lies over the grave is all torn and rotten, and is not worth 2d*'. Despite the '*ill speech*' to which this upsetting and embarrassing state of affairs gave rise, two years later the monument had not yet even been commissioned, let alone built.[14] John II was full of good intentions – '*there shall be a tomb and somewhat else over my father's grave, on whose soul God have mercy, that there shall none be like it in Norfolk*' – but his plans depended on money which he did not have.[15] Margaret was keenly aware of the stigma, particularly since her friend Elizabeth Clere and her old enemy John Heydon had both recently made lavish gifts to the church at Bromholm, '*and if there should nothing be done for your father, it would be too great a shame for us all, and in chief to see him lie as he does*'.[16] Nevertheless, however exercised she was, there was no sign that she might relent and pay for the tomb herself. Nor was this the only family expense which Margaret now refused to shoulder: in 1477 she told John II that she was no longer willing to support his youngest brother William from her own resources. William's school fees had not been paid for more than six months, and he needed new clothes, but Margaret insisted that it was her eldest son's duty as head of the family to meet the cost of his brother's upbringing: '*I would you should remember it and purvey therefor*', she wrote; '*as for me, I will not*'.[17] Five years earlier, in the midst of their first altercations over Sporle, John II had had similar arguments with his mother about which of them should provide for his sister Anne, in terms of either her board and lodging or the cost of finding her a husband. Concerned though he was to do the right thing, it was clear that John II felt more than a little resentful of the suggestion that the burden should lie on his shoulders alone: '*I will purvey for her*', he told John III, '*and yet she is not my daughter*'.[18]

The question of Anne's future was one issue at least which had been resolved by the summer of 1477. She was now twenty-three, and various potential matches had been suggested for her over the previous five years, ever since her mother and brothers had been prompted into action by the fear that she might otherwise follow too closely in the footsteps of her disgraced sister Margery. The first sign of any concern over Anne's behaviour had come in the autumn of 1471, when Margaret asked John III to find employment in London for their servant John Pamping, ostensibly because '*he loses his time here*' in Norfolk. She made it abundantly clear, however, that there was more to her request than she was prepared to commit to paper. '*. . . for divers other causes I would he were hence in haste, for all manner of haps*', she wrote. '*Construe you, etc. I shall tell you more hereafter.*'[19] Two years later, John II felt able to be less discreet: '*I pray you take good heed to my sister Anne lest the old love between her and Pamping renew*', he told his brother in November 1473.[20] Pamping had worked hard for the family for more than a decade, attending John Paston in the Fleet Prison in 1465 and helping John III to defend Caister against the Duke of Norfolk's forces. Nevertheless, despite his loyalty and his capabilities, Margaret and her sons were not prepared to take any chances; the parallels between Anne's situation and Margery's romance with Richard Calle were too close for anyone's comfort. Yet again, a young Paston daughter had fallen in love with an older man whose undoubted personal qualities could not make up for the crucial issue of his status, or lack of it. This time, however, there would be no clandestine marriage. By the autumn of 1472 Pamping had gone from Margaret's household to serve John II in London and Calais, and a year after that he left the Pastons' employment altogether. Once the couple had been separated, the next priority was to find Anne a more suitable husband – not an easy task, given the precariousness of the family's finances, and therefore the difficulty of providing her with an acceptable dowry. One possibility which emerged very quickly was a match with Judge Yelverton's grandson William, an alliance which would serve to cement the reconciliation between Yelverton and the Pastons after the long years of conflict over Fastolf's will. Even leaving aside the question of Anne's feelings for Pamping, it was clear that the Yelverton marriage would not be a love-match on either side; '*as for Yelverton*', John II reported in November 1473, '*he said but late that he would have her if she had her money, and else not*'.[21] Nevertheless, the proposal had Margaret's backing and, in the end, she got her way: in the spring of 1477 Anne Paston finally became Anne Yelverton.

By that stage, however, negotiations for another marriage were causing much greater tension within the family. It had been apparent for some time that John III – unlike his elder brother – was keen to find himself a wife. Domesticity did not hold any fears for him; despite the occasional frustrations of his mother's household, life in Norfolk had never left him restless as it did John II. His eagerness to marry was partly a matter of personal preference, but it was also grounded in pragmatic judgement: a wife with a dowry would allow him at last to take possession of the manor earmarked for him in his father's will, and to set up his own household there with some measure of independence from his family. His problem was that, personable and talented though he was, he was a younger son. It had to be assumed that one day, even if it was in the far distant future, his older brother would marry and produce an heir, and consequently John III's prospects – and therefore his appeal as a potential husband – were limited. Property attracted property in the marriage market, and certainly John III could not offer enough of an estate to secure the hand of an heiress. The question was whether he could find a bride whose family would provide a sufficient dowry to establish the new couple's household on a solid financial footing, but would also be prepared to accept the limitations of the resources which he himself would bring to the marriage. The difficulties he faced were obvious as early as 1467, when he made a tentative approach to Alice Boleyn, the daughter of a local man who had made his fortune as a mercer in London and used the money to establish his family at the north Norfolk manor of Blickling. The response John III received was disheartening: Alice's mother would not overrule her daughter if Alice herself were determined on the match, John II reported from London, but would *'never advise her thereto in no wise'*.[22] The Pastons' financial and political problems over the next few years did nothing to improve John III's chances, and by 1470 he sounded half-jokingly despairing on the subject: '*I pray get us a wife somewhere*', he asked his brother that spring.[23] Other proposals came and went: in the summer of 1474 John III was juggling two potential matches in London, one a widow named Agnes – he did not even seem to be sure of her surname – at Blackfriars, the other a draper's daughter named Elizabeth Eberton. This seemed promising, not least because London merchants who were rich in cash but short on the status conferred by land and birth might be prepared to offer a substantial sum to secure their daughter's marriage to a gentleman, even a relatively impoverished one such as John III. However, despite his best efforts, nothing came of either possibility, nor of any of the other options he pursued, and by February 1476 he was ruefully asking his brother to keep an eye out for *'some old thrifty alewife'* for him.[24] Then, at the beginning of 1477, he met Margery Brews.

Margery – who was probably in her late teens, and certainly not more than twenty – was the daughter of a Norfolk knight, Sir Thomas Brews. She was not an heiress, and had three sisters for whom her father would also have to provide, but her family was of good local standing. So far, so moderately encouraging, although John III had been here before and, on those previous occasions, had made no further progress. However, this rapidly proved to be different from all of his previous courtships: he and Margery fell headlong in love. By February, Margery's mother Elizabeth Brews – who was clearly already as fond of John III as her daughter was smitten – was scolding him for making her life so difficult while the financial terms of the marriage contract had yet to be agreed. '. . . *you have made her such advocate for you*', she told him, '*that I may never have rest night nor day for calling and crying upon to bring the said matter to effect*'.[25] For his part, John III was just as impatient. At nearly thirty-three, he had been overwhelmed by the strength of his feelings for Margery, and sounded almost breathless as he wrote urgently to his mother about the progress of negotiations. '*Mother, the matter is in a reasonable good way*', he reported from the Brews' home at Topcroft, ten miles or so south of Norwich, '*and I trust, with God's mercy and with your good help, that it shall take effect better to my advantage than I told you of at Mautby, for I trow there is not a kinder woman living than I shall have to my mother-in-law if the matter take, nor yet a kinder father-in-law than I shall have, though he be hard to me as yet*'.[26] John III's optimism was touching, but Margery's father was determined to drive a tough bargain – or, from his point of view, a fair one: '*I were right loath to bestow so much upon one daughter that the other her sisters should fare the worse*', he wrote in March. The difficulty was that Swainsthorpe, the manor bequeathed to John III in his father's will, had by now been mortgaged, and a sum of £120 was required to pledge it out before the couple could live there and receive an income from the land. Thomas Brews was unhappy at the prospect that almost all of his daughter's dowry might be consumed by the cost of recovering the manor, telling John II that he '*would be sorry to see either my cousin your brother or my daughter driven to live so mean a life as they should do if the £120 should be paid of their marriage money*'.[27] On the other hand, if Sir Thomas himself put up the cash to reclaim Swainsthorpe, perhaps as a loan to be repaid over a period of some years, he would require a *quid pro quo* from the Pastons in the form of a larger jointure for his daughter than simply that single estate.

The details of the settlement hardly mattered to Margery and John III. Margery said as much in two tender, heartfelt letters to her '*good, true and loving Valentine*': her mother had argued their case as well as she could, she reported, but her father would not budge from his demands, '*for the which, God knows, I am full sorry. But, if that you love me, as I trust verily that you do, you will not leave me therefor; for if that you had not half the livelihood that you have . . . I would not forsake you*'.[28] Meanwhile, Margaret was worried that, despite all his experience, her son's judgement would prove to be equally clouded by his emotions. '*I know well, if it be not concluded in right short* time, that, as for my son, he intends to do right well by my cousin Margery and not so well by himself, she told Elizabeth Brews.[29] The two mothers were now determined that the marriage should take place – partly because of the evident intensity of the personal commitment between John III and Margery; partly because it would not reflect well on either family if negotiations which had been so widely reported within local society came to nothing; and partly because, in essence, it was a good match for both sides. Elizabeth Brews therefore renewed her efforts to persuade her husband to compromise, and Margaret agreed to supplement Margery's prospective jointure by granting her own manor of Sparham to the couple, on top of the estate which her husband had left John III at Swainsthorpe.

Given Margaret's customary strictures about financial caution, this was unlooked-for generosity. When objections to the cost of the match were eventually raised, they came from a much less likely source. Over the years, John II had applied himself cheerfully to the task of trying to find a bride for his brother – an assignment which he certainly found more diverting than looking for a wife for himself. '*I always shall be your herald*', he told John III in 1467, and he had been as good as his word, suggesting names of potential brides and making courtly overtures to a number of gentlewomen on his brother's behalf.[30] However, once it became clear that the wooing of Margery Brews had already been accomplished, and that it was now a question of agreeing a financial settlement to enable the wedding to take place, John II suddenly seemed a great deal less sanguine. At first, he had appeared reluctant to take the relationship seriously, referring to Margery as just one among three possible matches currently under consideration for his brother, and comparing the candidates' merits with almost ostentatious flippancy ('*I had liefer you had her than the Lady Waldegrave; nevertheless, she sings well with a harp*').[31] But his letter crossed in transit with one from John III, which – in asking John II's indulgence for the scribblings produced by a love-addled brain – left no room for doubt about the depth of his feelings. In response, John II abandoned his frivolous tone, and, along with it, his usual lightness of spirits. He was happy at the prospect of John III's marriage to Margery, he told his mother, '*considered her person, her youth, and the stock that she is come of, the love on both sides, the tender favour that she is in with her father and mother, the kindness of her father and mother to her in departing with her, the favour also and good conceit that they have in my brother, the worshipful and virtuous disposition of her father and mother, which prognosticates that of likelihood the maid should be virtuous and good*'.[32] This uncharacteristically solemn exposition of Margery's virtues proved to be a prelude to his serious reservations about the financial agreement which his mother and brother were proposing to conclude with the Brews family. Margaret's decision to grant Sparham to John III and Margery and their future children was overhasty and ill-considered, he said: what if, for example, the couple had a daughter, and Margery then died; any son John III might have by a second marriage would then have no right to inherit the estate, despite being his father's heir. It was not, he said, that he minded his mother giving away property which otherwise might have been his own; '*I would be as glad that one gave you a manor of £20 by year as if he gave it to myself, by my troth*', he told John III. Nevertheless, an unmistakable coolness and distance had abruptly replaced the familiar blithe fluency of his letters to his brother. '*This matter is driven thus far forth without my counsel*', he wrote; '*I pray you make an end without my counsel. If it be well, I would be glad; if it be otherwise, it is pity. I pray you trouble me no more in this matter.*'[33]

John II's sudden sternness – which was disconcertingly reminiscent of his father – owed a lot to the fact that, in reality, he was not the irresponsible figure of his parents' worst imaginings. He was probably telling the truth when he claimed that he had no objection in principle to the idea of Margaret granting his brother part of the Mautby inheritance: he was nothing if not generous, and told John III with a characteristic flourish that '*I will be to Sir Thomas Brews and my lady his wife a very son-in-law for your sake*'.[34] However, the negotiations were well under way by the time he was consulted, and it was already too late, he felt, for his legitimate concerns about the detail of the proposals to be addressed. Undoubtedly, too, there were other, more personal reasons for his anger. He had endured years of recrimination, first from his father and latterly from his mother, about his carelessness with money. Margaret had never acknowledged the fact that his financial struggles were not entirely – perhaps not at all – of his own making, and by the summer of 1477 she was refusing to lend him a single penny to help him deal with his debts. In the circumstances, her readiness to hand over an entire manor to his brother could only be hurtful. If so, it was a hurt which was compounded, in prospect at least, by the impact which John III's marriage would have on his own life. If his brother were now to become a husband and father, and head of a family in his own right, John II would lose the constant support of his right-hand man and probably his best friend. John III had been his partner in business, in fun, and literally his brother-in-arms, through all the troubles of the previous ten years. John II was certainly not in any straightforward sense envious of his brother's situation, but John III's romance with Margery unquestionably left John II a much lonelier figure. The estrangement between the brothers did not last long: bridges were rebuilt once John III and Margery finally married in the autumn of 1477, and John II was genuinely delighted when Margery gave birth to the couple's first child, Christopher, in August 1478. Nevertheless, that summer there was real feeling as well as brotherly teasing in John II's reproach that *'you have now wife and child, and so much to care for that you forget me'.*[35]

Even if there was little prospect that John III's domestic contentment would encourage his older brother to emulate his example, it seemed that the rest of the family did not share John II's reluctance. Anne – like John III, if somewhat less happily – had settled into marriage by 1478. Their sister Margery Calle had already been married for almost ten years, and had three sons, John, William and Richard – a new family to make up for the fact that her relationship with her mother and brothers had never recovered from the shock of her inappropriate choice of husband. Edmund, now in his late twenties, was actively looking for a wife, so far without success, although he had managed along the way to father a son by a married woman named in his brothers' letters only as *'Mistress Dixon'.*[36] Their youngest brother William was a student at Eton, the great school founded almost forty years earlier by Henry VI – an educational opportunity which William perhaps owed to Bishop Wainfleet, who had been provost there in the 1440s and still maintained close links with the college. Despite the fact that he was not yet twenty, William already seemed to have an eye on his matrimonial chances: in February 1479 he met a girl at a wedding, and asked John III to investigate her prospects – and offer an opinion on her looks – on his behalf. Meanwhile, Walter was studying at Oxford. Their mother had high hopes of him: *'I trust to have more joy of him than I have of them that are older'*, she had written with some asperity several years earlier. The plan had always been that Walter should enter the Church once he had taken his degree, although Margaret urged him not to put himself forward for ordination until he was old enough to be sure of the commitment. *'I will love him better to be a good secular man than to be a lewd priest'*, she said.[37] In June 1479 he graduated as a Bachelor of Arts, an achievement celebrated with a feast at which he faced a double disappointment: his brother John III, to whom he seems to have been particularly close, was unable to attend because a mix-up in their correspondence meant that he was not informed of the date; and the venison Walter had been promised for the meal failed to materialise. Nevertheless, *'my guests held them pleased with such meat as they had, blessed be God'*, he told John III cheerfully.[38] It had now been decided – thanks, perhaps, to his mother's concerns about his vocation for the priesthood – that Walter should instead train as a lawyer, studies which he was due to begin that autumn. By then, however, fate had taken a decisive hand in the family's plans.

Plague was an inescapable fact of life, but a no less terrifying one for that. England had suffered recurrent epidemics ever since the Black Death had first struck more than a hundred years earlier, but the outbreak which swept the country in 1479 was particularly virulent – one of the worst, in fact, since the cataclysmic mortality of 1348–9. In November John III reported to his older brother that '*the people die sore in Norwich, and specially about my house; but my wife and my women come not out, and flee further we cannot, for at Swainsthorpe since my departing thence they have died and been sick nigh in every house in the town*'.[39] By the time John III wrote, the Pastons already knew at first hand how terrible the consequences of infection might be. In early August, only weeks after his graduation, Walter Paston had fallen ill, and was brought from Oxford to be cared for at home in Norwich. By 18 August, it was clear that he would not survive. When he dictated his will that day, his youth was heartbreakingly evident in the fact that he had so little to leave: he carefully distributed his clothes among his teachers and friends in Oxford, and bequeathed his small share of the Paston estates to his favourite brother John III. Shortly after the document was completed, Walter died.

Over the next three days, the family gathered at Margaret's side to prepare for his funeral. His siblings were joined by their uncle William – John Paston's younger brother, who had helped him in the early days of the Fastolf dispute, and was now living in London where his legal and administrative career continued to flourish. Missing, however – presumably because the journey would have been too much for her – was their grandmother Agnes, now in her late seventies, who had left Norfolk several years earlier to take up residence with her son at his London home. On 21 August, while the Pastons were in church to hear mass for Walter's soul, a messenger arrived with news that Agnes too had died. When Edmund wrote to send word of this second bereavement to John III, who was not yet in Norwich, there was yet more distressing information to add to his letter: '*my sister*' – Anne, it seems likely –'*is delivered, and the child passed to God, who send us his grace*'.[40]

As if three deaths spanning four generations of the family within a single week were not enough, Agnes's will also threatened to precipitate John II into yet another bitter dispute over property. His uncle William's insistence that he should be the one to care for Agnes in her old age had been rooted

not only in filial duty but also in his determination to pursue his own claim
to a greater share of the Paston lands – a claim which dated back to the acri-
mony over Judge William's will thirty-five years earlier. Agnes always maintained that her husband's dying wish had been to leave more of his estates
to his younger sons, but once John Paston had succeeded in overruling her,
citing the terms of his father's written will, there was little that his brother
could do to secure possession of the contested properties. However, there
was everything still to play for in terms of the lands which Agnes herself
held – the three manors of her own inheritance, as well as Paston estates
including Oxnead, with its new manor house. John II had been aware of his
uncle William's intentions for ten years: '*he and I be as good as fallen out*', he
told Margaret in the autumn of 1469, just after the siege at Caister, '*for he
has let me plainly know that he shall have all my grandam's livelihood of her
inheritance and of her jointure also*'.[41] That particular argument did not
prove to be a permanent breach, but the relationship between uncle and
nephew remained uneasy. William was still willing to lend John II money,
something which proved a lifeline during the difficult years before the
recovery of Caister. However, the debts left John II acutely uncomfortable,
since he was no longer sure how far his uncle could be trusted. They also
served to emphasise the financial and political resources on which William
would be able to draw in any future battle for Agnes's estates. In August
1479, William served notice that it was a battle he was determined to fight:
he moved to stake his claim on the very day that news of Agnes's death
reached Norwich.

William's legal challenge was a blow which John II could well have done
without. Together with his own continuing litigation against the Duke of
Suffolk over Hellesdon and Drayton, it meant that he was obliged to return
to London in mid-October. For once, he seemed deeply reluctant to be
there. He was yet again hopelessly short of money, to such an extent that he
was having to borrow cash for his living expenses; he did not even have
enough to cover the cost of his journey home, he told his mother and brother. The letter they received from him displayed none of his usual sunny confidence. For the first four days of his stay '*I was in such fear of the sickness*', he
wrote; '*and also found my chamber and stuff not so clean as I thought, which
troubled me sore*'. Confronted with the plague which was still gripping the
capital, and the interminable pressure of his own business, he sounded
frightened, exhausted and alone. His lack of money, he said, had '*troubled
me so that it has made me more than half sick, as God help me*'.[42]

He was right to be fearful. Less than a month later, John II died, at the age of just thirty-seven. His brother came immediately to bring his body back to his family in Norfolk, but John II had left instructions that he should be buried where he died, in London. John III had never sounded so lost as when he contemplated his lonely journey home: *'I have much more to write, but my empty head will not let me remember it . . .'*[43]

CHAPTER 13

– *our trusty and wellbeloved knight* –

Margaret was suddenly getting old. She had suffered bouts of ill-health a little more frequently over the past few years – at the beginning of 1475, for example, asking John III to seek permission from the Bishop of Norwich for her to hear mass in her own private chapel, '*because it is far to the church and I am sickly, and the parson is often out*'.[1] In May 1478, at the age of fifty-six, she was so ill that she drew up her will, fearing that death was imminent – even if, by the end of the month, she had recovered enough to write a typically robust letter to John II on the subject of his father's tomb. The deaths of the summer and autumn of 1479, however, were hammer-blows which hit her hard. She had already come to the painful realisation that her eldest son was unlikely to return home on any kind of permanent footing, but that did not mean that she had reconciled herself to his absence. Now, suddenly, she had lost him completely. Her younger son Walter, on whom she had pinned her hopes for the future, had also been taken from her. The death of her elderly mother-in-law Agnes was less unexpected, and in any case Margaret had seen little of her since she had left Norwich for London five years earlier, but the two women had once been close, and her death can only have compounded Margaret's distress. Meanwhile, the consolations offered by the next generation of Pastons were fragile. Not only had Anne's baby died at birth, but John III and Margery had lost their young son Christopher some time after his arrival in the summer of 1478.

However, Margaret had never flinched in the face of adversity, and she did not do so now in the midst of overwhelming loss. Her grief did not prevent her from recognising the need to pay urgent attention to the practical issues which arose as a result of her eldest son's death. Shortly after the news reached Norwich, her son Edmund rode to two of the manors now in dispute with William Paston to claim them for John III as his brother's heir – and Edmund did so, a friend reported to John III in London, by the advice of '*my mistress your careful mother*'. Margaret also had a message for John III himself: '*my mistress your mother greets you well and sends you her blessing, requiring you to come out of that air as soon as you may*'.[2] The idea that she might now lose another son in the disease-ridden capital was too much to contemplate. John III could not comply with her request for his immediate return, but he did what he could to reassure her. '... *whereas you willed me ... to haste me out of the air that I am in, it is so that I must put me in God, for here must I be for a season*', he wrote; '*and in good faith I shall never, while God sends me life, dread more death than shame. And, thanked be God, the sickness is well ceased here, and also my business puts away my fear*'.[3]

Certainly, John III had plenty to distract his attention from the risks he was running. William was pursuing his claim to Agnes's lands with all the resources he could muster, and – whatever his personal feelings about the loss of his oldest nephew – John II's death undoubtedly presented him with a further opportunity to press his case. John II had been handling the dispute in person in London while his brother remained at home in Norfolk, and it would inevitably take John III some time to familiarise himself with the progress of negotiations – a delay which left the political initiative, temporarily at least, in William's hands. It was nevertheless clear that William's case was far from watertight. To argue that Agnes had the right to dispose of her own lands as she pleased was one thing, but the Paston lands she held – including Oxnead and lands in and around the village of Paston itself – were hers only for life, and, on her death, should have reverted as of right to the senior Paston line. William's claim depended on the allegation that he had been unjustly deprived of the estates which his father had left him on his deathbed nearly forty years earlier, and that he was therefore entitled to compensation in the form of the Paston property held by his mother. As always, however, his chances of victory had as much to do with the political support on which he could call as the technical viability of his case. Unfortunately for John III, William now enjoyed substantial wealth and influence as a result of his professional success. A decade earlier, he had married Lady Anne Beaufort, daughter of the Duke of Somerset who had been killed at the first battle of St Albans in 1455. It was a glamorous match which represented something of a coup for a younger son from a *parvenu* gentry family, even if its political and financial benefits were severely circumscribed by the fact that Anne's brothers had been executed and their lands forfeited as a result of their adherence to the Lancastrian cause.[4] Over the years, William himself had served as counsellor and trustee to the rich and powerful – among their number Sir John Fastolf in the 1450s; the Duke of Clarence, Archbishop Neville and the Earl of Oxford in the 1460s; and now, in the 1470s, the Duke of Buckingham, the widowed Duchess of Norfolk, and John Morton, the newly appointed Bishop of Ely. In fact, as John III soon discovered, Bishop Morton had agreed to act as one of two arbitrators in William's dispute with John II; the other was John II's own patron Lord Hastings. John III had almost no time to absorb the profound shock of his brother's death as he launched himself into the next round of political manoeuvres, petitioning both Hastings and the Bishop, and seeking support wherever he could find it. '*And if I may . . . cause the King to take my service and my quarrel together, I will*', he told his mother.[5]

Despite his efforts, it was clear as the months went by that there was little prospect of a speedy resolution to the conflict. William's contacts and his political experience made him too formidable an opponent to be brushed aside either swiftly or easily. Meanwhile, an all-too-familiar scenario unfolded at the disputed manors, as the two sides competed to assert their authority over tenants who were trapped helplessly in the middle. By the autumn of 1481 John III's wife Margery was sufficiently concerned about the situation at Marlingford, one of the manors of Agnes's own inheritance, to write to her husband twice in four days, warning him that his uncle's men were seizing wood and grain from the estate. Despite this aggression, word reached Norwich that William was now keen to find a settlement, but Margery remained sceptical about his sincerity: '*trust him not too much*', she told her husband, '*for he is not good*'.[6] Nevertheless, she was determined to do whatever she could to help. More than one family friend had suggested that the Duchess of Norfolk might agree to act as a peacemaker. So far, the Duchess had offered William her support, but Margery had recently been informed '*that my lady is near weary of her part*', and had been advised to speak to the Duchess herself – so long as she could do so diplomatically – on the grounds that '*one word of a woman should do more than the words of twenty men, if I could rule my tongue and speak no harm of my uncle*'.[7] Margery therefore proposed to take her mother-in-law Margaret and her mother Elizabeth Brews to petition the Duchess for help when she next visited Norwich. Margery, Margaret and Elizabeth together made a formidably persuasive combination; however, if the meeting did in the end take place, it achieved little, whether because the Duchess – whose fondness for John III does not seem to have survived the final recovery of Caister – was unwilling to compromise her support for William, or because William was unwilling to compromise his own campaign at the Duchess's request.

However exhausting their troubles, Margery and John III could at least take comfort in each other. Their relationship had settled happily and easily into warm domesticity, but it had not lost its romance. If some of Margery's letters to her husband were conventionally formal in address ('*Right reverend and worshipful sir . . .*'), others were not: '*Mine own sweetheart*', she called him in November 1481.[8] Even where the address was properly decorous, the postscript might not be: '*Sir, I pray you if you tarry long at London that it will please you to send for me*', she added at the end of one letter, '*for I think long since I lay in your arms*'.[9] By now, Margery was not the only one waiting impatiently at home for John III's return. They had had to cope with the loss of their firstborn son Christopher, but since then Margery had given birth to two more children, William and Elizabeth. The babies were flourishing, she told John III that autumn, and his mother, too, was in good health, albeit that she '*thinks long she hears no word from you*', Margery reported.[10]

Perhaps inevitably, Margaret's relationship with her son and daughter-in-law was gradually becoming more demanding as the years went on. Her grip on her affairs was as competent as ever, but she was weary, and increasingly preoccupied with her coming end. Given the prominent and destructive role which contested wills had played in her life, it was hardly surprising that she was deeply concerned to ensure the fulfilment of her own wishes after her death – and, in particular, that her heir, John III, should respect her bequests to her younger children and her servants. If there was anyone in the world Margaret could trust to honour her intentions to the last detail, it was John III – and yet her need for certainty was so great that she would take nothing for granted. At the end of a visit which her son and his family paid to her household at Mautby, Margaret broached the subject with her daughter-in-law, asking Margery to speak to John III on her behalf once they returned home. He wrote immediately – half exasperated, half concerned – to try to put her mind at rest. '. . . *mother*,' he said, '*it pleased you to have certain words to my wife at her departing touching your remembrance of the shortness that you think your days of, and also of the mind that you have towards my brothers and sister . . . and also of your servants, wherein you willed her to be a means to me that I would tender and favour the same. Mother, saving your pleasure, there needs no ambassadors nor means between you and me . . .*' He would of course do whatever she wanted, he told her; he could scarcely believe that it might occur to her to doubt him, still less that she might feel unable to approach him directly, '*for I know well no one man alive has called so often upon you as I to make your will, and put each thing in certainty that you would have done for yourself and to your children and servants*'. He even suggested – whether to jolly her along or jolt her out of her insistent concern with her own mortality – that she was as likely to outlive him as the other way around.[11]

Nevertheless, it was easy to see why she might worry about her legacy. Ten years after her husband's death, his grave had been covered only with a tattered cloth; and, for all the grandeur of Sir John Fastolf's intentions, his college at Caister had in the end been swallowed up by Bishop Wainfleet's foundation at Oxford. Margaret's plans were on a much more modest scale, but to her they were no less important. The final version of her will, completed in February 1482, was characteristically purposeful. She was meticulously exact where it mattered most: she was precise to the last detail, for example, about the stone which was to be placed over the site where she wished to be buried in the south aisle of Mautby church. She was determined that she, at least, should have a fitting tomb *'within a year next after my decease'* – but, more than that, both the location and the design of her grave would proclaim her heritage as the last heir of the Mautby line.[12] The Mautby arms were to be carved in the middle of the marble tombstone, with four more shields at its corners – displaying the Mautby arms impaled with those of Paston, Berney, Loveyn and Beauchamp – to represent her own marriage and those of her father, grandfather and great-grandfather. Margaret had thrown herself without reservation into her life as a Paston, and had done everything she could to help secure the Paston name among the old-established families of Norfolk landed society. However, she had never forgotten that – unlike her husband – she herself had been born into one of those old-established families, and it was among her ancestors that she now wished to be buried.

Her gifts to her family were as practical and unsentimental as she was. She made individual bequests where goods were valuable enough to be specified, but there was a limit to the detail into which she was prepared to go. Male testators, occupied principally with the important business of apportioning estates, often paid little attention to the disposition of their personal possessions: Margaret's brother-in-law William Paston, for example, did not include a single personal gift when he drafted his will in 1496. Women, on the other hand, frequently went into painstaking detail about the household goods they wished to distribute to members of their family. The will of Margaret's sister-in-law Elizabeth Paston, now Elizabeth Browne, contained an exhaustive itemised list of the silver plate, clothes, beds, bedlinen, carpets, vestments, altar-cloths, napkins and tablecloths, tables, stools, coffers, candlesticks, tableware and kitchenware which she intended her daughter Mary to have when she married *'except'*, Elizabeth added as an afterthought, '*such stuff as cannot be kept from moths*', of which Mary was to take possession straight away.[13]

By comparison, Margaret's will seemed almost austere. As her oldest surviving son, John III would of course inherit her estates, but she also gave him a silver-gilt standing cup with '*a knob like a garlic head*' on its lid, and six silver goblets; and to his wife Margery she left her mass-book, her altar-cloths, and silver vessels to hold the consecrated bread and wine at the Eucharist. To their children, William and Elizabeth, Margaret left the sum of 100 marks. Her son Edmund had at last found himself a wife, a young widow named Catherine Clippesby, and the couple now had a baby son. All three were remembered in the will: for Edmund, there was silver plate and a featherbed; for Catherine, a fine purple girdle and some kitchenware; and to her grandson, Robert, Margaret left her swans – birds so highly valued as a delicacy that a licence from the King was needed to keep them. Edmund's family were also to receive a small income of five marks a year from Margaret's lands. Her daughter Anne Yelverton was to have a share of her silver plate, a girdle, her primer, her enamelled silver beads, a bed, and some pots and pans, as well as £10 '*to her proper use*'. To her youngest son William, Margaret left yet more silver, a featherbed, and 100 marks with which to buy '*as much land to him and to his heirs as may be had with the same money*'. Margaret was tough-minded, but she had never been unemotional: she put aside ten marks for her illegitimate granddaughter Constance, John II's only child, and £20 for John Calle, eldest son of her estranged daughter Margery. To Margery herself, Margaret left nothing. It is possible that she had already died – or perhaps Margaret could still not bring herself to forgive her daughter's defiance. Beyond these bequests, and a handful of others – her quartz beads '*gaudied with silver and gilt*' to her goddaughter, and gifts for her servants – Margaret was prepared to allow John III discretion to exercise his judgement as her chief executor: '*I will that the residue of the stuff of my household unbequeathed be divided equally between Edmund and William, my sons, and Anne my daughter*', she wrote. John III himself, as the head of the family, had much less need of such practical assistance, but Margaret instructed that he should nevertheless be given £10 '*for his labour*' in the execution of the will.[14]

That left only the question of religious and charitable donations to ease her soul through the pains of purgatory. Those too were careful, measured and precise. There were bequests to the churches at her own manors – principally, of course, Mautby, where she directed that '*the said aisle in which my body shall be buried be new roofed, leaded and glassed, and the walls thereof heightened conveniently and workmanly'.* She left money to be shared among her tenants, a few pence per household; to the churches of the two parishes in which she had lived at Norwich; and to the four orders of friars at Norwich and Yarmouth. Her executors were to pay for the provision of masses for her soul for seven years after her death, and she specified that twelve of her poorest tenants, *'apparelled in white gowns with hoods according',* should hold torches around her coffin during her funeral. Her poor tenants were not only the most in need of her help, but the closest to God on account of their poverty, and their prayers were therefore particularly efficacious; the same (on account of their sickness) was true of the inmates of the leper houses at the city gates of Norwich and Yarmouth, each of whom was to receive 3d. All that remained was to commit her soul *'to God Almighty, and to Our Lady his blessed mother, St Michael, St John Baptist, and to all saints',* and to confirm that her will was composed *'with perfect advisement and good deliberation'.*[15] It is the last surviving document to which she put her seal. On 4 November 1484, at the age of sixty-two, Margaret died.

For John III, his mother's death marked the passing of an era. He was not left alone: he had a new and happy family of his own to console him. But he had been devoted to his mother and brother, with whom he had spent most of his life working shoulder-to-shoulder in defence of the family's interests – and now they were both gone. Margaret's death also, of course, left John III much wealthier. In theory, he enjoyed what neither his father nor his brother ever had – control of all the family's estates – since he now inherited Margaret's Mautby lands and the Paston manors which she had held during her eighteen years of widowhood, on top of the properties formerly held by his grandmother. In practice, of course, given the determined challenge of his uncle William, Agnes's estates were not simply John III's to command, but he was at least spared his elder brother's peculiarly stressful existence as an heir whose inheritance was for the most part tantalisingly out of reach. Despite their father's fears, John II's stewardship of the family's affairs had been far from disastrous, particularly in terms of his unsparing efforts to retrieve Caister from the political wreckage of the dispute over Fastolf's will. Nevertheless, it was clear that Paston interests were finally in the hands of the person best equipped to look after them. Over the years since their father's death, John III's abilities, his judgement and his generosity of spirit had quietly made him the backbone of the family. His talents now also attracted the attention and the friendship of one of the most powerful men in the country. By 1483 Lord Hastings valued John III's service so highly that he sent him to assist his ailing brother, Sir Ralph Hastings, in command of the fortress of Guines just outside Calais. Towards the end of April Sir Ralph recovered his health, and Hastings was keen to have John III back: '*I trust he may now spare you*', he wrote warmly, signing the letter '*your true friend Hastings*'.[16] For his own part, Ralph Hastings was more than sorry to see John III go, particularly since he fell ill again almost immediately, but by the time he wrote on 9 May – to '*my faithful loving good cousin John Paston*' – it had become frighteningly apparent why his brother wished to have men he could trust around him in England.[17]

King Edward had turned forty in the spring of the previous year. One of the mottoes which he had chosen for himself was '*confort et liesse*' – 'comfort and delight' – and in the spring of 1483 it emerged that the King had taken his maxim too far for his own or his country's good. Years of over-indulging his physical appetites had transformed Edward from a golden boy into a bloated man whose remarkable good looks and athletic build were blurring into dissolution. Excess, it turned out, had taken its toll on his health as well as his appearance. The King was suddenly taken ill at the end of March. He rallied enough after the first seizure – perhaps a stroke – to revise his will, but on 9 April, three weeks before his forty-first birthday, he died, leaving his twelve-year-old son to inherit his throne. It was an appalling shock for a country which had had little more than ten years to settle back into stability since the upheavals of 1470–1, and the powerful regime which King Edward had built during that time abruptly fractured.

The difficulty was that the new boy-King, Edward V, was – from a political point of view – at the worst possible age. It would be only two or three years before a plausible claim could be made that he was old enough to rule for himself; but, on the other hand, he was plenty young enough for those around him to exert a controlling influence over the exercise of his authority for some time to come. Any manoeuvring for position among the nobility would have to be done quickly before the new government took irreversible shape. The fact that the reign of the last monarch to have inherited the throne in childhood – Henry VI – had ended in disaster did not help to calm the atmosphere of rising panic. Nor did it help that the young King, who was at Ludlow when his father died, was currently in the care of his mother's large and assertive family, the Woodvilles. They were therefore better placed than anyone else to secure their position at the King's side; that fact, however, ensured that they were also regarded with suspicion and hostility by other leading members of the nobility, including the dead King's two most trusted lieutenants, his friend Lord Hastings and his younger brother the Duke of Gloucester. Both Gloucester and Hastings feared for their future under a Woodville-dominated regime, and only days after Edward's death they resolved on a pre-emptive coup. The new King was riding to London with his Woodville uncle, Earl Rivers, when on 30 April the royal party was met at Stony Stratford in Buckinghamshire by the Duke of Gloucester, accompanied by the Duke of Buckingham and at the head of a substantial retinue. Rivers was expecting to accompany his nephew to London to prepare for the coronation; instead, he was arrested. The King arrived in the capital on 4 May with Gloucester at his side, to be welcomed into the City by Lord Hastings. Less than a week later, Gloucester was named Protector, while Rivers and other members of the Woodville family were imprisoned, and their lands and offices confiscated.

The fall of the Woodvilles was an indication of the profound trauma which Edward IV's sudden death had precipitated within the political establishment, but they had been able to rally little support in their own defence, and the coup had been executed rapidly and ruthlessly. The stage now seemed set for the continuation of Yorkist rule in the name of Edward V under the leadership of his father's two most loyal servants. Together, Gloucester and Hastings already dominated large areas of the country, Gloucester as the greatest magnate in the north, and Hastings as the pre-eminent force in the midlands. They also had the active support of the Duke of Buckingham, who could trace his descent back to the royal line of Edward III, but had so far found little favour under the Yorkist regime, whether because his father and grandfather had been killed fighting for the Lancastrian cause, or because Edward IV had not been convinced of his political judgement. Buckingham was married to Rivers's sister Catherine Woodville, but he showed no inclination to throw in his lot with his wife's family. Instead, by positioning himself at the heart of the new government, Buckingham stood to reap major political rewards for the first time in his career – something which became apparent immediately when he took over from his brother-in-law Rivers as the leading power in Wales and the Welsh borders.

For John Paston III, as for other loyal subjects of the Yorkist crown, there was no reason to question his own allegiance to the newly established Protectorate. It was a long time since he had had any significant contact with Earl Rivers, and it seemed that the dramatic events of the past two months had served to secure the influence in government of his current patron Lord Hastings. However, it would be some time before calm was fully restored, and meanwhile the political atmosphere remained tense. Sir Ralph Hastings had recognised as much when he wrote to John III, in suitably circumspect terms, from Guines on 9 May: '*praying you to advertise my lord*' – his brother Hastings – '*to see well to himself, etc*'.[18] A month later, Sir Ralph's anxiety was vindicated in horrifying fashion. On Friday 13 June, during a council meeting at the Tower of London, the Duke of Gloucester suddenly accused Lord Hastings of treason. Hastings was given no chance to respond to the allegations, still less any kind of formal hearing: on Gloucester's orders he was immediately bundled outside onto Tower Hill and beheaded. The execution proved to be the first move in a second coup – this time a *coup d'état*, designed to place Gloucester on the throne in his nephew's place. The Duke summoned an army from his northern estates, and, while his troops were mustering, proclaimed that Edward V and his siblings were illegitimate, on the grounds that their father was already promised elsewhere in marriage at the time of his secret wedding to Elizabeth Woodville. On 26 June, Gloucester took his seat on the marble throne in the Great Hall of the Palace of Westminster. Ten days later, with his own men now in control of the capital, he was crowned as King Richard III.

It was an utterly shocking turn of events, of which it is no easier to make sense with the benefit of hindsight than it was for the new King's terrified subjects. Gloucester's entire political career had been shaped and defined by his uncompromising loyalty to his brother, but he had responded to the crisis of the King's unexpected death by murdering Edward's best friend and deposing his son in order to take the crown for himself. The public justification for his actions was patently bogus. Probably the most plausible explanation is that Gloucester – under extreme pressure of time and circumstance – felt himself forced into radical action by the realisation that the destruction of the Woodvilles could secure his position only in the short term, since it was more than likely that the young King would one day seek retribution against those he perceived to be responsible for the political destruction of his mother's family. Gloucester seems to have been driven by a combination of fear, panic and an emerging conviction that his own rule was the only means of safeguarding the stability of a realm so recently recovered from the devastation of civil war. If he needed to remove Lord Hastings – who would never accept the deposition of Edward IV's son – in order to clear his own path to the throne, that was a price the Duke was prepared to pay. He was undoubtedly encouraged to reach that conclusion by the Duke of Buckingham, who had gained a great deal from the fall of the Woodvilles, and stood to gain a great deal more from Hastings's death.

If Gloucester did believe that his usurpation was the route to political security for himself and for the country, his mistake quickly became apparent. The newly crowned Richard III was an able man who did his utmost to govern as effectively as his dead brother had done. However, this Yorkist King had achieved the throne by dividing the Yorkist regime against itself, and, without legitimacy, he could not hope to rebuild political unity. Less than a month into his reign, evidence was discovered of a plot to rescue Edward V and his brother, the ten-year-old Duke of York, from the Tower, where they had been housed in preparation for Edward's now-abandoned coronation. The conspiracy served to emphasise the fact that, for as long as they were alive, Richard's nephews would be a powerful focus for resistance to his rule. On the other hand, it was not an easy matter to dispose of the threat which they embodied. In the past, the killing of deposed kings – as in the case of Henry VI in 1471 – had been tacitly accepted as a fact of life, a necessary evil on the road to political recovery. However, the murder of two children who bore no responsibility for the conflict in which they had been caught up was unlikely to be accepted with any kind of equanimity – and the simultaneous deaths of two healthy boys could not easily be represented as the result of accident or coincidence. Instead, they disappeared. It is impossible to know exactly what happened, beyond the fact that sightings of them in the Tower became less and less frequent, until they were no longer seen at all. Certainly, by the end of September 1483 it was widely believed that they were dead. It quickly became apparent, however, that their removal from the political stage had not eliminated their capacity to undermine Richard's authority. Even in the absence of conclusive proof that the Princes had been murdered, rumours alone were enough to alienate support further from a King who now seemed to have the innocent blood of his own nephews on his hands.

That autumn, the instability of Richard's regime was publicly exposed by a full-scale rebellion against his government. The most frightening aspect of the revolt from the King's point of view was that it came from within, not outside, the Yorkist establishment. The rebels included prominent members of Edward IV's household in the south of England, and at their head – in what was for Richard a devastating personal betrayal – was the Duke of Buckingham, whose vaulting personal ambition had made him a destabilising force throughout the entire crisis. The disappearance of Edward V and his brother proved to be no defence against this rising. Instead, Richard had achieved the unlikely feat of making a credible contender for the throne out of Henry Tudor, the last scraping of the

Lancastrian barrel. Tudor, who was in exile in Brittany, was the only surviving male heir of the Lancastrian dynasty: his mother, Margaret
Beaufort, was the great-granddaughter of John of Gaunt, Duke of
Lancaster and father of King Henry IV. However, the Beaufort line was
descended from Gaunt's third marriage to his long-standing mistress
Catherine Swynford, and the couple's children had been legitimised after
their parents' wedding with the explicit proviso that they should have no
right to inherit the crown. Even if this technical disqualification could be
set aside, arguments for the superiority of the Lancastrian claim to the
throne over that of the house of York had depended on the fact that Henry
VI was descended from the third son of King Edward III in the male line,
whereas the Yorkist descent from the second son of Edward III came
through a woman. Given that Henry Tudor's descent from the third son of
Edward III also came through a woman, it was indisputable that the Yorkist
claim should take precedence.[19] In the autumn of 1483, none of that mattered. What mattered was that all those who could not accept the disappearance of Edward IV's sons and the destruction of half of his regime
were now looking to Henry Tudor as the only viable claimant around
whom to rally opposition to Richard. Extraordinarily, the Lancastrian heir
had now become a Yorkist candidate for the throne – a new political per-
sona which Tudor immediately sought to bolster by promising to marry
Edward IV's oldest daughter Elizabeth.

In the face of this challenge, Richard could call on the support of his
powerful northern retinue, and a few magnates whose personal interests
were closely linked to the fortunes of his regime. In East Anglia, his principal representative was John Howard, whom he had created Duke of
Norfolk in June 1483. Anne Mowbray, the daughter and heiress of the last
Duke, had died two years earlier at the age of only eight, and Howard,
whose mother was the dead Duke's great-aunt, was the next heir. However,
the terms of the little Duchess's marriage to Edward IV's second son –
which had taken place in 1478, when the bride was five and the groom four
– had been so generous to her young husband that he kept his wife's title
and estates after her death. Despite Howard's twenty years of loyal service
to the Yorkist regime, Edward IV had preferred to appropriate the dukedom for his own family rather than allow Howard to succeed his Mowbray
cousin. The deposition of Edward V therefore opened the way for Howard
to claim his inheritance, and he supported the usurpation from the first:
his son Thomas was among those who carried out the arrest and execution
of Lord Hastings, and he himself served as High Steward at King Richard's

coronation. He was rewarded with not only the dukedom of Norfolk, but also the estates of Earl Rivers, who had been executed a few days after Hastings's death, and the East Anglian lands of the Earl of Oxford, who was still in captivity at Hammes Castle. By 10 October 1483, with the rebels gathering their forces in Kent, Howard was raising as many men as he could in defence of the King to whom he owed his sudden promotion. One of those who received a letter was John Paston III: '*I pray you*', Howard wrote, '*that with all diligence you make you ready and come hither, and bring with you six tall fellows in harness; and you shall not lose your labour, that knows God, who have you in his keeping*'. The letter was signed '*Your friend, J. Norfolk*'.[20]

Howard's relationship with the Paston family went back decades, but it was not unequivocally positive: it was one of Howard's servants, after all, who had attacked John Paston with a dagger over the disputed parliamentary election of 1461. Nevertheless, the new Duke's personal dealings with John III had begun in more propitious circumstances when they were both in the old Duke's service in the early 1460s; Howard had even lent '*young Paston*' three shillings when they were travelling together in Norfolk's household in the winter of 1463.[21] However, if Howard hoped that shared memories – or his new eminence – would persuade John III to arm himself in support of King Richard, he was to be disappointed. For John III, there was too much to lose, and nothing to be gained, by risking his life on the battlefield. Twelve years earlier, he had fought at Barnet in the service of the Earl of Oxford, to whom the Pastons owed a great deal and from whom they hoped for much more under a future Lancastrian government. It was a gamble that had failed, and spectacularly so. Now, John III had little incentive to repeat the experience, since he owed nothing to John Howard – quite the reverse, in fact, given the role which Howard had played in Lord Hastings's fall. Howard's efforts at recruitment were successful enough that the rebels were defeated by early November, but it was a victory achieved without Paston help. If John III needed any reminder of the dangers of political involvement in such unstable times, it was provided by his aunt Elizabeth's husband, Sir George Browne, who had been a knight of the body to Edward IV, and was so close to his royal master that he carried the banner of St George at the King's funeral in April 1483. Six months later, he and his stepson Edward Poynings, Elizabeth's son by her first marriage, joined the rebellion against King Edward's usurping brother. Elizabeth Paston had lost her first husband on the field at St Albans in 1461; now, she lost her second to the executioner's axe, and her son into exile.

It was hardly surprising, therefore, that John III maintained a low political profile during the months that followed. He concentrated on pursuing his case against his uncle William over his grandmother's lands, drawing up a petition which declared that '*the said William has, contrary to truth and conscience, vexed and troubled and put to cost and charge the said John now by the space of five years save a quarter*', and detailing losses arising from the dispute which, he alleged, came to a total of more than £7,000, '*beside grief, great labour and dis-ease that the said John has daily been put unto*'.[22] However, neither John III himself nor his uncle – whose Beaufort marriage brought him uncomfortably close connections to the camp of the King's rival-in-exile, Henry Tudor – was in a position to press his claim to a successful conclusion. In November 1484 John III was also confronted with the loss of his mother. It is impossible to recapture in any detail the emotional impact of Margaret's death on the family as a whole, since in the letters – or rather the absence of them – there is silence. Apart from anything else, John III now spent most of his time at home with his wife and children, and, once Margaret herself was gone, there was neither the opportunity nor the need for the kind of sustained correspondence which had become second nature during the long years of the Fastolf dispute.

Even had his mother and brother still been alive, the continuing volatility of the political world meant that John III might well have hesitated before committing too many of his thoughts to paper. The suppression of the revolt of 1483 had brought no lasting security to King Richard's beleaguered regime. The King was attempting to use his northern supporters to reimpose his authority across the south of England – a short-term fix which was already stirring up widespread resentment at the appointment of outsiders to positions of local influence, and thereby emphasising the limitations of his own power base. Meanwhile, the threat of further insurrection in support of Henry Tudor was becoming more menacing. In the summer of 1484 Richard exerted all the diplomatic pressure he could bring to bear on the Duke of Brittany in the attempt to secure Tudor's arrest, but Henry instead escaped to France, where it became alarmingly clear that the new King, Louis XI's son Charles VIII, was prepared to provide him with both money and troops. Tudor was joined at the French court not only by the Yorkist loyalists who had fled after the failed rebellion of 1483, but by the Pastons' former lord, the Earl of Oxford. In November 1484, after ten years of imprisonment at Hammes, Oxford finally made his escape by the brilliantly simple manoeuvre of persuading the captain of the castle to abandon his post and defect to Tudor's cause. The Earl had last tried to leave the castle six years earlier by jumping from the battlements. Now he was a free man, riding out of Hammes with his jailer at his side, to be followed a couple of months later by most of the soldiers of the garrison. By the summer of 1485, King Richard's regime was, if not haemorrhaging support, then at least badly incapacitated, and Henry Tudor was gathering an invasion force in Normandy. His fleet landed in south Wales on 7 August.

For the second time, John Howard set about raising troops to defend his King. Once again he wrote to his '*wellbeloved friend*' John Paston III, summoning him to join his muster and requiring him to '*bring with you such company of tall men as you may goodly make at my cost and charge*'. This time, in haste and with a hint of desperation, he signed himself '*Your lover, J. Norfolk*'.[23] For the second time, John III did not respond. Nor did he join his old lord the Earl of Oxford in opposition to the King. When the two armies met near Market Bosworth in Leicestershire on 22 August, the only Paston on the field was Elizabeth Paston's son Edward Poynings, who had accompanied Henry Tudor on his return from France. The fundamental weakness in King Richard's position was that his authority was too flawed and fragile to command the unquestioning support of his subjects, many of whom, like John III, were waiting to see what would happen before committing themselves irrevocably to his cause. The vanguard of Richard's army was led by John Howard, the new Duke of Norfolk, but many other nobles had not rallied to his side, and, disastrously, not all of those who did so proved to be reliable allies. When the battle began, neither the men under the command of the Earl of Northumberland nor the forces of Lord Stanley – who had ostensibly remained loyal to Richard despite being married to Henry Tudor's mother Margaret Beaufort – joined the fighting. Stanley's men did not intervene until the King himself charged at the heart of his enemy's army, planning to kill Tudor and thereby end the conflict with a single decisive blow. Richard fought so hard, pressing forward on foot even after his horse was killed under him, that he came within feet of his rival. As he did so, he discovered that he had been betrayed: Stanley intended not to destroy Henry Tudor, but to save him. Richard's men were overwhelmed by the superior numbers of Stanley's troops, and the King himself was cut down in the mêlée. Among the heavy casualties sustained by Richard's defeated army was his loyal servant John Howard.

Yet again, England had a new King. Richard's naked body was exposed in public for two days before being unceremoniously buried in an unmarked grave at the Grey Friars' church in Leicester, while Henry Tudor rode south to take possession of the capital. There, on 30 October, he was crowned as

King Henry VII. By then, with the new regime beginning to take shape around him, John Paston III had already been forced to show his hand. Henry himself – who had spent the last fourteen of his twenty-eight years in exile as an impoverished refugee – had little experience even of the country of which he was now King, let alone of the demands of government, but he set about establishing his authority through the resources most immediately at his disposal. In East Anglia, that meant the regional influence of the Earl of Oxford, who was restored to his estates and appointed Lord Admiral of England. Oxford, at forty-three, had also spent the last fourteen years on the continent, at first in exile and then as a prisoner at Hammes. However, he at least had political associations from the years before 1471 – associations such as his relationship with John III – on which he could now draw in the service of the new King. His task, and that of his royal master, was also made easier by the fact that Henry's accession in many ways represented a restoration of the Yorkist regime which had been shattered by Richard III's usurpation – albeit that Richard's actions had turned the natural political order on its head to such an extent that it was now a Yorkist regime with Lancastrian leadership. John Paston III was ideally placed to benefit from this hybrid political heritage: he had fought for the Lancastrian cause at Barnet under the Earl of Oxford's command, before refashioning himself as a loyal subject of King Edward in the service of Lord Hastings. He therefore represented the Yorkist establishment through which the country had been governed until 1483, while at the same time his Lancastrian past recommended him to Oxford, who knew his abilities of old. The combination of Henry's decisive victory and the return of his own former lord seems to have persuaded John III finally to commit himself unequivocally to the new regime. On 12 September 1485, less than a month after the fighting at Bosworth, he was appointed sheriff of Norfolk and Suffolk by King Henry, almost certainly at Oxford's suggestion. By the following summer John III was an esquire of the body in the new royal household; five months after that, the Earl of Oxford was addressing him as 'my right trusty and wellbeloved counsellor'.[24] It was not long before John III's brothers Edmund and William followed him into the Earl's service.

However, political commitment brought risks as well as rewards, especially once the aftershocks of the conflict of 1485 began to make themselves felt. In the spring of 1486, Francis, Viscount Lovell – one of King Richard's closest friends and the former chamberlain of his household – raised a rebellion in Yorkshire. The rising was quickly suppressed, but Lovell himself escaped, and John III was charged with keeping watch on the East Anglian coasts in case the fugitive tried to reach the continent. By the beginning of 1487, it emerged that the information which John III had gathered about Lovell's movements and adherents was both out-of-date and inaccurate – circumstances which prompted an icy letter of reproof from the Earl of Oxford. Lovell, it transpired, was already in Flanders, where he took refuge with the dowager Duchess Margaret of Burgundy, sister of Edward IV and Richard III. Despite Henry Tudor's claims to be the heir of Edward IV's political legacy, which were underpinned in January 1486 by his marriage to Edward's daughter Elizabeth, Margaret refused to accept that his dubious title to the throne should prevail at the expense of her own family. The fact that Henry had deposed her brother with French support also meant that it served Burgundian interests to destabilise his government. Margaret therefore gave her assistance to a planned invasion of England under Lovell's leadership. As their figurehead, the rebels adopted a young man who claimed to be Edward, Earl of Warwick, son of the dead Duke of Clarence and the next Yorkist heir in the male line after the Princes who had disappeared in the Tower. It was a simple matter for King Henry to demonstrate that this pretender – whose real name was Lambert Simnel – was an impostor, and he did so in February 1487 by producing the real Earl of Warwick from his apartments at the Tower and parading him through the streets of the capital. The truth of Simnel's identity, however, was not enough to defuse the threat which Lovell and his allies posed to Henry's regime – a threat which was reinforced two months later by the defection of John, Earl of Lincoln, the eldest son of the Duke of Suffolk. Lincoln, too, had Yorkist blood in his veins through his mother Elizabeth, another sister of Edward IV and Richard III, and in April 1487 he fled to join Lord Lovell in Flanders at the court of his aunt, Duchess Margaret.

As Lovell and Lincoln prepared their assault on England, John Paston III was appointed to a commission charged with the task of raising men in Norfolk to resist the invasion. At the end of April, however, he found himself in danger of being swept away by increasingly treacherous currents of speculation and suspicion. Towards the end of the month he was observed leaving Yarmouth by boat – an event of no moment whatsoever under normal circumstances. With the King's enemies massing their forces in Flanders, however, John III's decision to travel by sea was enough to call his intentions into question. '*Sir, it is so that there has been a great rumour and marvellous noise of your departing from Yarmouth*', he was warned by a servant on 29 April; '*for some said that you were departed in a Dutch ship and some said in a Spanish ship and some said in your ship, and some said against your will you were departed'*. The atmosphere was so feverish that even those with most reason to trust him were ready to jump to threatening conclusions. The steward of King Henry's household, Lord Fitzwalter, was a Norfolk man – promoted to a new eminence by the change of regime – who had extended his friendship to John III ever since they had met more than a decade earlier, to such an extent that it had even seemed possible at one stage that John III might marry his sister-in-law. However, when Fitzwalter heard of John III's embarkation at Yarmouth in the spring of 1487, he *'imagined and purposed many grievous things against your mastership'*, John III was told.[25] It became clear soon enough that he had not absconded to the continent, and by the middle of May the muster of troops in King Henry's name was well under way. Nevertheless, there was widespread uncertainty about how many local gentlemen would prove willing to take up arms against the rebels, and it was apparent that John III remained under suspicion. *'. . . you be sore taken in some place, saying that you intend such things as is like to follow great mischief'*, his friend Edmund Bedingfield reported.[26] It may have been John III's personal generosity which raised doubts about his political reliability. Lord Lovell's mother-in-law, Lady Fitzhugh, was the sister of both Lady Hastings and the Countess of Oxford, the wives of John III's two most recent patrons, and it was perhaps through this connection that John III came to offer her his service – a relationship which Lady Fitzhugh valued so highly that she addressed him as *'son Paston'*, and signed herself *'your loving mother'*.[27] His unstinting friendship, both to Lady Fitzhugh and to her daughter, gave rise to politically damaging innuendo: Bedingfield's letter, for example, written on 16 May, reported the spread of rumours that John III had recently been seen returning from a visit to Lady Lovell. Whether or not it was true, the allegation could scarcely have been more dangerous. Ten days earlier, her husband had landed in Ireland with two thousand German mercenaries provided by Duchess Margaret of Burgundy. In Dublin, on 24 May, Lambert Simnel was crowned King Edward VI of England, and less than a fortnight later the rebels set sail for the Lancashire coast.

Perhaps John III had always intended to serve in King Henry's army under the Earl of Oxford's command, or perhaps he was prompted to do so by the need to silence the whispers about his suspected disloyalty. Either way, he demonstrated both his allegiance and his courage in unequivocal terms on 16 June when the King's troops met the rebel contingent at the village of Stoke, near Newark in Nottinghamshire. Oxford's men, John III among them, formed the vanguard of the King's forces and bore the brunt of a brutal engagement. Thousands were killed before the greater numbers and superior equipment of the royal army finally began to tell. After almost three hours of heavy fighting, the rebels were routed. The Earl of Lincoln was killed; Lord Lovell disappeared without trace; and the sorry figure of Lambert Simnel was captured, and put to work in the King's kitchens. Once the battle was over, fifty-two gentlemen were knighted in the field by King Henry in recognition of their service. John Paston III was one of their number.

The King's victory at Stoke was a turning-point, which at last established his rule on secure foundations. It did the same for John III's political career. He did not abandon his association with Lady Fitzhugh or her daughter Lady Lovell – now searching in vain for her missing husband – but no one now questioned his loyalty. He resumed his friendship with Lord Fitzwalter, its warmth unimpaired by the tensions of 1487, and rose high in the service of the Earl of Oxford, becoming steward of the Earl's Norfolk estates and his deputy as Lord Admiral – an office in which John III's responsibilities ranged from the rescue of shipwrecks and the arrest of '*men of war roving upon the coast*' to the disposal of the valuable carcass of a whale found in shallow water off a north Norfolk beach ('*a great fish and a royal . . . eleven fathoms and more of length and two fathoms of bigness and deepness in the middle fish*').[28] The new distinctions of John III's public career also seemed to bode well for his private quarrel with his uncle, although William Paston too had benefited greatly from the change of regime. His wife's formidable cousin Margaret Beaufort was now, as the King's mother, an extremely powerful figure who took an active interest in the affairs of her extended family. It was thanks to Margaret, for example, that William's eldest daughter Mary married the heir of the Earl of Westmorland – a wedding which took place in the presence of the King himself – although the lasting significance of the match was limited by the fact that Mary died before her twentieth birthday, succumbing to measles in the winter of 1489.

Perhaps, in the end, his grandmother's manors were saved for John III by an accident of fate. William had no sons – his heirs were his two surviving daughters, Agnes and Elizabeth – and the knowledge that his estates would be divided between two families, neither of which would bear the Paston name, almost certainly encouraged him to accept a settlement in money rather than land. An arbitration was under way by 1489, in which John III's hand was strengthened by the support of an unlikely ally. His father's old enemy John Heydon had died in September 1479 – perhaps, like John II and Walter Paston, a victim of the devastating plague which swept the country that year. A decade after the old man's death, the Paston–Heydon feud was decisively consigned to history when Heydon's son and heir Henry agreed a marriage between his own daughter Bridget and John III's young son William – an alliance which also secured Heydon's help in the conflict over Agnes's lands. The negotiations over the disputed manors and the arrangements for the wedding were pursued in parallel, Heydon writing warmly to John III not only about the progress of *'your matter between you and your uncle'*, but to ask *'in what silk or cloth you will have these two innocents married in . . .'*.[29] The match was an excellent one, not least because Bridget's large dowry helped to ease the financial burden of John III's eventual agreement with his uncle. John III's pleasure at seeing his son so advantageously married was tempered shortly afterwards by harrowing loss, when his beloved wife Margery died in 1495. She was not yet forty. John III eventually married again, but it seems possible that this second match – to a wealthy widow named Agnes Morley – had more to do with his temporarily straitened financial circumstances than any kind of personal inclination.[30]

By 1500 John III was in his mid-fifties. The Paston name was respected and honoured, and its influence felt within the highest political circles. No one would ever again speak of the family as *'churls of Gimingham'*; their place among the *'right noble and worshipful blood'* of the realm was assured. That spring, one more mark of distinction was accorded to a trusted servant of the crown. A marriage had been contracted between the heir to the throne, King Henry's oldest son Prince Arthur, and Catherine of Aragon, the fifteen-year-old daughter of the Spanish monarchs Ferdinand of Aragon and Isabella of Castile. In March a royal letter arrived in Norfolk, summoning John III to attend the Princess's arrival:

> *Trusty and wellbeloved, we greet you well, letting you know that our dearest cousins the King and Queen of Spain have signified unto us by their sundry letters that the right excellent Princess, the Lady Catherine their daughter, shall be transported from the parts of Spain aforesaid to this our Realm about the month of May next coming for the solemnisation of matrimony between our dearest son the Prince and the said Princess. Wherefore we, considering that it is right fitting and necessary, as well for the honour of us as for the laud and praise of our said Realm, to have the said Princess honourably received at her arrival, have appointed you to be one among others to give attendance for the receiving of the said Princess; willing and desiring you to prepare yourself for that intent, and so to continue in a readiness*

*upon an hour's warning, till that by our letters we shall advertise you of the
day and time of her arrival and where you shall give your said attendance;
and not to fail therein as you tender our pleasure, the honour of yourself,
and of this our foresaid Realm.*[31]

John Paston III was now the King's '*trusty and wellbeloved knight*', called to
give personal service at a royal wedding. His grandfather – growing up as the
son of a '*good plain husbandman*' – could have hoped for nothing more.

– *letters of good consequence in history* –

John Paston III died, at the age of sixty, on 28 August 1504. He was survived by his second wife Agnes, and probably by his youngest brother William, who had served the Earl of Oxford for almost twenty years until he was sent home to his family in 1503 when he became '*crazed in his mind*'.[1] John III's other siblings, Edmund, Margery and Anne, had predeceased him: Anne had died ten years earlier and Edmund only six months before John III himself. The date of Margery's death is unknown, but her husband Richard Calle was still living in 1503. John III was also survived by his two children, his daughter Elizabeth – who married William Clere, grandson of Margaret Paston's friend Elizabeth Clere – and his son and heir William, who followed his father into royal service. William was knighted before 1520, when he was among those who attended King Henry VIII at the Field of the Cloth of Gold. He and his wife Bridget Heydon had a large family of five sons – Erasmus, Henry, John, Clement and Thomas – and seven daughters.[2] Erasmus Paston died before his father, but his younger brother Clement gave distinguished military and naval service to the crown, and built a new house at Oxnead which became the family's main seat when it was inherited after Clement's death by his nephew, Erasmus's son William.[3] The family continued to prosper until the mid-seventeenth century when Erasmus's great-great-grandson, another Sir William Paston, committed himself to the royalist cause in the Civil War and, as a result, forfeited a great deal of the family's property under the parliamentary regime. William himself survived, but he was forced to sell Caister Castle in 1659 in the attempt to pay off his debts. However, the family's loyalty to the Stuart monarchy meant that they benefited spectacularly from the restoration of King Charles II. William's son, Sir Robert, became a Gentleman of the Privy Chamber at King Charles's court, and was created Lord Paston and Viscount Yarmouth in 1673. Six years later he was further rewarded, becoming the first Earl of Yarmouth.

Robert's son William, the second Earl of Yarmouth, at first emulated his father's success. He married Charlotte Jemima Henrietta Maria Fitzroy –

one of Charles II's illegitimate daughters – and in 1687, at the age of thirty-three, became Treasurer of the royal household of James II, King Charles's brother and heir. However, King James's attempts to promote a restoration of Catholicism precipitated an overwhelming political crisis, and in 1688 the King was driven into exile, leaving the throne to be taken by his Protestant daughter Mary and her Dutch husband William of Orange. William Paston's career fell with his King: he was imprisoned in the Tower of London on charges of treason in 1690 and again in 1692. He escaped execution, and even achieved some measure of political rehabilitation, but he lost both his fortune and his family. He was estranged from his mother – 'her son gives her no respects or holds any correspondence with her, though she lives not above two miles from him', it was reported in 1693[4] – and his son Charles died before him, leaving no male heirs of his own to inherit the family name or his father's title. Isolated and impoverished, William died on Christmas Day in 1732.

John Paston III had once, in dangerous times, reminded his brother of the uncertainty of the world with a cheerful jingle:

> But Fortune with her smiling countenance strange
> Of all our purpose may make a sudden change.[5]

Fortune's wheel was a ubiquitous motif in medieval culture, and for the Paston brothers in 1471 it had seemed to offer the consoling prospect that triumph must one day follow the disasters against which they were struggling. Almost three centuries later, however, the wheel came full circle for the Paston family itself. From the moment when William Paston first left Paston village to embark on his legal career, it took nearly a hundred years to establish beyond question the family's position as gentlemen, landowners, and valued servants of kings and nobles. It took seven generations more for the Pastons to reach the apotheosis of a peerage in their own right. Just one generation after that – with the lonely death of another William Paston – title, wealth and family were gone.

To the fifteenth-century Pastons, it seemed that lasting remembrance would depend on the physical embodiment of their achievements: on the houses in which they lived and the memorials which marked their graves. Little now remains of the buildings and monuments on which they lavished such care. Judge William's house at Oxnead is long gone; the manor house at Gresham is nothing but overgrown foundations; and Caister Castle is a ruin, its elegant tower overlooking no more than an outline of the great house traced in brick on the grass below. Not a single fifteenth-century Paston tomb survives. The chantry chapels and monastic institutions to which so many of the family entrusted their graves were swept away by the Reformation; and, although Mautby church still stands, its south aisle – where Margaret Paston was buried under a tombstone made to her own precise specification – no longer exists. What did survive, against all the odds, was not brick or marble but paper. As a result, the Pastons now occupy a unique place in the history of medieval England.

'So violent and motley was life', the great historian Johan Huizinga famously wrote of the late Middle Ages, 'that it bore the mixed smell of blood and of roses.' The extraordinary vicissitudes of the Pastons' experience tempt any reader of their letters to agree. But Huizinga saw the people of the Middle Ages as alien beings, oscillating 'between the fear of hell and the most naïve joy, between cruelty and tenderness, between harsh asceticism and insane attachments to the delights of this world, between hatred and goodness, always running to extremes'.[6] In the Paston letters there is a chorus of voices – rational, humane, amused, sceptical, pragmatic and resilient – speaking across the centuries to contradict him.

Select Bibliography

This bibliography lists the main primary and secondary sources for the lives of the Pastons themselves, followed by a selection of further reading on fifteenth-century England. Some of the more specialist works cited in the endnotes have not been repeated here.

The Pastons

UNPRINTED PRIMARY SOURCES
London: Public Record Office

C1	Early Chancery Proceedings
E28	Exchequer, Council and Privy Seal
KB9	King's Bench, Ancient Indictments
KB27	King's Bench, *Coram Rege* Rolls

Oxford: Magdalen College
   Fastolf MSS
   Hickling MSS

PRINTED PRIMARY SOURCES
Calendar of the Close Rolls, 1399–1509, 18 vols. (London, 1927–63)
Calendar of the Fine Rolls, 1399–1509, 11 vols. (London, 1931–62)
Calendar of the Patent Rolls, 1399–1509, 17 vols. (London, 1903–16)
Davis, N. (ed.), *Paston Letters and Papers of the Fifteenth Century*, 2 vols. (Oxford, 1971–6, reprinted 2004)
Davis, N. (ed.), *The Paston Letters: a selection in modern spelling* (Oxford, 1983)
Fenn, J. (ed.), *Original Letters, written during the reigns of Henry VI, Edward IV, and Richard III by various persons of rank or consequence . . .* , 5 vols. (London, 1787–1823)
Gairdner, J. (ed.), *The Paston Letters*, 6 vols. (London, 1904; reprinted Gloucester, 1983)
Harvey, J. H. (ed.), *William Worcestre: Itineraries* (Oxford, 1969)
List of Sheriffs for England and Wales, PRO Lists and Indexes, 9 (1898)
Rotuli Parliamentorum, 6 vols., Record Commission
Williams, C. H. (ed.), *Year Books of Henry VI (1 Henry VI)*, Selden Society (London, 1933)

SECONDARY SOURCES
Barron, C., 'Who were the Pastons?', *Journal of the Society of Archivists*, 4 (1972), 530–5
Bennett, H. S., *The Pastons and their England* (Cambridge, 1922)

Blomefield, F., *An Essay towards a Topographical History of the County of Norfolk*, 11 vols. (London, 1805–10)

Britnell, R. H., 'The Pastons and their Norfolk', *Agricultural History Review*, 36 (1988), 132–44

Castor, H., *The King, the Crown, and the Duchy of Lancaster: Public Authority and Private Power, 1399–1461* (Oxford, 2000), Part II

Cokayne, G. E., *The Complete Peerage*, ed. V. Gibbs *et al.*, 13 vols. (London, 1910–40), vol. XII pt. 2, 889–93 (Earldom of Yarmouth)

Davis, V., *William Waynflete* (Woodbridge, 1993)

Gies, F. and J., *A Medieval Family* (New York, 1998)

Hughey, R., introduction to *The Correspondence of Lady Katherine Paston, 1603–1627*, Norfolk Record Society (Norwich, 1941)

Lewis, P. S., 'Sir John Fastolf's lawsuit over Titchwell, 1448–55', *Historical Journal*, 1 (1958), 1–20

McFarlane, K. B., 'The investment of Sir John Fastolf's profits of war', and 'William Worcester: a preliminary survey', in his *England in the Fifteenth Century* (London, 1981), 175–97 and 199–224

Richmond, C., *The Paston Family in the Fifteenth Century: The First Phase* (Cambridge, 1990)

Richmond, C., *The Paston Family in the Fifteenth Century: Fastolf's Will* (Cambridge, 1996)

Richmond, C., *The Paston Family in the Fifteenth Century: Endings* (Manchester, 2000)

Serpell, M., 'Sir John Fenn, his friends and the Paston Letters', *Antiquaries Journal*, 63 (1983), 95–121

Smith, A. R., 'Litigation and politics: Sir John Fastolf's defence of his English property', in A. J. Pollard (ed.), *Property and Politics* (Gloucester, 1984), 59–75

Smith, A. R., '"The greatest man of that age": the acquisition of Sir John Fastolf's East Anglian estates', in R. E. Archer and S. Walker (eds.), *Rulers and Ruled in Late Medieval England* (London, 1995), 137–54

Stoker, D., '"Innumerable letters of good consequence in history": the discovery and first publication of the Paston letters', *The Library: Transactions of the Bibliographical Society*, xvii (1995), 107–55

Virgoe, R., *Private Life in the Fifteenth Century: Illustrated Letters of the Paston Family* (London, 1989)

Fifteenth-Century England: Politics and the Wars of the Roses

Carpenter, C. *The Wars of the Roses: Politics and the Constitution in England, c. 1437–1509* (Cambridge, 1997)

Chrimes, S. B., *Henry VII* (London, 1972)

Curry, A., *The Hundred Years' War* (London, 1993)

Goodman, A., *The Wars of the Roses: Military Activity and English Society, 1452–97* (London, 1981)

Griffiths, R., *The Reign of Henry VI* (London, 1981)

Gunn, S. J., *Early Tudor Government, 1485–1558* (Basingstoke, 1995)

Haigh, P. A., *The Military Campaigns of the Wars of the Roses* (Stroud, 1995)

Harriss, G. L. (ed.), *Henry V: The Practice of Kingship* (Oxford, 1985)

Hicks, M. A., *False, Fleeting, Perjur'd Clarence: George, Duke of Clarence, 1449–1478* (Gloucester, 1980)

Horrox, R., *Richard III: A Study of Service* (Cambridge, 1989)

McFarlane, K. B., *England in the Fifteenth Century: Collected Essays* (London, 1981)

Maurer, H. E., *Margaret of Anjou: Queenship and Power in Late Medieval England* (Woodbridge, 2003)

Pollard, A. J. (ed.), *The Wars of the Roses* (London, 1995)

Pollard, A. J., *Late Medieval England, 1399–1509* (Harlow, 2000)

Ross, C., *Edward IV* (London, 1975)

Ross, C., *Richard III* (London, 1981)

Scofield, C. L., *The Life and Reign of Edward the Fourth*, 2 vols. (London, 1923)

Watts, J. L., *Henry VI and the Politics of Kingship* (Cambridge, 1996)

Fifteenth-Century England: Society, Economy and Culture

Bolton, J. L., *The Medieval English Economy, 1150–1500* (London, 1980)

Duffy, E., *The Stripping of the Altars: Traditional Religion in England, 1400–1580* (New Haven and London, 1992)

Dyer, C., *Standards of Living in the Later Middle Ages: Social Change in England, c. 1200–1520* (Cambridge, 1989)

Dyer, C., *Everyday Life in Medieval England* (London, 1994)

Hanawalt, B., *The Ties that Bound: Peasant Families in Medieval England* (Oxford, 1986)

Harding, A., *The Law Courts of Medieval England* (London, 1973)

Horrox, R. (ed.), *Fifteenth-Century Attitudes: Perceptions of Society in Late Medieval England* (Cambridge, 1994)

Horrox, R. (ed.), *The Black Death* (Manchester, 1994)

Keen, M., *Chivalry* (New Haven and London, 1984)

Keen, M., *English Society in the Later Middle Ages, 1348–1500* (London, 1990)

Marks, R. and Williamson, P. (eds.), *Gothic: Art for England, 1400–1547* (London, 2003)

Orme, N., *Medieval Childhood* (New Haven and London, 2001)

Platt, C., *The English Medieval Town* (London, 1976)

Rawcliffe, C., *Medicine and Society in Later Medieval England* (Stroud, 1995)

Reeves, C., *Pleasures and Pastimes in Medieval England* (Stroud, 1995)

Webb, D., *Pilgrimage in Medieval England* (London, 2000)

Woolgar, C. M., *The Great Household in Late Medieval England* (New Haven and London, 1999)

Notes

References are given for direct quotations from contemporary texts, and for material taken from unpublished documents. Otherwise, the principal sources used are listed in the bibliography.

The main source for the lives of the Paston family is the edition of their letters by Norman Davis (*Paston Letters and Papers of the Fifteenth Century*, 2 vols., Oxford, 1971–6, abbreviated here as *PL* Davis). Some documents omitted by Davis are printed in James Gairdner's earlier edition (*The Paston Letters*, 6 vols., London, 1904, abbreviated as *PL* Gairdner). Apart from references to the introductions by Davis and Gairdner (where page numbers are used), notes refer to individual letters, which are numbered consecutively throughout the volumes of each edition.

PROLOGUE

1 *PL* Davis, vol. I, p. xxvi.

2 *PL* Davis, vol. I, p. xxiv.

3 D. Stoker, '"Innumerable letters of good consequence in history": the discovery and first publication of the Paston letters', *The Library: Transactions of the Bibliographical Society*, xvii (1995), p. 119.

4 J. Fenn (ed.), *Original Letters, written during the reigns of Henry VI, Edward IV, and Richard III by various persons of rank or consequence . . .*, 2 vols (London, 1787). There had been some discussion between Fenn and his publishers about the timing of publication – whether to wait until the spring when the members of fashionable society would return to London from their country estates, or whether the fact that most books were published in the spring for that very reason would provide unhelpful competition. Fenn's brother-in-law John Frere, who was acting as his agent and adviser in London, saw no reason to delay publication: '*I should think its coming out before other works might find it purchased among people who don't care to buy everything that comes out, which it might lose if it had to stand the market with four or five other books. I have often heard people say – "Bless me! What number of guinea-quartos are come out this spring – 'tis impossible to buy them all!"*'. Stoker, '"Innumerable letters"', p. 136.

5 *PL* Gairdner, vol. I, p. 1.

6 Stoker, '"Innumerable letters"', p. 143.

7 Stoker, '"Innumerable letters"', p. 108.

8 *PL* Davis, vol. I, p. xxiv.

9 Stoker, '"Innumerable letters"', p. 147.

10 *PL* Davis, vol. I, p. xxvi.

11 C. Carpenter (ed.), *Kingsford's Stonor Letters and Papers, 1290–1483* (Cambridge, 1996); J. Kirby (ed.), *The Plumpton Letters and Papers* (Camden Society, fifth series, vol. VIII, 1996); A. Hanham (ed.), *The Cely Papers, 1472–1488* (Early English Text Society, 273, 1975); C. Carpenter (ed.), *The Armburgh Papers* (Woodbridge, 1998).

12 *PL* Davis 127.

13 *PL* Davis 127.

14 *PL* Davis 73.

15 *PL* Davis 128.

16 W. Shakespeare, *Richard III*, act V, scene 8, l. 23; *PL* Davis 261.

ONE

1 *PL* Davis, vol. I, p. xli. The document survives in the form of a nineteenth-century transcription of a manuscript which has since gone missing.

2 R. Horrox (trans. and ed.), *The Black Death* (Manchester, 1994), p. 250.

3 Horrox (ed.), *The Black Death*, pp. 340–1.

4 *PL* Davis 423.

5 C. H. Williams (ed.), *Year Books of Henry VI (1 Henry VI)*, Selden Society (London, 1933), pp. xxxi–xxxii, 100–6. Joan, the daughter of Thomas Holland, Earl of Kent, had married the Duke of York in 1393 when she was ten and he was fifty-two. After York died in 1402, she married William, Lord Willoughby, and in 1410, having been widowed for a second time before her thirtieth birthday, she took Henry, Lord Scrope of Masham, as her third husband. Scrope was beheaded in August 1415 for treason as a result of his involvement in the Southampton Plot against Henry V on the eve of the Agincourt campaign. Joan married Henry Broomfleet a few months later.

6 Trial by battle was still very occasionally used in cases – often treason cases – where a convicted criminal tried to save his own neck by informing on his associates. The informer (or 'approver') was required to fight in person against those he accused of complicity in his crime. Judicial combat involving an approver took place in London in 1455–6, but it was probably the last such trial ever staged in England. The case in which William Paston was involved in 1423 was different in that it involved land rights rather than charges of felony or treason, and as a result several procedural differences were noted in the Year Book. The champions' heads were not shaved before the duel, for example, as that of an approver would have been, and the red '*baston*', or staff, which was carried with a red shield behind each champion into the court did not have a knob at one end, as it would have done in the case of an approver. The compiler of the Year Book noted that '*it was said by J. Martin*' – one of the judges – '*when he saw the baston, that really the baston should have a knob on the end*'. However, '*there was no reply*', and the difference of opinion remained unresolved. For all details of the case, see Williams (ed.), *Year Books of Henry VI (1 Henry VI)*, pp. 95–100.

7 Williams (ed.), *Year Books of Henry VI (1 Henry VI)*, p. 96.

NOTES

8 L. O. Pike, *A History of Crime in England*, 2 vols. (London, 1873), I, p. 389.

9 *PL* Gairdner, vol. VI, appendix 1. William's mother Beatrice had died in 1409, and her brother Geoffrey Somerton in 1416. William's only remaining family after his father's death was his paternal aunt, Clement's sister Martha.

10 *PL* Davis, vol. I, p. xli.

11 For quotation, see C. Richmond, *The Paston Family in the Fifteenth Century: The First Phase* (Cambridge, 1990), p. 86.

12 Richmond, *The Paston Family: The First Phase*, p. 90.

13 *PL* Davis 870D.

14 *PL* Davis 5.

15 *PL* Davis 867.

16 *PL* Davis 867, 5.

17 *PL* Davis 867. William's refusal to abandon court proceedings also scuppered a proposed arbitration in the East Beckham case several years later.

18 *PL* Davis 4.

19 *PL* Davis 2.

20 *PL* Davis 7.

21 *PL* Davis 13.

22 *PL* Davis, vol. I, p. xli.

TWO

1 Gonville Hall was refounded in the sixteenth century as Gonville and Caius College. A seventh college, King's, was founded by Henry VI in 1441, and another, Queens', by his wife Margaret of Anjou in 1448.

2 Judge William made this very point in a case he heard in the court of Common Pleas in 1436. A defendant claimed that a writ sued against him was inadmissible because it incorrectly described him as a 'husbandman' instead of a 'gentleman'. Opposing counsel argued that, irrespective of the defendant's wealth, 'husbandman' was a technically correct description of his occupation, since he and his sons took an active part in the cultivation of their own lands – and supported the argument by pointing out that a writ issued against a Serjeant of the Kitchen in the King's household might properly describe him as a 'cook'. The Chief Justice observed that an officer of the royal household would find it offensive to be described as a cook rather than a gentleman, but Judge Paston said that such a writ would be good in law because it referred to the defendant's '*mystery*', or craft; a Serjeant of the King's Kitchen, he said, was by definition both a gentleman *and* a cook. For details of the case, see R.L. Storey, 'Gentlemen-bureaucrats', in C.H. Clough (ed.), *Profession, Vocation and Culture in Later Medieval England* (Liverpool, 1982), pp. 91–2.

3 *PL* Davis 14.

4 *PL* Davis 439.

5 *PL* Davis 13. The report of John and Margaret's meeting is the main business of Agnes's only surviving letter to William (see above, chapter 1).

6 *PL* Davis 125.

7 *PL* Davis 125.

311

8 *PL* Davis 126. 'Scarlet' was a type of woollen cloth of the highest quality, usually brightly coloured, but not yet exclusively associated with the colour red.

9 *PL* Davis 155.

10 *PL* Davis 346.

11 *PL* Davis 127.

12 *PL* Davis 432.

13 *PL* Davis 31.

14 *PL* Davis 32.

15 Even the will of January 1444 had not been properly revised; the text of the 1441/2 draft was not changed to take account of the time that had passed since it was written (as reflected, for example, in his children's ages, and the birth of his first grandson): *PL* Davis 12; *PL* Gairdner vol. VI, appendix 2, II.

16 *PL* Davis 32.

17 *PL* Davis 31.

18 *PL* Davis 33.

19 *PL* Davis 32.

20 *PL* Davis 33.

THREE

1 The parish church was probably St Mary Coslany, to which both Margaret and John Wyndham left legacies. The Pastons later rented a house near St Peter Hungate, and made substantial donations to the rebuilding of that church.

2 Public Record Office (hereafter PRO) KB27/762 rot. 75.

3 *PL* Davis 129.

4 *PL* Davis 129.

5 *PL* Davis 129.

6 *PL* Davis 129.

7 For the reconstruction of the missing words, see C. Barron, 'Who were the Pastons?', *Journal of the Society of Archivists*, 4 (1972).

8 *PL* Davis 23.

9 *PL* Davis 14. Clifford's Inn was one of the Inns of Chancery, which offered elementary training in the law (as opposed to the specialist professional instruction at the four Inns of Court).

10 *PL* Davis 79.

11 *PL* Davis 127.

12 Margaret and John Paston took possession of Matlask and Bessingham in 1446 after the death of her grandmother Eleanor. The Mautby manor of West Beckham, which also lay two miles from Baconsthorpe and Gresham, passed on Eleanor's death to Margaret's uncle Edmund Mautby; Margaret finally inherited it when he died in 1479.

13 *PL* Davis 38.

14 *PL* Davis 128.

15 *PL* Davis 79. Davis gives this letter a suggested date of 1447, but 1448 is much more likely: only after Moleyns's seizure of Gresham in February 1448 did Daniel's position

in relation to Suffolk become important enough to the Pastons to be discussed in these terms.

16 During the divorce hearing, Thomas and Alice both testified that they had not consummated their marriage during the seven years they lived together. Alice confessed that the father of her baby was Richard Stapleton, a Woodhouse servant, with whom, she said, she had had sex only once. The baby died soon after birth. Alice entered a convent, where she remained until her death fifty years later. Tuddenham never remarried. For full details of the case, see R. Virgoe, 'The Divorce of Sir Thomas Tuddenham', *Norfolk Archaeology*, 34 (1969).

17 *PL* Davis 128. The hostility between Daniel and Tuddenham, and the rivalry between Heydon and the Pastons, became further entangled when Heydon's father-in-law Edmund Winter married Tuddenham's mother-in-law Alice Woodhouse after she was widowed in 1431.

18 For John at Winchester in early July 1448 see *PL* Davis 453: a letter from James Gresham, written in London, which Davis dates to 3 July 1450. However, that was the day on which Jack Cade's rebels arrived in the city – frightening circumstances of which there is no hint in Gresham's letter. John's petitions to Bishop Wainfleet (for which, see *PL* Davis 873) instead indicate a date of 1448 for his visit to Winchester. *PL* Davis 454, which is part of the same correspondence, must also therefore have been written in that year.

19 *PL* Davis 36, 39.

20 *PL* Davis 130.

21 *PL* Davis 443.

22 *PL* Davis 444.

23 *PL* Davis 36; PRO KB9/262 mm. 45–6.

24 *PL* Davis 444.

25 PRO KB9/262 mm. 45–6.

26 *PL* Davis 131.

27 *PL* Davis 131.

28 *PL* Davis 131.

29 *PL* Davis 132.

30 *PL* Davis 36.

31 *PL* Davis 133 (and, for Moleyns's letter itself, see *PL* Davis 875).

32 *PL* Davis 132.

33 *PL* Davis 133.

34 *PL* Davis 37. Edmund's will is *PL* Davis 80.

35 *PL* Davis 37.

36 *PL* Davis 135.

37 *PL* Davis 135.

38 *PL* Davis 136.

39 E.F. Jacob, *The Fifteenth Century* (Oxford, 1961), p. 493.

40 *PL* Gairdner 117.

41 *PL* Davis 450.

41 *PL* Davis 450.

43 J. L. Watts, 'Ideas, Principles and Politics', in A.J. Pollard (ed.), *The Wars of the Roses* (London, 1995), p. 110.

44 *PL* Davis 450.

45 *PL* Davis 450.

46 *PL* Davis 133.

FOUR

1 *PL* Davis 692; R. A. Griffiths, *The Reign of Henry VI* (London, 1981), p. 636.

2 *PL* Davis 455.

3 *PL* Davis 136.

4 *PL* Gairdner 122.

5 *PL* Davis 455.

6 *PL* Davis 39.

7 For details of all these indictments, see PRO KB27/758 Rex rot. 9; KB27/762 Rex rot. 29; KB27/766 rot. 90; KB27/798 Rex roti. 9, 26; KB9/265 mm. 44–5; KB9/272 m. 3; *PL* Davis 137.

8 *PL* Davis 458.

9 PRO KB27/758 Rex rot. 9.

10 *PL* Davis 447.

11 *PL* Davis 459.

12 *PL* Davis 460.

13 *PL* Davis 461.

14 *PL* Davis 460, 463.

15 *PL* Davis 463, 460.

16 *PL* Davis 460, and see also Yelverton's letter 463: '*This is supposed verily to be Heydon's work, that will set him verily to do the utterest against you and John Damme in the worst wise that he can*'.

17 *PL* Davis 460.

18 *PL* Davis 463.

19 *PL* Davis 467.

20 *PL* Davis 878.

21 *PL* Gairdner 162.

22 *PL* Davis 878, 877.

23 *PL* Gairdner 162.

24 At the November hearings, John Wyndham and his servant Thomas Hawes were charged with assaulting James Gloys in the street in Norwich two years earlier. Gloys was said to have '*despaired of his life*' – a reminder that legal language was employed to maximise the gravity of the charges in relation to relevant statute law, not to provide an accurate description of events. By Margaret's account of the incident, Gloys was not so much in fear of his life as having to be held back from the fight. PRO KB9/272 m. 2; and see above, chapter 3.

25 *PL* Gairdner 162.

26 Magdalen College, Oxford, Hickling MS 104.

27 *PL* Gairdner 167.

28 *PL* Gairdner 162; *PL* Davis 881.

29 *PL* Gairdner 169.

30 *PL* Davis 471.

31 *PL* Davis 472.

32 *PL* Davis 472.

33 *PL* Davis 39.

34 *PL* Davis 473.

35 *PL* Davis 137.

36 *PL* Davis 474.

37 *PL* Davis 138.

38 *PL* Davis 139.

39 *PL* Gairdner 192.

40 *PL* Davis 477.

41 *PL* Gairdner 192.

42 *PL* Davis 478.

43 *PL* Gairdner 192.

44 Magdalen College, Oxford, Hickling MS 104.

45 *PL* Davis 479.

46 This was the third time Alice Chaucer had been widowed. Her first husband, Sir John Philip, died at Harfleur a few months after their marriage in 1415, when Alice was eleven. Her second husband, the Earl of Salisbury, was killed at the siege of Orléans in 1428 (an engagement in which Suffolk served under his command). John de la Pole, her son by Suffolk, was her only child.

FIVE

1 According to the ancient Greek recipe on which the medieval formulation was based, treacle had more than sixty ingredients, including flesh of roasted viper, which were prepared over forty days and left to mature for up to twelve years. The usual prescription during epidemics was that patients should take a dose twice a day mixed into wine, ale or rosewater.

2 *PL* Davis 141.

3 *PL* Davis 144. '*Sir Thomas*' was Fastolf's chaplain: priests, like knights, were addressed by the honorific title 'sir'. For the redating of this letter from Davis's suggested date of 1452 to 1451, see C. Richmond, *The Paston Family in the Fifteenth Century: Endings* (Manchester, 2000), p. 106n.

4 *PL* Davis 483.

5 *PL* Davis 485.

6 *PL* Davis 484.

7 PRO KB27/750 rot. 104.

8 *PL* Davis 40, 48; PRO KB9/272 m. 52.

9 *PL* Davis 40.

10 *PL* Davis 48.

11 *PL* Davis 43.

12 *PL* Davis 43, 40, 48; PRO KB27/790 Rex rot. 43v; KB9/85/2 m. 8.

13 *PL* Davis 43 (see also 42, 44).

14 *PL* Davis 46.

15 PRO KB27/774 Rex rot. 30v.

16 *PL* Davis 882, 41.

17 *PL* Davis 46, 41, 882.

18 *PL* Davis 882.

19 *PL* Davis 487.

20 *PL* Davis 140. Davis suggests that this letter was written on 3 June 1451, but Margaret's reference to Charles Nowell indicates a date of 18 May 1452.

21 Jane Boys was presumably trying to salvage what she could of her dignity and reputation by claiming that she had freely agreed to marry Langstrother. John Paston, for one, did not believe her testimony; he helped to bring charges against Langstrother in 1451, and gave Southwell a harrowing account of the evidence he had gathered: '*These be proofs that Jane Boys was ravished against her will, and not by her own assent*', he wrote. '*One is that she, the time of her taking when she was set upon her horse, she reviled Langstrother and called him knave, and wept and cried out upon him piteously to her, and said as shrewdly to him as could come to her mind, and fell down off her horse unto that she was bound . . . Item, when she was bound she called upon her mother, which followed her as far as she might on her feet, and when the said Jane saw she might go no further she cried to her mother and said that whatsoever fell of her she should never be wedded to that knave, to die for it. Item, . . . in all other places where she might see any people, she cried out upon him and let people know whose daughter she was and how she was ravished against her will, desiring the people to follow her and rescue her.*' *PL* Davis 45 (redated to 4 or 18 July 1451: see PRO KB27/762 Rex rot. 1). Richard Southwell later married Jane's sister Amy Wichingham.

22 *PL* Davis 140. Margaret's reminder about the girdle – a request first passed on to her husband by John Osbern in Davis 487 (written 14 May 1452) – confirms the date of 1452 for this letter.

23 *PL* Davis 41.

24 *PL* Davis 81.

25 *PL* Davis 142 (redated to 4 July 1452 by the references to Roger Church and Margery's girdle).

26 *PL* Davis 48 (and see also PRO KB9/85/2 m. 14).

27 PRO E28/84; KB27/775 Coram Rege rot. 20v.

28 For these indictments, see PRO KB9/85/2 mm. 8, 14, 17–17v, 25, 6, 30, 33, 35, 37; KB9/118/1 mm. 16, 22, 23, 24, 28, 29, 36; KB9/118/2 m. 30; *PL* Davis 48.

29 PRO KB9/118/2 mm. 163–4.

30 PRO KB9/118/2 mm. 57, 36, 30, 28, 25, 24, 21, 18.

31 *PL* Davis 146.

32 *PL* Davis 147.

33 *PL* Davis 26.

34 *PL* Davis 148.

35 *PL* Davis 149.

36 *PL* Davis 150.

37 *PL* Davis 151.

38 *PL* Davis 150.

39 *PL* Davis 150.

40 *PL* Davis 446.

41 *PL* Davis 446.

42 *PL* Davis 84. For the other proposals over the years 1449–54, see *PL* Davis 19, 145, 150, 493, 27, 499, 50.

43 *PL* Gairdner 235.

44 *PL* Gairdner 230.

45 *PL* Gairdner 235.

46 *PL* Davis 48. The petition alleged that on 5 November 1453 twenty of Ledham's men – 'and no man of reputation among them' – 'came under colour of hunting and broke up gates and closes of Osbert Mundford at Bradeston. And twelve persons of the same fellowship, with bows bent and arrows ready in their hands, abided alone between the manor of Bradeston and the church, and there kept them from seven of the clock in the morning unto three of the clock after noon, lying in wait upon the servants of the said Osbert Mundford, lord of the said manor, so that none dared come out for doubt of their lives'. Two days later eight of the men allegedly lay in wait 'privily in a hole' to ambush two of Mundford's servants on their way back from Acle market, 'and thereupon chased them so that if they had not been well horsed and well escaped they had been dead and slain'.

47 *PL* Davis 48.

48 PRO KB27/782 rot. 114. Daniel was able to secure the annulment of the sentence of outlawry in 1457, on the grounds that he had been serving in Scotland in the spring of 1454 and had therefore been unable to appear in court to answer the summons.

49 PRO KB9/272 mm. 2–5.

50 *PL* Davis 83.

51 *PL* Davis 83.

SIX

1 The volumes included a Bible and works by Livy, Julius Caesar and Aristotle, as well as a 'book of King Arthur' and the *Roman de la Rose*. *PL* Davis 64; H.S. Bennett, *The Pastons and Their England* (Cambridge, 1922), p. 111.

2 *PL* Gairdner 389; K.B. McFarlane, 'The investment of Sir John Fastolf's profits of war', in his *England in the Fifteenth Century* (London, 1981), p. 190n.

3 *PL* Gairdner 223.

4 For Scales's handwritten appeal to their former friendship, see above, chapter 4. The Hickling dispute was still unresolved when Fastolf died.

5 *PL* Gairdner 174.

6 *PL* Gairdner 164, 173. Fastolf believed that Dalling had forged the inquisition which found in Hull's favour in 1448. It was nevertheless clear that there were problems with his own title to the estate: see P.S. Lewis, 'Sir John Fastolf's lawsuit over Titchwell, 1448–55', *Historical Journal*, 1 (1958).

7 *PL* Davis 537.

8 *PL* Davis 506.

9 *PL* Davis 507.

10 *PL* Davis 132 (and see 130).

11 *PL* Gairdner 251.

12 *PL* Davis 509.

13 *PL* Davis 516.

14 *PL* Davis 520.

15 *PL* Davis 525.

16 *PL* Davis 536.

17 *PL* Davis 509.

18 *PL* Davis 28.

19 *PL* Davis 121.

20 *PL* Davis 512.

21 *PL* Gairdner 282.

22 *PL* Gairdner 283.

23 *PL* Davis 522.

24 *PL* Gairdner 287.

25 *PL* Davis 527.

26 *PL* Davis 528.

27 *PL* Davis 528. The word used in the original text was '*wood*' as a wild bullock, a now-obsolete adjective meaning 'mad' in both modern senses – that is, insane and/or violently angry.

28 *PL* Gairdner 299.

29 *PL* Gairdner 322.

30 *PL* Davis 553. Many of the surviving letters from 1456–8 are difficult to date conclusively and precisely. They are attributed here to the most plausible date within that period.

31 *PL* Davis 556.

32 *PL* Davis 571, 572. (Worcester's text gives the last phrase in Latin – '*de malo in peius*'.)

33 *PL* Davis 572.

34 *PL* Davis 566.

35 Fastolf's Yorkshire estates had formerly belonged to his wife Millicent Scrope; for John's visit there, see *PL* Davis 53.

36 *PL* Davis 550.

37 *PL* Davis 558.

38 *PL* Davis 537.

39 The college was to be dedicated to St John the Baptist. At great expense, Fastolf had acquired one of the saint's fingers, which was kept in the chapel (also of St John) at Caister.

40 *PL* Davis 570.

41 *PL* Gairdner 340 (dated to 1457 by reference to Davis 569 and 570). The royal administration was allegedly demanding the vast sum of 500 marks for each 100 marks of annual landed income with which the college was to be endowed. Fastolf was planning an endowment to produce a net income of 300 marks a year, which would

mean paying at least 1,500 marks – the equivalent of £1,000 – for the licence, an amount which might justifiably be thought outrageously high.

42 PRO C1/19/115.

43 *PL* Davis 25.

44 *PL* Davis 569.

45 There is a difficulty about the date of this written will, since *PL* Davis 54 reports that it was sealed on 14 June in the thirty-fifth year of the reign of Henry VI – the thirty-fifth year being 1457. However, all other evidence dates the will to 14 June 1459, which suggests that the reference in Davis 54 is no more than a slip of the pen.

46 *PL* Gairdner 385.

47 *PL* Davis 578.

48 *PL* Davis 54; 4,000 marks was the equivalent of £2,666. The purchase price of land was usually calculated as twenty times its annual income. On that basis, Fastolf's estates (including his properties in London and elsewhere as well as in Norfolk and Suffolk) would have been worth about £20,000 on the open market.

49 *PL* Davis 25.

50 *PL* Gairdner 385.

51 During a period of '*great sickness*' while Fastolf was still living at Southwark, for example, a proclamation was made on his instructions at St Paul's Cathedral offering restitution to anyone he had wronged, and a number of people came forward to ask for redress. When they did so, however, Fastolf gave them '*sharp and bitter answer*' – whether because illness had made him more than usually irritable, or because by then he had recovered and was therefore no longer so acutely conscious of the need to make amends before his time ran out. The presumably confused and disappointed petitioners '*naught had but rebukes*'. C. Richmond, *The Paston Family in the Fifteenth Century: Fastolf's Will* (Cambridge, 1996), p. 88n.

52 The unsettling effects of this deliberately maintained ambiguity were apparent in a letter which John Paston received from Henry Windsor, a chancery clerk who had served Fastolf for some time, asking whether Fastolf intended to keep his promise that Windsor should have charge of one of the inns he owned in London. '*. . . if it please you to remember my master, at your best leisure, whether his old promise shall stand as touching my preferring to the Boar's Head in Southwark,*' Windsor wrote. '*Sir, I would have been at another place, and of my master's own motion he said that I should set upon the Boar's Head; in the which matter I report me to William Worcester, Bocking and William Barker, and most specially to my master's own remembrance*'. *PL* Davis 574.

53 *PL* Davis 578 – and see also Fastolf's own detailed list of instructions for John on a variety of legal and other matters, written on 3 July 1459 (*PL* Davis 579).

54 *PL* Davis 583. Brackley wrote the last sentence in Latin: '*Haec verba replicat saepius cum magno stomacho, etc*'.

55 *PL* Davis 901.

SEVEN

1 Richmond, *The Paston Family: Fastolf's Will*, p. 137.

2 *PL* Davis 54; *PL* Gairdner 387.

3 *PL* Davis 86. William Paston and William Worcester must have left Caister on Tuesday to arrive in London by 8 a.m. on Friday as William Paston described. Thomas Howes later alleged that Worcester spent that Tuesday night at Caister (see Davis 901) but his declaration was made seven years after the event to serve a particular political purpose, and his evidence cannot therefore be taken to override that of William Paston's letter.

4 *PL* Davis 86.

5 Elizabeth Heveningham's son was not happy at the prospect of his mother's remarriage ('*he has said as much thereagainst as he dares do to have her good mothership*'), and Margaret had tried to help him dissuade her from the match, offering to show her a copy of Wyndham's pedigree to demonstrate that he was not the worshipful gentleman he claimed to be. Nevertheless, Wyndham had both the support of the dowager Duchess of Suffolk and the money to pay off the Heveningham family's debts, and the marriage went ahead despite all objections. *PL* Davis 152.

6 *PL* Davis 584.

7 *PL* Davis 153.

8 The passage in full reads: '*Propter Deum caveatis a confidentia in illo nigro Hibernico oculis obliquo et lusco, qui utinam corde, ore et opere non esset obliquior, qui heri misit litteram Colino Gallico, de quibus dicitur quod singuli caccant uno ano*'. *PL* Davis 612.

9 *PL* Davis 86. For Worcester's absence when Fastolf died, see *PL* Davis 612.

10 *PL* Davis 88.

11 *PL* Davis 604. Worcester poured his heart out in another letter to a friend at around the same time: '. . . *I was not put in favour nor trust to command and give in my master's name and for his sake a gown cloth to none of his friends, servants or almsfolk, but must beg and pray as I were a stranger. If I caused Master Paston and my uncle the parson that they have such authority as they have, they ought be the fainer and desirous of the continuance of my authority, that is as great as theirs or greater, whatsoever Friar Brackley or they say, and so it is too openly known of record . . . Those that I have helped to be cherished with my master be now my adversaries; there shows no gentleness of blood nor noble condition in that point namely, etc . . . Suppose you that such gifts and grants my master made to me for my relief in recompense of my service, that I will let it pass, and my master's servants, with his poor kinsfolk, so simply rewarded? I shall be for them to my simple power as my master charged me.*' *PL* Davis 888.

12 *PL* Davis 604.

13 Or (another version given elsewhere in the same letter) '*Who that ever says so, I say he lies falsely in his head*'. *PL* Davis 705.

14 *PL* Davis 88.

15 *PL* Davis 88.

16 *PL* Davis 705. Yelverton was particularly exercised by the fact that Brackley had been telling people that Yelverton himself had started the quarrel with John. Brackley was quick to defend himself: '"*For sooth," said I, "when I came into the chamber there, the first word I heard was this, that you said to my master J.P., "Who that ever says so, I say*

he lies falsely in his head"'. Yelverton's point was the reasonable one that the first word heard by Brackley was not necessarily the first word of the argument – '"*Yes*," *said the justice, "you should have told what moved me to say so to him*"'– but Brackley replied that '*I could not tell that I had not heard*'. Yelverton retorted that he should have troubled to find out, but Brackley – the kind of man who knew what he thought without having to think about it first – said, '*Sir, it belonged not to me to examine the matter, for I knew well I should not be judge in the matter*'. Leaving aside the fact that Brackley had leaped to judgement in any case and passed on his conclusions as fact, Yelverton focused on the issue of loyalty and friendship: '"*No*," says he *hardily, "you shall not be judge, but if you had owed me as good will as you did and do to Paston, you would then have searched the cause of my great grief, why I said as I said, etc; but I have seen the day you loved me better than him, for he gave you never cause of such love as I have done*"'.

17 *PL* Davis 88.
18 *PL* Davis 89.
19 *PL* Davis 705.
20 *PL* Davis 89.
21 *PL* Davis 609.
22 *PL* Davis 154.
23 *PL* Davis 157.
24 *PL* Davis 624.
25 *PL* Davis 612. '*Item, dicit quod cum pater vester fuerit iudex ditissimus, quasi nihil fecistis pro eo in distribuendo elemosinam pro anima eius, et cum nihil feceritis pro patre vestro, quomodo pro Magistro Fastolf aliquid facietis?*'
26 Jasper Tudor and his brother Edmund, Earl of Richmond, were the sons of Henry V's Queen, Catherine de Valois, by her second marriage to Owen Tudor, a Welsh esquire who had been brought up in Henry V's household.
27 *PL* Davis 114.
28 *PL* Davis 114.
29 *PL* Davis 317. The letter was written in the name of one of John's sons, but corrections to the text in John's own hand make clear that he was responsible for drafting it.
30 *PL* Davis 158.

EIGHT

1 '*Je n'ai pas souvenance d'avoir jamais vu un plus bel homme*'. C. L. Scofield, *The Life and Reign of Edward the Fourth*, 2 vols (London, 1923), I, p. 127.
2 *PL* Davis 114.
3 *PL* Davis 632.
4 R. E. Archer, '"How ladies . . . who live on their manors ought to manage their households and estastes": women as landholders and administrators in the later middle ages', in P. J. P. Goldberg (ed.), *Woman is a Worthy Wight: Women in English Society, c.1200–1500* (Stroud, 1992), p. 154.
5 *PL* Davis 611. '*Ipse enim* [the Bishop of Norwich] *cum Ducissa Suffolchie et aliis perso-*

nis prenominatis sunt Reginae et Principi maxime favorabiles cum totis suis viribus . . .
Item, bonum esset quod iuvenis Dux Suffolchie cum suis militibus et armigeris uteretur
suis calcaribus et iam probaretur in bello cui esset fidelis, an caro vel piscis'.

6 *PL* Davis 231.

7 *PL* Davis 58.

8 *PL* Davis 636, 160. For the presence of the Paston household at Hellesdon in late June
and early July, see Davis 635 and 159.

9 *PL* Davis 59.

10 *PL* Davis 117.

11 *PL* Davis 163.

12 *PL* Davis 163.

13 *PL* Davis 167.

14 *PL* Davis 168.

15 *PL* Davis 168.

16 *PL* Davis 169.

17 *PL* Davis 662.

18 *PL* Davis 677. Davis suggests a date of 1463 for this letter, but the issue of leasing land
at Boyton, which Playter mentions in the middle of the letter, connects it with Davis
653, written at the end of December 1461. Playter was therefore writing in January
1462.

19 *PL* Davis 661.

20 *PL* Davis 644. Davis placed the whole of the Cotton episode in the autumn of 1461,
but it has since been redated to 1462 by reference to the King's Bench proceedings
which resulted from the incident: see Richmond, *The Paston Family: Endings*, pp.
199–200n. The letters redated to 1462 as a result are Davis 166, 644, 645, 647, 648 and
737.

21 *PL* Davis 645.

22 *PL* Davis 647. The John Paston who went with Richard Calle to Cotton has previously been taken to be John Paston II, the eldest son of the family, but the evidence suggests that it was in fact John Paston III. John Paston's later petition to the Duke of
Norfolk on the subject of the conflict at Cotton (Davis 65, redated to some time after
March 1463 because of the redating of the incident itself from 1461 to 1462) remarks
that the son John sent with Calle to Cotton was '*a servant of my lord's*'. It was John
III, not John II, who was by that stage in the service of the Duke of Norfolk. John's
instruction to Calle and his son to go to Cotton is given in Davis 66 (which must,
therefore, date from before 8 October 1462), and it is '*John Paston the younger*' to
whom he refers. It was John III who called himself John Paston junior, or the
younger (see Davis 318, 319), whereas John II signed himself John Paston the older
(see Davis 231, 232, 234, 235). The '*John Paston junior*' to whom Calle addressed his
letter about events at Cotton (Davis 737) was therefore John III.

23 *PL* Davis 648.

24 *PL* Davis 737. There is one apparent difficulty with redating this letter to 1462: Calle
refers to '*the day after All Saints. which shall be on Tuesday next coming*'. Davis took
Calle to mean that the day *after* All Saints' day was a Tuesday, which would fit his

suggested date of 1461. However, if Calle meant that All Saints' day itself was a Tuesday, as it was in 1462, the difficulty disappears – and the substance of his comments about the conflict at Cotton clearly places the letter in the autumn of that year.

25 *PL* Davis 166.

26 *PL* Davis 120 (redated to 16 March 1462: see Richmond, *The Paston Family: Fastolf's Will*, pp. 150–1).

27 *PL* Davis 680.

28 *PL* Davis 652. Davis was uncertain of the year, but the substance of the letter best fits 1463.

29 *PL* Davis 88.

30 *PL* Gairdner 565. '*iste iuratus non intellexit in tota vita sua tantam liberalitem in dicto domino Johanne Fastolf.*

31 *PL* Davis 119.

32 *PL* Davis 118.

33 *PL* Davis 177.

34 *PL* Davis 671. The precise date of this letter is uncertain, beyond the fact that it was written between 1462 and 1466. However, Russe's comments best fit the circumstances of 1464.

35 '*Shrewdly*' often carries a sense of malicious intent, but here seems simply to indicate the poor quality of their work.

36 *PL* Davis 70. For the redating of John's quarrel with his eldest son, see below, chapter 9.

37 *PL* Davis 688.

38 *PL* Davis 73. The letter was written on '*the Thursday before St Peter's Day*'. Davis took this to be the feast of Saints Peter and Paul on 29 June, and therefore dated the letter to 27 June. However, internal evidence suggests it was written much earlier in the year – especially its closeness in tone to Davis 72 (written 15 January), and the fact that John says he hopes to make progress in the probate case '*before Easter*'. It seems much more likely that he was writing on 21 February, the day before the feast of St Peter's Chair.

39 *PL* Davis 180.

40 *PL* Davis 181, 180.

41 *PL* Davis 184.

42 *PL* Davis 690.

43 *PL* Davis 188.

44 *PL* Davis 74.

45 *PL* Davis 190, 191.

46 *PL* Davis 323. In 1465 Elizabeth Venour was embroiled in a protracted legal battle with a rival claimant, William Babington, over her right to the wardenship – a fight which became a cause célèbre as a result of her colourful love-life. As a wealthy heiress and widow, Elizabeth was an appealing prospect as a potential wife, and in 1462 she was allegedly abducted and forcibly married by a man named Richard Worth. Worth was outlawed for the offence and took sanctuary at Westminster Abbey, but Elizabeth's

decision to join him there allowed Babington to claim that she had colluded in her own kidnapping, and that she should forfeit her possessions as a result. When the case went to trial, Elizabeth initially refused to leave Worth, but divorced him when it became clear that she otherwise risked losing her inheritance. Babington subsequently won the case, but Elizabeth launched an appeal, and in 1466 an out-of-court settlement was agreed by which Elizabeth kept the wardenship, on condition that Babington would inherit the office after her death if (as proved to be the case) she remained childless. Worth then petitioned the Pope for an annulment of their divorce, and the couple lived out the rest of their days together. For Elizabeth Venour and the Fleet Prison itself, see M. Bassett, 'The Fleet Prison in the middle ages', *University of Toronto Law Journal*, vol. V, no. 2 (1944).

47 *PL* Davis 77.

48 *PL* Davis 192.

49 *PL* Davis 180.

50 *PL* Davis 194.

51 *PL* Davis 196.

52 *PL* Davis 196.

53 *PL* Davis 196.

54 *PL* Davis 688.

55 *PL* Davis 30.

56 '*pro Johannes Fastolf milite ditissimo qui egit contra istud concilium*'.

57 C. F. Bühler (ed.), *The Dicts and Sayings of the Philosophers*, Early English Text Society (London, 1941), pp. xxiv, 54; Richmond, *The Paston Family: The First Phase*, pp. 259–60.

NINE

1 *PL* Gairdner 637.

2 *PL* Davis 153.

3 *PL* Davis 116.

4 *PL* Davis 231.

5 See above, chapter 8.

6 *PL* Davis 116.

7 *PL* Davis 643.

8 *PL* Davis 232.

9 *PL* Davis 172.

10 *PL* Davis 680.

11 *PL* Davis 175.

12 *PL* Davis 176.

13 *PL* Davis 72.

14 *PL* Davis 72.

15 *PL* Davis 73 (redated to 21 February 1465).

16 *PL* Davis 234. Davis suggests a date of March 1464 for this letter, but its contents best fit the situation a year later when John II had been barred from home by his father.

17 Margaret says that the time of year when John II was banished from the house was

'*about St Thomas's mass*'. The difficulty in interpreting her comment is that there were several saints named Thomas, some of whom had more than one feast day. Nevertheless, it is possible to narrow down the options because the major feasts of the most prominent saints of that name – St Thomas the apostle and St Thomas Becket – were concentrated in December and July. Given the intensity of John Paston's anger at his eldest son in January and February 1465, it seems likely that the breach between them had taken place not long before, which suggests that Margaret was referring to one of the feasts of St Thomas in December 1464.

18 *PL* Davis 178.

19 *PL* Davis 179.

20 *PL* Davis 690.

21 *PL* Davis 897, 896. In the mid-sixteenth century John Paston III's great-grandson Sir William Paston named one of his sons Wulstan in honour of this Norman 'ancestor'. R. Hughey (ed.), *The Correspondence of Lady Katherine Paston, 1603–1627*, Norfolk Record Society (Norwich, 1941), pp. 19, 36–7.

22 *PL* Davis 896.

23 *PL* Davis 198.

24 *PL* Davis 279.

25 *PL* Davis 329. Davis tentatively suggests a date of 1468 for this letter. However, John III's comments about a man named Hugh Fenn link it with Davis 749, which must have been written before George Neville lost the chancellorship in June 1467. Both letters can therefore be dated to March 1467.

26 *PL* Davis 236.

27 Letter now lost; extract quoted in headnote to *PL* Davis 236.

28 *PL* Davis 236.

29 *PL* Davis 327.

30 *PL* Davis 745.

31 *PL* Davis 323.

32 *PL* Davis 330, 329. Margaret mentions a '*little John*' in her household in two letters before this date, without further comment on his identity. In 1472 John III also mentions '*little Jack*' as one among a list of people to whom John II should send greetings in London (see *PL* Davis 187, 194, 354).

33 *PL* Davis 327.

34 *PL* Davis 325.

35 *PL* Davis 720. John Paston and John II were together in London when this letter was written, which rules out Davis's suggested date of February 1465, given that the two were estranged at this point. It is much more likely that the letter was written a year later, on 6 February 1466.

36 *PL* Davis 748.

37 *PL* Davis 741 (redated to 1467, by reference to Davis 92), 748.

38 C. Ross, *Edward IV* (London, 1975), p. 63n.

39 *PL* Davis 199.

40 *PL* Davis 199.

41 *PL* Davis 901A.

42 *PL* Davis 237.

43 *PL* Davis 330.

44 *PL* Davis 902.

45 *PL* Davis 752.

46 For the last three years of his life, Howes was rector of Pulham Market in south Norfolk. He commissioned a stained-glass window for the church there depicting Sir John Fastolf and his wife Millicent, with an inscription asking onlookers to pray for their souls, and declaring that Fastolf *'did many good things during his lifetime'* (*'multa bona fecit in tempore vitae'*). Richmond, *The Paston Family: Fastolf's Will*, pp. 184–6.

47 *PL* Davis 238.

48 *PL* Davis 759.

49 *PL* Davis 200.

50 *PL* Davis 752.

51 *PL* Davis 764. The letter is undated, but a reference to a man named Roger Ree as sheriff of Norfolk and Suffolk means that it cannot have been written earlier than his appointment to office in November 1468. The King visited Norfolk in June 1469, and the events which followed (for which, see below) mean that the letter cannot have been written after that point. The most likely dating is therefore some time in the early months of 1469, when John II's relationship with the Hautes was already established.

52 *PL* Davis 200, 201.

53 *PL* Davis 904.

54 *PL* Davis 201.

55 *PL* Davis 331.

56 *PL* Davis 332.

57 *PL* Davis 332.

58 *PL* Davis 331, 333.

59 J. Kirby (ed.), *The Plumpton Letters and Papers* (Camden Society, fifth series, vol. VIII, 1996), p. 40.

60 *PL* Davis 240.

61 *PL* Davis 333.

62 *PL* Davis 333.

63 *PL* Davis 333.

64 *PL* Davis 333.

65 A. R. Myers (ed.), *English Historical Documents, 1327–1485* (London, 1969), p. 300; Scofield, *Edward the Fourth*, I, p. 495.

66 *PL* Gairdner 719.

67 *PL* Davis 762.

68 *PL* Davis 763.

TEN

1 J. H. Harvey (ed.), *William Worcestre: Itineraries* (Oxford, 1969), p. 187. Worcester reported that the Duke's army was 3,000 strong, but such figures were used to give an impression of imposing scale rather than an accurate headcount, and it is clear, by

comparison with what is known about the armies which fought on international campaigns, that a single nobleman could not have mustered a force of that size. It is impossible to be sure how many men the Duke had at his disposal during the siege, but, by extrapolation from Worcester's list of local knights and esquires who offered him their support (*Itineraries*, p. 189), a total of two or three hundred is not implausible.

2 *PL* Davis 202.

3 *PL* Davis 241.

4 *PL* Davis 242.

5 *PL* Davis 242.

6 *PL* Davis 204.

7 *PL* Davis 243.

8 *PL* Davis 244.

9 *PL* Davis 786.

10 *PL* Davis 334.

11 *PL* Davis 335.

12 *PL* Davis 335.

13 *PL* Davis 205.

14 *PL* Davis 245.

15 *PL* Davis 328 (redated to October 1469 by reference to Davis 335 and 205; cf. Richmond, *The Paston Family: Endings*, p. 135n).

16 *PL* Davis 201.

17 *PL* Davis 332.

18 *PL* Davis 861.

19 *PL* Davis 203.

20 *PL* Davis 203.

21 *PL* Davis 335.

22 *PL* Davis 208 (redated to 1469 by reference to Davis 328 – see above, note 15).

23 *PL* Davis 336.

24 *PL* Davis 245.

25 *PL* Davis 248.

26 *PL* Davis 337.

27 *PL* Davis 338.

28 *PL* Davis 248.

29 *PL* Davis 339.

30 *PL* Davis 912.

31 *PL* Davis 252.

32 *PL* Davis 248.

33 *PL* Davis 787.

34 From a report by Sforza di Bettini, the Milanese ambassador to France: Myers (ed.), *English Historical Documents*, p. 304; and see Scofield, *Edward the Fourth*, I, p. 529.

35 Proclamation quoted in Scofield, *Edward the Fourth*, I, p. 537.

36 G. E. Cokayne, *The Complete Peerage*, ed. V. Gibbs et al., 13 vols. (London, 1910-40), vol. IX, p. 91.

37 *PL* Davis 345.

38 *PL* Davis 217 (redated to 1470 by reference to Davis 345).

39 *PL* Davis 258.

40 *PL* Davis 258.

41 *PL* Davis 213 (redated to 1470: see Davis, vol. II, p. xxv).

42 *Calendar of the Close Rolls, 1468–76*, pp. 163–5.

43 *PL* Davis 727. Davis's suggested date of 1468 is too early, since the letter must have been written after Bishop Wainfleet's intervention in the dispute. 1471 is the most likely year, although it is not impossible that Worcester was writing in 1470.

44 Quotation from the *Arrival of Edward IV* – an exactly contemporary, largely eye-witness account, albeit a partisan Yorkist one. See Ross, *Edward IV*, pp. 157, 162n.

45 Quotation from the *Arrival of Edward IV*: see Ross, *Edward IV*, p. 165.

46 Henry Beaufort, the Duke of Somerset who had commanded the Lancastrian army at Towton, had been executed in 1464 for his role in leading the unsuccessful Lancastrian resistance in the north. The Duke who joined Queen Margaret in 1471 was his younger brother, Edmund Beaufort.

47 *PL* Davis 261.

48 *PL* Davis 346. John II signed the letter '*your humblest servant, J. of Geldeston*' – using his birthplace to identify himself to his mother rather than his name – in case the paper fell into unfriendly hands.

ELEVEN

1 *PL* Davis 263.

2 *PL* Davis 347.

3 *PL* Davis 263.

4 *PL* Davis 267.

5 *PL* Davis 266.

6 *PL* Davis 264.

7 *PL* Davis 266.

8 *PL* Davis 263.

9 *PL* Davis 209.

10 *PL* Davis 256 (August 1470).

11 *PL* Davis 394.

12 *PL* Davis 395.

13 *PL* Davis 353.

14 *PL* Davis 263.

15 *PL* Davis 268.

16 *PL* Davis 216.

17 *PL* Davis 209.

18 *PL* Davis 212 (29 November 1471). Margaret's much calmer letter of 20 November (*PL* Davis 211), which does not mention the issue of the loan, seems likely to have been addressed to John III, rather than John II as Davis suggests.

19 *PL* Davis 212.

20 *PL* Davis 266.

21 *PL* Davis 350 (written shortly before Christmas 1471).

22 *PL* Davis 355.

23 *PL* Davis 214 (which Davis dates 'about 1472'; but the substance of the letter makes clear that it must have been written shortly after John III's letter no. 355 of 16 October).

24 *PL* Davis 354.

25 *PL* Davis 269.

26 *PL* Davis 270.

27 *PL* Davis 271.

28 *PL* Davis 357.

29 *PL* Davis 358.

30 In fact, the legal situation was a great deal more complicated even than this. It was true that, in the absence of a male heir, daughters had equal rights to a share of the estate, irrespective of seniority. However, the earldom of Warwick itself was the inheritance of the Earl's wife Anne Beauchamp, who was still alive, and whose rights should therefore have taken precedence over those of her daughters. Many of the Earl's own Neville estates, meanwhile, were held in tail male, and should therefore have passed to his nephew, John Neville's son George, as his next male heir. Nevertheless, neither the widowed Countess of Warwick nor George Neville was in any position to insist on their rights, and the claims of Isabel and Anne Neville (and therefore of their husbands Clarence and Gloucester) were ratified in parliament once the settlement had been agreed.

31 *PL* Davis 274. John II's difficulties were compounded by the fact that, although he had not sold the timber at Sporle, he had mortgaged the manor for a year to a local lawyer, Roger Townsend, thinking that he would be able to redeem it with the £100 he believed Margaret had promised him. Now that she was withholding the money, the whole manor was potentially at risk.

32 *PL* Davis 212.

33 *PL* Davis 274.

34 *PL* Davis 279.

35 *PL* Davis 277.

36 *PL* Davis 282.

37 *PL* Davis 275.

38 *PL* Davis 277.

39 *PL* Davis 272.

40 *PL* Davis 354.

41 *PL* Davis 355.

42 *PL* Davis 356.

43 *PL* Davis 355.

44 *PL* Davis 101.

45 Certainly, John III had been deeply committed to ensuring that John Daubeney's will was dealt with properly and promptly. In March 1470 he reported to John II (*PL* Davis 339) that Daubeney's executors could not act until they received confirmation that he had owed no money to his employers, and was clearly much exercised at the

prospect that his brother might not get round to producing the document with any urgency: '*You may do it well enough, so God help me, for I know well you owe him money and he not you, if so be that he were true when he died, and I know well we found him never untrue in his life. But his friends and other of the country put great default in me that there is nothing done for him, saying that he might do no more for us but lose his life in your service and mine, and now he is half forgotten among us; wherefore I pray you let this be sped.*' Another possibility – not mutually exclusive with this one – is that John III made the journey to Santiago in the retinue of Earl Rivers (Lord Scales), who was said to have visited the shrine at some point in 1473.

46 *PL* Davis 282.

47 *PL* Davis 284.

48 *PL* Davis 286.

49 *PL* Davis 770.

50 *PL* Davis 285.

51 *PL* Davis 221.

52 *PL* Davis 221.

53 *PL* Davis 291.

54 *PL* Davis 221.

55 *PL* Davis 291.

56 Ross, *Edward IV*, p. 218.

57 *PL* Davis 224.

58 *PL* Davis 289.

59 *PL* Davis 293.

60 *PL* Davis 365.

61 *PL* Davis 366.

62 *PL* Davis 365.

63 *PL* Davis 293.

64 *PL* Davis 365.

65 *PL* Davis 366.

66 *PL* Davis 294.

67 It has always been assumed that the Duke died at his home at Framlingham in Suffolk, but there seems to be no concrete evidence to confirm the supposition. John II and John III were both nearby when he died, since they reported the news to Margaret the next morning (*PL* Davis 295), but it seems unlikely that they would have been at Framlingham given their breach with Norfolk two months earlier. However, John III had previously reported that the Duchess intended to spend her pregnancy at Norwich (*PL* Davis 365), and certainly both John II and John III were there on 20 January, three days after the Duke's death (*PL* Davis 367). It therefore seems probable that the Duke and members of his household were staying in Norwich with his wife when he died.

68 *PL* Davis 295.

69 *PL* Davis 368.

70 *PL* Davis 296.

71 *PL* Davis 298, 372.

72 *PL* Davis 371.

73 *PL* Davis 299.

74 *PL* Davis 299.

75 *PL* Davis 300.

TWELVE

1 *PL* Davis 379. It was presumably because of his shortage of money that, in the same year, the Duke sold a magnificent jewel to his brother-in-law King Edward for £160 ('*an image of Our Lady, of gold, with Our Lord in her arms, and the images of St John the Baptist and St Catherine on either side of Our Lady, and two other images with seven angels thereto pertaining, the same image of Our Lady sitting upon a cushion of silver and over-gilt in a pavilion of gold garnished with six sapphires, six rubies, twenty-four great pearls upon five cushions of gold, twenty small pearls upon the crown, four little pearls in little diamonds, a ruby and two emeralds, thirteen very little pearls set in other places, and a ruby set in Our Lady's breast*'). Scofield, *Edward the Fourth*, II, p. 433.

2 *PL* Davis 782.

3 *PL* Davis 297.

4 *PL* Davis 302.

5 *PL* Davis 312.

6 *PL* Davis 278.

7 *PL* Davis 774.

8 *PL* Davis 755.

9 *PL* Davis 228.

10 *PL* Davis 366.

11 *PL* Davis 298.

12 *PL* Davis 227.

13 *PL* Davis 227. This was the second time John II had mortgaged Sporle to the local lawyer Roger Townsend. He had successfully redeemed the manor after the first mortgage in 1472 (for which, see chapter 11, note 32), but was now concerned about whether he would again be able to recover the property.

14 *PL* Davis 371.

15 *PL* Davis 311.

16 *PL* Davis 228.

17 *PL* Davis 227.

18 *PL* Davis 270.

19 *PL* Davis 209.

20 *PL* Davis 283.

21 *PL* Davis 282.

22 *PL* Davis 236. Sir Geoffrey Boleyn bought the manor of Blickling from Sir John Fastolf in 1452. Boleyn's great-granddaughter Anne married King Henry VIII in 1533.

23 *PL* Davis 339.

24 *PL* Davis 369.

25 *PL* Davis 791.

26 *PL* Davis 374.

27 *PL* Davis 773 (and see also Davis 376). The word '*cousin*' denoted a much less specific family relationship than it does in modern usage. Given the extent of intermarriage among the gentry of any region, it was always likely that some form of kinship existed between families from the same area, and '*cousin*' was therefore often used as a term of respectful address.

28 *PL* Davis 415, 416. Margery's letters are the earliest surviving Valentine messages in the English language. Her mother had invited John III to stay for St Valentine's Day itself, when '*every bird chooses him a mate*', she said. *PL* Davis 791.

29 *PL* Davis 226.

30 *PL* Davis 236.

31 *PL* Davis 303.

32 *PL* Davis 304.

33 *PL* Davis 306.

34 *PL* Davis 305.

35 *PL* Davis 312.

36 *PL* Davis 302, 381.

37 *PL* Davis 220.

38 *PL* Davis 404.

39 *PL* Davis 381.

40 *PL* Davis 397.

41 *PL* Davis 245. John Paston's youngest brother Clement had died in the late 1460s, soon after John himself. By the 1470s, therefore, William Paston was the only surviving son of Judge William and Agnes.

42 *PL* Davis 315.

43 *PL* Davis 383. John II was buried in the church of the White Friars, just off Fleet Street. John III had intended to bring his brother's body back to Norfolk along with that of his grandmother, who had also died in London. In the end, it was just Agnes's coffin which was brought back, for burial in the Lady Chapel of the White Friars' Church in Norwich, beside her parents and her youngest son Clement.

THIRTEEN

1 *PL* Davis 222. The right to private worship was one which held social cachet, and the Pastons must previously have secured such permission when James Gloys was their resident chaplain. Nevertheless, the fact that Margaret couched her request this time in terms of her own infirmity seems significant.

2 *PL* Davis 793.

3 *PL* Davis 384.

4 Anne Beaufort's oldest brother Henry was executed in 1464 for his part in leading the Lancastrian resistance against Edward IV in the north of England. Her second brother Edmund was captured and beheaded after the Battle of Tewkesbury in 1471.

5 *PL* Davis 383.

6 *PL* Davis 417.

7 *PL* Davis 418.

8 *PL* Davis 417, 418.

9 *PL* Davis 417.

10 *PL* Davis 417.

11 *PL* Davis 386.

12 *PL* Davis 230.

13 *PL* Davis 123.

14 *PL* Davis 230.

15 *PL* Davis 230.

16 *PL* Davis 795.

17 *PL* Davis 796.

18 *PL* Davis 796.

19 Henry's father Edmund Tudor was the son of Henry V's Queen, Catherine de Valois, by her second marriage to the Welsh esquire Owen Tudor. Edmund and his brother Jasper were therefore half-brothers of King Henry VI, but they had no claim to the throne in their own right, since their relationship with King Henry came through their French mother rather than the royal line of England.

20 *PL* Davis 799.

21 A. Crawford (ed.), *The Household Books of John Howard, Duke of Norfolk, 1462–71, 1481–3* (Stroud, 1992), p. 183.

22 *PL* Davis 387.

23 *PL* Davis 801.

24 *PL* Davis 807.

25 *PL* Davis 810.

26 *PL* Davis 811.

27 *PL* Davis 813 (and see above, chapter 4, note 26, for Thomas, Lord Scales addressing Sir John Fastolf as '*father*' as a term of respect). The three women – Alice Fitzhugh, Catherine Hastings and Margaret de Vere – were all Nevilles, sisters of the kingmaking Earl of Warwick.

28 *PL* Davis 823, 816, 420. By law, half of the whale belonged to the local men who found it, and the other half to the crown – '*fish royal*' being a technical legal term which included sturgeon and porpoise as well as whales. There was initial uncertainty about whether the crown's share should be taken by the King himself or by Oxford in right of the Admiralty, but the Earl graciously abdicated his claim.

29 *PL* Davis 830. Henry Heydon was married to Anne Boleyn, whose sister Alice had refused John III's suit more than twenty years earlier (see above, chapter 9).

30 The fact that Agnes made no mention of any Paston connections when she wrote her own will after John III's death may suggest that it was an essentially pragmatic match. She asked to be buried beside her first husband, John Harvey. *PL* Davis 930.

31 *PL* Davis 839.

EPILOGUE

1 *PL* Davis 848. The Earl himself was both concerned and solicitous: '*your brother William, my servant, is so troubled with sickness and crazed in his mind that I may not keep him about me, whereof I am right sorry, and at this time send him to you*', he told

John III; *'praying especially that he may be kept surely and tenderly with you to such time as God fortune him to be better assured of himself, and his mind more sadly disposed, which I pray God may be in short time'.*

2 Sir William's choice of name for his eldest son was an unusual one, which probably derived from a family connection to the great Dutch scholar Desiderius Erasmus. John Paston III was a friend of the wealthy London merchant Henry Colet, whose son John was one of the leading English humanists in the early sixteenth century. John Colet developed a close relationship with Erasmus during the years which the latter spent in England, and the friendship between the Paston and Colet families may therefore have meant that Sir William Paston also knew Erasmus well.

3 It was this William Paston who named his second son Wulstan, after the family's fictional Norman ancestor (see above, chapter 9).

4 *Complete Peerage*, vol. XII, part 2, p. 890.

5 *PL* Davis 350.

6 J. Huizinga, *The Waning of the Middle Ages* (Harmondsworth, 1968), p. 25.

Index